AN EAST ASIAN
RENAISSANCE

AN EAST ASIAN RENAISSANCE

IDEAS FOR ECONOMIC GROWTH

INDERMIT GILL
HOMI KHARAS

TOGETHER WITH
DEEPAK BHATTASALI • MILAN BRAHMBHATT
GAURAV DATT • MONA HADDAD • EDWARD MOUNTFIELD
RADU TATUCU • EKATERINA VOSTROKNUTOVA

1 2 3 4 5 10 09 08 07

This volume is a product of the staff of the International Bank for Reconstruction and Development / The World Bank. The findings, interpretations, and conclusions expressed in this volume do not necessarily reflect the views of the Executive Directors of The World Bank or the governments they represent.

The World Bank does not guarantee the accuracy of the data included in this work. The boundaries, colors, denominations, and other information shown on any map in this work do not imply any judgement on the part of The World Bank concerning the legal status of any territory or the endorsement or acceptance of such boundaries.

ISBN10: 0-8213-6747-1
ISBN13:978-0-8213-6747-6
eISBN10: 0-8213-6748-X
DOI: 10.1596/978-0-8213-6747-6

Library of Congress Cataloging-in-Publication Data

Gill, Indermit Singh, 1961-
   An East Asian renaissance : ideas for economic growth / Indermit Gill
and Homi Kharas ; together with Deepak Bhattasali . . . [et al.].
        p. cm.
   Includes bibliographical references and index.
   ISBN-13: 978-0-8213-6747-6
   ISBN-10: 0-8213-6747-1
   ISBN-10: 0-8213-6748-X (electronic)
  1. East Asia—Economic policy. 2. East Asia—Economic conditions.
I. Kharas, Homi J., 1954- II. Bhattasali, Deepak. III. World Bank. IV.
Title.
   HC460.5.G55 2007
   338.95—dc22

                                      2006037026

Cover designer: Drew Fasick
Photo on lower left of cover: ©Curt Carnemark/World Bank

CONTENTS

Boxes

Figures

Tables

ACKNOWLEDGMENTS

This book is a product of the Office of the Chief Economist, East Asia and Pacific Region of the World Bank. It is the result of a collective effort by a World Bank team led by Homi Kharas (Chief Economist) and Indermit Gill (Economic Adviser). The lead authors by chapter are Indermit Gill and Homi Kharas (Overview), Indermit Gill and Radu Tatucu (Chapter 1), Mona Haddad (Chapter 2), Milan Brahmbhatt (Chapter 3), Homi Kharas, Ramkishen Rajan, and Ekaterina Vostroknutova (Chapter 4), Deepak Bhattasali and Indermit Gill (Chapter 5), Gaurav Datt, Sisira Jayasuriya, and Tao Kong (Chapter 6), and Edward Mountfield and Ceren Ozer (Chapter 7).

The authors have relied on background papers by Joshua Aizenman, Caroline Freund, Gordon Hansen, Govind Hariharan, Albert Hu, Françoise Lemoine, Reza Siregar, Shujiro Urata, Sjamsu Rahardja, Giok Ling Ooi, and Wei-Kang Wong.

Antonio Ollero and Radu Tatucu have provided excellent research assistance for various chapters. Adelma Bowrin, Marlyn Caluag, and Doris Chung have supplied cheerful and effective help with the administration and budget for the task.

Valuable comments at various stages of the project were received from Richard Baldwin, Peter Drysdale, Ronald Jones, Tommy Koh, Arun Mahizhnan, and Soogil Young.

At the World Bank, among the many colleagues who have contributed with their ideas and inputs are Vivi Alatas, Rosa Alonso i Terme, Mohamad Al-Arief, Premachandra

Athukorala, Robert Blake, Paul Brenton, Andrew Burns, Ed Campos, Shubham Chaudhuri, Lester Dally, Aniruddha Dasgupta, Christian Delvoie, Shanta Devarajan, Sanjay Dhar, Uri Dadush, Paavo Eliste, Melissa Fossberg, Swati Ghosh, Marcelo Giugale, Bert Hofman, Yukon Huang, Magda Lovei, Xubei Luo, Kazi Matin, Raja Mitra, Elisabeth Mealey, Ijaz Nabi, Richard Newfarmer, Vikram Nehru, Barbara Nunberg, Brian Pinto, Martin Rama, Kaspar Richter, Apurva Sanghi, Kalpana Seethepalli, Luis Serven, Robert Taliercio, Dominique van der Mensbrugghe, Keshav Varma, William Wallace, Jacob Young, and Shahid Yusuf.

The book has also benefited from the suggestions of participants at a concept note review meeting in December 2005, a retreat in April 2006 among World Bank staff working in the East Asia and Pacific Region's Poverty Reduction and Economic Management and the Financial Sector and Private Sector Development units, a discussion of the book at the National University of Singapore's Center for Applied and Policy Economics (SCAPE) Workshop in September 2006, and at a retreat among the World Bank's East Asia and Pacific Region managers in November 2006. The authors also acknowledge the participation of others at seminars within the Bank.

Jolan Falk of Creative Force and Bruno Bonansea and Jeffrey Lecksell of the World Bank Cartography Unit have been instrumental in the map design and creation. We would also like to thank Edward Leman for kindly providing some data used in Chapter 5.

Susan Graham, Patricia Katayama, and Stuart Tucker have provided invaluable ideas and assistance during the production phase, and Robert Zimmermann has edited and improved the manuscript.

The team leaders are responsible for any errors. The opinions expressed in the book are those of the authors and do not represent the views of the management of the World Bank, its executive directors, or the countries they represent.

ABBREVIATIONS, AND ACRONYMS

ASEAN	Association of Southeast Asian Nations
ASEAN+3	ASEAN nations, plus China, Japan, and the Republic of Korea
FDI	foreign direct investment
G-7	finance ministers of the G-8, less Russia
GDP	gross domestic product
IIT	intraindustry trade index
KN	Lao kip
kW, kWh	kilowatt, kilowatt hour
Lao PDR	Lao People's Democratic Republic
Mercosur	Southern Cone Common Market
MR	metropolitan region
NIE	newly industrializing economy
OEM	original equipment manufacturing
PPP	purchasing power parity
PRODY	productivity index
R&D	research and development
RCA	revealed comparative advantage
SITC	standard international trade classification
TFP	total factor productivity
US$	United States dollar
USPTO	United States Patent and Trademark Office
Y	Chinese yuan
¥	Japanese yen

All dollars are U.S. dollars unless otherwise noted.

The economic performance of East Asia since the late 1990s has been remarkable. The region has responded by increasing regional integration. Economies are growing, and societies are being transformed. But problems are emerging in domestic integration. This book seeks to identify how East Asian governments should adapt development strategies to address these breathtaking changes.

OVERVIEW
The Unfolding of a Renaissance

A Renaissance Unfolds

Less than 10 years ago, in 1997–98, a financial crisis brought four economies in East Asia to their knees.[1] Many predicted that the structural weaknesses that the crisis laid bare—corruption, cronyism, nepotism—would condemn the region to stagnation as had happened in Latin America after a debt crisis in the mid-1980s.[2] Emerging East Asia was expected to lose years of growth, just as Latin America had lost a decade. Instead, the growth record of the emerging economies of the region since 1998 has been remarkable: gross domestic product (GDP) has almost doubled, rising by over 9 percent per year, to reach US$4 trillion in current dollars by 2005.[3]

Other indicators of performance are equally impressive. Exports have increased to one-fifth of the world's total, or a value of more than US$2 trillion per year, making emerging East Asia one of the most open trading regions in the world. The region is the largest destination for foreign direct investment (FDI) and has US$1.6 trillion worth of foreign exchange reserves. Its capital markets have grown, and its domestic financial sector assets amount to US$9.6 trillion. There are 300 million fewer people living in poverty (measured as per capita expenditures of at least US$2 a day) now than there were in 1998. A middle class has emerged with a lively democratic voice in economic affairs. Business-friendly reforms are moving ahead throughout the region, and confidence in economic prospects is high.

1

An economic renaissance is unfolding in the region. Like the renaissance in Europe, a period of intellectual discovery that produced new ideas and economic development, innovation is getting similar attention in East Asia (see box 1). The pace of change in trade and finance, ideas and technology, urban development, household finances, and the demands on the public sector is breathtaking. If current growth trends prevail, East Asia will be as large in terms of the world economy (40 percent) by 2025 as it was in 1820, around the time that it began a long decline in global importance.[4]

In a world in which development seems so ephemeral, how is it that a dozen countries in East Asia have all been successful? (The Democratic People's Republic of Korea and Myanmar are the only exceptions.) Common economic characteristics cannot be the whole explanation since the diversity among these countries is enormous. Emerging East Asia includes China, with 1.3 billion people, and Mongolia with 2.5 million. Per capita incomes range from US$400 in the Lao People's Democratic Republic to US$24,000 in Singapore. Hong Kong (China) is perhaps the most laissez-faire economy in the world, while Vietnam is one of the few remaining socialist economies. What is going on? Is there something special about East Asia that makes these economies grow?

There is a large literature that has attempted to answer this question. Perhaps the most widely quoted recent study is *The East Asian Miracle*, a volume published by the World Bank (1993). *The East Asian Miracle* sought to explain the superior eco-

■ BOX 1 **Renaissance Then and Now**

The European Renaissance began in the thriving city-states of Italy in the 15th century and spread rapidly to Central and Western Europe. It was characterized by the absorption of knowledge, especially mathematics, from Arabia and India, the importance of the idea of living well in the present, and an acceleration in the exchange of ideas due to the advent of printing. The Renaissance marked the advent of broad structural forces of urbanization, globalization, and new modes of production.

In retrospect, many historians believe that undesirable social conditions associated with the pre-Renaissance Middle Ages—particularly poverty, strife, corruption, and the persecution of minorities—may have actually worsened during the European Renaissance. While the well-off viewed the changes as a break from the Middle Ages, much of the rest of society saw it as a time of intensification of social maladies.

The East Asian renaissance now unfolding is also marked by the accelerated absorption of knowledge (from America and Europe), a focus on living well, and the more rapid dissemination of ideas due to the computer, the general-purpose technology that easily rivals the printing press. A lesson from European history is that these changes must be accompanied by greater social cohesion for the East Asian renaissance to be transformed into a golden age.

Source: Cannistraro and Reich 2003.

nomic accomplishments of eight high-performing Asian economies. It concluded that, in large measure, these economies achieved high growth by "getting the basics right." But it went on to claim that fundamental policies were only part of the story and that "in one form or another, the government intervened—systematically and through multiple channels—to foster development" (p. 5). *The East Asian Miracle* concluded by noting that a willingness to experiment and adapt policies to changing circumstances is a key element in economic success. This insight provides the rationale for our study. How should governments in East Asia adapt their policies today to reflect the profound changes in the region and in the world since 1990?

A Changing Economic Landscape

It is clear that the economic landscape in East Asia is quite different in 2006 than it was in 1990. The region is much richer than it was. So, the size of the regional market is larger. Individuals are also richer, and the demand for consumer durables is growing. At the same time, the economic center of gravity—production, trade, and finance—has shifted toward China and Northeast Asia. *Regionalism* within East Asia has risen sharply in the guise of formal economic trade agreements between two or more countries. In the last 10 years, 24 new agreements have been concluded, and 34 more are under negotiation. In part, regionalism has its roots in the currency and financial crisis of 1997–98, a determining moment when many policy makers saw for the first time the risks that come with the benefits of globalization, or integration with the world at large. But perhaps more significant is a trend toward *regionalization*, a market-driven process that has seen trade, finance, and innovation accelerating within East Asia at the same time that globalization has taken hold.

East Asian countries that have successfully integrated into the global economy are now integrating regionally. Remarkably, this regional integration is occurring in addition to, not at the expense of global integration. And, in many aspects, this second integration is evolving at an even more rapid pace than the first. Individually, East Asian countries appear to have learned the lessons of the economic crisis and have fortified themselves for continued international integration. Collectively, these countries have sought regional integration to stay globally competitive.

While many of the countries have reduced poverty and reached middle-income status, the rapid economic growth driven by international integration has been accompanied by growing domestic friction stemming from urban squalor and environmental strains, rising inequality, and corruption. This has meant that, as East Asian countries have kept their economies competitive by augmenting global integration with regional integration, they are being challenged to keep this growth sustained through a third integration, one at the domestic level that is aimed at keeping societies cohesive.

A Richer Region with a Growing Middle Class

In 1990, developing East Asia had a GDP of US$1.2 trillion (see figure 1). Today, the total is US$4 trillion. If one adds Australia, Japan, and New Zealand, the region has a combined GDP of US$9.5 trillion, close to one-quarter of the world's output. Because of this growth, the region has become more middle income. Once Vietnam reaches middle-income levels, which might occur as early as 2010, more than 95 percent of East Asians will reside in a middle-income country. The region's economic future depends on the prospects and performance of middle-income countries. While this book is about all of developing East Asia, it is especially aimed at the region's middle-income countries—China, Indonesia, Malaysia, the Philippines, and Thailand.

The fact that East Asia is increasingly a middle-income region with more countries looking for strategies to move to rich-country status is important because patterns of growth change as income levels change. Research suggests that two

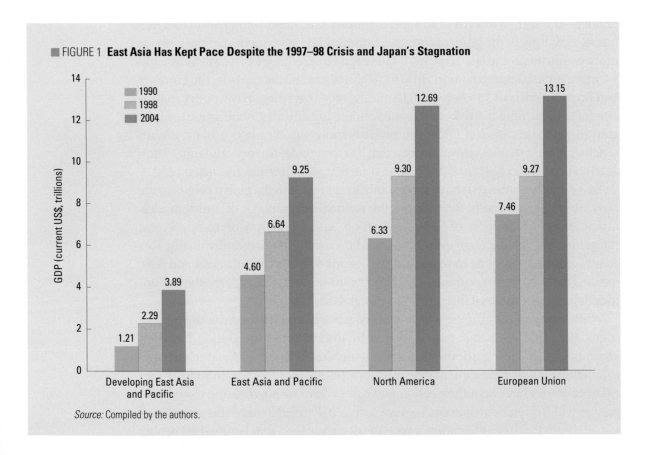

■ FIGURE 1 **East Asia Has Kept Pace Despite the 1997–98 Crisis and Japan's Stagnation**

Source: Compiled by the authors.

trends are at work in driving the sectoral pattern of growth. On the one hand, as countries get richer, there is a demand for a greater variety of goods, many of which may be produced domestically; so, there is a force toward sectoral diversification. On the other hand, countries only become richer if they specialize in what they do best. Which tendency dominates is an empirical question; researchers speculate that the answer depends on the extent of scale economies in production relative to the love of variety in consumption.

One recent study shows that countries initially diversify, meaning that value added and employment are spread out more and more through the economy.[5] At a turning point that differs across countries, but that occurs *systematically* at middle-income levels, countries begin to specialize in production and employment once more. Scale economies in production appear to win out. This suggests that new strategies that favor specialization must be adopted at some point by middle-income countries if they are to become rich.

The idea that middle-income countries have to do something different if they are to prosper is consistent with the finding that middle-income countries have grown less rapidly than either rich or poor countries, and this accounts for the lack of economic convergence in the twentieth century world. Middle-income countries, it is argued, are squeezed between the low-wage poor-country competitors that dominate in mature industries and the rich-country innovators that dominate in industries undergoing rapid technological change.[6]

This is the challenge that confronts East Asian countries today, especially those in Southeast Asia. There is reason for optimism. The newly industrializing economies in East Asia successfully made this transition from middle income to rich, showing that such a transition is possible under the proper circumstances and the correct policies. And, within Asia, experience suggests that there is not such a sharp distinction between the domination of low-income countries in manufacturing and the domination of rich countries in the knowledge economy. The newly industrializing economies remain successful manufacturers, even in quite mature industries, while China and India show that success in the knowledge economy is not reserved only for rich countries. For middle-income countries, it seems the trick is to straddle both strategies.

China Is Driving Regionalization and Regionalism

The story of China was not included in *The East Asian Miracle* because the transition experience there was considered sui generis.[7] But China is the biggest development story in the world today and a major economic presence in the region, representing one-half of developing East Asia's GDP and one-third of its exports. Especially since its accession to the World Trade Organization in November 2001, China has offered major opportunities as a rapidly growing market for Asian exports. It is also a major competitor. Policy makers throughout the region are rethinking national strategies as they adjust to China's economic growth.

China has a special place in the story of East Asia because of its absolute size, its unusual openness for a continental economy, and its orientation toward the region. China is now the world's third largest trader, and it is the largest trader in East Asia, having overtaken Japan in 2004. For East Asian countries, China has become a major trading partner. It is the second export market for Japan and that country's largest supplier, and it is the largest export market for the Republic of Korea and that country's second largest supplier. China's imports have been growing at about 18 percent per year for the past decade, and its imports-to-GDP ratio has reached 34 percent, a figure triple that of Japan (9 percent) and the United States (12 percent), two other large economies. China sources more than half of its imports from East Asia. It is because of China that more than half of East Asian trade occurs within the region, a degree of integration paralleling that in the European Union.

Most analysts have concluded that intraregional trade in East Asia has been market driven and, hence, best described not as the product of regionalism, but of regionalization, the natural by-product of the fact that the East Asian economies are among the most rapidly growing and most open economies in the world.[8] East Asian countries have been the strongest proponents of multilateral and unilateral trade liberalization, and it is only recently that regional trade agreements have proliferated. It appears that this has been closely linked to the changing pattern of trade and investment in the region and, hence, to real economic forces, not any political considerations favoring regional approaches, nor a backlash against globalization following the Asian crisis.

An increasing share of trade in the region is comprised of parts and components that are shipped from one country to the next for further assembly in regional production networks.[9] These production networks were initiated in the mid-1980s after the Plaza Accord, and their development accelerated when China and other East Asian economies started applying more favorable policies toward foreign investment. By 1990, foreign affiliates were accounting for 30 to 90 percent of total manufactured exports from China and other middle-income countries in East Asia. Japanese multinational companies now send more than 80 percent of their exports from Asian affiliates to other Asian countries and obtain 95 percent of their imports from Asian producers.

This nexus between trade and FDI has become a powerful driver of regionalism.[10] Regional agreements have ensured market access among the countries spanned by regional production networks and have permitted deeper tariff cuts—essentially free trade—on components. At the same time, regional trade agreements have sought to reduce the obstacles to foreign investment, the trade in services, and skilled labor mobility, which are critical to the establishment of regional production networks, but which have been too sensitive as issues to be tackled in multilateral trade talks. Regional trade agreements therefore have complemented multilateral trade agreements.

The economic landscape of East Asia has changed profoundly since the early 1990s. The region is large in size, and income levels have risen across the board. It is more open than ever, and intraregional trade is expanding rapidly. At the same time, East Asia's share of exports to the rest of the world has also risen, albeit not as sharply. East Asia integrated globally first and is now integrating regionally (see figure 2). China is at the center of this development, but the institutional framework for regional cooperation is relatively immature, and the ad hoc arrangements may have costly side effects. Is there something more to be learned about managing these complexities?

A Changing Intellectual Landscape

In the real world of policy making in East Asia, there is a major debate on regional integration and cooperation that revolves around trade liberalization, the overly complex "noodle bowl" rules of origin in regional trade agreements, tax subsidies for foreign investors, and a new regional financial architecture. At the same time, policy makers are concerned with what needs to be done domestically to manage the stresses associated with integration and rapid growth, including congestion, corruption, and the lack of social cohesion. For the most part, economists have had little to add to these debates and have learned more from East Asia's success than they have taught. The tried-and-true recipes for economic success that emerge from neoclassical growth models—macroeconomic stability and savings, openness and education—seem inadequate for providing relevant insights into the policy debate. For much of East Asia (the Democratic People's Republic of Korea and Myanmar are the exceptions), these principles are important, but obvious. Nevertheless, the thinking on economic development evolved in the 1990s, and a growing body of empirical evidence suggests that this new thinking does not merely consist of theoretical niceties, but has the makings of a powerful paradigm that may help guide practical policy.

It is instructive to take a short detour to understand modern economic theories that model what is traded (new international trade theory), what makes rich coun-

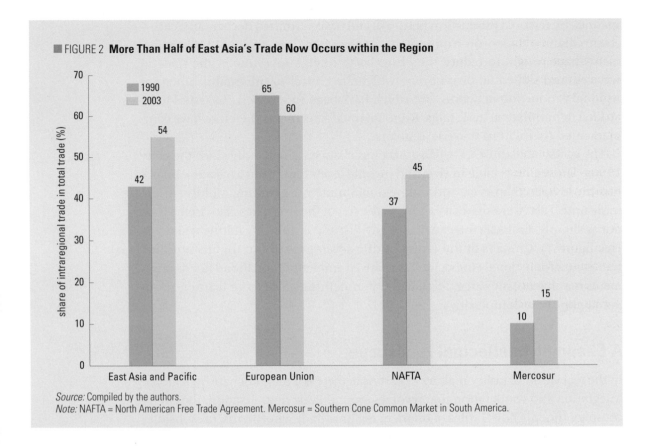

■ FIGURE 2 **More Than Half of East Asia's Trade Now Occurs within the Region**

Source: Compiled by the authors.
Note: NAFTA = North American Free Trade Agreement. Mercosur = Southern Cone Common Market in South America.

tries continue to grow rapidly, often more rapidly than poor or middle-income countries (new growth theory), and where growth occurs (the new economic geography). At their heart, these theories have one element in common: by relaxing the assumption of constant returns to scale and emphasizing scale economies, they are able to handle the complexities of the marketplace in a more realistic fashion. Scale economies refer to the tendency for production costs to fall as the volume of production rises or for product development costs to fall as new varieties are introduced. The ability to model scale economies, in turn, is built on new models of imperfect competition that can be solved even in the presence of increasing returns. For the middle-income countries in East Asia, the insights provided may be useful in adapting growth strategies as the countries deal with the challenges of specialization.

Figure 3 presents a summary of the principal forces analyzed in modern theories of industrial organization, international trade, economic growth, and economic geography. Growth occurs as a result of the exploitation of scale economies through specialization and innovation and is reflected in international integration via the trade in goods, money, and ideas. This integration triggers spatial and social changes that have an impact on domestic integration and the process of urbanization and income distribution. If they are well managed, these social and spatial trends may, in turn, feed back into more scale economies through agglomeration of production and incentives for more rapid skill formation. If managed badly, spatial and social problems may lead to the waste of the economic benefits of scale economies through congestion, pollution, social discord, and corruption, sharply reducing the resources available for investment and growth.

Scale economies do seem to play an important role in East Asia. One source of scale economies is in product markets. There can be efficiency gains from larger production volumes (plant level scale economies). More scale economies result from the ability of large producers to reduce fixed costs of branding, marketing, and product development per unit of production (firm level scale economies). When firms locate close to each other, they can create markets for more specialized intermediate goods, and they can benefit from lower transport costs (agglomeration economies).

Another source of scale economies is in labor markets. Workers in large cities have higher productivity because they are able to move to jobs they are best

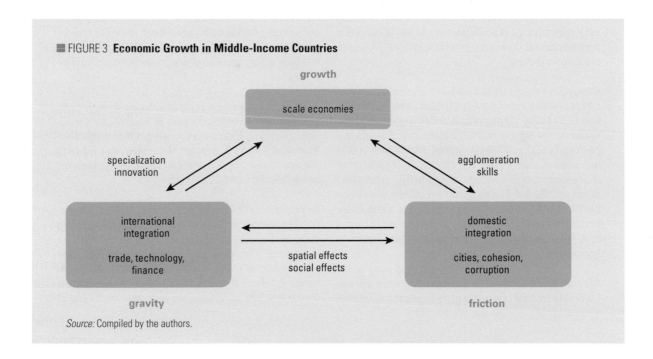

■ FIGURE 3 **Economic Growth in Middle-Income Countries**

Source: Compiled by the authors.

suited for, they get training in skills demanded by the marketplace, and they can get information about other similar firms more easily.

All these forces can be seen in operation in East Asia. One extraordinary example comes from the experience of Dongguan, a city in southern China. Dongguan has grown by 22 percent per year for the last 25 years. Cumulatively, the city's economy now is 144 times as big as it was in 1980, all thanks to its ability to exploit economies of scale and avoid social diseconomies through good public policy (see box 2).

■ BOX 2 **Growth, Gravity, and Friction in the Pearl River Delta**

In 1978, what is today the city of Dongguan, in China's Guangdong Province, was a collection of villages and small towns spread over 2,500 square kilometers along the Pearl River, midway between Guangzhou, to the north, and Shenzen and Hong Kong (China), to the south. The area's population of 400,000 relied primarily on fishing and farming, and, while they were far from being among the poorest in China, neither were the people prosperous. Dongguan today has a population of nearly 7 million. More than 5 million of the inhabitants are migrants who work in the thousands of factories that dot the city, churning out a dizzying range of products in such huge volumes that media accounts in recent years have labeled Dongguan the world's factory.

Dongguan's economy has grown at an average annual rate of over 20 percent in the last two decades. GDP in 2004 was US$14 billion. If one only includes registered urban residents (as is done in official statistics), Dongguan's per-capita GDP of US$9,000 in 2004 made it the wealthiest city in China. Even if the city's fluid population of migrant workers is included, per capita GDP in 2004 was still over US$2,000. The development of Dongguan since the 1970s and, in particular, the last decade, exemplifies, perhaps in exaggerated fashion, the economic forces that have been shaping East Asia's middle-income economies.

Growth: scale economies and agglomeration effects. Favorable location and factor prices undoubtedly played

a role in the early growth of Dongguan. For the first decade and a half after China's reforms began, small and medium enterprises from Hong Kong (China) and Taiwan (China) set up manufacturing operations in Dongguan. They were attracted by Dongguan's proximity, the availability of cheap land, and the plentiful supply of low-cost labor. Dongguan's sustained, rapid growth through the 1990s may best be understood in terms of the economies of scale in the production of intermediate goods and differentiated products and the agglomeration effects within industries, spanning upstream and downstream firms, and across industries that, because of advances in technology, reductions in transport costs, and improvements in logistics, have come to characterize global production processes.

There are many internal scale economies. A single plant in Dongguan manufactures over 30 percent of the magnetic recording heads used in hard drives worldwide. Another produces 60 percent of the electronic learning devices sold in the U.S. market. Yet another produces nearly 30 million mobile phones.

Agglomeration or external scale effects are equally visible. The benefits in the form of knowledge spillovers and the lower logistics costs that result from locating close to input providers and export traders have resulted in the development of globally important industry clusters in knitted woolens, footwear, furniture, and toys. But the cluster that has dominated the industrial landscape of

■ BOX 2 (*Continued*)

Dongguan since the mid-1990s is the telecommunications, electronics, and computer components cluster: 95 percent of the parts and components needed for the manufacture and processing of personal computers may be sourced within the Dongguan city limits, and, for several specific products, Dongguan's factories account for over 40 percent of global production.

Gravity: foreign investment and trade. Dongguan's growth has been generated through its links with the regional and global economy. The development of electronics and furniture clusters would not have occurred without the involvement of and investment by Taiwanese firms. Similarly, firms in Hong Kong (China) have been instrumental in the growth of the apparel and toy clusters. More important than the financial investment made by foreign firms—a total of over US$15 billion in the last two decades—has been the technical know-how, knowledge of the market, and relations with customers that these firms have provided. The result is that, in 2004, Dongguan's exports totaled over US$35 billion. Imports, mostly parts and components from other countries in East Asia, were nearly US$30 billion.

Friction: income disparities, urban congestion, and corruption. The growth and structural transformation of the magnitude and at the pace experienced by Dongguan has created frictions that need to be managed. Growth in manufacturing is intensive in infrastructure and resources. Dongguan's annual consumption of electricity and water in 2004, 35.2 billion kilowatt hours and 1.5 billion cubic meters, respectively, has exceeded that of many countries. The conversion of land to industrial use is putting stresses on the environment. In 2004, Dongguan discharged 225 million tons of industrial waste water, nearly 200,000 tons of sulfur dioxide emissions, and nearly 30,000 tons of solid industrial wastes. Agglomeration may lead eventually to congestion. Land is no longer as cheap in Dongguan as it once was, and labor is no longer as compliant nor as easily available. Shortages of labor, especially skilled labor, are being reported with increasing frequency.

It is not only the physical landscape that is transformed. Growth may also fundamentally alter the social fabric and institutional foundations of governance. The drive to capture the profits and economic rents associated with scale economies, while central in attracting investment, ideas, and contacts, may also engender corruption and crime. Dongguan in the 1990s was often described as having the atmosphere of a frontier gold-rush city. No direct statistics are available, but media accounts and case-based research suggest that corruption was common, whether in acquiring land for the construction of factories or in facilitating the evasion of taxes and labor and environmental standards. Crime rates were higher than in other parts of China. And the uneven distribution of the economic surpluses generated by the growth—attributable partly to market-based incentives that reward individual effort, but also partly to uneven influence—has led to large disparities in income, itself a possible source of social tension. Household surveys indicate that the mean per capita income among Dongguan's 1.6 million registered urban residents was 20,564 Yuan in 2004. Successful local entrepreneurs, whose incomes were unlikely to have been captured in the households surveys, undoubtedly earned much more. A typical migrant worker in Dongguan's factories, on the other hand, earned less than 10,000 Yuan, working much longer hours with fewer protections and much less access to public services.

What makes the Dongguan story particularly compelling, however, is the extent to which the city has been striving to address these challenges. Environmental and labor standards are increasingly being enforced: in 2004, 90 percent of the industrial waste water in Dongguan met discharge standards, as did 86 percent of the solid wastes; 93 percent of sulfur dioxide emissions met emissions standards (see table 1). Through its Labor Bureau, the city is trying to ensure the protection of worker rights and facilitate worker-firm matches. And the city is investing its sizable revenues from land rents and local taxes—over US$1 billion in 2004—in relieving congestion and improving infrastructure such as roads, port facilities, and industrial parks.

(Continued)

■ BOX 2 **Growth, Gravity, and Friction in the Pearl River Delta (*Continued*)**

■ TABLE 1 **The Story of Dongguan in Numbers**

Indicator	Value	Indicator	Value
Average annual GDP growth, 1980–2005 (%)	22	GDP (US$ billions)	14.4
Population, registered residents (millions)	1.6	Population, estimated (millions)	7.0
GDP per-registered resident (US$)	8,999	GDP per-capita (US$)	2,070
Exports (US$ billions)	35.2	Imports (US$ billions)	29.3
Government revenues (US$ billions)	1.0	Government expenditures (US$ billions)	1.2
Magnetic heads, computer cases (% of world output)	40	Scanners and minimotors (% of world output)	20
Copper-clad boards and disk drives (% of world output)	30	Keyboards (% of world output)	16
AC capacitors and flyback transformers (% of world output)	25	Motherboards (% of world output)	15
		Water consumption (m³ billions)	1.5
Electricity consumption (billion kWh)	35.2	Industrial waste water (million tons)	225.0
Sulfur dioxide emissions ('000 tons)	199.4	Industrial waste water meeting discharge standards (%)	90.1
Industrial solid wastes ('000 tons)	28.6		
Days with good air quality (%)	97.8	Industrial solid wastes meeting discharge standards (%)	86.5
Sulfur dioxide emissions meeting emissions standards (%)	92.9		

Sources: China, National Bureau of Statistics 2005; data from the government of Dongguan.

The result is that, in a 2005 World Bank survey of over 12,000 firms in 120 Chinese cities, Dongguan ranked among the top 10 in terms of a broad measure of the investment climate.[25] Even more telling is the fact that Dongguan ranked second in terms of a narrower measure of government efficiency based on estimates of the effective tax burden and the costs of corruption and bureaucratic delays faced by firms.

Sources: Shubham Chaudhuri, personal contribution.

New International Trade

New international trade theory was developed originally to explain the observation that more trade takes place between countries at similar income levels than between countries with different income levels and factor endowments. This is of growing relevance in East Asia because most trade occurs between middle-income countries. The main idea is the recognition that scale economies in more specialized products represent an additional factor in determining what is exported and what is imported. Economists would say that trade is increasingly being based on differences both in factor endowments (classical comparative advantage) and in economies of scale in production (modern competitive advantage).

The notion that trade is closely linked with new technology and with product variety is an important departure from the traditional assumption that trade reflects factor endowments. It provides an explanation for intraindustry trade because products with small differences still fall under the same broad industrial classification, yet may be made in different countries and traded for each other. It also supplies an explanation for the trade in intermediate goods because there are many more intermediate goods than final goods, and, so, it is in intermediates that a lot of product diversification occurs.

With economies of scale, trade allows the exploitation of technological advantages by increasing the size of the potential market. More trading opportunities therefore encourage specialization in production. At the same time, specialized producers innovate more, and the greater the degree of innovation, the greater the extent of trade. One key insight is that trade often involves the exchange of new or different product varieties and therefore depends on the speed of the introduction of new products. If the ability to develop new products depends on the variety of products already in existence, then technology spillovers may emerge that drive trade and growth.

New Economic Growth

The new growth theory starts with the recognition that, in standard neoclassical economics, there is little room for the entrepreneur. Entrepreneurs develop new ideas, technologies, markets, and business processes. In doing so, they expect to be rewarded. But rewards to entrepreneurs are ruled out in a context of perfect competition with constant returns to scale, so there are no incentives for entrepreneurial activity. To escape this awkward result, neoclassical models have to assume an exogenous growth rate of technology. This means that such models have nothing to say about the long-run growth of frontier economies and emphasize new capital accumulation exclusively so that developing countries may reach high-income status. In such formulations of the economy, schooling and investment are all that count for growth.[11]

New growth theory tries to model how innovations actually happen in a real economy by allowing for some economic rewards that go to entrepreneurs. It attempts to explain the observation that around 60 percent of export growth seems to take place through new product varieties, rather than through the exportation of greater volumes of the same goods.[12] The models link the quantity of resources applied to innovation with the output in terms of new ideas and processes and then link the impact of these new ideas to growth. Different models emphasize different aspects of these key relationships. The main concepts are that innovation requires effort and that ideas are different from goods and factors in that they may be used simultaneously by many people. And, even when ideas may not be used freely to produce goods (say, because of patent or copyright reasons), they may still be used freely and widely to produce other new ideas. In any case, as societies accumulate knowledge (the stock of useful ideas), they may grow seemingly without limit. In contrast, there are strict limits to a pattern of growth that is based only on the accumulation of people and capital.

The concept of ideas as drivers of economic growth is closely tied to the notion of learning and skills, and, so, the first versions of endogenous growth theory emphasized education as the precondition for absorbing new ideas.[13] If the rate of growth of new ideas depends on the stock of human capital, then countries may avoid diminishing returns to investment and continue to grow through capital accumulation. Later versions take this further and disaggregate between primary, secondary, and university education. They break down new ideas into innovations and imitations and associate the latter with technological catching up and basic education, while the former requires higher-level university education and research institutions.

What makes firms innovate and decide to invest in acquiring new technologies? Again, the difference between frontier firms and catch-up firms is important. Frontier firms enjoy economic rents accruing from the fact that they are the best in the business. They have little incentive to innovate unless they become concerned about potential competitors encroaching on their markets. Competition, openness to trade, and deregulation so as to facilitate new entrants may spur innovation in such firms, thereby ensuring that they remain on the frontier.

Catch-up firms, on the other hand, face a different set of incentives. If they are able to come close to frontier technology by innovating, then the extra profits that accrue to them make it worth their while to put a lot of resources into the endeavor. But, if they are so far behind that the likelihood of earning extra profits is slim, while their existing position is threatened by new entrants, they may react to intense competition by simply giving up innovation completely. The growth effect of new entry is still positive, however, because the new entrants themselves raise productivity.

Importantly, evidence from developed and developing countries seems to support some of the predictions of these models.[14] This evidence suggests that, indeed, structural reforms such as new competition policy, delicensing, trade liberalization, entry and exit strategies, and education attainment may have a direct impact on economic growth by influencing the degree to which firms make an effort to innovate or imitate. Moreover, the theory suggests that this impact is conditional on the situation of the firms and the nature of the industry. More advanced firms need competition to encourage frontier innovation. But intense competition seems to be less important for imitation. In that case, a set of institutions is required that facilitates the implementation and adoption of existing technology.

New Economic Geography

The new economic geography concerns itself with the choices firms make about location.[15] In geography models, firms tend to concentrate production in one location so as to enjoy plant-level economies of scale, and they like to be near their customers and suppliers in order to reduce transport costs.[16] But, once a market has reached a certain scale, this encourages other firms to locate there to take advantage of market size, thereby giving rise to "agglomeration economies," or advantages of coalescing geographically. Agglomeration is also associated with more intense competition and the easier entry of new firms. However, agglomeration may also create problems—what we call the costs of grime, crime, and time. The formation or growth of secondary cities may be made stronger by rising pollution, breakdowns in law and order, and congestion in a major city. In general, the number of cities and their locations depend heavily on specific characteristics that are difficult to model. What is clear is that ports and other transport nodes have served as the foundation for cities, and, once established, these cities have tended to grow. Transport costs continue to be important in determining the size and nature of cities.

The new economic geography emphasizes the agglomeration economies that arise from the colocation of firms and the role of cities in the spread of new ideas and processes.[17] There is particular interest in economies of scale in the production of intermediate goods, which renders it desirable to locate final goods production in the same place, enhancing the size of the market and thereby encouraging more firms to locate in the same city.

The new economic geography suggests that history matters. The existence of a large manufacturing sector represents an incentive to suppliers to locate in a country to take advantage of the larger market and greater potential access, and these would reinforce the original advantage. But modelers have recognized that factors of production, especially labor, are not mobile between countries in the same way they are mobile within countries; thus, cost structures may drive firms from larger, higher-wage centers or countries to smaller, lower-wage centers or countries.[18] The lower the transport costs firms face, the less likely firms will all congregate in a rich country or city.

This is the core of the first attempt to model the shifting location of production in East Asia that was put forward in the now famous flying geese analogy.[19] According to this model, a lead economy (Japan) develops new technologies and production capabilities, but, as it develops, it shifts these techniques to economies with cheaper labor. In this way, mature industries migrate from more to less well developed economies, while the lead economy specializes in more sophisticated, complex industries. This model was used to explain the evolution of the four Asian tigers, Hong Kong (China), the Republic of Korea, Singapore, and Taiwan (China), which did, indeed, gradually take over many of the industries that Japan had specialized in through 1960.

One drawback of the flying geese model is that it focuses on interindustry relocation and trade, but does not explain intraindustry trade. Nor does it explain why some industries, such as garments and textiles, have moved quickly to low-wage countries, while other industries, such as automobiles, have not. The emphasis on savings of labor costs implies economic determinism, whereby economies would naturally follow a predetermined homogeneous trajectory. But this allows for catching up, not overtaking, and offers a minimal role for policy.

In the new economic geography, by contrast, there is less determinism. One feature of these models is multiple equilibria, and small changes in initial conditions may have large effects. History and luck matter a lot in terms of which cities and countries are selected as the location for firms. And, given the presence of unexhausted economies of scale, the selected areas will have a persistent advantage into the future and an ability to reward workers with higher wages. Small wonder, then, that policy makers are so concerned about national competitiveness.

Distributional Consequences

The new theories built around economies of scale do not address questions of income distribution directly. The formulations tend to be formally centered on a representative agent and usually do not recognize the heterogeneity of firms and workers within economies. This is the aspect that recent research has been emphasizing. In any case, there is no doubt that income distribution is affected profoundly by the existence or lack of scale economies and the manner in which they are exploited.

At the heart of the analysis of distributional impact is the notion that economies of scale allow for economic rents, which are the surpluses above and beyond the income needed to pay owners of labor and capital. Economic surpluses allow entrepreneurs to be rewarded for innovation and perhaps represent a source of surplus that may be taxed, without distortion, for public funding of public goods. Similarly, the taxes may be used to finance the investments in urban infrastructure that are needed to exploit agglomeration economies. In each of these cases, the presence of economic rents is a desirable, indeed, necessary ingredient allowing for sustained rapid growth through the exploitation of economies of scale.

But the distributional impacts are not always positive. Economies of scale may exist in one part of an economy, but not in other parts; economists have argued that they are more likely to be present in manufacturing and in urban areas, but are largely absent in agriculture and the rural sector.[20] If this is true, then it provides one explanation for the persistence of urban-rural wage differences.[21] Economies of scale may also result in a premium for skilled workers relative to unskilled workers, especially if the skilled workers are key personnel in innovation or imitation that generates temporary excess profits for firms facing imperfect competition. If this is true, then it provides an explanation for widening income gaps in relatively open and rapidly growing economies. The spatial and social aspects of growth, driven by the exploitation of economies of scale, figure prominently in this report.

As we argue above, the licensing of new entrants, exit policies, trade liberalization, and competition among incumbents may affect the degree to which firms are able to extract economic surpluses from their innovation efforts. If firms are able to extract surpluses, then they will try to influence government policy to favor their own interests. Economic rents attract rent-seeking behavior.

It is noteworthy that the distributional implications outlined above have little overlap with the distributional outcomes in neoclassical models. In those models, international trade is based on factor endowments. Poorer countries export labor-intensive goods, and the returns to unskilled labor would be bid up. This model has successfully explained East Asia's growth-with-equity experience and is still the best explanation for developments in poor countries in the region. But neoclassical models do not seem to provide adequate insight into what is happening to distribution in the middle-income economies of East Asia today.

Avoiding the Middle-Income Trap

Modern growth theory predicts that middle-income countries in East Asia should witness three transformations: first, diversification will slow and then reverse, as countries become more specialized in production and employment; second, investment will become less important, and innovation should accelerate; third, education systems will shift from equipping workers with skills that allow them to adjust to new technologies to preparing them to shape new products and processes. These would be the observable outcomes associated with a successful shift in strategy as countries progress through middle-income status.

In the absence of economies of scale, East Asian middle-income countries would face an uphill struggle to maintain their historically impressive growth. Strategies based on factor accumulation are likely to deliver steadily worse results, which is a natural occurrence as the marginal productivity of capital declines. Latin America and the Middle East are examples of middle-income regions that, for decades, have been unable to escape this trap.

Exploiting economies of scale offers a way out. But do such economies exist for middle-income countries on a scale that is sufficiently sizable to make a difference in aggregate economic growth? This section describes key economic developments in the region through the lens of theories based on economies of scale. We argue that the pattern of trade, the flow of ideas and innovations, the new financial architecture, and the performance of cities are all consistent with East Asian economies displaying a shift toward growth that is founded on economies of scale. Equally, the distributional consequences—the change from growth with equity to rising income inequality within countries—and the concerns about corruption are also symptomatic of economies of scale.

Economies of scale are not easily measured, but, when measures exist, it is clear that economies of scale are playing a central role in East Asia's success. Electronics, computers, and communications are all sectors that exhibit sizable scale economies. Economic historians have argued that most technological progress takes the form of small, incremental improvements.[22] These could hardly give East Asian economies the impetus they need. But certain technological improvements are radical: the steam engine, electricity, and now computers.[23] East Asia is at the center of recent radical changes. In the short run, as major producers, they stand to gain from economies of scale in production. In the medium term, as users close to the innovators, they stand to gain by quickly learning how to use the new technologies. It is not surprising that, in addition to being one of the world's largest producers of high-technology goods, an East Asian country, Korea, is also the world's most connected economy. It is also not surprising that some East Asian economies have focused on technologies that have enabled them successfully to grow through middle-income status to become high-income economies over the past generation.

Trade and Technology

Dramatic changes are taking place in the composition of East Asian trade, and, at the same time, the value of trade is expanding. Low-skill, labor-intensive products, such as garments and textiles, toys and sports equipment, and wood and paper products, are becoming less important, even for China, and now account for only 15 percent of total exports. Instead, exports of higher-skill and higher-technology products, such as computers, office equipment, and communications equipment, are growing the most rapidly. Falling under the broad category of machinery in international trade statistics, these goods account for over half of East Asian exports.

This trade pattern in machinery may best be explained by two related technological developments that have profoundly affected the way in which goods are produced and sold worldwide: scale economies and vertical specialization. Scale economies in machinery exist at the plant level (determined by engineering), the firm level (for example, the availability of internal research and development [R&D] facilities), and the economy-wide level (agglomeration economies in cities). Industrial engineers have concluded that scale economies exist in products such as scientific instruments, electrical machinery, nonelectrical machinery, iron and steel, and pharmaceuticals (see figure 4).[24] These are precisely the products in which the share of East Asian exports has increased. On the other hand, products such as wood, footwear, leather, apparel, and textiles show no tendency toward scale economies; these industries have seen their export shares fall.

Vertical specialization describes the potential for breaking down production into different components that may later be combined into final goods. If each component is produced in a specialized plant located where the cost is the lowest and the variety and innovation are the highest, then the final good may be produced at a lower cost and higher quality. If vertical specialization leads to the production of components outside the firm, this is called outsourcing. If the production takes place in another country, it is called offshoring. To be cost effective, offshoring requires low transport costs in terms of logistics and trade tariffs. In addition, a buyer must be assured that the selected component manufacturer is, indeed, the producer at the lowest cost and, so, must incur information and search costs that need to be efficiently covered.

Offshoring has also been fostered by changes in business models. To ensure a constant inventory of supplies, vertically integrating firms used to take over factory production lines. Now, lean production techniques, pioneered by Toyota, emphasize instead innovation and high quality among parts suppliers and combine this with sophisticated logistics so as to reduce inventory costs to a minimum. These developments lend themselves to the exploitation of scale economies at the plant level, and to industry- and economy-wide agglomeration economies. Similar manufacturers congregate in one location, each helping the

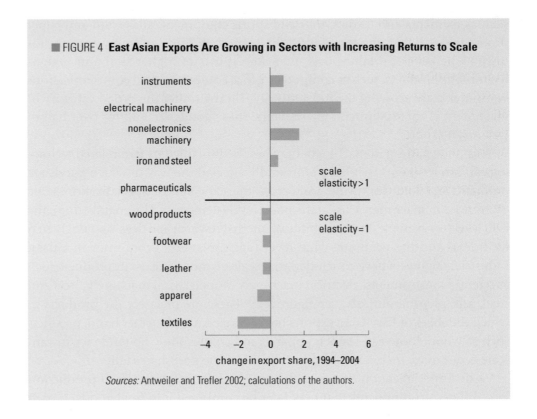

■ FIGURE 4 **East Asian Exports Are Growing in Sectors with Increasing Returns to Scale**

Sources: Antweiler and Trefler 2002; calculations of the authors.

other to develop a local talent pool of skilled labor, and each innovating and building on the innovations of the others.

In East Asia, countries are competing vigorously to become part of the offshoring trend. Cost advantages, such as low wages, continue to play a role. Other factors are also critical, however, including a friendly environment for affiliates created through foreign investment, excellent logistics, predictable economic policies that permit low tariffs and good duty-drawback schemes in cases where local inputs are taxed, and a well-developed service sector to link component deliveries. Because such a wide range of factors is at play, no single country within East Asia dominates entire production chains. Each country has found a niche and is participating and sharing in regional growth opportunities.

In the presence of significant offshoring, the trade in intermediate goods rises more rapidly than does total output. Trade is measured in terms of the gross value of output. If a product is shipped to another country, worked into the next stage of production, and then shipped to yet a third country for final assembly, it might be counted several times in international trade statistics. This is, indeed, what is happening globally. The world trade in parts and components increased in value from US$400 billion in 1992 to over US$1 trillion in 2003. Taking a somewhat broader definition, Yeats (2001) concludes that intermediate goods account for 30 percent of the world trade in manufactures. In East Asia, the same phenomenon is at work (see figure 5). The trade in parts and components has grown more rapidly than has the trade in final goods. In industries with the highest scale economies, such as electrical machinery, the trade in parts and components now accounts for 80 percent of the total exports of the sector. Firm-level surveys in a sample of five low- and middle-income countries in East Asia suggest that outsourcing is almost 40 percent more prevalent in East Asia than it is in the rest of the world.[26]

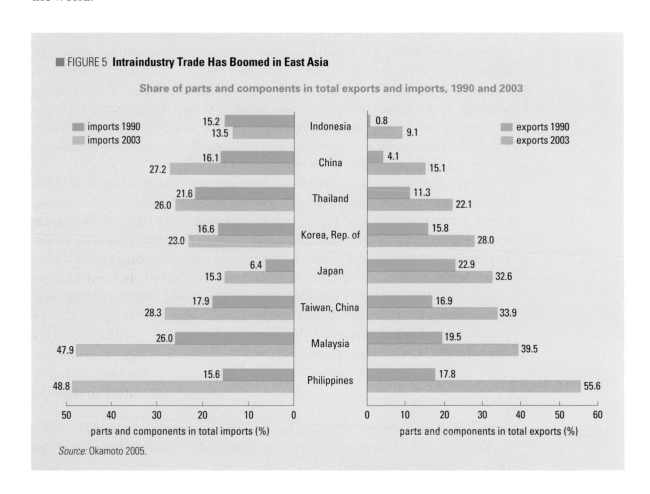

■ FIGURE 5 **Intraindustry Trade Has Boomed in East Asia**

Share of parts and components in total exports and imports, 1990 and 2003

imports 1990
imports 2003

exports 1990
exports 2003

Country	imports 1990	imports 2003	exports 1990	exports 2003
Indonesia	15.2	13.5	0.8	9.1
China	16.1	27.2	4.1	15.1
Thailand	21.6	26.0	11.3	22.1
Korea, Rep. of	16.6	23.0	15.8	28.0
Japan	6.4	15.3	22.9	32.6
Taiwan, China	17.9	28.3	16.9	33.9
Malaysia	26.0	47.9	19.5	39.5
Philippines	15.6	48.8	17.8	55.6

parts and components in total imports (%)

parts and components in total exports (%)

Source: Okamoto 2005.

If trade is driven by economies of scale, one major implication is that relatively small changes in trade costs may lead to significant changes in the volume of trade flows. Some studies of multinationals put the elasticity at between 2 and 4, that is, a 1 percent decrease in trade costs may increase trade volumes by up to 4 percent. This puts a premium on efforts to reduce trade costs. East Asian countries have done this. Since the 1997–98 crisis, trade costs have been systematically brought down. In fact, tariffs in East Asia have fallen, on average, by more than 50 percent since 1994 and now account for a little over 5 percent of import value. By contrast, in Latin America, tariffs actually increased slightly over this period in a backlash against globalization.

Because most of East Asia has efficient ports and infrastructure, freight costs as a percent of import value are lower there, on average, than they are in any other region. But freight costs do increase with distance, and this is why production networks tend to be regionally concentrated and not involve countries that are more remote. Thus, Venables (2006) points out that the elasticity of trade with respect to distance means that a distance of 8,000 kilometers will choke off more than 90 percent of the trade that would be observed over a 1,000 kilometer distance. Similar distance elasticities hold for other economic interactions such as equity holdings, FDI, and technology transfers. An exception occurs if a service component is involved, such as design or research. Services may be transported through a global telecommunications network that no longer prices according to distance. But, for the flow of goods, proximity remains a benefit.

One result of all these forces is that, within East Asia, there is far more trade than may reasonably be explained by conventional economic theories. Statistically, China, Hong Kong (China), Korea, and Japan import 8 to 10 times more from within the region than one might predict on the basis of many economic models. The tendency to import more from neighboring countries is more pronounced in the trade for parts and components relative to total trade, but the key tendencies remain the same: there is a regional dimension to trade that one is unable to explain using traditional economic models, and, in the case of China, this regional dimension has increased radically in the decade 1994 to 2004, the period when the level of China's imports began surging.[27]

Ideas and Innovation

Firms in East Asia rely extensively on knowledge from abroad, especially from the developed world, where 80 percent of the money on global R&D is spent. Countries (and firms) have used different mechanisms to acquire technology, depending on the sector and the stage of development. One important mechanism in East Asia has been exports and imports. It is well known that export firms tend to be more efficient than their nonexporting domestic counterparts, sometimes by substantial margins. But the causality of this relationship is difficult to gauge. It may be that more efficient firms naturally become exporters to exploit economies of scale. In this case, the technological innovation precedes and, indeed, causes exports. Or it may be that exporting firms must constantly innovate to meet the intense competition that arises from operating in the global marketplace. Both tendencies appear to be at work in East Asia.

Many exporting firms, especially in Korea and Taiwan (China), operate under contracts to foreign buyers who specify precise designs. This sort of original equipment manufacturing may have accounted for 70–80 percent of Korea's electronics exports around 1990 and for 40 percent of the computer hardware exports of Taiwan (China). By undertaking original equipment manufacturing production, firms achieved economies of scale and built up their technological capabilities with the assistance of foreign buyers. Once established, they developed the ability to do their own designing (original design manufacturing) and, increasingly, brand their own products (original brand manufacturing), thereby moving up the value chain. This path through manufacturing, design, and branding has been labeled supplier-oriented industrial upgrading.

The mechanism of vertical technology transfers operates domestically, as well as internationally. When there is an efficient domestic producer, such as a foreign multinational, there is strong evidence that vertical technology transfers to domestic suppliers take place.[28] Higher standards for product quality, precision, and on-time delivery, coupled with constant pressures for cost efficiencies, provide strong incentives for local suppliers to upgrade production management and technology.

According to the replies of 43 percent of a broad sample of firms in the region, East Asian firms themselves believe that the key source of new technology is the importation of new machinery.[29] Some of this occurs through parent companies when firms are bought by foreign partners using FDI. The evidence in case studies indicates that such acquisitions lead to higher output, employment, wages, and productivity, along with higher investment levels; in one study on Indonesia, the gains in productivity from foreign acquisition were estimated at an average of 46 percent.[30] The total benefits to an economy may be even higher if a foreign acquisition has a positive effect on higher productivity for domestic competitors via imitation or the hiring away of workers with experience in the new technologies. But these gains may also be offset if foreign investment reduces the market available to local firms and causes them to forego economies of scale. On balance, the evidence for so-called horizontal technology transfers is mixed.

Finally, R&D within the region provides an important source of innovation. Spending on R&D has almost doubled in East Asia over the last decade and now averages 1.2 percent of GDP (see figure 6). But this conceals large differences between countries. As one might expect, richer economies such as the newly industrializing economies spend a significantly higher share of GDP on R&D (2.2 percent), and, in an encouraging sign, the rate of growth in this R&D spending has been quite rapid by international comparison. However, among the middle-income countries, only China (1.4 percent of GDP) and Malaysia (0.7 percent) show substantial R&D spending. Southeast Asian countries generally spend much less. This is a concern since a rising number of studies suggest that R&D may yield great benefits (some studies show social returns at upwards of 78 percent) even among middle-income countries, especially when the spending facilitates the absorption of knowledge from abroad.

In determining effectiveness, the pattern of R&D is as important as the volume. Many East Asian economies follow the same pattern as developed countries in that over 60 percent of R&D is carried out within the business sector, while only 20 percent is performed by government, and another 20 percent in institutions of higher education.[31] Business, rather than government, also bears the brunt of the R&D costs. Interestingly, the East Asian economies have developed this pattern at a lower income level than is typically the case. Economies in other middle-income regions, such as Eastern Europe and Latin America, show only one-half to two-thirds as much participation in R&D by business. The presumption is that the commercial returns to R&D are likely to be higher if the share of business in the spending is higher. This augurs well for East Asia.

Innovation is more rapid when domestic capacity for knowledge absorption is high. This requires an educated labor force and quality academic institutions, the protection of intellectual property rights, and effective collaboration between research institutions and the private sector. Under these conditions, R&D spending translates into more patents. Indeed, the number of patents has skyrocketed recently in East Asia. Moreover, the number is generally higher in East Asian economies, relative to population size and per capita income, than global norms. In East Asia, the patents are concentrated in electronics, computers, and communications, although, in some countries, such as China, drugs and medical goods are also important. These patents are not merely window dressing, but have real economic value. According to one measure of patent quality, which involves an analysis of patent citations in other countries, patents in Japan, Korea, and Taiwan (China) are 70–90 percent as

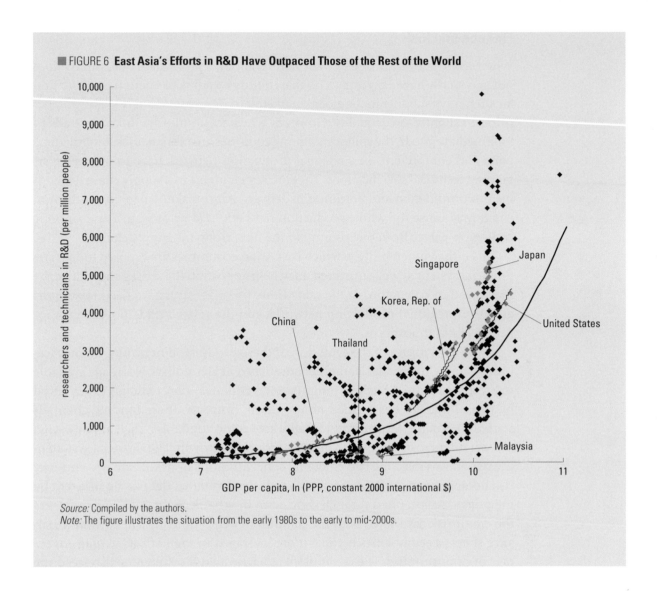

■ FIGURE 6 **East Asia's Efforts in R&D Have Outpaced Those of the Rest of the World**

Source: Compiled by the authors.
Note: The figure illustrates the situation from the early 1980s to the early to mid-2000s.

productive globally as U.S. patents, the recognized leader. Nonetheless, this may underestimate the impact of East Asian patents because, in common with patents elsewhere, patents in East Asia tend to be used or cited more often if they are registered in adjacent locations rather than in far-off countries. This geographical localization of patent knowledge spillovers means that East Asian economies stand to gain much more from the fact that the number of original patents has been rising rapidly in Northeast Asia. The regional transmission of knowledge is accelerating.

Finance and Risk

When economies are linked by trade in final goods, a problem in one country does not necessarily have a big impact on that country's trading partners. It is easy to find an alternative supplier in the global marketplace. The cost is simply slightly higher prices or slightly lower quality. However, when economies are linked by trade in intermediate goods, the spillovers among countries are more serious. Intermediate parts and components in a regional production network have to meet precise, tailored technical specifications. They are key elements in a supply chain depending on coordination and timeliness in delivery. Any breakdown in the production chain may cause the whole production network to slow or stop. The economic contagion passes from one country to the next along the supply chain.

This is the vulnerability to which East Asian economies are exposed today. The financial system, if well structured, may help apportion these risks and reduce the likelihood of contagion. At the same time, financial structures need to support growth in regional production networks and the related trade flows, and they need to fund innovation.

In the early stages of the evolution of these production networks, finance followed trade. Crossborder lending, denominated in U.S. dollars, was made available to local banks and directly to multinational affiliates. The credit risk experienced by these large entities seemed minor. Soon, however, these funding channels started to expand. More credit was allocated to nontradables, such as real estate, as asset prices rose, along with broader economic growth. The financial system in the region was masking two emerging concentrations of risk. There was currency risk because of the rising foreign exchange denominated debt being incurred by the private sector, often through short-term interbank credit lines, and there was the credit risk associated with the buildup of debt and equity in corporate balance sheets as companies became more leveraged in their efforts to take advantage of opportunities. The credit risk was aggravated if companies also faced the exchange risk involved in receiving revenues denominated in local currencies and carrying liabilities denominated in foreign exchange.

When the currency and financial crisis of 1997–98 hit the region, the economic damage spread quickly across countries. The regional financial system was unable to isolate or disperse the shocks. As Alan Greenspan famously remarked, "East Asia had no spare tire."[32] Since then, policy makers have become determined to erect defenses against economic volatility. The currency risk has been reduced by a movement toward more flexible exchange rates and by building massive international reserves to permit monetary authorities to manage exchange rates and avoid excessive volatility. In this way, Asian currencies have gradually changed in value and avoided sharp swings over short periods, giving companies plenty of room to adjust to market forces. The foreign exchange reserves in emerging East Asia now total US$1.6 trillion, and most of the middle-income economies in the region have more than enough reserves to cover all their debt liabilities for at least one year.

The credit risk has not been addressed as successfully. Banks are healthier and have plenty of liquidity. Across the region, indicators of financial sector performance have vastly improved, such as measures of asset quality, capital adequacy, and bank profitability. Average capital-loan ratios in banks in five East Asian crisis countries rose to 15 percent in 2005. Interest margins, a key determinant of profitability, increased to almost 4 percent. Nonperforming loans have fallen to moderate levels. Corporations, too, have improved their balance sheets through reduced leverage and higher operating margins. Debt-equity ratios in East Asia, which had reached 90 percent in the years before the financial crisis, had fallen to about 50 percent by 2005. But banks have been reluctant to lend to many borrowers, and almost 20 percent of firms (even more among exporting firms) report that the limited access to and high cost of finance have become major obstacles to business expansion.

Today, financial structures in Asian economies are more up to the task of addressing the key vulnerabilities associated with integration. Because of the greater reserves and diversified sources of finance among countries, the region is much less susceptible to capital flow reversals and less affected by fluctuations in the dollar-yen exchange rate (see figure 7). However, lacking the availability of a well-developed corporate bond market, the majority of firms that are not investment grade now face problems in gaining access to finance for expansion and innovation. East Asia finally has a spare tire, but it is still not a full-sized spare.

Cities and Livability

Most economic activity takes place in cities. It has been estimated that cities in East Asia generate about three-quarters of annual output and between one-half and two-thirds of exports. Often, much of this is concentrated in single primate cities: Bangkok accounts for 40 percent of Thailand's GDP; Manila, for 30 percent in the Philippines; Ho Chi Minh City, for 20 percent in Vietnam; and Shanghai, for 11 percent in China. Four East Asian cities have one-quarter or more of the total national population: Seoul, Taipei, Tokyo, and Ulaanbaatar. Seven of the world's 21 megacities (those with populations in excess of 10 million) are in East Asia. Per

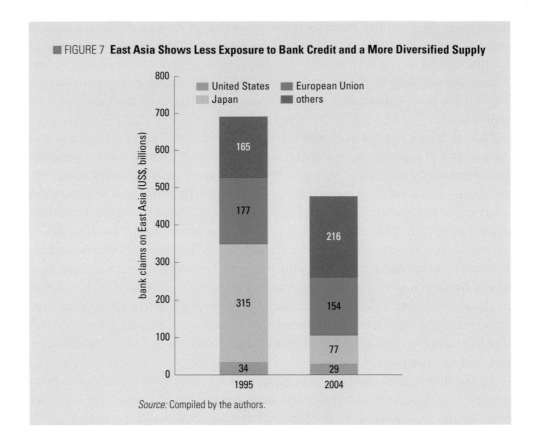

■ FIGURE 7 **East Asia Shows Less Exposure to Bank Credit and a More Diversified Supply**

Source: Compiled by the authors.

capita incomes in cities are a multiple of economy-wide averages, and the average city dweller consumes almost twice as much as the average rural inhabitant.

East Asian cities have been able to deliver the agglomeration economies that are required for rapid growth, and have done well as connectors to the outside world. A study of 120 cities in China that, together, account for three-quarters of economy-wide output shows that the productivity of firms rises significantly when they are located in large cities.[33] Another study shows that distance to a port is a powerful determinant of income levels in Chinese cities: on average, cities that are more than 400 miles from the coast have half the per capita GDP of otherwise similar coastal port cities.[34] These more remote cities also attract less foreign investment: 80 percent of China's FDI has gone into coastal provinces, and 60 percent of Vietnam's FDI has gone to only three cities: Dong Nai, Hanoi, and Ho Chi Minh City. The function of providing a gateway for commerce is critical for a region dependent on exports to drive growth.[35] East Asia, excluding Japan, is home to 16 of the largest 25 seaports in the world, 14 of the largest 25 container ports, and 7 of the largest 25 cargo airports.

More generally, there is a strong empirical relationship globally between indexes of city livability and a country's GDP per capita, suggesting that long-term growth is only feasible if city attributes in terms of congestion, pollution, and safety are improved alongside urban economic management. East Asian cities tend to register around the global average adjusted for current income level and so need to progress substantially to sustain higher living standards. Cities such as Bangkok and Manila have only half the average rapid-transit road network relative to wealthier, more efficient cities such as Hong Kong (China) and Singapore. The problems are worse in smaller cities. Even within countries, cities vary in their management effectiveness and livability. It is becoming clearer that what is good for people is good for business: Shanghai, a popular destination for businesses, has recently been voted the most livable city in China.

Thus, cities have been able to accommodate or even lead in the rapid growth trend in East Asia. Will they continue to do so? The challenge is immense. Because of rapid economic growth, East Asian countries have reached levels of industrialization and per capita income that are generally associated with greater urbanization. East Asian cities are witnessing an urbanization "catch-up" that will be the largest rural-to-urban shift in population in human history. In the next two decades, cities in East Asia will swell by 2 million people *every month*. The strains are already apparent in terms of slums, poor services, and large informal labor markets. This extraordinary urbanization will require an extraordinary response from policy makers in municipal, provincial, and national governments.

Most urban growth is not occurring in major metropolitan areas, which have been relatively well managed. These areas are reaching natural limits. Instead, according to forecasters, about half of new urbanites will settle in cities of less than 500,000 inhabitants. While this will give better spatial balance to East Asian growth, it poses questions about how well these smaller cities will deliver scale economies or, conversely, whether they will waste gains in agglomeration by tolerating congestion, crime, and poor city management. It appears that there is great diversity in the performance of smaller cities in their provision of basic services and overall governance. Unless these smaller cities are able to raise their game and connect up with existing trade networks, it will be difficult for East Asia to maintain its strong growth performance over the next quarter century.

Cohesion and Inequality

For many years, East Asian growth was associated with rapid poverty reduction and equity. In 2005, some 150 million East Asians (8 percent of the regional population) were living in absolute poverty (below US$1 per day), while 585 million were living on less than US$2 per day. If present trends continue, East Asia may be able to come close to eliminating absolute poverty within a decade and the broader problem of poverty within a generation.

Yet, the concerns about social cohesion within the region are becoming more serious, not less. Inequality is rising in the region in terms not only of incomes, but also of education attainment and access to basic services. Poorer regions and rural areas are falling further behind their urban counterparts. Ethnic minorities are not participating in the generalized growth. Despite the huge differences in income per capita among East Asian countries, more than three-quarters of the inequality in living standards among East Asian citizens is accounted for by within-country inequality (see figure 8). In China, inequality has risen both within rural and urban regions and between them. In short, despite successful global integration and increasing regional integration, many East Asian countries are failing in the achievement of domestic integration. Why is this so?

The rise of inequality in the region can be explained in terms of the growth processes driven by economies of scale. With increasing returns to scale activities located in cities, income growth in urban areas has generally outpaced that in rural areas. There are other geographic disparities however. We have already referred to the strong links between trade opportunities, as measured by distance to a seaport, and income levels within countries. A growing share of this trade in East Asia is in the form of trade in intermediate inputs, which can have a much greater impact on wages and employment than trade in final goods. There is compelling evidence that trade in inputs shifts demand away from less skilled labor and toward skilled workers.[36] In a study of five East Asian economies— Hong Kong (China), Korea, the Philippines, Singapore, and Thailand—during 1985–98, Te Velde and Morrissey (2004) find that trade boosted wage inequality.[37] For Indonesia, Bourguignon and Goh (2004) find that wages are higher and earnings stability is greater among people employed in the more traded sectors.

It is clear that a sizeable fraction of the within-country inequality is arising from the growing inequality in urban incomes. Part of this is caused by the higher wage premiums for skilled workers. In China and Vietnam, the returns to university education have climbed steeply over the last decade. However, this may be a transitory phenomenon created by rigidities in the supply of college education.

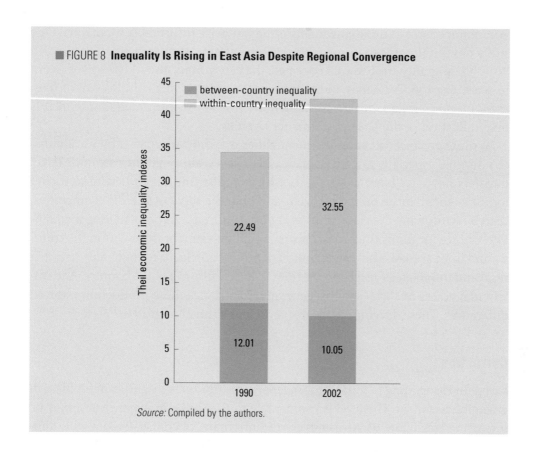

■ FIGURE 8 **Inequality Is Rising in East Asia Despite Regional Convergence**

Source: Compiled by the authors.

Neither Indonesia nor Thailand, where the number of graduates has soared, display any trend toward greater skill premiums.

Another source of inequality in urban areas is labor market restructuring. Countries that are more successful in trade and integration also show more turnover and labor force restructuring. This is typical of highly innovative systems. What happens to workers in this case? In a study of five cities in China where enormous labor market restructuring has occurred during the reform of state-owned enterprises, Giles, Park, and Cai (2006) have found that workers younger than 40 years of age who were reemployed were able to raise their average earnings, while those over 40 got lower wages. Two-thirds of workers were not able to find new jobs within a 12-month period, suffering considerable income losses. The pattern is quite different in Vietnam, where workers laid off from state enterprises have been able to improve their incomes, and workers remaining with their enterprises have achieved wage and productivity gains.

A major source of urban inequality is the extensive informal labor market. One study has put the size of this market in China at almost 40 percent of the total.[38] Women, migrants, the less well educated, the very young, and older workers seem to work disproportionately in the informal market. If this is indicative of fragmentation in urban labor markets, then the size of the informal labor market is one indication of the poor performance of cities.

In more advanced economies, inequalities may be partly offset by fiscal transfers directed especially toward poor areas. However, although they are quite large, transfers have not been designed to achieve redistribution in East Asia. Richer localities spend more on their citizens and on basic services and other amenities, thereby reinforcing their positions as choice locations and perpetuating inequalities. Choice locations thus attract more capital investment from within the country and from abroad. The concentration of production leads to inequality between rural and urban areas and between cities in different parts of the country. And differential access to social services generally exacerbates these production-induced differences. These developments may represent a threat to growth.

Corruption

Except in Hong Kong (China) and Singapore, corruption is a significant problem in emerging East Asia. The level is comparable to that in Latin America and may be increasing (see figure 9). Measures of corruption are, of course, fraught with difficulties, but a growing body of evidence appears to indicate that corruption is a serious issue in the region.[39] Can East Asian growth prevail under these circumstances?

Some have argued that there is an Asian paradox: how is it possible for high levels of corruption to coexist alongside rapid economic growth? Part of the answer seems to lie with the organized nature of corruption. Political scientists hypothesize that, if corruption is organized and centralized, then economic rents may be extracted from firms, while also ensuring that the corruption does not become so corrosive that firms move elsewhere or otherwise become unviable. In essence, a centralized corrupt organization has an incentive to promote economic growth, even as it extorts benefits from firms.

This model appears to fit East Asia quite well. Surveys show that a high proportion of firms in Cambodia (56 percent), Indonesia (41 percent), the Philippines (35 percent), and China (27 percent) report that corruption is a major or severe constraint to doing business.[40] But these same firms report that government effectiveness and regulatory quality are better than one might expect given the degree of corruption. The impression is one of widespread, but orderly corruption.

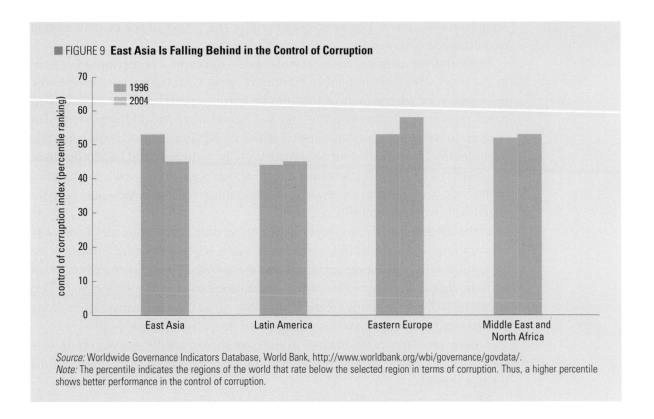

■ FIGURE 9 **East Asia Is Falling Behind in the Control of Corruption**

Source: Worldwide Governance Indicators Database, World Bank, http://www.worldbank.org/wbi/governance/govdata/.
Note: The percentile indicates the regions of the world that rate below the selected region in terms of corruption. Thus, a higher percentile shows better performance in the control of corruption.

Such a picture has been associated with strong central governments in the region. Presidents Marcos and Suharto are estimated to have embezzled billions of dollars through an organized system of corruption whereby all bribes flowed to the top and were then divided among government bureaucrats. The demise of industrial planning in 1993 weakened the information linking bureaucrats and businesses in Korea.[41] In the new democratic political system of Korea, corruption became more disorganized. Some pin the dramatic collapse of Hanbo Steel in early 1997 on the demise of government protection. In China, too, there are reports that large-scale corruption rings account for 30–60 percent of all the cases of graft uncovered by authorities.[42]

The notion that organized, predictable corruption is less damaging than disorganized corruption to economic growth presents challenges to middle-income East Asian countries. Centralized corruption is a more exposed target for public attack. By some measures, East Asians are even less tolerant of corruption than citizens of Western democracies. They have demanded and obtained broad improvements in political rights and the recognition of civil liberties over the past 20 years.

They have also pushed aggressively to reduce the power of the center through decentralized government.

Decentralization brings its own challenges to the control of corruption, at least in the short term. Subnational authorities in most East Asian countries are now responsible for a large share of total public spending and have significant rights to tax, regulate, and otherwise affect the business climate. World Bank investment climate surveys among firms show that the dispersion in productivity among localities in China and Indonesia is significant. In Indonesia and the Philippines, two countries that have implemented the most extensive decentralization programs in the region, the surveys among firms suggest that decentralization may be associated with worse corruption.

In the longer term, democracy and greater freedom of the press may have a significant impact on controlling corruption. Greater press freedom brings public corruption to light, while democracy allows the public to punish corrupt politicians by removing them from office. When institutions such as the judiciary are also strengthened, civil servants are no longer able to act with impunity. Hong Kong (China) and Singapore have long histories of the prosecution of public servants, and, more recently, Indonesia and Korea have shown a willingness to prosecute even the highest officials. China and Vietnam have also moved aggressively against corrupt officials.

But democracy and the institutions needed to find and root out corruption require time to mature. In the shorter term, the risk facing East Asia is that the "rule of man" has been largely swept away, while the "rule of law" has yet to become firmly established. The transition from centralized, corrupt governments to decentralized, uncorrupt governments may not be symmetric, and countries in the region risk becoming mired in this state of inefficiency, whereby governments are decentralized, but corrupt. Especially strong anticorruption efforts may be needed to ensure that this transition is short. Otherwise, the price in terms of growth may be high.

Growth, Gravity, and Friction in Action

Advancing steadily beyond middle-income status requires harnessing economies of scale. For most countries, this implies reliance on the "force of gravity" to connect countries globally and regionally (see table 2). Such strong regional forces are found in East Asia in trade, innovation, and financial links. However, countries must also reinvest economic rents efficiently to overcome the domestic friction associated with the social and spatial effects of rapid growth. In the region, frictional constraints are manifested in clogged cities, fraying social cohesion, and growing corruption.

■ TABLE 2 **Gravity and Friction: Facts and Implications**

	Facts	Implications
Gravity		
Trade	East Asia is the most open developing region for trade in goods	Liberalize trade in business services
	The trade in parts and components and intra-industry trade have grown rapidly	Make logistics more efficient
	China and Japan are the region's twin engines	Enhance market access through regional integration; keep rules of origin simple
Innovation	Internationally competitive firms (exporters) are driving industrial growth	Knowledge is now more easily accessible for all East Asians
	FDI and skills are driving innovation	Keep outward orientation and competitiveness
	Northeast Asia is producing more patents	Upgrade tertiary education
Finance	Bank claims on the corporate sector have fallen since the 1997–98 financial crisis	Local credit risks need to become better identified and managed
	Foreign exchange reserves have soared since the financial crisis	Regional cooperation may be a more efficient way to address the fear of floating exchange rates
	Bank-dominated financial systems do not support innovative enterprises	Develop more effective securities markets, including corporate bond markets
Friction		
Cities	Cities have three times the productivity of rural areas, reflecting agglomeration economies	Urban growth will drive regional differences
	Large cities are coming under stress	Make large cities more livable
	Secondary cities are growing more rapidly	Improve domestic connectedness and the economic management of small cities
Cohesion	Within-country inequality is significant because of urban-rural and coastal-interior gaps	Access to services, especially education, should not depend on location as much as it does
	Within-country inequality is rising because of rising within-urban and within-rural inequality	Labor market segmentation by space and social groups must be reduced
	Poverty rates have been falling rapidly in cities	Rapid skill formation may be able to offset the high postsecondary wage premium
Corruption	The tolerance for corruption is falling in East Asia	Corruption is seen as a threat to growth, and the perceptions of corruption are worsening
	East Asia's decentralization is progressing more rapidly than the institutionalization of checks and balances	Corruption may become a more serious obstacle to growth unless transparency and accountability develop at the local level
	The contestability of political power has grown in East Asia	Speed up the transition from the rule of man to the rule of law

Source: Compiled by the authors.

Toward a Third Integration

The notion that economies of scale are an important driver of economic growth in East Asia has major implications for public policy. This is so because there are winners and losers in the industrialization process.[43] Economies of scale may persist and provide the basis for future growth; so, the possible gains from public policy that attracts more capital and investment to a country are accentuated. Where economies of scale are important, small shifts in policy may have large payoffs. The temptation among policy makers to act so as to gain an advantage is huge. But the converse is also true. Bad policies may have large negative consequences that persist. Policy choices need to be grounded in a thorough understanding of what works and what does not.

For East Asia's low-income economies, the basic principles of openness, macroeconomic stability, and high savings and investment in physical and human capital continue to offer a promising path to progress. These economies will benefit for some time from the cost advantages they offer in global and regional trade. As regional production networks permit more fragmentation in production across countries, giving rise to an ever finer division of labor globally, low-income countries will find more opportunities. Their prospects in a rapidly growing region are bright. But the current benevolent integration into production networks should not be taken for granted by these countries. Suppliers may start relocating to be closer to final producers, such as China, if low-income countries do not buttress their cost advantages in low wages by instituting efficient logistics and more attractive business climates.

For the region's middle-income economies, there must be an evolution in the application of these strategies. Table 3 lists the implications involved in moving from a phase of exploiting comparative advantage to one in which countries also exploit economies of scale. This means recognizing the sensitivity of intraindustry trade to transport costs, the growing importance of investments in R&D and of an emphasis on proper education in science and technology, and the need to diversify capital markets to ensure appropriately priced finance.

Specialization. Low tariffs and efficient infrastructure to reduce transport costs have been the pillars of integration and regional production networks in the region. In fact, given the emphasis on the trade in intermediate goods and the benefits of agglomeration, openness takes on added importance for middle-income countries. However, scale economies put more emphasis on the significance of market size. Access to foreign markets becomes more essential than the static efficiency gains that unilateral liberalization may bring. In the absence of any likeli-

■ TABLE 3 **The Growing Complexity of Development: Economies of Scale**

Force	Growing complexity			Strategic imperatives	
	From: Exploiting comparative advantage	**+**	**To: Also exploiting scale economies**	**New opportunities**	**Policy priorities**
Specialization	Labor-intensive exports	+	Parts and components trade	Regional production networks	Logistics
Ideas and human capital	Basic and secondary education	+	Postsecondary education	Regional knowledge spillovers	Scientists and engineers
Managing economies	High savings and low deficits	+	Risk management	Regional financial stability	Corporate bond markets

Source: Compiled by the authors.

hood of global free trade, it is therefore not surprising that countries in the region are turning to regional agreements to enlarge markets. This also explains why the Association of Southeast Asian Nations is committed to a single free trade area so as to offset the advantages that China, with its large domestic market, appears to offer investors. Regional agreements may provide strategic advantages.

Ideas and human capital. Human capital accumulation is always desirable, no matter what form it takes. In economies where new ideas and innovations are key, higher education takes on a special dimension. Greater quantity and higher quality in knowledge workers—principally, but not only, scientists and engineers— will help countries absorb new ideas more rapidly and grow more quickly. Given the likely externalities and the benefits of early entry into growth industries, countries facing scarce supplies of skilled labor are also well advised to open their doors to immigration. Singapore has already taken this decision with its commitment to attracting global talent.

Economic management. The ideal macroeconomic environment for supporting regional production networks has three features: stable exchange rates to eliminate currency risk and build the foundations for a single market, capital convertibility to allow savings to be efficiently allocated across the region, and an independent monetary policy to minimize recessions and give firms the confidence that investments in innovative activities will pay off. However, it is a well-known axiom of economics that this trinity is impossible to achieve. The region seems to be moving in a sensible direction toward greater long-term flexibility in exchange rates, while minimizing short-term volatility through the accumulation of foreign exchange reserves, managed interventions, and broader regional surveillance and financial cooperation.

In many ways, these suggestions are not new, and the middle-income countries in East Asia have already started to implement them. There are areas where less progress has been made and some warning flags are being waved. In Southeast Asia, there are indications that spending on R&D is inadequate. Countries such as Indonesia are not participating vigorously in regional production networks and are weak in exports of intermediate goods, perhaps because customs processes and logistics are still cumbersome. In Northeast Asia, there are many opportunities for extending regional networks. In China, for example, there is efficient trade in the coastal cities, but not in the interior cities. Regional agreements are under discussion, but there is a concern that progress is slowing and that regional approaches have not yielded the expected gains in regulatory harmonization. The regional institutional framework is weak.

Despite these caveats and notwithstanding the considerable efforts that must still be made to create structures for trade, innovation, and finance that will support regional production networks, there is reason to be optimistic. The East Asian economies are moving toward appropriate solutions in these areas. There is less reason to be optimistic about the remaining domestic challenges. It is fashionable these days to equate the growth challenge with the problem of the development of institutions. But institutional development is an abstract notion. Table 4 lists the three specific areas of friction in the middle-income countries that are aggressively pursuing economic growth: congestion, inequality, and corruption. Modern growth theory makes a good case for expecting these areas to be problems even if governments are taking appropriate steps, but governments would be wrong to assume that the friction is best ignored.

Agglomeration. Large cities in the region must improve their livability, and smaller cities must be well managed and well connected so as to absorb productively the large numbers of people expected to relocate there. Small cities show a wide dispersion in performance, which presents an unexploited opportunity for more rapid growth. Cities need to deliver basic services and provide the infrastructure and regulations necessary so that firms are able to do business unmolested and without paying high costs due to inefficiencies of grime, crime, and time. While crime is not a pressing problem, pollution and congestion must not be left unaddressed if major East Asian cities are to support higher living standards. China appears to have recognized the importance of livable, well-connected cities.

■ TABLE 4 **The Growing Complexity of Development: The Distribution of Economic Rents**

	Growing complexity			Strategic imperatives	
Force	**From: Letting markets work**	**+**	**To: Also addressing coordination failures**	**Pressing challenges**	**Policy priorities**
Agglomeration	Megacities	+	Midsized and small cities	Congestion	Connected small and midsized cities
Social and spatial effects	Unskilled wage growth	+	Urban skilled wage growth	Inequality	Access to social services
Managing societies	Small centralized governments	+	Decentralized governments	Corruption	Transparency and accountability

Source: Compiled by the authors.

Social and spatial effects. A second institutional priority is the improvement of social cohesion. Rising within-country inequality is producing a concentration of production and regional inequalities that may become long-lasting and detrimental to overall growth. Existing patterns of fiscal decentralization do not effectively address these imbalances and should be improved. More broadly, the institutional environment for delivering basic social services in an equitable way is important to ensuring equality in opportunity, an outcome that would enhance growth prospects. Thailand has instituted relevant national programs that merit the attention of others.[44]

Better government. The third institutional priority is the control of corruption. The economic rents that are generated by economies of scale will not lead to sustained growth if they are dissipated in inefficient cities, unstable societies, or corrupt governments. The need for progress is greater in middle-income countries in Southeast Asia, where the process of decentralization may create short-term reversals unless new institutional mechanisms are found to increase public accountability and reduce impunity. There is little doubt that the appropriate solutions will take time and that progress in a number of areas is required. Countries will need to find their own paths forward. There are encouraging examples of success in Hong Kong (China), Korea, and Singapore.

East Asia has done well with global integration and has grown. The region is doing well with regional integration and is being transformed. But countries in the region have to do better with domestic integration and ensure that the growth and transformation is inclusive. East Asia needs a third integration, this one at home.

Notes

1. The crisis countries were Indonesia, the Republic of Korea, Malaysia, and Thailand.

2. See Stiglitz and Yusuf (2001).

3. East Asia refers to the member countries of the Association of Southeast Asian Nations (Brunei Darussalam, Cambodia, Indonesia, the Lao People's Democratic Republic, Malaysia, Myanmar, the Philippines, Singapore, Thailand, and Vietnam), plus China, Hong Kong (China), Japan, the Republic of Korea, Mongolia, and Taiwan (China). Emerging East Asia refers to East Asia, minus Japan. Developing East Asia refers to emerging East Asia, minus Hong Kong (China), Korea, Singapore, and Taiwan (China).

4. See Maddison (2003).

5. See Imbs and Wacziarg (2003).

6. See Garrett (2004).

7. Throughout this book, data on China refer to mainland China and Hong Kong (China). Because these two economies are so closely linked, a bias in favor of integration would result if they were treated as separate entities.

8. See Kawai (2005), Kharas, Aldaz-Carroll, and Rahardja (2007).

9. See Urata (2006).

10. See Gaulier, Lemoine, and Ünal-Kesenci (2005).

11. See Romer (1994); Warsh (2006) provides a highly readable and accurate account of the intellectual advances associated with these insights.

12. See Hummels and Klenow (2005).

13. See Lucas (1988).

14. See Aghion and Howitt (2006).

15. Krugman (1998) gives an excellent summary. See also Fujita, Krugman, and Venables (1999).

16. The median landlocked country has transport costs that are 55 percent higher than the transport costs in the median coastal economy. See Gallup and Sachs (1999).

17. As Venables (2006) puts it, a world characterized by diminishing returns to activity would not have cities.

18. See Venables (2006). Dispersion forces are usually not sector specific, though some agglomeration forces are. This gives rise to cities that are specialized by entire sectors. London is an example. So, perhaps, is New York.

19. See Akamatsu (1961).

20. Hayami (2006) provides some counterexamples to this proposition, showing how economies of scale may also be prevalent in rural development. But this is an exception, not the rule.

21. Krugman (1998) shows simulations for regional wage disparities in a model of locational choice. Venables (2006) points out that immobile factors, especially labor, bear the responsibility for much of the costs of poor geography. If labor is 10 percent of gross costs, then a 50 percent difference in overall productivity will translate into a 500 percent difference in wages.

22. See Helpman (2004).

23. These have been called general-purpose technologies by Bresnahan and Trajtenberg (1995).

24. Antweiler and Trefler (2002) offer a description of sectors with scale economies.

25. See World Bank investment climate surveys, http://iresearch.worldbank.org/ics/jsp/index.jsp; see also World Bank (2006).

26. See Hallward-Driemeier, Dwor-Frécaut, and Colaço (2003).

27. See Kharas, Aldaz-Carroll, and Rahardja (2007).

28. Blalock and Gertler (2004) find strong evidence for vertical technology transfers from multinational corporations to local suppliers in Indonesia.

29. World Bank investment climate surveys for Cambodia, China, Indonesia, Malaysia, Mongolia, the Philippines, and Thailand. See http://iresearch.worldbank.org/ics/jsp/index.jsp.

30. See Arnold and Javorcik (2005).

31. Indonesia is a notable exception to this trend. There, 80 percent of R&D is undertaken by the government.

32. The then chairman of the Board of Governors of the Federal Reserve of the United States made the remark during a speech entitled "Lessons from the Global Crises" and given at the annual meeting of the International Monetary Fund that was held in September 1999.

33. See World Bank (2006) and Rosenthal and Strange (2004). A doubling in city size is associated with a productivity increase of between 3 and 8 percent. So, for example, a person or a firm that moves from a city of 100,000 to a city of 10 million might expect a 40 percent increase in productivity. These effects seem to be larger in technology sectors.

34. See Leman (2005).

35. For example, see Redding and Venables (2004). A 1 percent improvement in a country's market access (which increases its exports by 1 percent) raises per capita income by about 0.25 percent.

36. Feenstra and Hanson (2001).

37. The positive effect of the trade ratio was significant in the pooled regression of the authors. The effect of FDI was insignificant in the pooled regression, but significant for Thailand. See Te Velde and Morrissey (2004).

38. See Park, Cai, and Zhao (2006).

39. See, for example, Transparency International (2005) on the corruption perceptions index and Kaufmann, Kraay, and Mastruzzi (2005) on the control of corruption index.

40. See the Investment Climate (Enterprise) Survey Database, World Bank, and International Finance Corporation, http://www.enterprisesurveys.org/.

41. See Kang (2002) and Chang (2001).

42. See Pei (2006).

43. See Rodrik (2004).

44. See World Bank (2005).

References

Aghion, Philippe, and Peter Howitt. 2006. "Appropriate Growth Policy: A Unifying Framework." *Journal of the European Economic Association* 4 (2–3): 269–314.

Akamatsu, Kaname. 1961. "A Theory of Unbalanced Growth in the World Economy." *Weltwirtschaftliches Archiv* 86 (2): 196–217.

———. 1962. "A Historical Pattern of Economic Growth in Developing Countries." *Journal of Developing Economies* 1(1): 3–25.

Antweiler, Werner, and Daniel Trefler. 2002. "Increasing Returns and All That: A View from Trade." *American Economic Review* 92 (1): 93–119.

Arnold, Jens Matthias, and Beata Smarzynska Javorcik. 2005. "Gifted Kids or Pushy Parents?: Foreign Acquisitions and Plant Performance in Indonesia." CEPR Discussion Paper 5065, Center for Economic Policy Research, London.

Blalock, Garrick, and Paul J. Gertler. 2004. "Learning from Exporting Revisited in a Less Developed Setting." *Journal of Development Economics* 75 (2): 397–416.

Bourguignon, François, and Chorching Goh. 2004. "Trade and Labor Market Vulnerability in Indonesia, Republic of Korea, and Thailand." In *East Asia Integrates: A Trade Policy Agenda for Shared Growth*, ed. Kathie Krumm and Homi Kharas, 171–88. Washington, DC: World Bank.

Bresnahan, Timothy F., and Manuel Trajtenberg. 1995. "General Purpose Technologies: 'Engines of Growth?'" NBER Working Paper 4148, National Bureau of Economic Research, Cambridge, MA.

Cannistraro, Philip V., and John J. Reich. 2003. *The Western Perspective: A History of Civilization in the West.* 2nd ed. Belmont, CA: Wadsworth Publishing.

Chang, Ha-Joon. 2001. "State, Capital, and Investments in Korea." In *Corruption: The Boom and Bust of East Asia,* ed. José Edgardo Campos, 45–68. Manila: Ateneo de Manila University Press.

China, National Bureau of Statistics. 2005. *Guangdong Statistical Yearbook 2005*. Beijing: China Statistics Publishing House.

Feenstra, Robert C. and Gordon H. Hanson. 2001. "Global Production Sharing and Rising Inequality: A Survey of Trade and Wages." NBER Working Paper 8372. National Bureau of Economic Research.

Fujita, Masahisa, Paul R. Krugman, and Anthony J. Venables. 1999. *The Spatial Economy: Cities, Regions and International Trade*. Cambridge, MA: MIT Press.

Gallup, John Luke, and Jeffrey D. Sachs. 1999. "Geography and Economic Development." With Andrew D. Mellinger. In *Annual World Bank Conference on Development Economics 1998*, ed. Boris Pleskovic and Joseph E. Stiglitz, 127–78. Washington, DC: World Bank.

Garrett, Geoffrey. 2004. "Globalization's Missing Middle." *Foreign Affairs* 83 (6): 84–96.

Gaulier, Guillaume, Françoise Lemoine, and Deniz Ünal-Kesenci. 2005. "China's Integration in East Asia: Production Sharing, FDI, and High-Tech Trade." CEPII Working Paper 2005–09, Centre d'Etudes Prospectives et d'Informations Internationales, Paris.

Giles, John T., Albert Park, and Fang Cai. 2006. "How Has Economic Restructuring Affected China's Urban Workers?" *China Quarterly* 185 (March): 61–95.

Hallward-Driemeier, Mary, Dominique Dwor-Frécaut, and Francis X. Colaço. 2003. "Asian Manufacturing Recovery: A Firm-Level Analysis." Conference edition, March 26, World Bank, Washington, DC.

Hayami, Yujiro. 2006. "A Rural-Based Development in East Asia under Globalization." In *East Asian Visions: Perspectives on Economic Development*, ed. Indermit S. Gill, Yukon Huang, and Homi Kharas, chap. 5. Washington, DC: World Bank.

Helpman, Elhanan. 2004. *The Mystery of Economic Growth*. Cambridge, MA: Harvard University Press.

Hummels, David, and Peter Klenow. 2005. "The Variety and Quality of a Nation's Exports." *American Economic Review* 95 (3): 704–23.

Imbs, Jean, and Romain Wacziarg. 2003. "Stages of Diversification." *American Economic Review* 93 (1): 63–86.

Kang, David C. 2002. *Crony Capitalism: Corruption and Development in South Korea and the Philippines*. Cambridge: Cambridge University Press.

Kaufmann, Daniel, Aart Kraay, and Massimo Mastruzzi. 2005. "Governance Matters IV: Governance Indicators for 1996–2004." Policy Research Working Paper 3630, World Bank, Washington, DC.

Kawai, Masahiro. 2005. "East Asian Economic Regionalism: Progress and Challenges." *Journal of Asian Economics* 16 (1): 29–55.

Kharas, Homi, Enrique Aldaz-Carroll, and Sjamsu Rahardja. 2007. "East Asia: Regional Integration among Open Economies." In *Economic Integration in Asia and India*, ed. Masahisa Fujita. Basingstoke, United Kingdom: Palgrave Macmillan.

Krugman, Paul R. 1998. "What's New about the New Economic Geography?" *Oxford Review of Economic Policy* 14 (2): 7–17.

Leman, Edward. 2005. "Metropolitan Regions: New Challenges for an Urbanizing China." Paper presented at the World Bank and Institute of Applied Economic Research "Urban Research Symposium," Brasilia, April 4.

Lucas Jr., Robert E. 1988. "On the Mechanics of Economic Development." *Journal of Monetary Economics* 22 (1): 3–42.

Maddison, Angus. 2003. *The World Economy: Historical Statistics*. Paris: Organisation for Economic Co-operation and Development.

Okamoto, Yumiko. 2005. "Emergence of the 'Intra-Mediate Trade': Implications for the Asia-Pacific Region." Paper presented at the East-West Center and the Rosenberg Institute of Global Finance, Brandeis University, "PAFTAD 30" conference, Honolulu, February 19–21. http://www.eastwestcenter.org/stored/misc/paftad_30_okamoto.pdf.

Park, Albert, Fang Cai, and Yaohui Zhao. 2006. "The Informalization of the Chinese Labor Market." Background paper for the China Poverty Assessment, World Bank, Washington, DC.

Pei, Minxin. 2006. *China's Trapped Transition: The Limits of Developmental Autocracy*. Cambridge, MA: Harvard University Press.

Redding, Stephen, and Anthony J. Venables. 2004. "Economic Geography and International Inequality." *Journal of International Economics* 62 (1): 53–82.

Rodrik, Dani. 2004. "Industrial Policy for the 21st Century." Unpublished working paper, September, John F. Kennedy School of Government, Harvard University, Cambridge, MA.

Romer, Paul M. 1994. "The Origins of Endogenous Growth." *Journal of Economic Perspectives* 8 (1): 3–22.

Rosenthal, Stuart S., and William C. Strange. 2004. "Evidence on the Nature and Sources of Agglomeration Economies." In *Cities and Geography.* Vol. 4 of *Handbook of Regional and Urban Economics,* ed. J. Vernon Henderson and Jacques-François Thisse, 2119–71. Amsterdam: Elsevier B. V.

Stiglitz, Joseph E., and Shahid Yusuf, eds. 2001. *Rethinking the East Asian Miracle.* Washington, DC: World Bank; New York: Oxford University Press.

Te Velde, Dirk Willem, and Dirk Bezemer. 2004. "Regional Integration and Foreign Direct Investment in Developing Countries." Unpublished working paper, Department for International Development, London. http://www.odi.org.uk/iedg/Projects/ec_prep2.pdf.

Te Velde, Dirk Willem, and Oliver Morrissey. 2004. "Foreign Direct Investment, Skills, and Wage Inequality in East Asia." *Journal of the Asia Pacific Economy* 9 (3): 348–69.

Transparency International. 2005. *Corruption Perceptions Index 2005.* Berlin: Transparency International. http://www.transparency.org/policy_research/surveys_indices/cpi.

Urata, Shujiro. 2006. "The Changing Patterns of International Trade in East Asia." Background paper, World Bank, Washington, DC.

Venables, Anthony J. 2006. "Shifts in Economic Geography and Their Causes." Paper presented at the Federal Reserve Bank of Kansas City Symposium, "The New Economic Geography: Effects and Policy Implications," Jackson Hole, WY, August 24–26.

Warsh, David. 2006. *Knowledge and the Wealth of Nations: A Story of Economic Discovery.* New York: WW Norton and Company.

World Bank. 1993. *The East Asian Miracle: Economic Growth and Public Policy.* World Bank Policy Research Reports. New York: Oxford University Press.

———. 2005. *World Development Report 2006: Equity and Development.* Washington, DC: World Bank; New York: Oxford University Press.

———. 2006. *Governance, Investment Climate, and Harmonious Society: Competitiveness Enhancements for 120 Cities in China.* Report Series 37759-CN. Washington, DC: Poverty Reduction and Economic Management Unit, Financial and Private Sector Development Unit, East Asia and Pacific Region, World Bank.

Yeats, Alexander J. 2001. "Just How Big Is Global Production Sharing?" In *Fragmentation: New Production Patterns in the World Economy,* ed. Sven W. Arndt and Henryk Kierzkowski, 108–43. New York: Oxford University Press.

MAP 1.1 East Asia Will Soon Be a Middle-Income Region

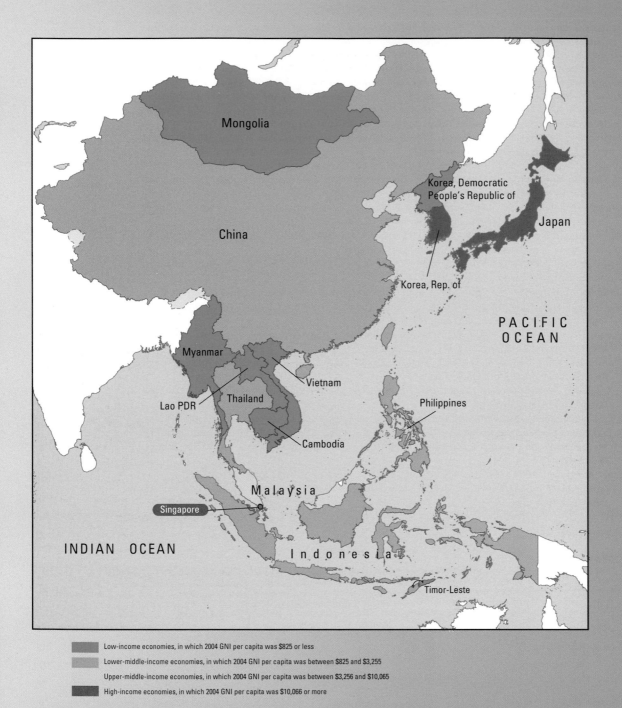

Mongolia

China

Korea, Democratic People's Republic of

Korea, Rep. of

Japan

PACIFIC OCEAN

Myanmar

Vietnam

Lao PDR

Thailand

Cambodia

Philippines

Malaysia

Singapore

INDIAN OCEAN

Indonesia

Timor-Leste

Low-income economies, in which 2004 GNI per capita was $825 or less

Lower-middle-income economies, in which 2004 GNI per capita was between $825 and $3,255

Upper-middle-income economies, in which 2004 GNI per capita was between $3,256 and $10,065

High-income economies, in which 2004 GNI per capita was $10,066 or more

Sources: World Development Indicators Database, World Bank, http://www.worldbank.org/data/datapubs/datapubs.html; Global Development Finance Database, World Bank, http://www.worldbank.org/data/datapubs/datapubs.html.

CHAPTER 1

GROWTH, GRAVITY, AND FRICTION

Recent theoretical advances may help explain the causes, consequences, and policy implications of the economic transformation that has made East Asia a predominantly middle-income region.

New Challenges, Fresh Insights

East Asia is a completely different region today compared to the place studied in *The East Asian Miracle* (World Bank 1993). In analyzing the rise of eight high-performing Asian economies, which did not include China, *The East Asian Miracle* pointed to strong fundamentals, international integration, and good government as the key factors of success in East Asia. But three subsequent developments necessitate a reexamination of East Asian growth: the biggest economic crisis of the 1990s, which showed that the governments were anything but infallible; the rise of China, the biggest economic development story of the 1990s; and the expansion of East Asia's cities fueled by the biggest rural-to-urban shift in population during the 1990s. The meteoric rise of China, the growing concentration of trade and investment flows within Asia, the sharp financial crisis of the 1990s, and the rapid growth of cities all reflect a vastly different reality, a richer middle-income region than the one at the beginning of the 1990s (see map 1.1).

This report, like three other World Bank studies since 1993 (see box 1.1), is a contribution to the debate on how development strategies should be adapted in response to such changes. This chapter outlines the changes in the region since 1990 and compares them with what has happened in other parts of the world. It then provides a summary of developments in economic theory that may help in determining the causes, consequences, and—with additional country-specific work—policy implications of these changes.

■ BOX 1.1 **Once Every Four Years: World Bank Regional Studies on East Asia**

Since the early 1990s, the World Bank has completed a major study of East Asian growth every four years: *The East Asian Miracle* (World Bank 1993), *Lessons from East Asia* (Leipziger 1997), and *Rethinking the East Asian Miracle* (Stiglitz and Yusuf 2001). The frequency befits the most dynamic region in the world. Each of these efforts has been different in nature, and this book again differs in both focus and format from the three previous World Bank publications.

The East Asian Miracle emphasized export-led growth, rapid capital accumulation, skill-building, capable governments, and contestable private sectors. The differences between *The East Asian Miracle* and this report may be summed up in three points:

■ First, while the 1993 report analyzed growth in eight high-performing Asian economies (Hong Kong [China], Indonesia, Japan, the Republic of Korea, Malaysia, Singapore, Taiwan [China], and Thailand), there was no explicit attempt to explain the experience of these countries in *regional* terms. While the report recognized that the countries learned from each other and, hence, adopted a pragmatic blend of market fundamentals and government intervention, there was no economic analysis of "neighborhood effects." The eight countries in *The East Asian Miracle* might have been anywhere; they happened to be in East Asia. In contrast, regional or neighborhood factors are a central feature of this book.

■ Second, *The East Asian Miracle* deliberately omitted the growth experience of China since China was so different from the eight high-performing Asian economies. The implications of China's rapid

rise are a central issue in this book precisely because China is so different from the other East Asian countries.

■ Third, the aim of the 1993 report was to help other regions learn the lessons of rapid growth in East Asia and, by extracting general, transplantable lessons, inform the development debates current at the time. This book is also intended to inform the debates on *regional integration in East Asia* that have become widespread in the region since the financial crisis of the late 1990s.

Lessons from East Asia consisted of country case studies. It attempted to examine how public policy lessons permeated the borders between countries in the region and to explain the adoption of development approaches with common elements in countries that were so different, such as postconflict Japan and Korea, small states such as Hong Kong (China) and Singapore, and postcommunist China and Vietnam. However, *Lessons from East Asia* did not stress the economic links within the region that are a central part of this book.

Rethinking the East Asian Miracle aimed at addressing questions raised by several commentators who, prompted by the financial crisis of 1997–98, were skeptical of the durability of the East Asian development approach. *Rethinking the East Asian Miracle* consisted of essays on several issues central to this report: trade, foreign direct investment, technology, industrialization, corporate governance, and regional trade and monetary arrangements. This book reexamines many of these issues, but systematically uses the insights afforded by recent advances in economic thought outlined below.

East Asia is being transformed from a set of countries that rapidly integrated with the world to a region that is aggressively exploiting the sources of dynamism that lie within Asia. Just as the region was drawn earlier to the developed world by prospects of a mutually beneficial exchange of goods, capital, and ideas, different parts of the region are now being pulled toward each other by the same motives and modes. The result is rapid regional integration in the exchange of goods, capital, and ideas that rivals the regional integration in the European Union and in North America. (The next section presents a brief overview of these developments.)

This integration is the main source of dynamism in the region and has given the region a second breath. But it is also a source of growing economic contagion. The East Asian crisis was the most visible reflection of this contagion, and it was a reminder that the transition from middle-income to high-income status is rarely linear. The experiences of countries in Eastern Europe and Latin America that have had periods of high growth make clear that developing countries will inevitably face pitfalls. Such pitfalls have slowed down some countries and have derailed most others.

In a high-performing region such as East Asia, it is perhaps easier to think of what is *not* a potential pitfall. Fiscal prudence is now almost a habit and is likely to remain one. Competitive exchange rates are seen by countries in the region as an important building block of economic policies to sustain growth, as is low inflation. Financial sector pitfalls have been faced and, by and large, recognized by most countries in East Asia. Labor market flexibility was long recognized as necessary and remains a policy priority. High savings rates are still ingrained in household and corporate behavior. The list of the region's strengths is long.

Latin America's prospects in the early 1970s as the region's countries entered middle-income status were similarly bright, but many Latin American economies have since disappointed. This report emphasizes three potential pitfalls—listless cities, conflict-ridden societies, and corrupt governments—that East Asia should take care to avoid.

As the challenges posed by economic development have changed, so too have the analytical tools available to development economists. An academic literature that has burgeoned since the publication of *The East Asian Miracle* emphasizes unexhausted economies of scale as a central force driving industrial organization, international trade, the geographical concentration of economic activity, and economic growth. While the new international trade theory was developed during the 1980s, empirical support—a prerequisite if a theory is to be taken seriously by serious policy makers—for its central propositions came more than a decade later. Developed during the 1990s, the new economic geography, which may be viewed as an extension of both international trade and growth theory, has utilized economies of scale as a central precept to understanding spatial differences and the role of cities. And, while endogenous growth theory emerged in the late 1980s, it has become sufficiently refined to be of use for development policy only since the 1990s.

All these insights are useful in disciplining investigations of East Asian economic growth, but, given its timing, *The East Asian Miracle* could not make full use of them. The debates of the period centered on whether the results yielded by government intervention are better than those provided by unfettered markets, and the report made a qualified case for selective government intervention. In fact, as pointed out by Krugman (1998), the type of economy outlined in the literature on increasing returns makes for a tempting target of government intervention. There is no presumption that the market will get it right. In some circumstances, small policy interventions may have large effects, and processes of concentration tend to produce winners and losers. So, there is an obvious incentive for governments to ensure that their countries emerge as winners.

Nevertheless, it remains difficult to draw general policy implications from even this body of thought. A background paper for this book (Gill, Hariharan, and Kharas 2006) discusses how the combination of new trade theory, new growth theory, and new economic geography yields several implications for public policy. Elsewhere below, this chapter summarizes relevant findings.

East Asia Since the Early 1990s: Selected Facts

The East Asia region has grown more rapidly and more steadily than any other region in the developing world during the last quarter century. As a result, by 2010, more than 95 percent of the region's population will be living in middle-income countries. A second key point is that intraregional trade and investment flows have grown more rapidly in East Asia than have the region's trade and financial links with the rest of the world. The most important reasons for this have been China's rapid rise, large size, and expanding relations with the rest of the world. A third point is that, in contrast to what was once considered East Asia's hallmark, growth with equity, recent economic growth has generally been accompanied by rising inequality. The aspects of development that have been receiving the most attention are a widening gap in incomes and living standards between less well educated and more well educated workers and between rural and urban residents.

Growing to Middle-Income Status

The developing countries of East Asia (in this chapter, only Japan is excluded in this grouping) have grown rapidly and resiliently during the last two decades, even if account is taken of the crisis of the late 1990s. The region is unique today in that it encompasses high-income, middle-income, and low-income countries.

The most resilient region. Over the last quarter century, during any five-year period, no other part of the world has grown more rapidly than East Asia. East Asian gross domestic product (GDP) per capita averaged between 5.5 and 8.0 percent during this time, and GDP growth ranged between 6.8 and 9.4 percent (see table 1.1). In the developing world, only South Asia's growth record comes close to matching East Asia's in terms of strength and resilience.

Even over a longer period, after accounting for year-to-year fluctuations such as the crisis of the 1990s and after broadening the comparison to include developed countries, East Asia's performance stands out as remarkably strong and steady. Table 1.2 catalogs, for some of the world's regions and for selected East Asian countries (China, Indonesia, Malaysia, the Philippines, and Thailand), the number of years between 1966 and 2004 during which per capita GDP growth was negative, between 0 and 2 percent, and above 2 percent. As may be seen, the East Asian region had negative growth only during two years.

Maddison (2003) estimates that East Asia's share of world GDP (adjusted for purchasing power parity) was about 40 percent between the years 1500 and 1800 and peaked in 1820. By 1950, the share was less than 15 percent. Today, the share is about 33 percent. If the world continues to grow at the same annual rate registered during the past four decades, that is, about 3.6 percent, East Asia GDP must grow at between 6 and 7 percent per year to regain the peak share of 42 percent by about 2025.

The most diverse region. While regional groupings are somewhat arbitrary, cross-country comparisons of per capita income trends and levels may be instructive.

■ TABLE 1.1 **East Asia Has Been Growing More Rapidly Than All Other Regions**
percent GDP growth, 1980–2004

Region	1980–84	1985–89	1990–94	1995–99	2000–04
East Asia and Pacific	7.2	7.8	9.4	6.8	7.2
Latin America and the Caribbean	1.4	2.2	3.6	2.4	2.2
Europe and Central Asia	—	—	−5.2	2.0	5.2
Middle East and North Africa	3.8	1.2	4.6	3.4	4.4
South Asia	5.4	6.0	5.0	5.8	5.6
Sub-Saharan Africa	1.6	2.4	0.6	3.6	3.4

Sources: World Development Indicators Database, World Bank, http://www.worldbank.org/data/datapubs/datapubs.html; Global Development Finance Database, World Bank, http://www.worldbank.org/data/datapubs/datapubs.html.
Note: — = no data are available.

■ TABLE 1.2 **East Asian Growth Has Been Strong and Steady**
per capita GDP growth, percent, 1966–2004

Region	Growth	Number of years in which the rate was:		
		Negative	0–2%	Above 2%
East Asia and Pacific	5.77	2	3	34
China	7.00	3	3	33
Indonesia	4.03	4	3	32
Malaysia	3.95	5	3	31
Philippines	1.28	6	21	12
Thailand	4.79	3	5	31
Latin America and the Caribbean	1.46	10	15	14
Middle East and North Africa[a]	1.23	8	13	9
South Asia	2.56	1	12	26
Sub-Saharan Africa	0.18	14	20	5
OECD[b]	2.49	0	18	21

Sources: World Development Indicators Database, World Bank, http://www.worldbank.org/data/datapubs/datapubs.html; Global Development Finance Database, World Bank, http://www.worldbank.org/data/datapubs/datapubs.html.
a. Data for Middle East and North Africa are from 1975 to 2004.
b. OECD = Organisation for Economic Co-operation and Development.

Figure 1.1, which plots the ratio of the incomes of selected countries to the respective regional average, shows that the developing nations of East Asia are the most diverse among nations in all regions. Combined with geographical proximity and noneconomic similarities, this diversity may be an important factor in the mutually beneficial exchange of goods, finance, and ideas.

Figure 1.1 also shows a rapid "club convergence" in developing East Asia (chart a). Most importantly, perhaps, the ratio of China's income to the East Asian average rose from 0.86 to 1.09 between 1991 and 2004. The largest changes were recorded by the richest countries: Hong Kong (China), Korea, and Singapore. Indonesia and the Philippines slipped from above the regional average to below. But, despite this convergence, per capita income in 2004 ranged from about US$27,000 in Hong Kong (China) and US$24,000 in Singapore to US$15,000 in Taiwan (China) and US$14,000 in Korea and to almost US$5,000 in Malaysia, about US$2,500 in Thailand, US$1,400 in China, US$1,100 in Indonesia and the Philippines, US$600 in Mongolia and Vietnam, and about US$400 in Cambodia and the Lao People's Democratic Republic. In other words, Hong Kong (China) still has a per capita income that is about 60 times that of Cambodia.

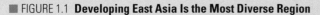
■ FIGURE 1.1 **Developing East Asia Is the Most Diverse Region**

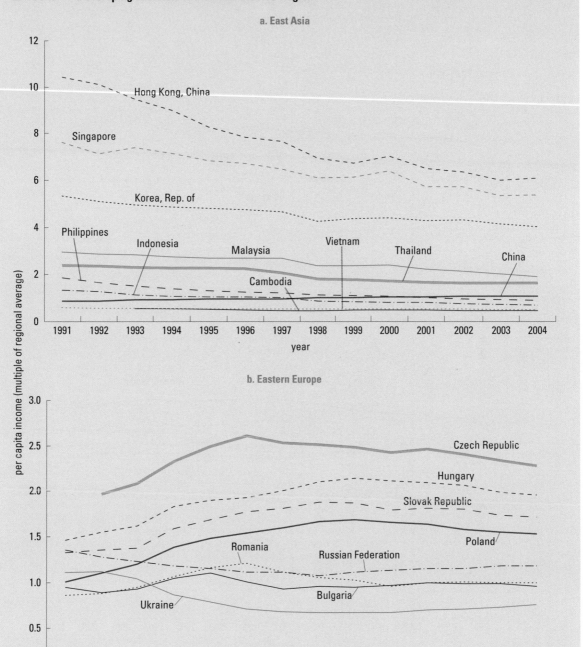

a. East Asia

b. Eastern Europe

(Continued)

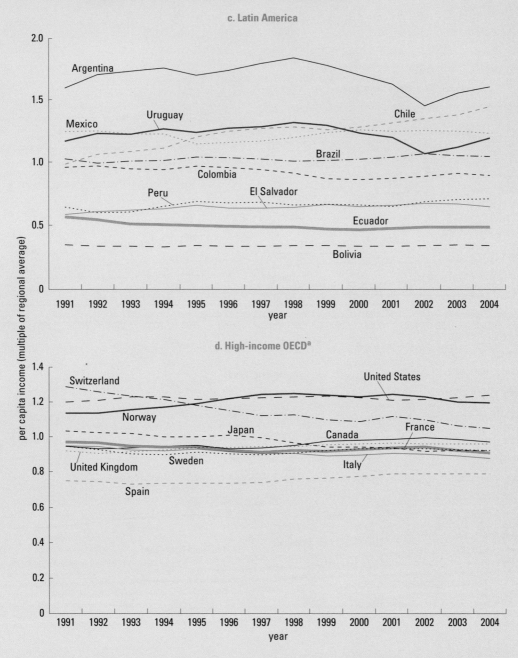

c. Latin America

d. High-income OECD[a]

Sources: Calculations of the authors based on World Development Indicators Database, World Bank,
http://www.worldbank.org/data/datapubs/datapubs.html (August 2005); Global Development Finance Database, World Bank,
http://www.worldbank.org/data/datapubs/datapubs.html (August 2005).
Note: The figure shows per capita income as a multiple of the respective regional average.
a. OECD = Organisation for Economic Co-operation and Development.

A region that will soon be mostly middle income. The median East Asian is already a citizen of a middle-income country. China, Indonesia, Malaysia, the Philippines, and Thailand all have per capita incomes between US$1,000 and US$10,000.[1] With Vietnam's per capita income expected to rise above US$1,000 by 2010, about 90 of every 100 East Asians will be living in a middle-income country, and, at current growth rates, fewer than 25 million of a total of about 2 billion East Asians will be living below the poverty line by 2020.

So, while this report is about all of East Asia, it is especially about the development challenges faced by middle-income countries. The focus is deliberate. During the last 50 years, many countries have moved from levels of income that are associated with abject poverty to levels that have earned them middle-income status. But, during this time, outside of Europe, only a handful have gone from low-income to high-income status. The part of the world that has been most disappointing is Latin America, where many countries reached middle-income levels and then, essentially, stopped growing. And the part of the world that has most notably defied this tendency is East Asia, where four of the most prominent high-performing economies are found: Hong Kong (China), Korea, Singapore, and Taiwan (China).

Figure 1.2 plots the per capita income levels of three groups of countries between 1900 and 2000: the eight largest Latin American countries that have reached middle-income levels (Argentina, Brazil, Chili, Colombia, Mexico, Peru, Uruguay, and the República Bolivariana de Venezuela), five East Asian economies that have reached high-income levels (Hong Kong [China], Japan, Korea, Singapore, and Taiwan [China]), and the five middle-income countries in East Asia (China, Indonesia, Malaysia, the Philippines, and Thailand). Figure 1.2 illustrates two noteworthy developments. The first is that, by the early 1970s, while the range of incomes differed considerably between the high-income East Asia Five and the Latin America Eight, the average per capita income of the two groups was roughly the same: about US$5,000. The second is that, by the early 2000s, the developing East Asia Five had caught up with the Latin America Eight, where the average per capita income had not changed much since the 1970s. Coincidentally, the range of incomes for the Latin America Eight and the developing East Asia Five was almost identical in 2000.

It is logical for policy makers in other East Asian countries that are attaining middle-income status to ask what the five Asian leaders did to transit successfully through middle-income stages of development, what the Latin America Eight did wrong, and what today's middle-income countries in East Asia might do to ensure

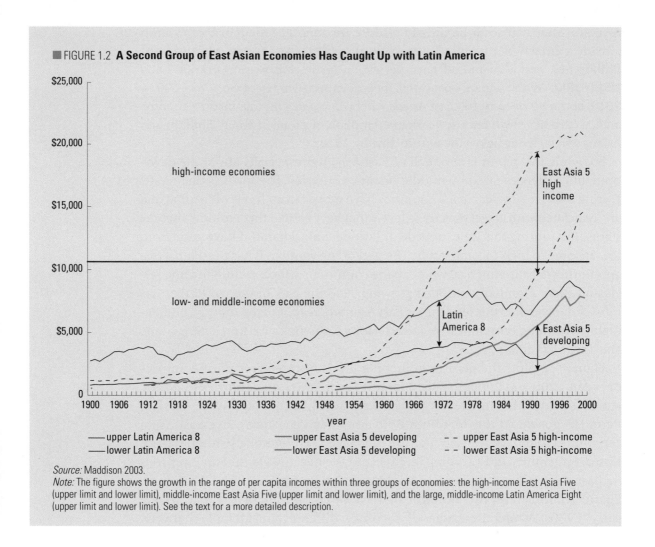

■ FIGURE 1.2 **A Second Group of East Asian Economies Has Caught Up with Latin America**

Source: Maddison 2003.
Note: The figure shows the growth in the range of per capita incomes within three groups of economies: the high-income East Asia Five (upper limit and lower limit), middle-income East Asia Five (upper limit and lower limit), and the large, middle-income Latin America Eight (upper limit and lower limit). See the text for a more detailed description.

a future that is more similar to the situation among their successful neighbors than among the countries across the Pacific.

Being Pulled Together by China

Many of these favorable patterns are simply a reflection of China's size. After all, about two-thirds of all East Asians live in China. But this is not the full story: China accounts for less than one-quarter of East Asia's gross national income of US$7,150 billion; Japan still weighs in with more than two-thirds. What has been happening in East Asia since the early 1990s has been the spreading out of the supply chain, and China is the destination of choice.

China's rise spurs regional trade integration. East Asia's share of world trade has increased from about 10 percent in the 1970s to more than 25 percent today, overtaking the North American Free Trade Area's share of about 20 percent and closing the gap with the European Union that still accounts for about one-third of world trade. Intraregional trade was only 35 percent of East Asia's trade in 1980; by 2004, this share was about 55 percent, second only to the European Union's intraregional share of 60 percent. A rapid rise of global trade, a steady rise in East Asia's share of world trade, and a big increase in the share of intraregional trade in East Asia all add up to a huge increase in the absolute amount of intraregional trade (see table 1.3). While GDP in the region has risen an average of almost 8 percent per year since 1980, intraregional trade has increased by more than 13.5 percent annually.

The growth of intraregional trade has been accompanied by the rising importance of intraindustry trade among East Asian countries. Between 1990 and 2004, the share of interindustry trade in the regional total fell from about 45 to 22 percent, and that of intraindustry trade rose from 55 to 78 percent. Related to this is the development of regional production and distribution networks in East Asia that, according to Ando and Kimura (2003), are both distinctive and relatively sophisticated compared with networks in other parts of the developing world. One indicator of the extent of these networks is the importance of parts and components in regional trade. Okamoto (2005) finds rapid growth in the trade in parts and components in the region between 1990 and 2003 (see table 1.4).

Korea and Taiwan (China) emerge as regional technology influences. East Asian countries have made considerable progress since 1990 in intellectual property rights and research and development (R&D). One measure of technological effort is the number of patents registered with the United States Patent and Trademark Office. Developing East Asia still lags behind Japan and the United States, which account for about 20 percent and 60 percent of registrations, respectively, but it is nonetheless remarkable that the developing East Asia share in the total had quadrupled from less than 2 percent to almost 8 percent by 2004. In contrast, Eastern Europe and Latin America appear to have made no inroads.

An important driver of the generation of useful ideas and of technological progress is the gross expenditure on R&D. As shown in figure 1.3, East Asian

■ TABLE 1.3 **The Intraregional Trade Share Has Risen in High- and Middle-Income Countries**
share of intraregional trade, percent, 1995 and 2004

Country	Intraregional exports		Intraregional imports		Summary of trends	
	1995	2004	1995	2004	Exports	Imports
High income						
Japan	36	41	35	44	◁	◁
Korea, Rep. of	37	42	39	42	◁	◁
Singapore	46	47	55	55	◁▷	◁▷
Taiwan, China	28	43	47	55	◀	◀
Middle income						
China	32	26	48	51	▽	◁
Indonesia	51	58	47	53	◀	◀
Malaysia	48	49	56	61	◁▷	◁
Philippines	36	52	46	56	◀	◀
Thailand	52	55	44	47	◁	◁
Low income						
Cambodia	69	12	87	78	▼	▼
Lao PDR	61	38	69	85	▼	◀
Mongolia	32	55	29	41	◀	◀
Vietnam	64	40	69	72	▼	◁

Source: Calculation of the authors based on Direction of Trade Statistics Database, International Monetary Fund and ESDS International, http://www.esds.
ac.uk/international/access/access.asp.
Note: Black arrows indicate sizable changes; open arrows indicate a small or no change.

■ TABLE 1.4 **Parts and Components Have Become More Important in East Asia's Trade**
share of total trade, percent, 1990 and 2003

Country	Share of exports		Share of imports	
	1990	2003	1990	2003
China	4.1	15.1	16.1	27.2
Indonesia	0.8	9.1	15.2	13.5
Japan	22.9	32.6	6.4	15.3
Korea, Rep. of	15.8	28.0	16.6	23.0
Malaysia	19.5	39.5	26.0	47.9
Philippines	17.8	55.6	15.6	48.8
Taiwan, China	16.9	33.9	17.9	28.3
Thailand	11.3	22.1	21.6	26.0

Source: Okamoto 2005.

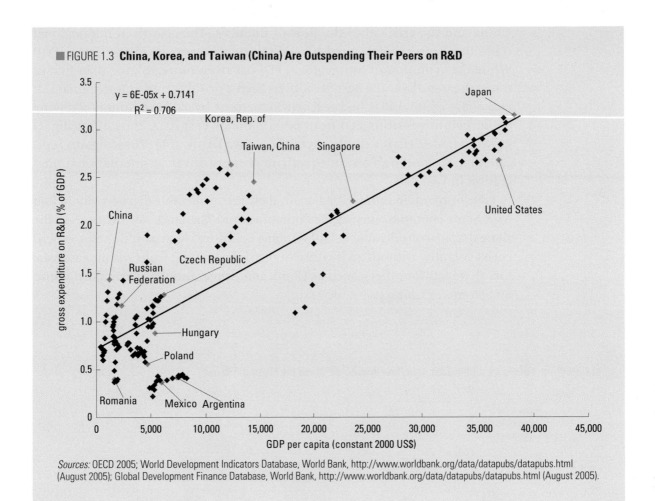

■ FIGURE 1.3 **China, Korea, and Taiwan (China) Are Outspending Their Peers on R&D**

$y = 6E\text{-}05x + 0.7141$

$R^2 = 0.706$

Sources: OECD 2005; World Development Indicators Database, World Bank, http://www.worldbank.org/data/datapubs/datapubs.html (August 2005); Global Development Finance Database, World Bank, http://www.worldbank.org/data/datapubs/datapubs.html (August 2005).

countries spend a greater share of their GDP on R&D than the average country in the sample; China, Japan, Korea, Singapore, and Taiwan (China) all lie above the line of best fit.

Hu (2006) finds strong evidence of the increasing regionalization of knowledge flows in East Asia. Korea and Taiwan (China), the region's leading innovators after Japan, have begun to cite each other's patents at least as frequently as they cite Japanese and U.S. patents. With the exception of Thailand, all the East Asian economies examined (China, Hong Kong [China], Malaysia, and Singapore) cite patents of Korea and Taiwan (China) as frequently as they cite patents of Japan and the United States. Clearly, intraregional knowledge flows have intensified substantially since the mid-1990s.

China and the crisis alter the flow of finances. The growth in intraregional trade has been accompanied by a similar expansion in intraregional FDI. While the evolution of intraregional FDI has been more volatile than that of trade, the trend over the past decade has been a positive one. Intraregional FDI as a share of total FDI had reached 57 percent by 2003. China is receiving about two-thirds of its FDI from other parts of East Asia, thus offsetting its growing trade deficit with these countries (see figure 1.4). These figures indicate that capital flows are an equally important driver of international integration in East Asia.

Like the trends in intraregional trade, there is considerable diversity within East Asia. Some countries, such as the Philippines and Thailand, saw increases in the share despite considerable volatility; some countries, such as Indonesia, experienced volatility without an increase in the share coming from within East Asia; this share fell for others, such as China and Korea, though it remained above 60 percent for China (see table 1.5).

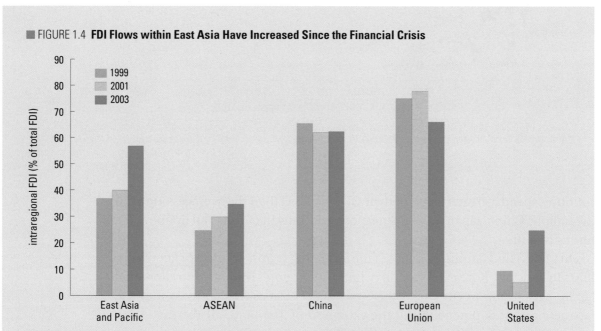

■ FIGURE 1.4 **FDI Flows within East Asia Have Increased Since the Financial Crisis**

Sources: UNCTAD 2003; Eurostat 2005; data of the U.S. Bureau of Economic Analysis (http://www.bea.gov/); China, National Bureau of Statistics 2005; ASEAN 2004; Rana 2005.
Note: The 2003 figure for East Asia is for 2002; figures for China include FDI from Japan; figures for the Association of Southeast Asian Nations (ASEAN) refer to FDI from East Asia to ASEAN and not strictly to intra-ASEAN FDI.

■ TABLE 1.5 **Regional FDI Patterns Have Changed during the Last Two Decades**
intraregional FDI as a share of total FDI, selected countries, 1985–2004

Country	Definition	Average share (%)			
		1985–89	1990–94	1995–99	2000–04
China	Inward FDI flows	76.5	83.2	73.2	61.4
Indonesia	Inward FDI approvals	40.6	47.1	38.0	41.8
Korea, Rep. of	Inward FDI approvals	53.1	29.7	26.3	25.8
Malaysia	Inward FDI flows	—	48.5	28.4	28.6
Philippines	Inward FDI registered at the central bank	25.9	38.9	43.3	41.9
Thailand	Inward FDI flows	71.0	62.3	51.9	94.4

Sources: Data on China: National Bureau of Statistics, various; Indonesia: Investment Coordinating Board; Korea: UNCTAD 2000 (for data up to 1997), Ministry of Commerce, Industry, and Energy (for data from 1998); Malaysia: BNM, various; the Philippines: Central Bank of the Philippines; Thailand: Bank of Thailand.
Note: — = no data are available.

Looking for a Middle Path

This integration-driven growth has been instrumental in reducing poverty and in raising the quality of life through the improved access to services that generally accompanies urbanization. But growth has also brought in its wake concerns about rising inequality, urban congestion, and corruption. These can be seen as sources of rising friction between the wealthy and other people, between rural and urban interests, and between public and private interests.

The per capita income of developing East Asia is still a fraction of the corresponding income of industrialized countries. So, the *distribution* of the fruits of economic growth should not excessively preoccupy policy makers. To put it crudely, it is important for countries in the region to adopt policies that help per capita incomes grow from US$1,000 to US$10,000 rather than those that simply prevent income inequality indexes from rising from 0.4 to 0.5. Nonetheless, it does not seem that distribution concerns may be altogether ignored without imperiling economic growth. As in other parts of the world, there are debates in the region about the distribution of the gains from growth between city dwellers and residents in the countryside, between educated and uneducated workers, and between those who have the ear of governments and those who do not. More broadly, worsening distribution may be a signal that growth opportunities are being missed and that the economy is not operating at full potential.

A big move into cities; a growing concern about livability. Urbanization is a natural correlate of development. As societies develop, they become increasingly urbanized and industrialized, while the relative importance of the agricultural sector frequently declines. After sub-Saharan Africa, East Asia experienced the largest annual average urban growth rate during 1960–2004. With an annual growth rate of 3.7 percent, East Asia's urban population has more than doubled every two decades. The Middle East and North Africa, South Asia, and Latin America have had comparably high urban population rates of growth of between 3.0 and 3.6 percent. East Asia's urban growth was three times as rapid as that of high-income countries in the Organisation for Economic Co-operation and Development. In East Asia, the share of urban areas in total population rose from 17 percent in 1980 to 40 percent in 2005.

The future promises even larger growth among urban populations in countries of the region. Urbanization in East Asia over the next two decades is likely to result in the largest rural-urban shift in population in human history. Indeed, it is expected that East Asian cities will have an additional 550 million persons by 2025, an increase equal in size to the entire population of Latin America.

This massive urbanization will bring opportunities for growth, but also raises big challenges. While East Asia's cities are as livable as those in Latin America today (controlling for per capital income), urbanization is still ahead for many countries in the region—whereas much of it has already occurred in Latin America (see figure 1.5). The literature on economic geography and endogenous growth emphasizes the benefits associated with agglomeration. But urbanization at such a scale may also easily lead to problems such as congestion, crime, and deteriorating public services. In East Asia, this might jeopardize entire economies because of the concentration of economic activity in cities. Today, Bangkok represents 40 percent of Thailand's GDP and 12 percent of the population; Manila has 30 percent of the GDP and 13 percent of the population of the Philippines; Ho Chi Minh City has 20 percent of Vietnam's GDP, but only 6 percent of the country's population; and Shanghai accounts for 11 percent of China's GDP, but less than 1 percent of China's population.

These considerations also raise questions with regard to the growing gap between prosperous megacities and the rest of a country, namely, rural areas and small- and medium-sized cities. Population growth in East Asian megacities raises important questions about urban sustainability and management. Many East Asian megacities are expected to grow by more than 50 percent by 2030 (see table 1.6). Cities such as Jakarta and Shanghai are likely to grow from around 12 million each in 2005 to more than 20 million each by 2030. Beijing is expected to expand from less than 10 million to more than 15 million inhabitants.

While East Asian cities differ in many ways, they share some attributes. Their population and wealth are growing rapidly; their governments are gaining administra-

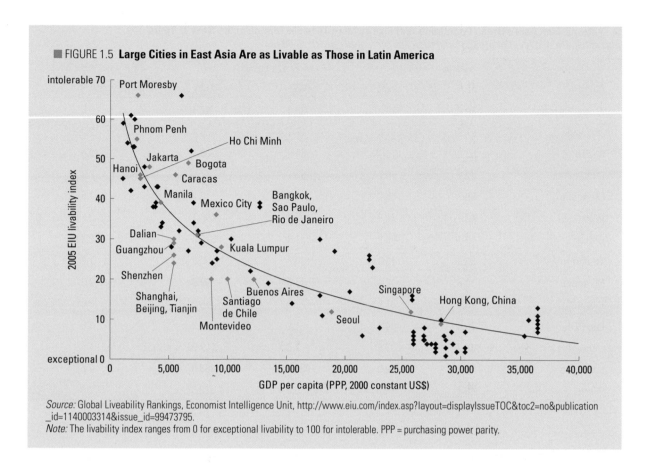

■ FIGURE 1.5 **Large Cities in East Asia Are as Livable as Those in Latin America**

Source: Global Liveability Rankings, Economist Intelligence Unit, http://www.eiu.com/index.asp?layout=displayIssueTOC&toc2=no&publication _id=1140003314&issue_id=99473795.

Note: The livability index ranges from 0 for exceptional livability to 100 for intolerable. PPP = purchasing power parity.

tive power; and they are the nerve centers for the regional production networks on which so much of East Asia's prosperity depends. Cities account for perhaps three-quarters of the economic growth in East Asia and all the demographic growth in most countries, including China, Indonesia, Malaysia, the Philippines, and Thailand. East Asia's economic growth will depend on how well cities handle the challenges associated with service delivery, infrastructure, land markets, the environment, the development of neighboring rural regions, employment creation, and urban poverty.

A big move out of poverty; a growing concern about inequality. East Asia is the poverty reduction champion of the world. Since 1999, headcount poverty (at US$2 a day) has fallen by about 250 million people. Put another way, between 2000 and 2006, about 1 million East Asians moved out of poverty *every week*. Consumption per person has more than doubled in real terms in the region since

■ TABLE 1.6 **East Asia's Urban Population Will Rise by More Than 500 Million in the Next 25 Years**
current share and level of urban population and projected growth, 2005–30

Country	Share urban (%)		Urban population (millions)		Annual growth rate
	2005	2030	2005	2030	2005–10
Korea, Rep. of	80.8	86.3	38.6	42.4	0.6
Malaysia	67.3	81.9	17.1	28.4	3.0
Japan	65.8	73.7	84.3	90.4	0.4
Philippines	62.7	76.7	52.1	87.5	2.8
Mongolia	56.7	65.7	1.5	2.2	1.5
Indonesia	48.1	68.9	107.2	186.7	3.6
China	40.4	60.3	531.8	872.6	2.7
Thailand	32.3	45.8	20.7	33.8	1.8
Myanmar	30.6	48.4	15.5	29.3	2.9
Vietnam	26.4	41.8	22.2	45.2	3.0
Lao PDR	20.6	34.0	1.2	3.2	4.0
Cambodia	19.7	37.0	2.8	7.9	4.9
East Asia	44.2	62.0	921.3	1,463.0	2.6
World	48.7	59.9	3,150.5	4,912.5	2.0

Source: World Urbanization Prospects: The 2005 Revision Population Database, United Nations Population Division, http://esa.un.org/unup/.

1990 (see table 1.7), and every country in the region experienced sizable improvements in human development between 1990 and 2003.[2] Approximately 150 million persons, or about 8 percent of East Asia, now live on less than US$1 a day. A big part of the story is China, though other countries, especially Vietnam, but also Cambodia and Lao PDR, have also effected poverty reduction on an unprecedented scale.

An ambitious region should perhaps have more ambitious poverty reduction targets. Using a poverty line of US$2 a day, an estimated 585 million East Asians are still poor: about 375 million in China, 100 million in Indonesia, 40 million in Vietnam, 35 million in the Philippines, and about 30 million in the other countries in the region.[3]

Strong and steady economic growth has been the principal reason for poverty reduction in the region, and growth-oriented policies will remain the main antipoverty program for the foreseeable future in most of the countries. But growing economies have also been associated with growing income disparities in East

■ TABLE 1.7 **The Number of East Asians Living on Less Than US$2 a Day Fell by 500 Million**
mean consumption and headcount poverty, 1990, 2000, and 2005

Year	East Asia and Pacific	China	Indonesia	Vietnam	Philippines	Thailand	Korea, Rep. of	Malaysia	Cambodia	Lao PDR
Population (millions)										
1990	1,585.4	1,143.3	178.2	66.2	62.6	55.6	42.9	18.2	10.3	4.2
2000	1,789.6	1,267.4	210.5	79.9	76.3	61.9	47.0	23.3	12.7	5.4
2005	1,868.5	1,307.7	226.1	86.1	83.7	65.1	48.3	25.5	14.1	6.1
Mean consumption (1993 US$ adjusted for purchasing power per person per day)										
1990	2.2	1.9	2.0	1.4	3.0	3.4	9.9	6.4	1.8	1.3
2000	3.7	3.5	2.4	2.4	3.5	4.1	16.3	10.0	2.3	1.8
2005	5.3	5.4	3.1	3.0	3.8	5.2	18.2	12.1	2.6	2.1
Poverty headcount index 1 (percentage of population living on less than US$1 a day)										
1990	28.8	31.5	20.6	50.8	19.1	12.5	<0.5	2.0	32.5	53.0
2000	13.8	15.4	9.9	15.2	13.5	5.2	<0.5	<0.5	22.6	33.9
2005	8.0	8.9	4.4	7.9	10.8	1.7	<0.5	<0.5	17.3	20.0
Poverty headcount index 2 (percentage of population living on less than US$2 a day)										
1990	66.9	69.9	71.1	87.0	53.5	47.0	<0.5	18.5	76.3	89.6
2000	45.8	44.8	59.5	63.5	47.2	35.6	<0.5	9.7	67.8	79.4
2005	31.3	28.6	44.4	49.1	41.9	22.8	<0.5	5.5	62.1	68.6
Persons living on less than US$1 a day (millions)										
1990	456.9	360.6	36.7	33.6	12.0	7.0	—	0.4	3.4	2.2
2005	149.7	117.0	9.9	6.8	9.0	1.1	—	—	2.4	1.2
Persons living on less than US$2 a day (millions)										
1990	1,060.8	799.6	126.7	57.6	33.5	26.1	—	3.4	7.9	3.7
2005	584.5	373.5	100.5	42.3	35.1	14.8	—	1.4	8.7	4.2

Source: World Bank staff estimates.
Note: — = no data are available.

Asia (see figure 1.6). By one measure, inequality rose by more than 22 percent between 1990 and 2002: Chapter 6 documents that the Theil index of inequality of per capita consumption in the region rose from 35 percent in 1990 to 43 percent in 2002. Other measures may show an even sharper increase.

The share of within-country inequality in the total increased between 1990 and 2002, while between-country inequality fell, thereby erasing a small fraction of

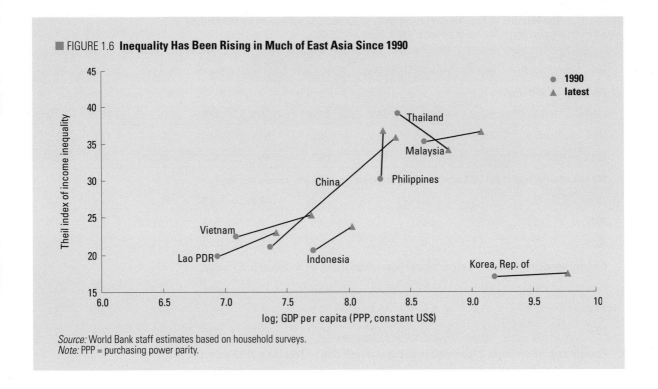

■ FIGURE 1.6 **Inequality Has Been Rising in Much of East Asia Since 1990**

Source: World Bank staff estimates based on household surveys.
Note: PPP = purchasing power parity.

the increase in within-country differentials in well-being. A (static) decomposition of inequality indicates that, in 1990, within-country inequality explained less than two-thirds of the inequality among East Asians. This had risen to more than three-fourths by 2002. Growth and regional integration seem to be helping to bring the average living standards of countries closer, while driving apart the differences within countries.

An aspect of inequality that is robust across all countries of the region is the rural-urban gap in income, consumption, poverty, education, and health. Urban mean consumption levels are between 50 percent (in countries such as Indonesia) and 100 percent (in countries such as China, the Philippines, and Thailand) higher than the rural levels. Rural poverty rates are between two and three times urban poverty rates, though poverty rates appear to have fallen equally rapidly in urban and rural areas since 1990. Poverty remains an overwhelmingly rural phenomenon in East Asia; the rural share of the poor (calculated using national poverty lines) ranges from about 75 percent in Indonesia and the Philippines to about 95 percent or more in Cambodia, China, and Vietnam. These ratios have not changed much since 1990. The urban schooling attainment rate is between 33 percent (the Philippines) and 50 percent (in countries such as China, Indonesia, and Thailand) and higher than the rural levels.

Bigger responsibilities for governments; a growing concern about corruption. One measure that illustrates the extent of corruption in a region is the control of corruption.[4] This measure shows the percentage of countries that are doing relatively worse in controlling corruption than a given country or region in the sample (that is, a higher percentage position indicates more control). East Asia's position deteriorated somewhat between 1996 and 2004. Indeed, in 1996, East Asia lagged behind only higher-income countries in the Organisation for Economic Co-operation and Development as far as control of corruption is concerned (see figure 1.7). By 2004, the regional average had declined to fourth, tied with Latin America.

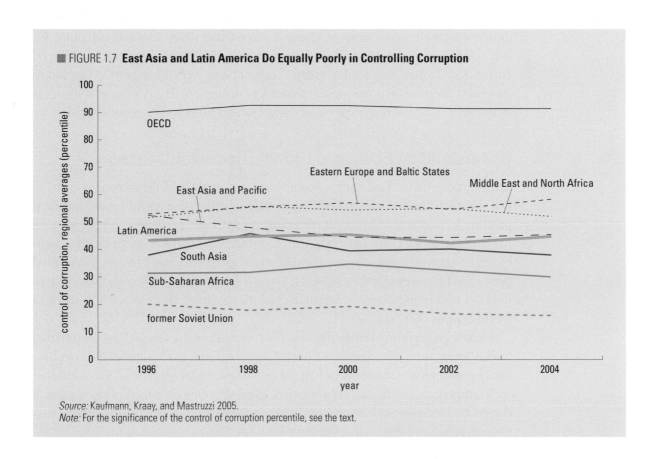

■ FIGURE 1.7 **East Asia and Latin America Do Equally Poorly in Controlling Corruption**

Source: Kaufmann, Kraay, and Mastruzzi 2005.
Note: For the significance of the control of corruption percentile, see the text.

Some have argued that East Asians are more tolerant of corruption than are people in other societies and that they do not consider some practices, such as giving small gifts to public officials, as corrupt. But there does not appear to be an empirical basis for such statements. Firms consider corruption a major obstacle to business in Cambodia, Indonesia, and the Philippines, and household surveys in Cambodia, Indonesia, and Thailand also find a strong intolerance for high-level corruption. Corruption has become a major issue in several political campaigns in the region, again suggesting that people care deeply about reducing it.

Regional averages mask considerable variation among countries, perhaps nowhere as much as in East Asia. East Asian countries span the range from the very clean to the very corrupt. Transparency International, for example, rates Singapore at better than 9 on a 0-to-10 scale in terms of perceived corruption, while Hong Kong (China), Japan, and Taiwan (China) get ratings of around 8, 7, and 6, respectively. At the opposite extreme are countries such as Cambodia, Indonesia, and the Philippines with ratings close to 2.

As East Asian economies become wealthier and more complex, citizens are demanding better government. Growth success translates into less tolerance for corrupt governments. In general, the region's successful developers have reduced corruption. It may also be that greater regional and global integration has led to increased pressure on governments to reduce corruption. In any case, governments in the region are likely to experience even stronger pressures to reduce corruption.

Understanding Economic Growth: Recent Advances

With rapid growth, East Asia is becoming a region of middle-income countries. But since East Asian countries still have only a fifth of the world's gross national product in dollar terms, they have found it profitable to strengthen their trade, investment, and technology links with North America and Western Europe, each of which account for about one-third of world gross national income. Continued per capita income growth of between 5 and 7 percent annually over the next two decades will help East Asia regain its historically high share of 43.4 percent of world output (see box 1.2).

Because of declining transport costs, the countries of the region have augmented global integration through rapidly escalating regional exchange levels in goods, finance, and ideas. Countries in East Asia now face the potential pitfalls associated with congestion, conflict, and corruption, the domestic side effects of rapid growth driven by international integration. The challenge ahead is to complement successful global and regional integration through domestic integration.

■ BOX 1.2 **"The East Asia Project": Achieving a Big Share in the World Economy**

For more than 300 of the past 500 years, East Asia's share in world GDP hovered around 30 percent, with a peak of 40 percent in 1820. India came in second with a share in world GDP of around 25 percent between 1500 and 1700. With the industrial revolution in the United Kingdom in the mid-to-late 18th century and the early 19th century and in most of Western Europe and in the United States throughout the 19th century, these two regions caught up rapidly with East Asia. East Asia had lost its lead to Western Europe by the mid-19th century and then was also overtaken by the United States at the beginning of the 20th century. By 1950, East Asia accounted for only 11.4 percent of world GDP. Since then, the region has effected an impressive rebound. By 2001, it again topped the list, accounting for almost 30 percent of the world economy in purchasing power terms (see figure 1.8).

Assuming that world GDP grows at the same rates of the last 30 years (that is, about 3.5 percent annually from 1975 to 2005), it will reach around US$109.1 trillion in 2025. For East Asia's share to account for 40 percent by that time, it would need to grow 5.9 percent annually. East Asia's annual growth during the last 30 years has been about 5.6 percent.

■ FIGURE 1.8 **Regional Share of World GDP**

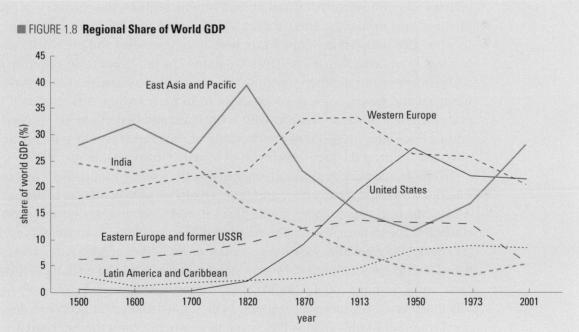

Source: Maddison 2003.
Note: The GDP figures are expressed in 1990 international Geary-Kharmis dollars.

This book considers the prospects in East Asia of this third integration to be as important as the prospects of the first two. To understand this assessment, one should examine recent advances in thinking and use the insights to frame and discipline the inquiry. This section summarizes relevant recent breakthroughs in economic theory and how they may help in understanding what is happening in East Asia.

Ever since Romer (1986) and Lucas (1988) revived broad academic interest in economic growth, some of the best minds in economics have been working on the problem of development. While economic growth remains a mystery, these efforts have yielded some insights. The next few pages attempt to summarize these developments within the backdrop of East Asia's experience over the last two decades and to discuss the potential policy implications of these advances.[5] Putting this work in the East Asian context is not difficult because East Asian economic growth already figures prominently in these efforts.

The renewed interest in economic development has been triggered by the observation that income levels across countries have not been converging as predicted by traditional neoclassical economic theory. This theory predicts that efforts to accumulate physical and human capital, improve the efficiency of production, and utilize the latest technologies should pay off in a narrowing of income gaps between developed and developing countries and eventually lead to roughly equal welfare levels across the globe. The fundamental implication of mainstream economic theory is that, in seeking the highest possible returns, financial and human capital would move from places where it is abundant to places where it is scarce, bringing with it the latest and best products, processes, and technologies. In this way, the working of the market would potently and effectively address the problems involved in achieving economic growth.

To ensure that markets would accomplish this, the role of governments is first and foremost to ensure "peace, easy taxes, and a tolerable administration of justice."[6] And, while openness to foreign trade, finance, and ideas makes good sense, neoclassical theorists recognize that money and skilled people may not move quickly enough and so emphasize the virtues of "more saving and more schooling." If countries did all this, it was thought, the newest technologies would be available to them. Developing countries could pick and choose among these ideas, and grow more rapidly than even those they were learning from. Capital and bright people in developed countries would not miss the chance to go where growth was high and bring their entrepreneurship and ideas along. This would happen until, in all the parts of the world where peace and justice prevailed, wealth gaps would narrow.

But this has not happened. With few exceptions (primarily the East Asian high-performing countries), income gaps between the West and the rest have grown. This does not mean the market has not worked at all: most countries have become richer, and poverty has fallen. Garrett (2004), for example, points out that, while the per capita GDP of high-income countries rose by about 50 percent between 1980 and 2000, that of low-income countries increased by more than 150 percent, and the income ratio between high- and low-income countries has been cut in half. But the average real per capita incomes of *middle-income* countries grew by less than 20 percent in the 1980s and 1990s; so, the distance between them and high-income countries *increased* by about 20 percent. Moreover, as often as capital has flowed downhill from richer to poorer countries, it has climbed uphill to rich countries even from middle-income countries that had peace, low taxes, a tolerable administration of justice, high savings, and rising levels of schooling. Adhering to classical and neoclassical advice seems to be necessary to grow, but is not sufficient to catch up to advanced countries.

Having demonstrated that they can institute the conditions for sustained growth and being so close to the few countries that have had success in achieving high-income levels, East Asia's middle-income countries should not settle for less than convergence with Western living standards. For this to happen in any reasonable length of time, middle-income countries must sustain high rates of income growth until they attain high-income levels. To do so, these countries may have to adjust their growth strategies (box 1.3).

■ BOX 1.3 **Middle-Income Status: A Period of Significant Change**

While the achievement of economic development requires constant learning and adjustment, recent findings point to the need for several major changes in strategy when countries reach per capita incomes between US$1,000 and US$10,000.

■ *From diversification to specialization.* Recent evidence indicates that countries generally appear to diversify in the early stages as they grow, but that this trend is reversed after per capita incomes reach levels around US$5,000–US$8,000, after which the countries begin to specialize again. This tipping point may arrive earlier or later depending on the country's size and export orientation. Thus, for example, Singapore started to specialize at a per capita income of around US$2,500. The reasons are likely related to economies of scale.

■ *From investment to innovation.* As firms in a country approach the technological frontier, regulatory policies that favored investment by incumbent firms should give way to regulations that encourage the entry of new firms and the exit of firms whose products or technologies have been rendered redundant by the new firms. This switchover must be well timed, and it will be difficult to implement because of vested interests.

■ *From basic to tertiary education.* As countries become more well informed about the products and the areas of production in which they should specialize and the related R&D activities which they should subsidize, governments must switch from general subsidies for schooling to more specific incentives for the creation of new products and processes. If policy makers are unable to reliably determine which R&D activities should be subsidized, second-best strategies include general subsidies for tertiary education.

Sources: Imbs and Wacziarg 2003; Aghion and Howitt 2005; Helpman 2006.

Do the recent advances in economic thought help in determining what East Asian countries need to reach high incomes? This report proposes that they do. At the risk of oversimplification, the insights provided by this work for middle-income countries in East Asia may be grouped into two categories: the role of *economies of scale* in growth and the importance of the efficient *distribution of economic rents.*

The remaining parts of this chapter discuss these two points. Chapters 2, 3, and 4 show that East Asia has done well in exploiting economies of scale, but might do even better. Chapters 5, 6, and 7 discuss how countries in the region might address distributional concerns so that the foundations for rapid growth are progressively strengthened.

Economies of Scale

The force behind convergence between rich and poor countries is the law of diminishing returns. Given that convergence has been slow, recent explanations point to the presence of increasing returns to scale in some activities or the absence of diminishing returns associated with a factor of production. Romer (1986, 1990) identifies knowledge as the factor exhibiting increasing returns and stresses the nonrival nature of ideas; that is, ideas are different from goods and factors because an idea may be used again and again and by many people at the same time. An idea, once formed, may be used by others as a starting point for new ideas.

Though ideas are nonrival, they are generally neither free nor nonexcludable. Coming up with useful ideas usually requires effort, and, through secrecy or the enforcement of intellectual property rights, it is possible to exclude people from using ideas to improve products or production processes, even if temporarily. This excludability results in knowledge that confers a monopoly power on the creators of the knowledge. By adding knowledge explicitly to formulations of economic growth, economists are able to recognize the centrality of ideas and the importance of increasing returns, but this also requires a recognition of the proliferation of imperfect competition. By the late 1980s, scale economies were standard features of the explanations of international trade. By the early 1990s, growth theorists had accepted the need to incorporate imperfect competition among firms into aggregate formulations of an economy. By the mid-1990s, theorists had shown how these ideas might be used to understand the spatial distribution of economic activity, including the rise and economic importance of cities. Table 1.8 provides a selective summary of this literature.

The formal recognition of scale economies, externalities, and imperfect competition makes economic theory conform more closely with the world in which

■ TABLE 1.8 **Recognizing the Importance of Scale Economies: Recent Theoretical Advances**

Subdiscipline	Decade	Key publications	Main insights
Industrial organization	1970s	Spence (1976); Dixit and Stiglitz (1977)	Formal models of increasing returns to scale and imperfect competition
International trade	1980s	Krugman (1980, 1981); Ethier (1982); Helpman and Krugman (1985); Grossman and Helpman (1995)	Increasing returns and imperfect competition explain intra-industry trade between countries with similar endowments; initial endowments may, through trade and specialization, influence the long-run rate of growth; trade unleashes forces of both convergence and divergence
Economic geography	1990s	Krugman (1991); Fujita, Krugman, and Venables (1999)	Increasing returns to scale activities are characterized by agglomeration and imperfect competition, while constant returns-to-scale sectors remain dispersed and competitive, helping to explain the spatial distribution of economic activity and the growth of cities
Endogenous growth	1980s	Romer (1986); Lucas (1988)	Perfect competition and knowledge- or human-capital-related externalities imply aggregate increasing returns and explain why growth rates may not fall over time and why wealth levels across countries do not converge
	1990s	Romer (1990); Grossman and Helpman (1991); Aghion and Howitt (1992)	Imperfect competition explains why the incentive to spend on R&D does not fall, and knowledge spillovers explain why R&D costs fall over time, resulting in more or better products that fuel growth
	2000s	Aghion and Howitt (2005)	Imperfect competition and Schumpeterian entry and exit of firms, with entrants bringing new technologies, explain how a country's growth and optimal policies will vary with distance to the technology frontier

Source: Gill, Hariharan, and Kharas 2006.

policy makers must live. For middle-income countries that have established peace, low taxes, and a reasonable administration of justice, there are three sets of implications from this work; these are determined by how economic growth relates to trade, innovation, and cities, as follows:

■ *Intraindustry trade.* The main insight provided by a formal recognition of increasing returns to scale and product differentiation is that trade may take place between economies that are similar in factor endowments; both interindustry *and* intraindustry trade may profitably take place. The principal implication is that countries may, in theory, profitably encourage some activities and ensure comparative advantage.

■ *Idea-driven economies.* The main insight is that the nonrival nature of ideas makes ideas different from other factors of production such as capital, land,

and labor in that the market may underinvest in the creation of new ideas. The principal implication is that governments should, theoretically, subsidize certain strands of R&D, for example, those that will ensure the continuance of the comparative advantage a country has acquired in certain areas.

- *City-based growth.* The main insight is that activities that display increasing returns due to factors external to a firm will tend to be concentrated in cities, while those displaying constant returns will remain more widely spread. The implication is that policies to keep cities business friendly and livable will become increasingly important as economies develop.

During the last decade, the thinking on economic growth has increasingly emphasized the interplay of scale economies, product differentiation, quality improvements, and the heterogeneity of firms within industries, for example, between exporters and nonexporters and between young and old firms. These profiles differ among countries depending on their distance to the technological frontier. This line of thought yields useful insights for middle-income countries. In general, economic theory has progressively recognized that economic growth has differential impacts on firms and workers depending on the sector, location, skill, and government relations of these firms and workers. The underlying reason is the love for variety in consumption and the economies of scale in production; the proximate causes are product differentiation, monopolistic power, specialization, and location externalities. The problem for governments is to address the divergence of market solutions from social optima because of scale economies and, because these lead to sizable economic rents, to the efficient and equitable distribution of economic rents.

Distribution of Economic Rents

While aggregate models have recognized scale economies, externalities, product differentiation, and imperfect competition among firms, recent trends have been toward more disaggregated models of an economy that recognize the differential impacts. Though perhaps an oversimplification, there may be some truth in the statement that these models tend to focus on the differences between skilled and unskilled workers, between firms that are large and those that are not, and between activities and people located in cities where the economic rents are high and those who live elsewhere. Put another way, while the section above on "economies of scale" discusses the scale of economic activities and imperfect competition among firms, this section discusses the distribution of economic rewards and imperfect allocation among workers and consumers. Table 1.9

■ TABLE 1.9 **Economic Growth and Distribution: Recent Theoretical Advances**

Subdiscipline	Channels	Key publications	Main insights
Correlation between growth and distribution			
International trade	Skill premiums	Ethier (1982); Helpman and Krugman (1985); Feenstra and Hanson (1996)	Trade in final goods takes place on Hecksher-Ohlin terms and reduces skilled-unskilled wage premiums in middle-income countries; trade in intermediate goods may increase these gaps
Industrial organization	Skill premiums	Acemoglu (1996)	Moves toward flatter organizations and team-based work within firms and the growing segregation of firms by skill levels across sectors likely reduce within-firm wage dispersion and raise across-firm wage gaps
Endogenous growth	Skill premiums	Aghion and Howitt (1998)	General-purpose technologies such as engines, lasers, and computers generate structural shifts that favor the more educated
		García-Peñalosa and Turnovsky (2006)	Higher saving or productivity leads to higher growth and inequality if the initial distribution of capital is less uniform than that of labor
Economic geography	Rural-urban differentials	Krugman (1991); Fujita, Krugman, and Venables (1999)	Increasing-returns-to-scale activities are characterized by rents and agglomerate in urban areas, while constant-returns-to-scale activities remain competitive and dispersed, thereby leading to large and persistent urban-rural differentials
Effects of distribution on growth			
Industrial organization	Investment	Loury (1981); Perotti (1992); Aghion and Bolton (1997)	Capital market imperfections imply that poor but talented individuals are unable to take advantage because of their inability to borrow and invest
Political economy	Incentives	Alesina and Rodrik (1994); Persson and Tabellini (1996)	Higher inequality leads to pressure for more redistribution, higher taxes, and lower growth
	Insecurity	Benabou (1996)	Inequality leads to sociopolitical conflict and, hence, less secure property rights that reduce investment

Source: Gill, Hariharan, and Kharas 2006.

attempts a summary of the advances achieved by economic theory in the efforts to understand these later.

The recognition of the distributional implications of economic growth that is driven by increasing returns and that leads to large economic rents allows economic theory to inform policy makers more accurately about the trade-offs and choices being faced. For middle-income countries that are growing rapidly and seeking to maintain this momentum, there are three aspects of distribution that have policy implications, as follows:

- *Spatial dispersion.* The main insight provided by the economics of geography is that there will be large and persisting differences between rural and urban areas at least until countries reach high-income levels. The implication for middle-income countries is that urbanization should be seen as a correlate of development, and rural-urban factor links and product market links should be strengthened. Combined with the implication that cities are central for growth, this implies a special effort on the part of governments to ensure the continued vibrancy of cities.
- *Socioeconomic disparities.* The insight provided by the new trade theory is that, while trade is essential for exploiting economies of scale, it will likely result in a widening skill premium in developed and middle-income developing countries. Greater trade and investment flows imply a greater potential for outsourcing, which raises skill premiums in both developed and developing countries. Countries that aggressively exploit economies of scale will likely experience rising inequality (within urban areas and between urban and rural incomes) even if they follow egalitarian human capital policies. The implication is that middle-income countries need to undertake especially aggressive efforts to ensure universal access to social services.
- *Reallocation of rents.* The insight provided by endogenous growth theory is that, for purely economic reasons, such as imperfections in credit markets and coordination failures, and perhaps also because of political economy considerations, there are grounds for growth-enhancing reallocations of economic rents. Choosing the appropriate activities and methods for taxation and the allocation of subsidies will involve learning and mistakes, but the solutions lie in closer, but more transparent relations between governments and the private sector, not attempts to build walls between them. The implication is that middle-income countries need to undertake especially strong efforts to address corruption.

Aggressive and well-implemented urban and social investments require governments that are well informed, efficient, and uncorrupt so that they are able both to tax economic rents appropriately and to spend the proceeds in ways that promote growth. Taxing urban economic rents and reinvesting the proceeds in the infrastructure of cities is an obvious way to reduce rural-urban differentials and keep cities livable, and social investments in education are the obvious way to ensure that the skill premiums associated with high growth in open economies remain reasonable.

Plan of This Report

The line of thinking developed in the literature during the last decade and a half may be summarized as follows:

- *Scale economies are important, and international integration is critical.* The literature on the role of unexhausted scale economies is persuasive, and scale economies are an important issue in the understanding of the nature and causes of growth in developing countries. The international flow of goods, ideas, and finance is necessary for the successful exploitation of scale economies in all countries, but especially in middle-income countries that have built the basic foundations for development.
- *Intraindustry trade reflects scale economies.* Scale economies are an important reason for the growth of intraindustry trade, alongside the more conventional interindustry trade based on relative factor abundance. For middle-income countries, trade is a potent instrument for obtaining access to new ideas, but it is important to recognize that such access depends on and may widen the differences between firms within a country and even within a specific sector.
- *Ideas are a key source of external economies.* New ideas are the most important source for the power to generate economic progress because, given their non-rival nature, ideas are the most important source of unexhausted scale economies. Growth means new products, especially intermediate goods, and new production structures. Middle-income levels generally include the stage of development in which economies appear to shift from increasing diversification to specialization and, hence, from an emphasis on investment to innovation.
- *Foreign capital is a critical facilitator of intraindustry trade and a conduit for knowledge.* Stable flows of finance within and between countries are a critical prerequisite of the specialization that enables the exploitation of scale economies, especially among partners in production networks. International flows of finance are also a potent instrument for accessing new technology, even though these flows may pose risks for middle-income countries.
- *Scale economies imply economic rents that are unevenly distributed within countries.* The sectoral location and the size of firms, the location of economic activities, and the skills of workers are critical correlates of the benefits of market-led growth. Scale economies, externalities, and distributional concerns imply a divergence between market solutions and social optima.
- *Cities reflect scale economies and are critical connectors.* The rise of cities may reasonably be interpreted as a reflection of the importance of economies of scale. Large cities and megacities serve as hotbeds of innovation as countries

approach the frontiers of world technology in economic activities in which their firms have become proficient. Cities, both small and large, facilitate the smooth flow of trade, finance, and ideas into and within developing countries. Vibrant cities are indispensable for middle-income countries that hope to match the achievements of the world's leading innovators.

- *Rural-urban differences are inevitable, and skill premiums tend to widen.* Growing intraindustry trade and the related FDI in middle-income countries have differential impacts on people depending on whether or not they are entrepreneurs or employees in sectors that exhibit scale economies and depending on whether they are skilled or unskilled. The rapid urbanization in East Asia's middle-income countries may represent an opportunity to expand the access of rural populations to the same social services and economic dynamism experienced by residents of large cities.

- *Societies must efficiently reinvest economic rents.* In middle-income countries, these investments should address the differential effects of rapid growth on workers and enterprises and, hence, be aimed at ensuring livable cities, innovative enterprises, and equitable societies. It is necessary for governments efficiently to regulate, tax, and reinvest the rents associated with activities that are characterized by scale economies and imperfect competition. This implies that it is increasingly important for governments to be both less corrupt and less centralized since the successful encouragement of selected activities requires close relations between private enterprises and government, not attempts to isolate government officials from business interests.

Developments in economic theory during the last two decades do inform the efforts of policy makers to blend discipline and discretion. In the next six chapters, these ideas—the importance of exploiting the advantages of bigness *and* recognizing the absence of sameness—are described and analyzed for the case of East Asia. Chapters 2, 3, and 4 discuss how East Asian countries are exploiting scale economies through international integration, especially with their East Asian neighbors, using the channels of trade, technology, and finance. These chapters discuss what East Asia is doing well, and what it may perhaps do more effectively. Chapters 5, 6, and 7 discuss the challenges of managing the domestic distribution of economic rents, taking up in turn the topics of cities, cohesion, and corruption. This report proposes that it is in these aspects of domestic integration that East Asia's developers must accomplish much more. As pointed out in other sections of this chapter, the experiences of the East Asian tigers since the 1960s show that this can be done, while the experiences of Latin American countries since the 1970s provide a cautionary tale of how things can go wrong.

Development economics has seen major advances during the last two decades, but many questions remain unanswered. It would be fair to say, however, that, since the early 1990s, East Asia is a favorite place for economists to look for answers to these questions. The reason is obvious: this is a part of the world where many countries have achieved success in increasing per capita incomes from about US$100 to more than US$1,000 and where some countries have raised per capita incomes from around US$1,000 to more than US$10,000. Countries in East Asia that have reached middle-income status have heeded Adam Smith and instituted the classical prerequisites of economic growth: "peace, easy taxes, and a tolerable administration of justice." They have also adhered to the neoclassical tenets of openness, macroeconomic stability, and broadly based investment in human capital. For such middle-income economies looking to become high-income countries, it is not helpful simply to repeat these messages. The subsequent chapters of this book draw upon modern economic growth theories, and are intended as a contribution to the efforts of developing countries in East Asia to grow through and beyond middle-income levels.

Notes

1. The World Bank classifies countries with per capita incomes below US$825 as low income, countries with incomes between US$826 and US$3,255 as lower middle income, countries with incomes between US$3,256 and US$10,665 as upper middle income, and countries with incomes over $10,066 as high income. Since 1950, among countries with more than 1 million inhabitants, only Hong Kong (China), Korea, Saudi Arabia, Singapore, and Taiwan (China) have gone from low- to high-income status.

2. See UNDP (2005).

3. These figures exclude the Democratic People's Republic of Korea and Myanmar.

4. The control of corruption "measures perceptions of corruption, conventionally defined as the exercise of public power for private gain. Despite this straightforward focus, the particular aspect of corruption measured by the various sources differs somewhat, ranging from the frequency of 'additional payments to get things done,' to the effects of corruption on the business environment, to measuring 'grand corruption' in the political arena or in the tendency of elite forms to engage in 'state capture' " (Kaufmann, Kraay, and Mastruzzi 2005: 131).

5. Helpman (2004) provides a discerning, though somewhat technical account of these developments, and Warsh (2006) offers an accurate account of the thinking that has led to these insights.

6. Smith (1755) wrote that "little else is requisite to carry a state to the highest degree of opulence from the lowest barbarism but peace, easy taxes, and a tolerable administration of justice: all the rest being brought about by the natural course of things." (See "Adam Smith Quotes," Adam Smith Institute, http://www.adamsmith.org.)

References

Acemoglu, Daron. 1996. "A Microfoundation for Social Increasing Returns in Human Capital Accumulation." *Quarterly Journal of Economics* 111 (3): 779–804.

Aghion, Philippe, and Patrick Bolton. 1997. "A Theory of Trickle-Down Growth and Development." *Review of Economic Studies* 64 (2): 151–72.

Aghion, Philippe, and Peter Howitt. 1992. "A Model of Growth through Creative Destruction." *Econometrica* 60 (2): 323–51.

———. 1998. *Endogenous Growth Theory.* Cambridge, MA: MIT Press.

———. 2005. "Growth with Quality-Improving Innovations: An Integrated Framework." In *Handbook of Economic Growth,* vol. 1A, ed. Philippe Aghion and Steven N. Durlauf, 67–110. Amsterdam: North-Holland.

———. 2006. "Appropriate Growth Policy: A Unifying Framework." *Journal of the European Economic Association* 4 (2–3): 269–314.

Alesina, Alberto, and Dani Rodrik. 1994. "Distributive Politics and Economic Growth." *Quarterly Journal of Economics* 109 (2): 465–90.

Ando, Mitsuyo, and Fukunari Kimura. 2003. "The Formation of International Production and Distribution Networks in East Asia." NBER Working Paper 10167, National Bureau of Economic Research, Cambridge, MA.

ASEAN (Association of Southeast Asian Nations). 2004. *Statistics of Foreign Direct Investment in ASEAN.* Jakarta: ASEAN Secretariat.

Benabou, Roland. 1996. "Inequality and Growth." In *NBER Macroeconomics Annual,* ed. Ben S. Bernanke and Julio Rotemberg, 11–74. Cambridge, MA: MIT Press.

BNM (Bank Negara Malaysia). Various issues. *Monthly Statistical Bulletin.* Kuala Lumpur: Bank Negara Malaysia.

China, National Bureau of Statistics. Various years. *State Statistical Yearbook.* Beijing: China Statistics Publishing House.

China, National Bureau of Statistics. 2005. *State Statistical Yearbook 2005.* Beijing: China Statistics Publishing House.

Dixit, Avinash K., and Joseph E. Stiglitz. 1977. "Monopolistic Competition and Optimum Product Diversity." *American Economic Review* 67 (3): 297–308.

Ethier, Wilfred J. 1982. "National and International Returns to Scale in the Modern Theory of International Trade." *American Economic Review* 72 (3): 389–405.

Eurostat. 2005. *European Union Foreign Direct Investment Yearbook 2005.* Luxembourg: Office for Official Publications of the European Communities.

Feenstra, Robert C., and Gordon H. Hanson. 1996. "Globalization, Outsourcing, and Wage Inequality." *American Economic Review* 86 (2): 240–45.

Fujita, Masahisa, Paul R. Krugman, and Anthony J. Venables. 1999. *The Spatial Economy: Cities, Regions and International Trade.* Cambridge, MA: MIT Press.

García-Peñalosa, Cecilia, and Stephen J. Turnovsky. 2006. "Growth and Income Inequality: A Canonical Model." *Economic Theory* 28 (1): 25–49.

Garrett, Geoffrey. 2004. "Globalization's Missing Middle." *Foreign Affairs* 83 (6): 84–96.

Gill, Indermit, Govind Hariharan, and Homi Kharas. 2006. "Growing Through Middle Income: Navigating the 'Horse Latitudes' of Economic Development." Background paper, World Bank, Washington, DC.

Grossman, Gene M., and Elhanan Helpman. 1991. *Innovation and Growth in the Global Economy.* Cambridge, MA: MIT Press.

———. 1995. "Technology and Trade." In *Handbook of International Economics,* vol. III, ed. Gene M. Grossman and Kenneth Rogoff, 1279–1337. Amsterdam: Elsevier Science.

Helpman, Elhanan. 2004. *The Mystery of Economic Growth.* Cambridge, MA: Harvard University Press.

———. 2006. "Trade, FDI, and the Organization of Firms." NBER Working Paper 12091, National Bureau of Economic Research, Cambridge, MA.

Helpman, Elhanan, and Paul R. Krugman. 1985. *Market Structure and Foreign Trade.* Cambridge, MA: MIT Press.

Hu, Albert Guangzhou. 2006. "Knowledge Flow in East Asia and Beyond." Background paper, World Bank, Washington, DC.

Imbs, Jean, and Romain Wacziarg. 2003. "Stages of Diversification." *American Economic Review* 93 (1): 63–86.

Kaufmann, Daniel, Aart Kraay, and Massimo Mastruzzi. 2005. "Governance Matters IV: Governance Indicators for 1996–2004." Policy Research Working Paper 3630, World Bank, Washington, DC.

Krugman, Paul R. 1980. "Scale Economies, Product Differentiation, and the Pattern of Trade." *American Economic Review* 70 (5): 950–59.

_____. 1981. "Intraindustry Specialization and the Gains from Trade." *Journal of Political Economy* 89 (5): 959–73.

_____. 1991. "Increasing Returns and Economic Geography." *Journal of Political Economy* 99 (3): 483–99.

_____. 1998. "The Role of Geography in Development." Paper presented at the Annual World Bank Conference on Development Economics, Washington, DC, April 20–21.

Leipziger, Danny M., ed. 1997. *Lessons from East Asia.* Studies in International Trade Policy. Ann Arbor, MI: University of Michigan Press.

Loury, Glenn C. 1981. "Intergenerational Transfers and the Distribution of Earnings." *Econometrica* 49 (4): 843–67.

Lucas, Robert E. 1988. "On the Mechanics of Economic Development." *Journal of Monetary Economics* 22 (1): 3–42.

Maddison, Angus. 2003. *The World Economy: Historical Statistics.* Paris: Organisation for Economic Co-operation and Development.

OECD (Organisation for Economic Co-operation and Development). 2005. "Main Science and Technology Indicators." 2005 (2) November, Organisation for Economic Co-operation and Development, Paris.

Okamoto, Yumiko. 2005. "Emergence of the 'Intra-Mediate Trade': Implications for the Asia-Pacific Region." Paper presented at the East-West Center and the Rosenberg Institute of Global Finance, Brandeis University, "PAFTAD 30" conference, Honolulu, February 19–21. http://www.eastwestcenter.org/stored/misc/paftad_30_okamoto.pdf.

Perotti, Roberto. 1992. "Fiscal Policy, Income Distribution, and Growth." Working Paper 636, Department of Economics, Columbia University, New York.

Persson, Torsten, and Guido Tabellini. 1996. "Federal Fiscal Constitutions: Risk Sharing and Redistribution." *Journal of Political Economy* 104 (5): 979–1009.

Rana, Pradumna B. 2005. "Economic Relations between South and East Asia: The Evolution of Pan-Asian Integration." Paper prepared for the high-level conference, "Asian Economic Integration," New Delhi, November 18–19.

Romer, Paul M. 1986. "Increasing Returns and Long-Run Growth." *Journal of Political Economy* 94 (5): 1002–37.

_____. 1990. "Endogenous Technological Change." *Journal of Political Economy* 98 (5): 71–102.

Smith, Adam. 1755. "Adam Smith Quotes." Adam Smith Institute.

Spence, Michael E. 1976. "Product Selection, Fixed Costs and Monopolistic Competition." *Review of Economic Studies* 43 (2): 217–35.

Stiglitz, Joseph E., and Shahid Yusuf, eds. 2001. *Rethinking the East Asian Miracle.* Washington, DC: World Bank; New York: Oxford University Press.

UNCTAD (United Nations Conference on Trade and Development). 2000. *Asia and the Pacific.* vol. VII of *World Investment Directory.* Geneva: United Nations.

_____. 2003. *World Investment Report 2003: FDI Policies for Development, National and International Perspectives.* Geneva: United Nations.

UNDP (United Nations Development Program). 2005. *Human Development Report 2005: International Cooperation at a Crossroads: Aid, Trade and Security in an Unequal World.* New York: United Nations Development Program.

Warsh, David. 2006. *Knowledge and the Wealth of Nations: A Story of Economic Discovery.* New York: W. W. Norton and Company.

World Bank. 1993. *The East Asian Miracle: Economic Growth and Public Policy.* World Bank Policy Research Reports. New York: Oxford University Press.

_____. 2005a. *World Development Indicators 2005.* Washington, DC: World Bank. http://devdata.worldbank.org/wdi2005/Cover.htm.

_____. 2005b. *Global Development Finance 2005: Mobilizing Finance and Managing Vulnerability.* Washington, DC: World Bank.

MAP 2.1 Trade Ties Make East Asia a Tightly Knit Region

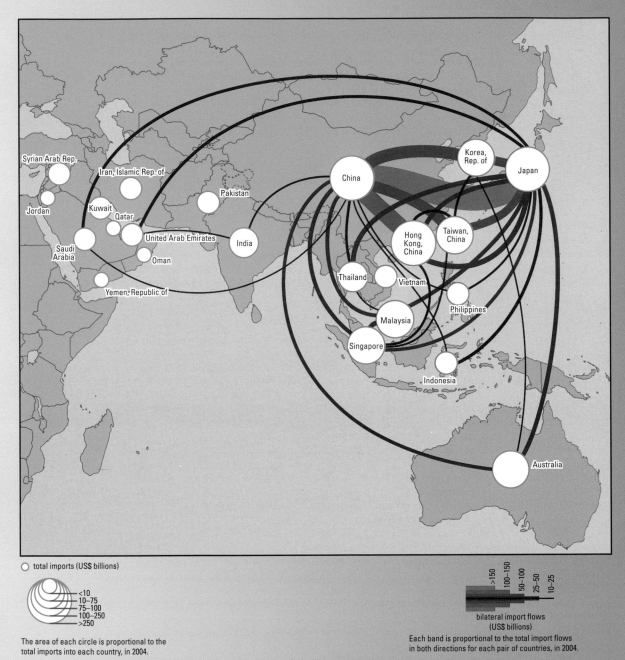

total imports (US$ billions)

<10
10–75
75–100
100–250
>250

The area of each circle is proportional to the
total imports into each country, in 2004.

>150
100–150
50–100
25–50
10–25

bilateral import flows
(US$ billions)

Each band is proportional to the total import flows
in both directions for each pair of countries, in 2004.

Source: Direction of Trade Statistics Database, International Monetary Fund and ESDS International, http://www.esds.ac.uk/international/access/
access.asp.

CHAPTER 2

TRADE

Vigorously growing sectors are relying on scale economies. Regional production networks have deepened trade ties by leading to rapid expansion in the trade in parts and components.

For the last four decades, trade has been the engine of economic growth for most of East Asia. In the 1960s, Japan emerged as the region's first major exporter, and it was followed in the 1970s by a second generation of countries (Hong Kong [China], the Republic of Korea, Singapore, Taiwan [China]), in the 1980s by a third generation (Indonesia, Malaysia, the Philippines, Thailand), and in the 1990s by a fourth generation (China, Vietnam). While unilateral liberalizations by individual countries helped initiate export-led development in the region, the increasing economic integration of East Asia has been an important factor in sustaining the region's growth.

The region's economies share a reliance on export-oriented industries. However, the economies have developed in ways that are distinct and also revealing of the region's underlying growth dynamic. Japan began as a producer of low-priced final consumer goods and later moved into capital-intensive intermediate and capital goods. Second-generation countries (with the partial exception of Korea) entered the global stage as subcontractors, assembling or producing final consumer goods using the intellectual property (brand names, patents, organizational capital) of European, Japanese, and U.S. firms. Their industrial roots lay in the fact that firms from high-wage countries relocated their production processes by moving labor-intensive manufacturing stages to East and Southeast Asia. As second-generation countries increased the skill and capital intensity of the goods and services they produced, they became sources of innovation in their own right. Industrialization in these economies has gone hand in hand with an expansion in the *varieties of goods* they produce by moving up a *quality ladder.*

Third- and fourth-generation exporters also entered global trade by providing subcontracting services to European, Japanese, and U.S. firms and competing in low-end consumer goods on the basis of lower unit labor costs. Over time, they have also become more specialized in producing components and other intermediate inputs for firms in Japan and in second-generation countries in East Asia and the Pacific through *production networks* managed by multinational firms in the region's entrepôts (Hong Kong [China], Singapore) and, increasingly, in the more industrialized East Asian economies (Japan, Korea, Taiwan [China]). Within these networks, intermediaries, be they multinationals or specialized traders, help coordinate production and lower transaction costs.

Trade within production networks contributes to *complementarity* among the development paths of countries in the region, even as it creates rivalry between countries for market share abroad. Income growth in one country increases the demand for intermediate inputs produced in nearby countries. By allowing input producers to enjoy *scale economies,* this lowers input production costs and enhances regional growth. In this way, *regional economic integration* has become a driver of growth.

One source of complementarity between production and trade in East Asian economies is the proximity of these economies to one another. Because of low transport costs and low trade barriers between the region's economies, growth in one East Asian economy tends to expand the trade between that economy and other East Asian economies rather than, say, Latin America. Low trade costs may magnify the advantages of fragmenting production, rendering the impact on trade of incremental reductions in trade barriers potentially large.

Production networks seem to be more extensive in East Asia than in other regions and are at the heart of the recent growth in intraregional trade (see map 2.1). This is due to a favorable policy setting (low tariffs, policies that encourage exports, such as duty drawback, and encouragement of export-oriented foreign direct investment [FDI]), first-mover advantages, and considerable intercountry unit labor cost differentials, combined with excellent logistics. Because of these advantages, East Asia has become a global production leader in products that exhibit increasing returns to scale, such as machinery, parts, and components.

The economic integration of China has deepened production fragmentation in East Asia to an unprecedented level. This vertical specialization has intensified the dynamism of East Asian economies and increased the economic interdependence within the region. From this perspective, China has been a positive force. But each East Asian country still depends heavily on extraregional exports of final goods. In those third markets, China is a fierce competitor.

Many questions arise within this East Asian model. Is China, on balance, a substitute or a complement for other East Asian producers? Can we identify the countries and the sectors that are most affected? Do countries engaging in production networks climb the technology ladder rapidly or do they become trapped on the same rung over time? What if China develops its own technological capabilities while it still has cheap labor for manufacturing? Will regional production networks collapse into Chinese production networks? Does the strong interdependence across countries make these countries vulnerable to shocks in each others' economies or do the main risks still lie with the health of global demand?

This chapter will (1) review the changing direction of trade and the changing commodity composition of trade, (2) assess how the region is responding to China's emergence as a major trader, and (3) evaluate the impact on technology and growth.

Trade Patterns in East Asia

The exports of emerging East Asia have been growing rapidly.[1] They doubled in the six years since the crisis and probably surpassed US$2 trillion in value in 2005. They now account for more than one-fifth of total world exports (see table 2.1). The value of East Asia's exports is greater than that of the total exports of Latin America, South Asia, Eastern Europe, the former Soviet Union, the Middle East and North Africa, and sub-Saharan Africa combined. The ratio of exports to gross domestic product (GDP) in the region, at slightly more than 50 percent, is the highest of any region in the world. Trade is East Asia's economic lifeblood and the source of its dramatic growth.

Improvements in transportation infrastructure have certainly played an important role in the expansion in trade in East Asia (see figure 2.1). Asia has the lowest freight costs among all developing regions, although the levels are still higher in Asia than they are in developed countries. Firms have taken advantage of low-cost shipping hubs in Hong Kong (China), Singapore, and, increasingly, other major cities in the region, such as Shanghai and the port of Tanjung Pelepas (serving Johore, Malaysia) to ship their goods. The distribution networks of traders in these hubs are an important factor in promoting the economic integration of the region and give the region an advantage over other developing regions, such as Africa and Latin America, which lack major entrepôts.

■ TABLE 2.1 **East Asia Is a Trade Powerhouse**
merchandise exports, current US$

	Value (US$ billion)			Share of world total (%)		
Region[a]	1990	1998	2004	1990	1998	2004
Emerging East Asia	427.7	939.0	1,847.6	12.3	17.1	20.2
Australia, Japan, and New Zealand	336.7	455.9	672.6	9.7	8.3	7.4
North America (3)	521.3	896.5	1,135.4	15.0	16.3	12.4
Eastern Europe (12)	34.5	119.0	291.2	1.0	2.2	3.2
Rest of Europe (28)	1,623.0	2,383.5	3,718.1	46.7	43.3	40.7
Former Soviet Union (15)	n.a.	115.6	284.9	n.a.	2.1	3.1
Memo: European Union (25)	1,535.2	2,322.4	3,670.8	44.2	42.2	40.1
Middle East (14)	138.4	144.5	389.6	4.0	2.6	4.3
North Africa (7)	38.6	34.4	82.8	1.1	0.6	0.9
Sub-Saharan Africa (48)	68.2	71.8	143.7	2.0	1.3	1.6
World	3,475.1	5,504.4	9,145.0	100.0	100.0	100.0

Source: World Bank 2005.
Note: n.a. = not applicable.
a. The number of countries is shown in parentheses.

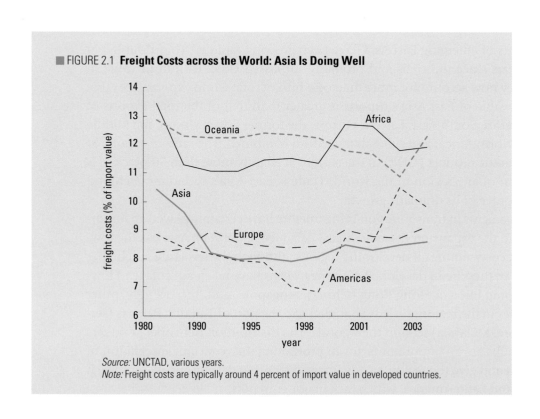

■ FIGURE 2.1 **Freight Costs across the World: Asia Is Doing Well**

Source: UNCTAD, various years.
Note: Freight costs are typically around 4 percent of import value in developed countries.

Reexports and exports on which final-stage value adding activities are undertaken close to a major port are facilitated when import tariffs are low and when export-oriented firms have access to duty drawback schemes. East Asia has always featured low tariffs and extensive duty drawbacks. The trend to openness has been accelerated recently by rapid reductions in import-weighted tariffs in China, Indonesia, Malaysia, the Philippines, and Thailand. In a bold move, countries in the region opted to continue to liberalize and reduce tariffs even after the 1997–98 crisis and now have average weighted tariffs at only slightly above 5 percent (see figure 2.2).

Trade middlemen may efficiently reduce the information and search costs incurred by buyers and sellers. Sometimes these traders manage the entire supply chain. The services they provide are valuable, especially when production involves multiple stages and many countries. A piece of evidence to support the idea that middlemen add more value when the supply chain lengthens is offered by Feenstra and Hanson (2004), who find that Hong Kong (China) traders charge

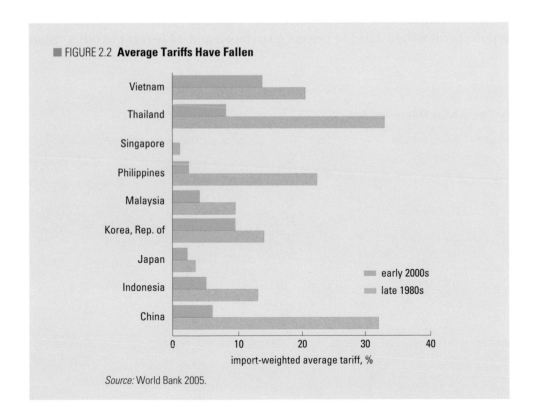

■ FIGURE 2.2 **Average Tariffs Have Fallen**

import-weighted average tariff, %

early 2000s
late 1980s

Source: World Bank 2005.

more on Chinese reexports in those export industries in which there is a higher share of processing exports from China.[2]

Much of the trade in the region is linked to the growth of FDI and the organization of regional production networks by multinational corporations. Figure 2.3 shows that the cumulative stock of FDI in the region has grown even more rapidly than have exports or GDP over the long term and that both exports and FDI have grown in economic importance. The 1997–98 crisis was accompanied by a fall in regional GDP and, consequently, a rise in the share of FDI (measured in U.S. dollars), but this aberration has been steadily offset as GDP has recovered.

The role of multinational corporations in trade and other economic aggregates is best exemplified by the case of China.[3] The share of multinational corporations in China's exports increased from 29 percent in 1994 to 55 percent in 2003 (see figure 2.4), while the corresponding share for imports increased from 46 to 56 percent. The high export and import orientation of multinational corporations differs according to the source and motive for investment. Affiliates of Japanese multinational corporations in Asia have a strong outward orientation; half their production is exported. Over 80 percent of these exports occur within Asia (47 percent go to Japan and 34 percent to other Asian

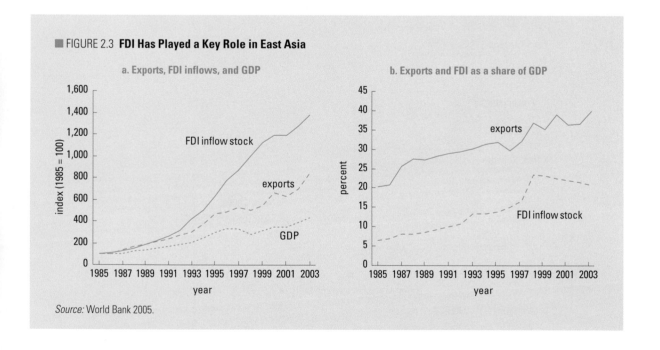

■ FIGURE 2.3 **FDI Has Played a Key Role in East Asia**

a. Exports, FDI inflows, and GDP

b. Exports and FDI as a share of GDP

Source: World Bank 2005.

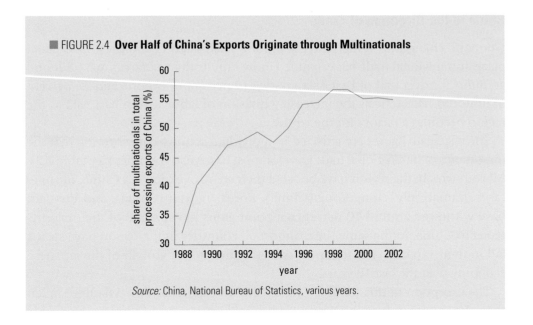

■ FIGURE 2.4 **Over Half of China's Exports Originate through Multinationals**

Source: China, National Bureau of Statistics, various years.

countries). Similarly, over 95 percent of Japanese multinational affiliate imports come from Asia (64 percent from Japan and 31 percent from other Asian countries). Much of this trade takes place within individual firms. Of the exports from the head offices of Japanese multinational corporations, 74 percent are destined to overseas affiliates, while 56 percent of the imports come from overseas affiliates. This high share of intrafirm trade indicates the closed nature of the regional production networks developed by Japanese multinational corporations, which have managed to fragment the stages of production and relocate each subprocess in the country offering the lowest unit cost. The same pattern now holds for multinational corporations from other East Asian economies, such as Hong Kong (China) and Singapore, which are emerging as important sources of FDI.

This Asian pattern of FDI contrasts with the traditional FDI that seeks to jump trade barriers and service domestic markets more effectively. From 1960 to the early 1980s, trade and capital flows between the United States and Europe tended to be substitutes rather than complements. That still holds for most European Union and U.S. FDI in Asia (especially China) and for Japanese affiliates in North America, which only export 14 percent of their production, producing the rest for the domestic market. In contrast, East Asian FDI has evolved so that trade and FDI flows move in parallel.

Shifts in the Direction of Trade

Dramatic changes in trade patterns among East Asian economies have taken place. Intraregional trade has expanded more rapidly than extraregional trade and accounts for over half of East Asia's trade (49 percent of exports and 55 percent of imports). This reflects the increasing division of labor within East Asia as the region becomes a factory for the world.

The aggregate figures are reflected in individual country data showing that the importance of intraregional trade grew for most East Asian countries (see table 2.2). All countries in the region have boosted their share of exports to China, in some cases dramatically. Hong Kong (China), Korea, Taiwan (China), and Vietnam have witnessed around 10 percentage point gains in the share of their exports going to China. At the same time, almost all countries in the region have seen a fall in their export shares to Japan, reflecting the slower growth of the Japanese economy over the last 10 years.

The exception to this trend is China. China's exports to East Asia have fallen since the country joined the World Trade Organization, and China has been able

■ TABLE 2.2 **East Asian Intraregional Exports Have Been Growing Thanks to China**
percent of total exports going to East Asia, China, and Japan

Exporter	East Asia 1990–94	East Asia 2000–04	China 1990–94	China 2000–04	Japan 1990–94	Japan 2000–04
East Asia	44.1	49.0	6.4	11.1	8.6	8.2
China	60.5	45.3	n.a.	n.a.	15.8	14.3
Hong Kong, China	47.0	55.5	29.9	39.3	5.4	5.4
Indonesia	62.0	56.9	3.6	5.4	32.9	21.0
Japan	34.6	43.1	3.7	10.0	n.a.	n.a.
Korea, Rep. of	40.8	46.6	4.2	15.6	15.7	9.8
Malaysia	54.7	54.2	2.5	5.3	13.6	11.5
Philippines	36.1	53.7	1.2	4.2	17.4	16.4
Singapore	48.2	56.4	2.0	6.1	7.8	7.0
Taiwan, China	42.7	55.2	0.0	10.3	11.3	9.2
Thailand	41.7	48.3	1.5	5.3	17.3	14.7
Vietnam	—	49.0	—	9.6	—	15.7

Source: Direction of Trade Statistics Database, International Monetary Fund and ESDS International, http://www.esds.ac.uk/international/access/access.asp.
Note: n.a. = not applicable. — = no data are available.

to access markets in the European Union and the United States. But China still exports a large share to other East Asian countries; almost half of its total exports went to East Asian trading partners between 2000 and 2004.

More intraregional trade should not be interpreted as a reorientation of exporters toward Asia and away from the rest of the world. There are other explanations for intraregional trade. Most importantly, the East Asian economy has been growing more rapidly than the economy of the rest of the world. So, it is natural to expect that, for all countries, the share of their exports going to East Asia would rise. This effect accounts for almost two-thirds of the intraregional effects noted above.[4] In addition, as East Asia becomes more generally open by, for instance, lowering tariffs across the board, one would expect a higher share of trade within the region. This accounts for another quarter of intraregional export growth. The change in orientation toward the region accounts for a relatively small share of intraregional exports. So, the rapid expansion of intraregional trade has not come at the expense of extraregional trade. Instead, East Asian countries are adding regional trade expansion to their already formidable global exports.

Much regional trade is accounted for by a triangular pattern of exports. There is back-and-forth trade in intermediate goods, whereby additional processing is undertaken at each stage until the final product is exported. This is evident in several sectors in which East Asian newly industrializing economies (NIEs) and Japan export a significant share of parts for electrical appliances, office and telecommunications equipment, and textiles and apparel to China and middle-income countries in the Association of Southeast Asian Nations (ASEAN), where the processing is completed. The final products are then exported to the European Union and the United States. This triangular trade may be quantified as the product of two indexes: the share of total intermediate exports from Japan and the NIEs going to China and ASEAN and the share of China's and ASEAN's total finished goods exports going to Canada, the European Union, and the United States.[5] The composite index captures both legs of the triangular trade. When the assembler countries in East Asia raise their share of intermediate goods, the index rises, and when they sell more to the rich countries outside the region, the index rises. The results are shown in Figure 2.5. Triangular trade has risen most sharply in electrical machinery, office and telecommunications equipment, and the metal industries. It has declined in automobiles, where a different process is at work. There, the triangular flows are reversed. Emerging East Asian countries are the exporters of parts to Japan, where final assembly is carried out.

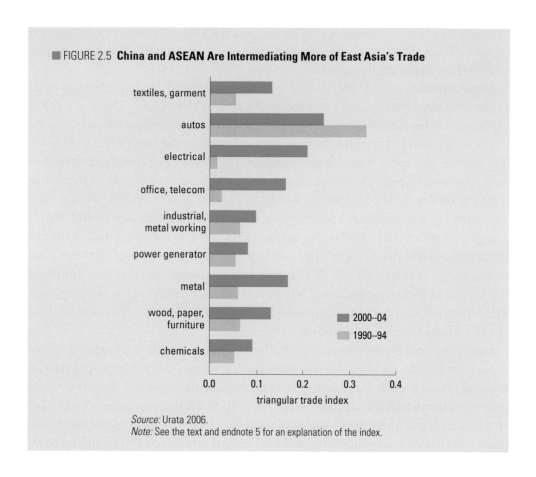

■ FIGURE 2.5 **China and ASEAN Are Intermediating More of East Asia's Trade**

Source: Urata 2006.
Note: See the text and endnote 5 for an explanation of the index.

Shifts in the Commodity Composition of Trade

The rapid expansion of trade by East Asian economies has been accompanied by substantial changes in the commodity composition of trade. From 1990–94 to 2000–04, exports shifted from light manufacturing, such as textiles and garments, wood, paper, and furniture, to more sophisticated manufactures, such as machinery (see table 2.3). Thus, machinery accounted for over 50 percent of East Asia's exports and 42 percent of imports. Within machinery, the exports of office and telecommunications equipment and electrical machinery grew particularly rapidly in ASEAN, the NIEs, and China. For China, the share of office and telecommunications equipment in overall exports increased from 6 to 22 percent, while the share of electrical machinery increased from 4 to 10 percent. ASEAN countries, with the exception of Indonesia, saw exports of office and telecommunications equipment and electrical machinery rise significantly, and

■ TABLE 2.3 **The Commodity Composition of Foreign Trade in East Asia**
percentage share of total trade

Composition	East Asia		China		Japan	
	1990–94	2000–04	1990–94	2000–04	1990–94	2000–04
Export Composition						
Agriculture	7.0	4.1	13.7	5.2	1.1	1.0
Mining, fuels	5.4	5.1	6.4	4.1	1.3	1.7
Total manufacture	86.1	88.7	78.5	90.1	95.8	93.0
Machinery	46.6	53.6	17.4	40.6	71.6	67.1
Textiles, garments	12.7	9.1	29.1	18.3	2.1	1.5
Import Composition						
Agriculture	12.9	8.9	9.3	7.7	23.3	15.6
Mining, fuels	15.4	16.8	7.7	13.7	27.9	25.5
Total manufacture	68.8	72.7	82.3	77.9	45.7	56.7
Machinery	34.3	41.8	42.0	45.0	16.9	27.6
Textiles, garments	7.3	5.4	9.4	4.4	6.6	6.5

Source: United Nations Commodity Trade Statistics Database, United Nations Statistics Division, http://unstats.un.org/unsd/comtrade/.

these accounted for a combined share ranging from 30 to 60 percent of total country exports. Similar to the changes in exports, the share of imports of machinery, in particular office and telecommunications equipment and electrical machinery, increased in total imports in many East Asian economies, including Japan.

Machinery has become an important trade commodity for countries in East Asia.[6] Innovative machinery products have played a significant role in the success of Japan and the NIEs in global trade. The same is now happening in China, where the share of machinery in total exports leaped to 41 percent in 2000–04 from 17 percent a decade earlier.

Machinery encompasses a broad range of products, and the growth in this sector has been accompanied by an equivalent evolution in the nature of the products traded. The products made in China are shifting to more sophisticated machinery and away from mass manufactured goods with low-technology inputs. For example, China now exports more personal computers and related accessories than metalworking tools. China is also exporting cellular phones, personal digital assistants, and flat-screen televisions instead of transistor radios. While much of this production involves the assembly of high-technology products

using low-skilled workers, there has been true improvement in China's technological capacity as well.

A considerable proportion of machinery exports encompasses intermediate
goods. For example, in electrical appliances, parts represent some 80 percent of
East Asian exports, while finished products account for only 20 percent. These
shares vary by sector, but they are indicative of the broader process of international
production fragmentation that is driving the commodity composition of trade.

The fragmentation of production across borders and the economic integration
of national economies have been coincident events in East Asia.[7] Several factors
explain this fragmentation:

- The desire to reduce costs by offshoring subprocesses to countries where unit
  labor costs are lowest; this may change as wage levels for different skills change
- The desire to locate production near sources of consumer demand and input
  supply
- The desire to centralize the production of finished goods or inputs to benefit
  from scale and other agglomeration economies, including thicker labor markets, and the more rapid learning of new technologies

As part of the production network in machinery, China has emerged as the
most important final assembly hub, while Japan and the NIEs are the major
sources of innovative intermediates. But the traditional production network is
changing. It is no longer a simple model whereby Japan and the NIEs supply
high-quality components and capital goods to developing East Asian countries,
which assemble them into finished goods for export to markets in the European
Union and the United States. A more sophisticated and complex network is developing, involving the transshipment of components.[8] An example of such a complex network is offered by the case of the production of hard drives in Thailand,
where parts from 11 different countries are combined. Once a drive is made, it is
exported elsewhere to be assembled into a finished personal computer. Clearly,
a significant amount of trade is involved in this process.

China's increase in machinery exports is exceptional (see table 2.4). Between
1993–04 and 2003–04, the world market share of China doubled in power generating equipment, tripled in industrial machinery, quadrupled in electrical
machinery, and quintupled in office and telecommunications equipment. By and
large, other East Asian countries also raised their world market shares in the same
products and at the same time as China. This is because these countries have been
able to avail themselves of China's rapidly growing internal market.

■ TABLE 2.4 **The Share of Exports of Selected East Asian Countries in World Markets**
percent

Country	Power generating equipment		Industrial machinery		Office, data, and telecom- munications		Electrical machinery		Road transportation	
	1993–94	2003–04	1993–94	2003–04	1993–94	2003–04	1993–94	2003–04	1993–94	2003–04
China	1.3	2.4	1.0	3.3	2.8	15.7	2.4	8.2	0.5	1.6
China (imports)	3.8	4.5	7.9	8.6	2.6	5.5	2.8	9.4	1.5	1.9
Indonesia	0.1	0.4	0.1	0.1	0.6	0.7	0.4	0.6	0.2	0.1
Malaysia	0.8	0.3	0.6	0.5	4.3	3.6	4.8	3.0	0.1	0.1
Philippines	0.0	0.1	0.0	0.1	0.4	1.1	1.5	2.7	0.1	0.2
Thailand	0.6	0.8	0.6	0.6	2.0	1.7	1.4	1.6	0.3	0.5

Source: United Nations Commodity Trade Statistics Database, United Nations Statistics Division, http://unstats.un.org/unsd/comtrade/.
Note: Lightly (dark) shaded figures indicate products with increasing (decreasing) market shares.

Machinery has come to represent a much larger share in total exports in all other countries in the region as well. As a result, the structure of exports has become more similar across the board. One way of gauging this phenomenon is to examine the export shares of specific products from individual countries and from the region as a whole. The correlation between the shares across all products (measured at the 4-digit level of the standard international trade classification [SITC]) is a measure of the similarity of the export structure between the country and the region. This export similarity index increased for all countries in East Asia between 1990–94 and 2000–04 (see figure 2.6). Indonesia is practically the only country that exhibits a different composition in export products. If the same exercise is carried out to compare the export composition of the East Asian countries to that of the rest of the world, there is much less correlation.

If East Asian countries have similar exports and they are trading more with each other, it follows that there must be back-and-forth trade in the same products between countries in the region. This is exactly what has happened. Within the region, the share of intraindustry trade rose steadily from 1990 to 2004, while the share of interindustry trade went down (see figure 2.7).[9] One type of intraindustry trade is called horizontal. This refers to trade in products that are similar in function, price, and quality, but differentiated by design or other minor characteristics. Such trade occurs to satisfy the consumer demand for variety. The other type of intraindustry trade is called vertical. Products of different quality and

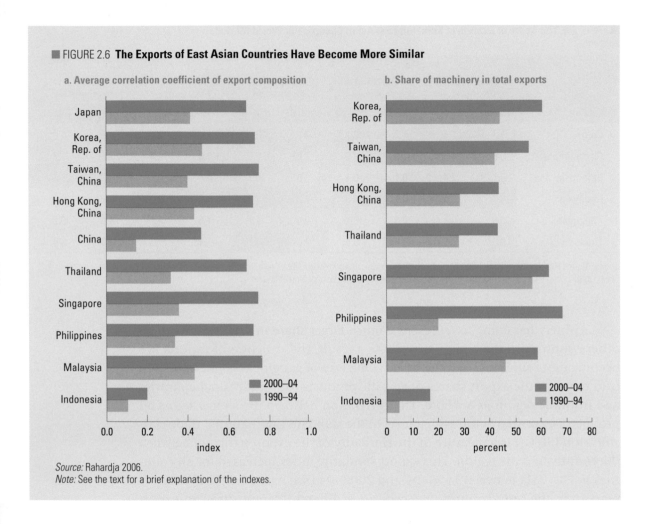

■ FIGURE 2.6 **The Exports of East Asian Countries Have Become More Similar**

a. Average correlation coefficient of export composition

b. Share of machinery in total exports

Source: Rahardja 2006.
Note: See the text for a brief explanation of the indexes.

prices are traded. An example of such trade involves standard color televisions and high-definition televisions, which are different in quality and price. Vertical intraindustry trade is common in footwear, garments, and electronics. But there is also considerable vertical intraindustry trade in parts and components, which can differ markedly from one another in quality and price. Ando and Kimura (2003) point out that the East Asian success story is mainly a vertical intraindustry trade phenomenon within which transactions are characterized by back-and-forth trade links whereby several countries in the region participate in various stages of single production chains.

Vertical intraindustry trade is a global phenomenon. The world trade in parts and components increased in value from US$400 billion in 1992 to over

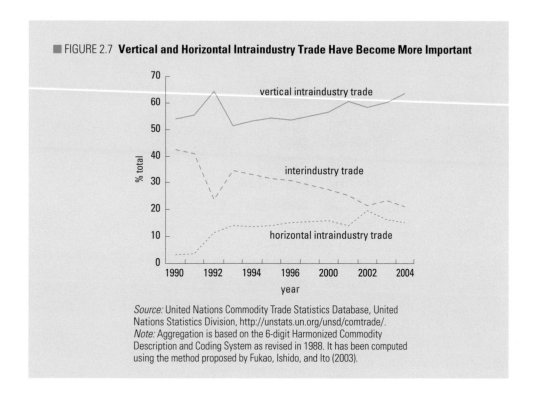

■ FIGURE 2.7 **Vertical and Horizontal Intraindustry Trade Have Become More Important**

Source: United Nations Commodity Trade Statistics Database, United Nations Statistics Division, http://unstats.un.org/unsd/comtrade/.
Note: Aggregation is based on the 6-digit Harmonized Commodity Description and Coding System as revised in 1988. It has been computed using the method proposed by Fukao, Ishido, and Ito (2003).

US$1,000 billion in 2003 and now accounts for a sizable portion of total exports in many countries (see figure 2.8). The share of East Asia in the total exports of components rose from 31 percent in 1992 to 43 percent in 2003 despite a decline in the share of Japan.

Within East Asia, there has also been a change in the trade in parts and components (see table 2.5). China has become a major exporter of parts and components, increasing its share of the regional market by 11 percentage points between 1993 and 2004, while it is also a principal importer, raising its market share of imports by 16 percentage points. On the export side, China, the NIEs, and middle-income ASEAN have all increased their market shares at the expense of Japan. On the import side, the NIEs and middle-income ASEAN have lost market share to China and Japan. The growth in the imports of parts and components is occurring in Japan mainly in the automobile sector, while, in China, it is mainly in electronics and telecommunications.

A reorientation in the export of components is taking place from developing East Asia to China. Over the past 10 years, the proportion of components in the exports to China has increased almost 5 times for Indonesia, 15 times for

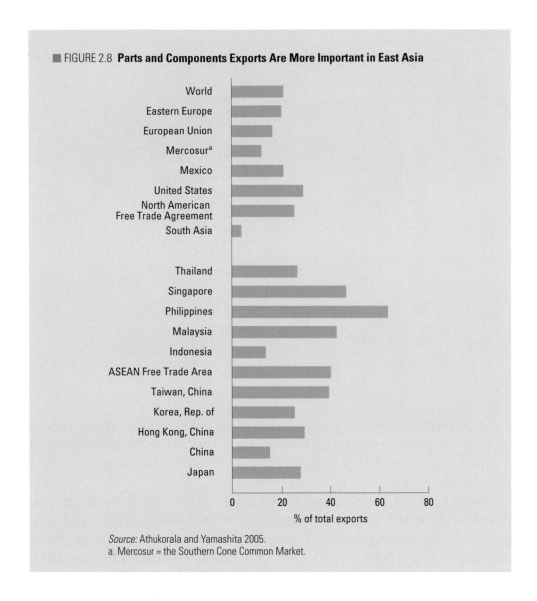

■ FIGURE 2.8 **Parts and Components Exports Are More Important in East Asia**

Source: Athukorala and Yamashita 2005.
a. Mercosur = the Southern Cone Common Market.

Thailand, 19 times for Malaysia, and 60 times for the Philippines. In 2003–04, countries in developing East Asia shipped almost 50 percent of their components within the region, a significant rise from the 33 percent in 1993–94. Other countries are also benefiting. For example, the proportion of components in the exports of Indonesia and the Philippines going to Malaysia increased by 2 and 10 times, respectively, during the decade.

■ TABLE 2.5 **Intra-Asian Trade in Parts and Components**

Exporters	Japan		NIEs		Importers ASEAN-4[a]		China		Asia	
	%, 2004	% point change, 1993–2004	%, 2004	% point change, 1993–2004	%, 2004	% point change, 1993–2004	%, 2004	% point change, 1993–2004	%, 2004	% point change, 1993–2004
Japan	n.a.	n.a.	11	−14	5	−8	7	+3	25	−22
NIEs	4	..	15	..	6	−2	15	+9	41	+7
ASEAN-4[a]	2	..	7	−1	2	+1	4	+4	16	+4
China	3	+2	10	+7	2	+1	n.a.	n.a.	16	+11
Asia	10	+3	44	−8	15	−7	25	+16	100	n.a.

Source: CEPII-BACI Database, Centre d'Etudes Prospectives et d'Informations Internationales, http://www.cepii.fr/francgraph/bdd/baci.htm.
Note: n.a. = not applicable. . . = negligible.
a. ASEAN-4 = Indonesia, Malaysia, the Philippines, and Thailand.

Responding to China

China's integration into the world economy is one of the most important developments affecting the structure and evolution of the global and regional trading systems. Over the past two decades, China's economy has grown at nearly 10 percent per year, driven primarily by the expansion of a modern, export-oriented industrial sector. Some 20 million Chinese workers move each year from rural underemployment to the modern sector, and nearly 300 million workers have yet to be reallocated; this is not a one-time shock, but an ongoing process that might continue into the next decade.[10]

China is now the sixth largest economy in the world and the third largest in trade (behind the United States and Germany). Its exports have grown even more rapidly than its economy, at rates exceeding 20 percent per year. As a result, China's share of world trade has increased from less than 1 percent two decades ago to more than 6 percent today. Between 1990 and 2002, its market share more than tripled in Japan (from 5 percent to 18 percent) and rose from 3 percent to 11 percent in the United States and from 2 percent to 7 percent in the European Union.

The structure of China's exports has also been changing away from the clothing, footwear, other light manufacturing, and fuels that dominated its trade in the 1980s and early 1990s toward office machinery, telecommunications, furniture, and industrial supplies in the late 1990s and automated data processing equipment and consumer electronics in recent years. Rodrik (2006) argues that China's success is not a simple story of specialization according to comparative advantage. Its export bundle is that of a country at a level of per capita income three times higher than the country's actual level. China has managed to latch on to the production of advanced, high-productivity exports beyond what is normally expected of a poor, labor-abundant country. This helps explain China's phenomenal growth and is at least partly a result of industrial policy.

With whom does China compete and in what product areas and markets? The answer to this question is critical in any assessment of the prospects of other countries in the region and in understanding whether China represents, on balance, an opportunity or a threat for other developing countries.

The majority of trade is still based on comparative advantage. Countries with similar income levels and, hence, similar wage levels tend to export similar products. So, one way of asking the question about China's competition is to investigate which countries exhibit similar export structures and the average income levels of these other countries.

For each good that a country exports, it is possible to construct an index of the income productivity of the export, or PRODY, to measure the productivity level associated with the country's pattern of specialization.[11] First, a weighted average of the per-capita GDPs of the countries exporting the product is computed wherein the weights reflect the revealed comparative advantage of each country in that product. This results in an index for the product at the world level. Then, an income productivity level that corresponds to the country's export basket is computed by calculating the export-weighted average of the index for that country.

In 2000–04, China's exports had an average PRODY of US$9,963. This implies that the country's exports are representative of an exporter with a real per capita income of about US$10,000. During this period, East Asia and the Pacific had an average PRODY of US$11,000. The average per capita income in the sample of countries in East Asia and the Pacific, weighted by exports, is US$9,679, indicating that their representative exports are associated with a higher-income level (by about 14 percent). The real income level represented by China's exports is below that of countries in East Asia and the Pacific, but growing somewhat more rapidly; it has increased by 20 percent over the last 10 years (see table 2.6).

Figure 2.9 shows that China is following the pattern of other East Asian countries in that it has a PRODY that is much higher than the actual income level. Most countries in the region exhibit this same characteristic to varying degrees. The Philippines appears to be the greatest outlier, with a bundle of exports far more sophisticated than is typical for a country at that income level. But the inference from these calculations is that China and, indeed, other East Asian exporters are competing more vigorously with higher-income countries than with countries at low wage levels. This is good news for low-income exporters and perhaps explains why low-income garment exporters such as Bangladesh and Cambodia have been able to compete with China despite the lifting of quotas once the Agreement on Textiles and Clothing expired on January 1, 2005.

■ TABLE 2.6 **Index of the Average Wage of Export**
trade-weighted average PRODY

Exporter	1990–94	2000–04	Change (%)
East Asia and Pacific	9,604	11,001	14.5
China	8,308	9,963	19.9
Latin America and the Caribbean	8,143	9,128	12.1
World	10,679	11,108	4.0

Source: Freund 2006.
Note: The data have been calculated using the PRODY index in 2000–04, weighted by the average industrial trade share of the respective region (or country) over the period.

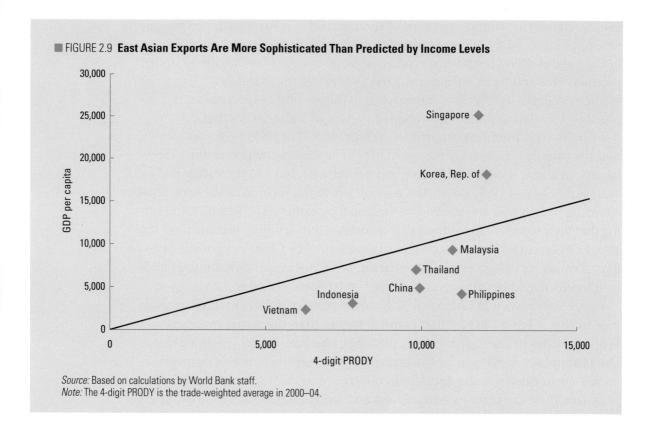

■ FIGURE 2.9 **East Asian Exports Are More Sophisticated Than Predicted by Income Levels**

Source: Based on calculations by World Bank staff.
Note: The 4-digit PRODY is the trade-weighted average in 2000–04.

Another way of looking at the competition posed by China is to examine how market shares for specific products have changed in specific markets. Figure 2.10 plots changes in China's market share in the European Union, Japan, North America, and the world market against the market shares of non-China emerging East Asia. Every industry is represented (at the 4-digit level of aggregation). Each dot on the scatter plots of figure 2.10 therefore shows whether China and other emerging East Asian exporters have been gaining or losing market share in a particular industry.

When one looks at each major developed market, that is, Europe, Japan, and North America, there is a distinct downward slope to the pattern of dots. This suggests that, for products in which China is gaining market share, other exporters are losing market share. Most of the dots are concentrated toward the lower right portion of the charts. But that pattern disappears if the world market is considered (see chart a). There, the majority of dots are scattered around the horizontal zero market share change line. The difference, of course, is that, in the world market, China itself is a potential market for other exporters. The inference is that

■ FIGURE 2.10 **East Asian Exporters Recoup in China What They Lose Elsewhere to China**

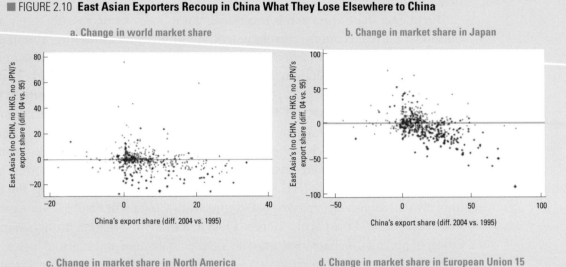

a. Change in world market share

b. Change in market share in Japan

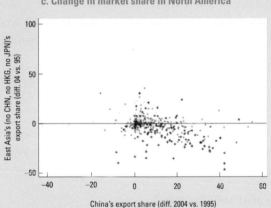

c. Change in market share in North America

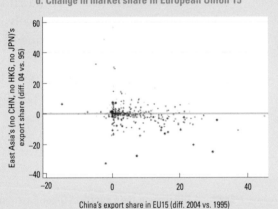

d. Change in market share in European Union 15

Source: Freund 2006.
Note: "East Asia" in the above scatter plots does not include China, Hong Kong (China), or Japan. The change in the export shares in all cases refers to the difference between the situation in 1995 and that in 2004. Each data point represents a 4-digit SITC category, and the size of the point is weighted by the export shares at the beginning of the period. Points appearing toward the lower right portion of each chart show products for which the market share of countries in East Asia and the Pacific (excluding China) have fallen, while China's market share has risen. This portion is densely populated in charts b, c, and d, indicating that there are many significant industries in Europe, Japan, and North America in which East Asia and the Pacific have lost market share, while China has gained. In chart a, this is not so much the case. See the text for an explanation.

exporters in East Asia are making up in the China market what they are losing in richer country markets.

The market share approach is suggestive, but it does not necessarily imply any causality or actual economic displacement. It implicitly assumes that, absent any other forces, market shares will remain constant. But it is possible that China might be increasing its market share at the expense of domestic producers instead of other exporters. If this were the case, total exports would expand and, by definition, the share of other exporters would decline even if the quantity of their exports did not change at all. This analytical gray area is likely to appear whenever a relatively aggregate industry category, such as the 4-digit classification, is used. For example, assume China sells primarily overcoats, while other emerging East Asian exporters sell mainly suits. At the 4-digit level, these products will seem to be competing, but it is unlikely that an increase in overcoat exports from China will displace suit exports from East Asia and the Pacific. Hence, a loss in a share in a market is only an indication of potential welfare losses, not an accurate statement about actual losses.

An estimation of China's impact on other emerging East Asian exporters may be rendered more systematically by controlling for other effects that have an impact on market shares. This kind of econometric investigation shows the following:[12]

- On average, export growth to non-China markets in industrial products is low when Chinese exports in these same products are significant and growing (see table 2.7).
- A coefficient of about −0.3 implies that, in a product area with a Chinese market share of 10 percent and Chinese export growth of 20 percent, export growth

■ TABLE 2.7 **Is China Displacing the Exports of Other East Asian and Pacific Countries?**

Statistic	All products	Nonindustrial products	Industrial products
Export supply effect	1.176***	1.090***	1.194***
	[43.70]	[28.91]	[38.67]
China export effect	−0.208***	0.102	−0.307***
	[2.94]	[1.43]	[3.55]
Observations	1338229	299056	1039173
R-squared	0.35	0.34	0.35

Source: Freund 2006.
Note: The regressions include export, year, and 4-digit product-fixed effects. The estimates thus rely entirely on cross-market variation in Chinese import penetration in a given product. Robust t-statistics are shown in brackets.
***significant at 1 percent.

in emerging East Asia would be reduced by 0.6 percentage points ($0.3 \times 0.1 \times 20$), a relatively small impact.

■ The negative impact has been strongest in the most recent period, 2000–04.

■ The negative impact is strongest in Japan and North America and in many developing-country markets, but is actually positive in Europe (see figure 2.11, chart a). This implies that Chinese exports may be opening up European product markets for other East Asian countries.

■ Among East Asian exporters, 12 of 19 seem to be negatively affected by China; the most serious impacts are in Korea, Singapore, and Taiwan (China) (see figure 2.11, chart b). But these countries are the ones that have also gained the most from increasing their exports to China and that have taken advantage of the triangular trade discussed earlier.

The same estimation method may be used to examine industry-specific effects. In about 16 industries of the 67 studied, China emerges as a major threat to other East Asian exporters. These industries are listed in table 2.8. They are mostly industries in which the exports from emerging East Asia to China are growing most rapidly. In fact, 11 of the 16 threat industries are in the top-20 list of the most rapidly growing export industries to China.

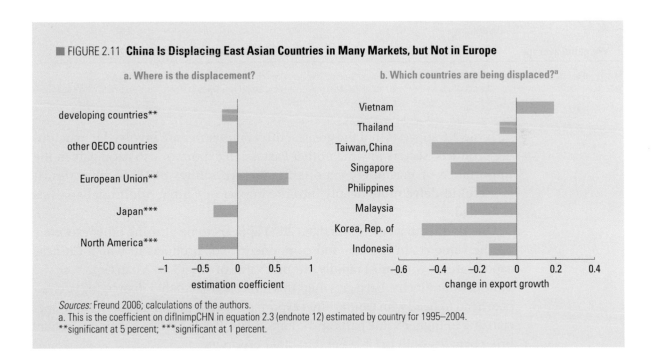

■ FIGURE 2.11 **China Is Displacing East Asian Countries in Many Markets, but Not in Europe**

a. Where is the displacement?

b. Which countries are being displaced?[a]

Sources: Freund 2006; calculations of the authors.
a. This is the coefficient on diflnimpCHN in equation 2.3 (endnote 12) estimated by country for 1995–2004.
**significant at 5 percent; ***significant at 1 percent.

■ TABLE 2.8 **The Threat Industries of China**

SITC code	Industry	Export growth from East Asia to China, 1990–94 to 2000–04 (annual %)
34	Gas, natural and manufactured	23.5
56	Fertilizers, manufactured	−23.1
59	Chemical materials and products n.e.s.	14.5
65	Textile yarn, fabrics, made-up articles n.e.s., related products	6.9
66	Nonmetallic mineral manufactures n.e.s.	14.4
69	Manufactures of metals n.e.s.	9.3
71	Power generating machinery and equipment	12.4
72	Machinery specialized for particular industries	11.0
73	Metalworking machinery	14.7
74	General industrial machinery, equipment, parts n.e.s.	9.6
75	Office machines, automatic data processing machines	29.2
76	Telecommunications, sound recording equipment	14.1
77	Electrical machinery, apparatus, appliances n.e.s.	27.0
81	Sanitary, plumbing, heating, lighting fixtures n.e.s.	1.4
89	Miscellaneous manufactured articles n.e.s.	7.5
95	Arms, ammunition	−3.4
Weighted average		14.2

Source: United Nations Commodity Trade Statistics Database, United Nations Statistics Division, http://unstats.un.org/unsd/comtrade/.
Note: The codes in italics indicate the industries on the top-20 list of the most rapidly growing export industries to China. n.e.s. = not elsewhere specified.

Table 2.8 suggests that the greatest threat industries are involved in machinery products, sectors in which other East Asian exporters also excel. Given the importance of machinery exports for the economies of these countries, it is useful to delve more deeply into the impact of China. Additional analysis is needed.[13]

One finding that emerges is that China appears to be pushing other exporters up the value chain in parts and components. For products in which Chinese exports are growing most rapidly, the unit value of other East Asian exports of the same commodity has been growing. This indicates that, rather than trying to compete head to head with China, other exporters are refining their products and specializing in higher-value parts and components. If this process continues, it may bring benefits both to China and to other exporters.

If one looks at finished machinery, however, a different story emerges. In finished products, the competition with China is much more significant. For finished goods in which Chinese exports are growing most rapidly, other East Asian exporters have had to lower their prices in response. This is not surprising. If the Chinese production of finished goods is the last stage of an efficient regional production network, then it follows that other producers will also have to match the efficiency gains and reflect these in lower prices if they wish to compete.

So far, it seems that efficiency gains and cost and price reductions in other countries have allowed these countries to maintain their market shares even as China's exports are growing rapidly. In those instances where market shares have fallen, this does not appear to be the result of the threat from China, but rather of the internal restructuring of the exporter economy. The exporters who have lost global market share are those who have also reduced revealed comparative advantage (RCA) in the export product.[14] Significant internal restructuring has been taking place in countries as they adapt to the changing global market. So, it is not surprising to see some countries losing market share in particular products even as China is increasing its market share in these products. The causality, however, is the reverse of what was feared. The initial exporter is moving up the value chain, thereby leaving space that China is filling.

But the dominant feature of the changes in the trade in machinery continues to be the evidence that the increase in China's exports of finished machinery products is linked to a substantial rise in the exports of parts and components from other emerging East Asian exporters. This triangular trade is the most notable empirical phenomenon of the last few years.

Trade and Growth

The trade performance of East Asia rests on the intricate production sharing networks and on the open trade and foreign investment regimes that allow these networks to materialize. But how much does this contribute to growth? Production networks may breed long-term vulnerabilities even as they promote short-term growth. There is a risk that specialization in one portion of a production network may limit the potential for an improvement in technology. There is also a risk that production networks may create a regional interdependence that makes East Asian countries hostage to the performance of their neighbors.

The evidence suggests that production networks are, indeed, increasing the sophistication of technology in the region and that the composition of exports is shifting toward the most efficiently produced products in each country. When the category of high-technology exports is examined, it is clear that East Asian producers are becoming more specialized in their exports relative to the rest of the world. Figure 2.12 shows the revealed comparative advantage (RCA) of high-technology exports from five middle-income economies. It indicates that, in all cases except Indonesia, the RCA is greater than 1, demonstrating that these economies have larger shares of high-technology exports than does the world as a whole and that the RCAs are growing. If one disaggregates further into high-technology exports and computes the RCA for individual items, a pattern emerges showing that more and more of the high-technology exports do, indeed, have RCAs greater than 1.

Because RCAs have a long tradition in the trade literature as indicators of export efficiency, the inference is that East Asian exporters are becoming more specialized and more efficient in their exports as they participate in regional production networks. At least in the short term, the technology and efficiency gains are positive. High RCAs suggest specialization in exports. This is what is happening. In China, for example, the top two export product areas—office machinery, and radios and televisions—account for 85 percent of all high-technology exports.

In addition to static efficiency gains, there is another mechanism through which trade may contribute to growth. Romer (1990), Grossman and Helpman (1991), and Jones (1995a, 1995b) emphasize the importance of the availability of a large variety of intermediate inputs. In the Jones model, the creation of new input vari-

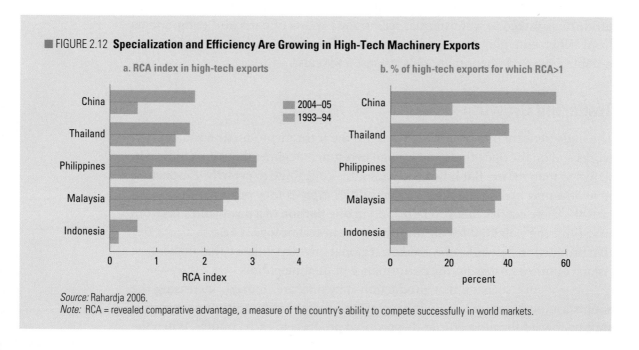

■ FIGURE 2.12 **Specialization and Efficiency Are Growing in High-Tech Machinery Exports**

a. RCA index in high-tech exports

2004–05
1993–94

China
Thailand
Philippines
Malaysia
Indonesia

RCA index

b. % of high-tech exports for which RCA>1

China
Thailand
Philippines
Malaysia
Indonesia

percent

Source: Rahardja 2006.
Note: RCA = revealed comparative advantage, a measure of the country's ability to compete successfully in world markets.

eties by firms sustains growth even in the absence of factor accumulation. This growth is made possible because, it is assumed, the research and development (R&D) costs of creating new varieties fall as the number of input varieties in existence rises. Thus, the creation of new input varieties today reduces the cost of creating new input varieties tomorrow, rendering growth self-sustaining.

Evidence from Korea and Taiwan (China) consistent with this theory that product varieties contribute to growth. Over the period 1975–91, one study finds that changes in sectoral product varieties are positively correlated with changes in sectoral total factor productivity (TFP).[15] Nearly all the sectors showing a positive correlation between changes in product variety and the TFP use differentiated manufacturing products as inputs, which is consistent with the Jones model. The sectors showing a zero or negative correlation are nearly all industries that primarily use natural resources and other raw materials as inputs. These results suggest that, as the variety of inputs to which firms have access increases, the firms will enjoy gains in the TFP. For these gains to become self-sustaining, the increases in variety must lower the R&D costs of creating new varieties. On this issue, there is little research. We do not yet know whether falling R&D costs in Korea, Taiwan (China), and other countries have been caused by the documented increases in input variety or by other factors entirely.

Further evidence on the relationship between product variety and productivity is offered by Feenstra and Kee (2006), who estimate the impact of export variety on TFP for a large sample of countries over the 1980–2000 period. They find that export variety and TFP are strongly and positively correlated. In Korea, for example, export variety, as measured by the growing number of new export products, has been growing substantially over time, and so has the TFP. Japan, on the other hand, has not had much growth in new products, and the TFP has been more or less flat. In fact, Korea's exports are now 95 percent as varied as Japan's, compared to 66 percent in the early 1980s. The TFP in Korea has grown to 53 percent of the level for Japan, compared to 47 percent in 1980.

Figure 2.13 shows partial regression plots of the TFP on export variety for a cross-section of countries (controlling for other regressors). While there is a clear, positive correlation between the two variables, it does appear that many emerging East Asian countries (Indonesia, Korea, Malaysia, the Philippines, Singapore, and Thailand) show up below the regression line, indicating that the TFP is lower than one would expect given the observed levels of export variety in these countries. In East Asia, only Japan is above the regression line. Thus, while the region exports a relatively wide variety of goods, this outcome has not translated into such high levels of the TFP as seen in other countries.

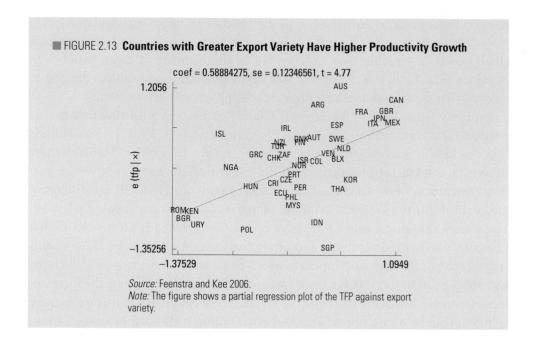

■ FIGURE 2.13 **Countries with Greater Export Variety Have Higher Productivity Growth**

Source: Feenstra and Kee 2006.
Note: The figure shows a partial regression plot of the TFP against export variety.

Perhaps this is good news and a reflection of the relatively recent experience with regional production networks. The cross-country regressions indicate long-term effects; so, one might expect that Asian countries have considerable room to grow based on their export mastery of many different products.

East Asian countries are consistently developing new export varieties at a more rapid pace than their competitors. Figure 2.14 shows the change in export variety in six East Asian economies compared to a sample of 44 countries. The figure shows, as one would suspect, that China is among the leaders in the development of new export varieties, but almost all other East Asian countries are following suit. The exception is the Philippines. Thailand has had one of the most rapid expansions in export varieties. In the early 1980s, it lagged behind other developing countries, but has since risen to the same level of diversity as Malaysia.

Recent research suggests that the introduction of new export products and the level of sophistication of exports might be related to the pace of economic growth across countries and over time.[16] Economies tend to follow a common path during the process of development; at the start, they possess highly concentrated export structures, but they introduce new export products as their income levels rise. Nonetheless, it is important not to equate the desirable pattern whereby new

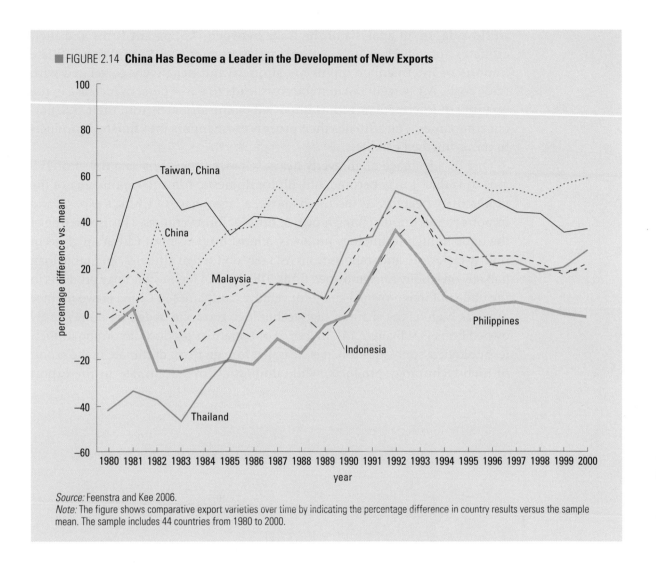

■ FIGURE 2.14 **China Has Become a Leader in the Development of New Exports**

Source: Feenstra and Kee 2006.
Note: The figure shows comparative export varieties over time by indicating the percentage difference in country results versus the sample mean. The sample includes 44 countries from 1980 to 2000.

export products are created with old concepts of export diversification. In East Asia, exports remain specialized so as to achieve economies of scale, but, with innovation, the composition of export structures may change.

Production networks are organized to minimize costs and achieve maximum efficiency and innovation over time. So, it is not surprising that, where production networks are dense, as in East Asia, outsourcing is especially sensitive to border trade barriers. In such an environment, small changes in border costs may have large effects on trade. This is exactly what has been found worldwide. In an analysis of the trade between U.S. parent firms and their affiliates abroad, Hanson, Mataloni, and Slaughter (2005) find that affiliate imports of intermediate inputs are strongly and negatively correlated with trade costs. A 1 percent fall in trade costs leads to a 2–4 percent increase in the quantity of intermediate inputs imported by the affiliates from their U.S. parent companies. The affiliates then process these inputs into finished products or more-finished products.

One disadvantage of an overly heavy reliance on exports as a driver of TFP growth is that it may become difficult for domestic firms to capture any of the productivity benefits. As discussed above, a large share of China's exports and imports comes through foreign-owned firms or joint ventures. This is also true of the trade in high-technology products; almost 80 percent of China's high-technology exports to and imports from Asia rely on foreign affiliates, and more than half rely on wholly foreign-owned firms. The share of high-technology products in the trade of foreign-owned and joint venture companies in China is two to three times as high as the share of high-technology products traded by domestically owned firms (see figure 2.15). Indeed, if one stratifies products according to their technological sophistication, it is clear that foreign firms dominate in the export of high-technology products, while domestic firms dominate in the export

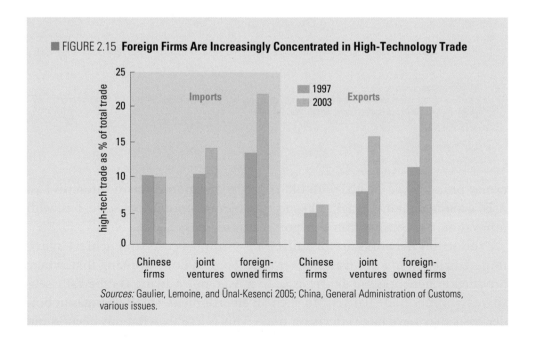

■ FIGURE 2.15 **Foreign Firms Are Increasingly Concentrated in High-Technology Trade**

Sources: Gaulier, Lemoine, and Ünal-Kesenci 2005; China, General Administration of Customs, various issues.

of low-technology products such as basic metals, textiles, and chemicals (see figure 2.16).

There is some concern that too much reliance on foreign firms may actually slow broader technological change. In some sectors, high-technology imports and FDI have been used as a substitute for local expenditures on R&D. But surveys of industrial firms in China in the 1990s confirm that productivity and innovation are highest when in-house R&D is raised to internalize effectively the new technologies being brought in from abroad. So, in several high-technology sectors, there has been only a limited effect on domestic innovative capacity.[17]

At the end of the 1990s, the Chinese authorities began to implement a new policy that put emphasis on the development of domestic innovative capacities. As a result, R&D expenditures increased, and their share in GDP rose from 0.7 percent in 1997 to 1.3 percent in 2002 and may have reached 1.5 percent in 2005. FDI may now help China to catch up because foreign firms investing in China have started to increase their involvement in R&D activities not only as a result of political pressure by the Chinese government to intensify technology transfers, but also as a result of evolving strategies of the firms themselves.

Institutional Support for Trade

East Asian trade has developed through market-based structures. It has been driven by unilateral openness in most countries in the region and a strong adherence to multilateral principles of nondiscrimination. But the significant supply-side integration of the region points to the growing vulnerability of each country with respect to the performance of its neighbors. Any firm in the region that is participating in a production network is exposed to the trade, economic, and political frictions among the Asian economies.[18] So far, tensions have not spilled over into the economic realm, but a new source of tension may arise in the region. The commercially important elements of East Asian regionalism, the ASEAN-China Free Trade Area and the ASEAN-Japan bilateral agreements are only now beginning to cut tariffs on a discriminatory, preferential basis. The discrimination has led to trade tensions in other regions. A more structured framework within East Asia might be desirable so as to manage any frictions that arise.

The ASEAN Free Trade Area was the only major free trade area until 2002, when Japan and Singapore agreed to a New Age Japan-Singapore Economic Partnership Agreement. Since then, there has been a surge in the number of new institutional trade agreements not only among countries within East Asia, but also outside the

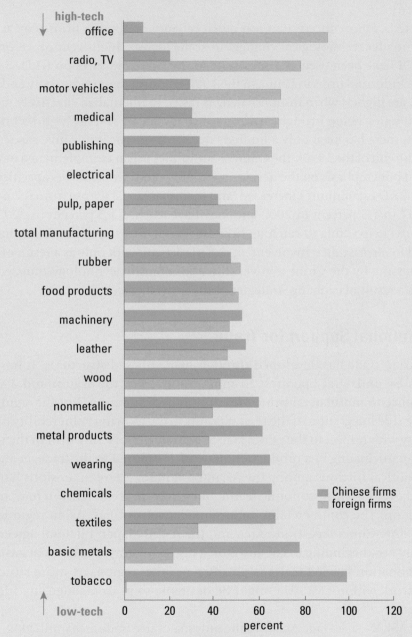

■ FIGURE 2.16 **Domestic Firms Dominate in China's Low-Technology Export Industries**

Source: China, General Administration of Customs, various issues.
Note: The product categories are adapted from SITC, Rev. 3 (2-digit), United Nations Statistics Division, http://unstats.un.org/unsd/cr/registry/regcst.asp?Cl=14.

region (see figure 2.17). In addition to individual country bilateral agreements, ASEAN as a group has become active in discussions on free trade areas in recent years. ASEAN and China enacted a free trade area in goods trade in July 2005, and they are currently negotiating a free trade area in services. ASEAN is also negotiating free trade areas with India, Japan, Korea, and others.

While free trade areas appear to have offered benefits to the region, it is too soon to quantify the full impact. The ASEAN Free Trade Area has been useful for low-income countries such as Cambodia and the Lao People's Democratic Republic because it has brought them into a more open regional trading system prior to accession to the World Trade Organization, of which Cambodia is now a member, and Lao PDR is in membership negotiations. Free trade areas also permit countries greater latitude to exclude sensitive products from trade liberalization. So, a substantial number of products, including important agricultural commodities such as rice, have been exempt from liberalization. Many agreements take the form of comprehensive economic partnerships that encompass trade and FDI facilitation, liberalization, and economic and technical cooperation. However, the implementation of these partnerships has been slow. A particular challenge is the development of straightforward rules of origin so that it is possible to realize the complex network of regional agreements without imposing undue administrative costs on firms.

The current blueprint for free trade agreements in the region is far less overarching than the corresponding agreements of the European Union or the North American Free Trade Agreement. In the latter instances, single sets of rules govern regional trade, and there are clear arrangements for dispute resolution. No single entity in East Asia now plays this role. Perhaps the most similar grouping is the ASEAN+3 (ASEAN countries, plus China, Japan, and Korea), but ASEAN+3 has focused more on financial cooperation than on trade. It is safe to say that the institutional underpinnings for Asia's complex production networks are not yet in place.

The Way Forward

East Asia's rapid export growth and the region's growing concentration in machinery and the redirection of exports among countries within the region are all based on the expanding regional production networks. These networks have centered on China, but the dynamism of China has offset on any of the threats China poses to its competitors in third markets. China is increasingly competing with higher-income exporters that are better able to adapt by mov-

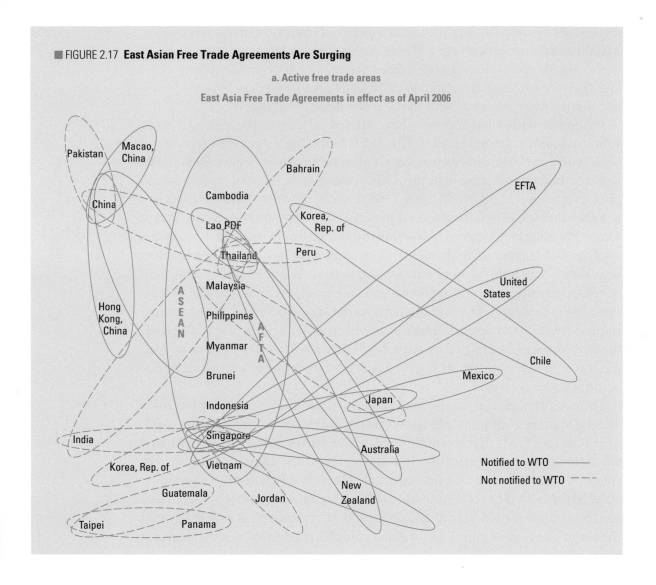

■ FIGURE 2.17 **East Asian Free Trade Agreements Are Surging**

a. Active free trade areas

East Asia Free Trade Agreements in effect as of April 2006

Pakistan

Macao, China

China

Bahrain

EFTA

Cambodia

Lao PDF

Korea, Rep. of

Thailand

Peru

Malaysia

United States

Hong Kong, China

ASEAN

Philippines

AFTA

Myanmar

Brunei

Chile

Mexico

Indonesia

Japan

India

Singapore

Australia

Korea, Rep. of

Vietnam

New Zealand

Guatemala

Jordan

Notified to WTO ———

Not notified to WTO – – –

Taipei

Panama

ing up the value chain. There is good evidence that this is happening in the region and is driving growth in all countries.

Production networks spawn specialization and physical concentration. They also trigger innovations, especially in intermediate goods, and this tends to accelerate growth. East Asia seems to be enjoying a phase of development during which export specialization is going hand in hand with a blossoming in the variety of exports. The export specialization is permitting the exploitation of economies of scale, while

■ FIGURE 2.17 (**Continued**)

b. Free trade areas under negotiation

East Asia Free Trade Agreements under negotiation as of April 2006

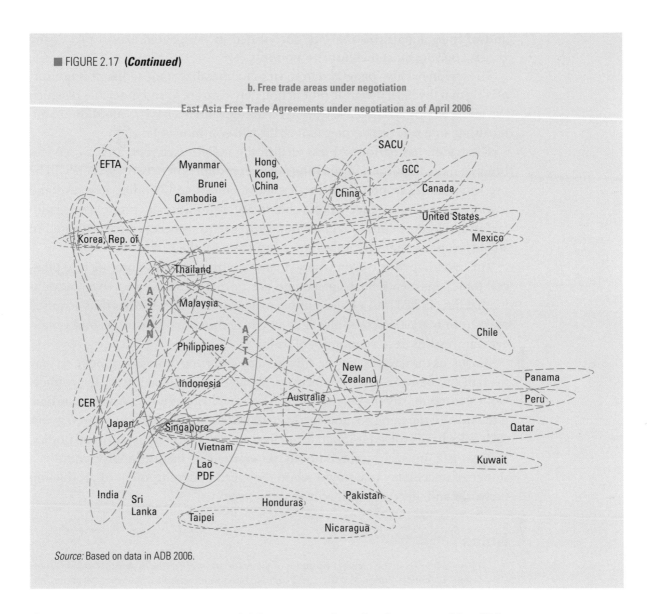

Source: Based on data in ADB 2006.

the increasing variety in exports is driving new product development. This will be a winning combination if it can be sustained.

Production networks may become more dense and extend into additional sectors only if the trade barriers remain low. East Asia has performed well in bringing down barriers to the trade in goods. International transport costs have been constrained, but there is still considerable scope in many countries to bring down the internal costs involved in the transport of goods from the factory gate to ports and of integrating firms that are not located in designated export processing zones. Logistics must therefore be a priority.

The region has also benefited from steps to liberalize trade tariffs. It is not surprising that the most dynamic production networks are found in sectors in which the tariffs are lowest. Because regional trade agreements have focused on manufacturing, one may only expect that tariffs will continue to fall.

The region has performed less well in the trade in services, and, as services become more important in stitching together production networks, there will be pressures on this front. Countries that move quickly to liberalize services stand to gain more because they will be able to attract additional component manufacturing. Because component manufacturers tend to become concentrated in single locations, there are important advantages for the first movers.

This is perhaps one reason why so many countries are now entering into bilateral trade agreements. Such agreements ensure market access. Moreover, a country that has entered into a large number of agreements and that has thus acquired maximum market access is also able to entice more manufacturers and obtain ever larger gains from economies of scale.

But just as the rewards may be enhanced by attracting more investment, so may the tensions between countries increase. Unlike conventional interindustry trade, vertical intraindustry trade generates winners and losers. Trade tensions may flare if the rules of the game are not clearly established and followed. In other regions, such rules have evolved through the deliberations of formal institutional bodies. In East Asia, no such umbrella body yet exists. This institutional vacuum is a source of uncertainty that might retard the speed of development of production networks and, hence, overall growth in the region.

Notes

1. East Asia refers to the member countries of the Association of Southeast Asian Nations (Brunei Darussalam, Cambodia, Indonesia, the Lao People's Democratic Republic, Malaysia, Myanmar, the Philippines, Singapore, Thailand, and Vietnam), plus China, Hong Kong (China), Japan, the Republic of Korea, Mongolia, and Taiwan (China). Emerging East Asia refers to East Asia, minus Japan. Developing East Asia refers to emerging East Asia, minus Hong Kong (China), Korea, and Singapore.

2. Processing exports are goods for export that are produced using imported intermediate inputs and for which production takes the form of processing or assembly.

3. On the impacts of FDI on trade, see, for example, Urata (2001) and Kawai and Urata (1998, 2004).

4. See Kharas, Aldaz-Carroll, and Rahardja (2007).

5. The triangular trade index is defined as: [(exports of intermediate goods from Japan and the NIEs to China and ASEAN) ÷ (exports of intermediate goods from Japan and the NIEs to the world)] × [(exports of finished goods from ASEAN and China to Canada, the European Union, and the United States) ÷ (exports of finished goods from emerging East Asia to the world)].

6. Machinery comprises all commodities classified under code 7 in the standard international trade classification (SITC); see http://unstats.un.org/unsd/cr/registry/regcst.asp?Cl=14.

7. Various terms have been used to describe production networks, including slicing up the value chain (Krugman 1995), outsourcing (Feenstra and Hanson 1996, 1997), the disintegration of production (Feenstra 1998), the fragmentation of production (Deardorff 1998; Jones and Kierzkowski 2001), and intraproduct specialization (Arndt 1997).

8. See, for example, Ando and Kimura (2003) and Athukorala and Yamashita (2005).

9. The intraindustry trade index (IIT) is computed as:

$$\text{IIT} = 1 - \left[\Sigma\Sigma\Sigma \left| X_{ijk} - M_{ijk} \right| \div \left(X_{ijk} + M_{ijk} \right) \right], \qquad 2.1$$

where X_{ijk} represents exports from industry i by country j to country k, and M_{ijk} represents the corresponding import values. The greater the degree of intraindustry trade, the greater the value of IIT. IIT tends to increase with the level of aggregation in terms of the number of countries under one group, such as East Asia, rather than individual countries. It also tends to increase with the level of product aggregation, say, from SITC 3-digit to SITC 2-digit. See Fukao, Ishido, and Ito (2003) for the classification of three types of trade; the 6-digit Harmonized Commodity Description and Coding System classification is used.

10. See Eichengreen, Rhee, and Tong (2004).

11. We follow Hausmann, Hwang, and Rodrik (2005) and create an index of the average real wage (as measured by per capita GDP at purchasing power parity) associated with exporters in a given industry. The index is created at the world level and is defined as follows:

$$PRODY_k = \sum_j \frac{\left(exports_{jk} / EXPORTS_j \right)}{\sum_j \left(exports_{jk} / EXPORTS_j \right)} GDPPC_j, \qquad 2.2$$

where k denotes the industry, j denotes the country, and $GDPPC$ is per capita GDP at purchasing power parity. $Exports_{jk}$ is exports of country j in industry k, and $EXPORTS_j$ is total exports of country j. Thus, the weight on GDPPC is a country's revealed comparative advantage or RCA (that is, the share of its export basket in a product over the sum of the export shares of all countries; see also endnote 14). Export weights alone would place too much weight on large exporters of k for whom k might still be a small portion of overall exports. We calculate $PRODY$ for each 4-digit SITC industry using average bilateral trade and average GDPPC using purchasing power parity data from 2000–04.

12. In our empirical analysis, we use bilateral trade data at the 4-digit SITC level from 1985 to 2004. We test whether Chinese exports to a particular country in a given category are affecting exports from East Asia and the Pacific to a greater extent than exports from other countries and areas. We also control for overall exporter supply growth. The advantage of this specification is that we are exploiting both cross-sectional and time series variation to estimate how the exports of East Asia and the Pacific are affected by China. If Chinese export growth is primarily displacing domestic producers or is not competing with East Asia and the Pacific for some other reason, we will not pick it up. While Chinese exports might not be pushing out the exports of East Asia and the Pacific (it may be that China is entering because East Asia and the Pacific are exiting), this is less likely since we are controlling for export supply growth.

We estimate the following equation:

$$dif \ln exp_{ijt}^k = \alpha_{it} + \beta_0 dif \ln impnonCHN_{jt}^k + \beta_1 dif \ln impCHN_{jt}^k + \varepsilon_{ijt}^k, \qquad 2.3$$

where i is the exporter, j is the importer, k is the industry, t is the time, *dif lnexp* is export growth, *dif lnimpnonch* is the growth in non-China exports to j in product k at time t, and *diflnimpCHN* is the growth in China's exports, multiplied by China's lagged market share in the specific sector and market. Weighting China's export growth by the lagged market share ensures that only sectors are picked in which China is a significant supplier. A negative coefficient on China (β_1) indicates that Chinese export growth is correlated with a decline in East Asian export growth in a given industry.

13. To what extent is the emergence of China as an important player in the global trade in machinery putting competitive pressures on prices? We estimate a linear regression model where we test whether the unit value of exports in machinery from Southeast Asian countries is affected by the quantity of China's exports. The model is given as:

$$\ln V_{ijkt} = \alpha_0 + \alpha_1 * F_{jk} + \alpha_2 \ln Q_{jkt-1} + \alpha_3 \left(F_{jk} * Q_{jkt-1} \right) + \alpha_4 \ln V_{ijt-1} + Z_{ijt}\beta + \varepsilon_{ijt}, \qquad 2.4$$

where V is the unit value of the exports, F is a dummy variable for the finished good, Q is the volume of exports from China, Z is a matrix of covariates, and ε is the error term. The subscripts i, j, k, and t represent the country (Indonesia, Malaysia, the Philippines, and Thailand), the product classification at the 6-digit level of the Harmonized Commodity Description and Coding System, the category (components or finished products), and the time (spanning from 1992 to 2004).

To control for observable characteristics, we include a set of covariates Z such as time, product, country dummies and their interactions, the importation of capital goods, world GDP per capita (excluding the reporter country i), the difference between country i GDP per capita and world GDP per capita, and world tariff rates. Note that we also include a lagged dependent variable on the right-hand side of equation (2.4) to allow for the possibility that a previous period has determined the current period of the unit value (a control for possible rigidity). Had we not included this variable as a regressor, the lagged volume of Chinese exports, Q, might have correlated with the error term. This problem arises because China's export volume at time $t-1$ might correlate with the world import price at $t-1$. We also include the share of imports of capital goods from China as a control for the possible existence of cheaper imports of capital goods from China. Assuming that the lagged volume of exports from China and the unit value, Q_{jt-1} and V_{ijt-1}, are predetermined, we estimate equation (2.4) using ordinary least squares.

Whether or not the increase in China's presence in the global trade in machinery has caused changes in the market share of exports in machinery from Southeast Asian countries, the exportation of machinery from China is rapidly gaining market share. However, the exports of machinery from countries in Southeast Asia are also increasing the presence of these countries in the global market. The empirical model for our analysis on this question is given as:

$$\Delta MS_{ijkt} = \delta_0 + \delta_1 * F_{jk} + \delta_2 \, \Delta CMS_{jt-1} + \delta_3 \left(F_{jk} * \Delta CMS_{jt-1} \right) + \delta_4 \Delta RCA_{ijkt-1} + W_{ijt}\Gamma + \xi_{ijkt} \qquad 2.5$$

On the left-hand side of equation (2.5), ΔMS is the change in the global market share of product category k at the 4-digit SITC, component, finished, in the exportation of commodity j from country i at time t. On the right-hand side, F is a dummy variable for finished goods, ΔCMS is China's change in global market share for product j at time t, ΔRCA is the change in the revealed comparative advantage (RCA) index (scale from 0 to 100), product j, category k, and Γ contains other covariates similar to Z in equation (2.4). To control for the degree of competitiveness of a particular product produced by a particular country, we include a lagged change in the RCA index in the right-hand side variable of equation (2.5).

The third objective is to examine the direction of specialization in the context of product fragmentation. The data suggest that several countries are becoming more competitive in producing components. Apart from the situation as regards China, the performance of the countries in Southeast Asia in the exportation of components compares more favorably with that in finished machinery. Therefore, we examine the extent to which China's shift in specialization in finished machinery is causing Southeast Asia to shift its exportation of components to China. The empirical model for this objective is given as:

$$SCC_{ijt} = \gamma_0 + \gamma_1 CMF_{jt-1} + \gamma_3 RCAC_{ijt-1} + W_{ijt}\Pi + \eta_{ijt} \qquad 2.6$$

On the left-hand side of equation (2.6), SCC is the share of exports in the components of product j from country i to China at time t (the share of the exports going to the world is 100 percent). On the right-hand side, CMF is China's global market share for finished machinery of product j at time $t-1$, $RCAC$ is the RCA index in components for country j (scale 0 to 100) at time $t-1$. Finally, matrix W contains covariates such as dummy variables for industry, location, time, and China's import tariffs.

For equation (2.6), we reclassify our product into a 3-digit SITC more broadly than we do in equation (2.5). This relatively more aggregate category reduces the extreme variation in market share relative to a more detailed product category, thereby allowing us to examine the effect of spillover more accurately. In our sample, we also retain products that have components in their classification. Finally, because some countries do not engage in the exportation of particular products, *SCC* is censored from below. Thus, we estimate equation (2.6) using Tobit, using zero as the lower censoring point.

We estimate equations (2.4) to (2.6) using pooled time series and cross-product data. The time series spans from 1992 to 2004, while the cross product varies depending on the estimated equation. Most of our trade data come from the United Nations Commodity Trade Statistics Database (http://unstats.un.org/unsd/comtrade/), and the rest have been obtained from the World Development Indicators Database (http://www.worldbank.org/data/datapubs/datapubs.html). Rahardja (2006) provides details on the estimation results.

14. RCA is a measure of a country's specialization in the exportation of a product relative to the rest of the world. The RCA of a good, *k,* is given as the ratio of the share of exports of good *k* in the total exports of country *i,* divided by the share of exports of good *k* in global exports. See also endnote 11.

15. See Feenstra et al. (1999).

16. See Lederman and Maloney (2006).

17. See Jefferson et al. (2003).

18. See Baldwin (2006a).

References

ADB (Asian Development Bank). 2006. *Asian Development Outlook 2006.* Manila: Asian Development Bank.

Akamatsu, Kaname. 1961. "A Theory of Unbalanced Growth in the World Economy." *Weltwirtschaftliches Archiv* 86 (2): 196–217.

Ando, Mitsuyo, and Fukunari Kimura. 2003. "The Formation of International Production and Distribution Networks in East Asia." NBER Working Paper 10167, National Bureau of Economic Research, Cambridge, MA.

Antweiler, Werner, and Daniel Trefler. 2002. "Increasing Returns and All That: A View from Trade." *American Economic Review* 92 (1): 93–119.

Arndt, Sven W. 1997. "Globalization and the Open Economy." *North American Journal of Economics and Finance* 8 (1): 71–79.

Athukorala, Prema-chandra, and Nobuaki Yamashita. 2005. "Production Fragmentation and Trade Integration: East Asia in a Global Context." Working Papers in Trade and Development 2005–07, Research School of Pacific and Asian Studies, Australian National University, Canberra.

Baldwin, Richard E. 2006a. "Managing the Noodle Bowl: The Fragility of East Asian Regionalism." CEPR Discussion Paper 5561, Center for Economic Policy Research, London.

_____. 2006b. "Implications of European Experiences with Regionalism for Future Economic Integration in Asia." Unpublished paper, Graduate Institute of International Studies, Geneva.

China, General Administration of Customs. Various issues. *China's Customs Statistics.* Hong Kong, China: Economic Information and Agency.

China, National Bureau of Statistics. Various years. *State Statistical Yearbook.* Beijing: China Statistics Publishing House.

Chodos, Daniel, Bailey Klinger, and Daniel Lederman. 2006. "International Trade and Innovation: A Review of Policy Issues, Empirical Evidence, and East Asia's Performance." Unpublished working paper, World Bank, Washington, DC.

Deardorff, Alan. 1998. "Determinants of Bilateral Trade: Does Gravity Work in a Neoclassical World?" In *The Regionalization of the World Economy,* ed. J. A. Frankel, Chapter 1. Chicago: University of Chicago Press.

Eaton, Jonathan, and Samuel Kortum. 2002. "Technology, Geography, and Trade." *Econometrica* 70 (5): 1741–80.

Eichengreen, Barry, Yeongseop Rhee, and Hui Tong. 2004. "The Impact of China on the Exports of Other Asian Countries." NBER Working Paper 10768, National Bureau of Economic Research, Cambridge, MA.

Feenstra, Robert C. 1998. "Integration of Trade and Disintegration of Production in the Global Economy." *Journal of Economic Perspectives* 12 (4): 31–50.

Feenstra, Robert C., and Gordon H. Hanson. 1996. "Foreign Investment, Outsourcing, and Relative Wages." In *The Political Economy of Trade Policy: Papers in Honor of Jagdish Bhagwati*, ed. Robert C. Feenstra, Gene M. Grossman, and Douglas A. Irwin, 89–127. Cambridge, MA: MIT Press.

———. 1997. "Foreign Direct Investment and Relative Wages: Evidence from Mexico's Maquiladoras." *Journal of International Economics* 42 (3–4): 371–93.

———. 2004. "Intermediaries in Entrepôt Trade: Hong-Kong Re-Exports of Chinese Goods." *Journal of Economics and Management Strategy* 13 (1): 3–35.

Feenstra, Robert C., and Hiau Looi Kee. 2006. "Export Variety and Country Productivity: Estimating the Monopolistic Competition Model with Endogenous Productivity." Unpublished paper, University of California–Davis, Davis, CA.

Feenstra, Robert C., Dorsati Madani, Tzu-Han Yang, and Chi-Yuan Liang. 1999. "Testing Endogenous Growth in South Korea and Taiwan." *Journal of Development Economics* 60 (2): 317–41.

Freund, Caroline. 2006. "The Effect of China's Exports on East Asian Trade with the World." Unpublished paper, World Bank, Washington, DC.

Fujita, Masahisa, Paul R. Krugman, and Anthony J. Venables. 1999. *The Spatial Economy: Cities, Regions and International Trade*. Cambridge, MA: MIT Press.

Fukao, Kyoji, Hikaru Ishido, and Keiko Ito. 2003. "Vertical Intra-Industry Trade and Foreign Direct Investment in East Asia." RIETI Discussion Paper 03-E-001, Research Institute of Economy, Trade, and Industry, Tokyo.

Gaulier, Guillaume, Françoise Lemoine, and Deniz Ünal-Kesenci. 2005. "China's Integration in East Asia: Production Sharing, FDI and High-Tech Trade." CEPII Working Paper 2005-09, Centre d'Etudes Prospectives et d'Informations Internationales, Paris.

———. 2006a. "The Emergence of China and Its Impact on Asian Trade." Background paper (June), World Bank, Washington, DC.

———. 2006b. "China's Emergence and the Reorganization of Trade Flows in Asia." CEPII Working Paper 2006-05, Centre d'Etudes Prospectives et d'Informations Internationales, Paris.

Grossman, Gene M., and Elhanan Helpman. 1991. *Innovation and Growth in the Global Economy*. Cambridge, MA: MIT Press.

Haddad, Mona. 2006. "Trade Integration in East Asia: The Role of China and Production Networks." Draft working paper, World Bank, Washington, DC.

Hanson, Gordon H. 2006. "Trade in the East Asia and Pacific Region." Unpublished paper, World Bank, Washington, DC.

Hanson, Gordon H., Raymond J. Mataloni, and Matthew J. Slaughter. 2005. "Vertical Production Networks in Multinational Firms." *Review of Economics and Statistics* 87 (4): 664–78.

Hausmann, Ricardo, J. Hwang, and Dani Rodrik. 2005. "What You Export Matters." NBER Working Paper 11905, National Bureau of Economic Research, Cambridge, MA.

Hiratsuka, Daisuke. 2005. "Vertical Intra-Regional Production Networks in East Asia: A Case Study of the Hard Disc Drive Industry." Working paper, Institute of Developing Economies, Japan External Trade Organization, Chiba City, Japan.

Hu, Albert Guangzhou, and Gary H. Jefferson. 2002. "FDI Impact and Spillover: Evidence from China's Electronic and Textiles Industries." *World Economy* 25 (8): 1063–76.

Hummels, David, Jun Ishii, and Kei-Mu Yi. 2001. "The Nature and Growth of Vertical Specialization in World Trade." *Journal of International Economics* 54 (1): 75–96.

Imbs, Jean, and Romain Wacziarg. 2003. "Stages of Diversification." *American Economic Review* 93 (1): 63–86.

Jefferson, Gary H., Albert Guangzhou Hu, Xiaojing Guan, and Xiaoyun Yu. 2003. "Ownership, Performance, and Innovation in China's Large and Medium-Size Industrial Enterprise Sector." *China Economic Review* 14 (1): 89–113.

Jones, Charles. 1995a. "Time Series Tests of Endogenous Growth Models." *Quarterly Journal of Economics* 110 (2): 495–526.

———. 1995b. "R&D Based Models of Economic Growth." *Journal of Political Economy* 103 (4): 759–84.

Jones, Ronald W., and Henryk Kierzkowski. 2001. "Globalization and the Consequences of International Fragmentation." In *Money, Capital Mobility, and Trade: Essays in Honor of Robert A. Mundell,* ed. Guillermo A. Calvo, Rudiger Dornbusch, and Maurice Obstfeld, 365–84. Cambridge, MA: MIT Press.

———. 2003. "International Fragmentation and the New Economic Geography." Unpublished paper, University of Rochester, Rochester, NY.

Kawai, M., and Shujiro Urata. 1998. "Are Trade and Direct Investment Substitutes or Complements?: An Empirical Analysis of Japanese Manufacturing Industries." In *Economic Development and Cooperation in the Pacific Basin: Trade, Investment and Environmental Issues,* ed. H. Lee and D. Roland-Holst, 251–93. Cambridge: Cambridge University Press.

———. 2004. "Trade and Foreign Direct Investment in East Asia." In *Exchange Rate Regimes and East Asia,* ed. G. de Brouwer and M. Kawai, 15–102. London: Routledge Curzon.

Kharas, Homi, Enrique Aldaz-Carroll, and Sjamsu Rahardja. 2007. "East Asia: Regional Integration among Open Economies." In *Economic Integration in Asia and India,* ed. Masahisa Fujita. Basingstoke, United Kingdom: Palgrave Macmillan.

Klinger, Bailey, and Daniel Lederman. 2006. "Diversification, Innovation, and Imitation Inside the Global Technological Frontier." Policy Research Working Paper 3872, World Bank, Washington, DC.

Krugman, Paul R. 1995. "Growing World Trade: Causes and Consequences." Brookings Papers on Economic Activity 1: 327–77.

Leamer, E. 1984. *Sources of Comparative Advantage.* Cambridge, MA: MIT Press.

Lederman, Daniel, and William F. Maloney. 2006. "Trade Structure and Growth." In *Natural Resources, Neither Curse Nor Destiny,* ed. Daniel Lederman and William F. Maloney, Chapter 2. Palo Alto, CA: Stanford University Press.

Melitz, Marc. 2003. "The Impact of Trade on Intra-Industry Reallocations and Aggregate Industry Productivity." *Econometrica* 71 (6): 1695–1725.

Pitigala, Nihal. 2006. "Opportunities in Production Sharing in Kenya." Unpublished paper, World Bank, Washington, DC.

Rahardja, Sjamsu. 2006. "Big Dragon, Little Dragons: The Role of China in Exporting Machinery to Developing Southeast Asia." Unpublished paper, World Bank, Washington, DC.

Redding, Stephen, and Anthony J. Venables. 2004. "Economic Geography and International Inequality." *Journal of International Economics* 62 (1): 53–82.

Rodrik, Dani. 2006. "What's So Special about China's Exports?" NBER Working Paper 11947, National Bureau of Economic Research, Cambridge, MA.

Romer, Paul M. 1990. "Endogenous Technological Change." *Journal of Political Economy* 98 (5): 71–102.

UNCTAD (United Nations Conference on Trade and Development). Various years. *Review of Maritime Transport.* Geneva: United Nations.

Urata, Shujiro. 2001. "Emergence of an FDI-Trade Nexus and Economic Growth in East Asia." In *Rethinking the East Asian Miracle,* ed. Joseph E. Stiglitz and Shahid Yusuf, 409–59. Washington, DC: World Bank; New York: Oxford University Press.

———. 2006. "The Changing Patterns of International Trade in East Asia." Background paper, World Bank, Washington, DC.

Venables, Anthony J. 1996. "Equilibrium Locations of Vertically Linked Industries." *International Economic Review* 37 (2): 341–60.

World Bank. 2005. *World Development Indicators 2005.* Washington, DC: World Bank. http://devdata. worldbank.org/wdi2005/Cover.htm.

Yeats, Alexander J. 2001. "Just How Big Is Global Production Sharing?" In *Fragmentation: New Production Patterns in the World Economy,* ed. Sven W. Arndt and Henryk Kierzkowski, 108–43. New York: Oxford University Press.

Yi, Kei-Mu. 2003. "Can Vertical Specialization Explain the Growth of World Trade?" *Journal of Political Economy* 111 (1): 52–102.

MAP 3.1 Telecommunications Flows in East Asia Suggest a Vigorous Exchange of Ideas
intra-Asian telecommunication traffic flows, 2004

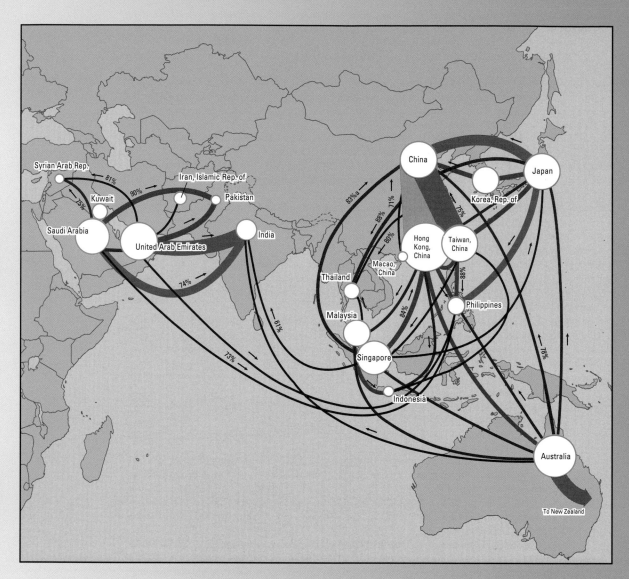

Key

All figures are given in millions of minutes of telecommunications traffic for the public telephone network.

The map shows all intra-Asian routes with a combined 2004 volume of more than 100 million minutes.

Traffic flows
(minutes, millions)

800   500   100

Each band is proportional to the total annual traffic on the public telephone network in both directions for each pair of countries.

total outgoing traffic
(minutes, millions)

— 100
— 500
— 1,500

The area of each circle is proportional to the volume of the total annual outgoing traffic from each country.

% of traffic

On routes where traffic in one direction accounts for more than 60 percent of the total, an arrow shows the direction of most of the traffic flows.

Not all thicknesses of lines represented; not all circle sizes represented.

Source: TeleGeography Research 2006.

CHAPTER 3

INNOVATION

Ideas and trade display the same gravity forces; innovation and investment require many of the same basics. Regional knowledge now also flows through patented processes and technologies.

The generation, diffusion, absorption, and application of new ideas are widely perceived as crucial drivers of economic growth and development. Modern growth theory stresses the importance of overcoming idea gaps relative to object gaps in the process of development, that is, overcoming barriers to the productive absorption of available ideas versus overcoming gaps in the availability of objects such as factories or raw materials. Innovation efforts by forward-looking firms are at the heart of new theories of endogenous economic growth emerging over the last couple of decades.[1] This chapter looks at innovation in East Asia, including the diverse activities being pursued, the problems being faced, and the innovation outcomes being achieved in economies at different levels of development, as well as lessons learned about policies and institutions that have been helpful in fostering innovation.[2]

In advanced economies and, increasingly, in leading emerging economies such as the Republic of Korea, Singapore, and Taiwan (China), business firms are among the principal engines for creating new ideas and learning through systematic, long-term, and large-scale investments in research and development (R&D), resulting in discoveries that add to global knowledge, that may be patented, and that are the principal sources of competitiveness and profitability. Most innovation by firms in developing countries, however, entails not advances in the frontier of global knowledge, but, instead, catching up to the global frontier through the adoption and adaptation of existing products, production processes, and methods that are new to the firm, though not to the world. This chapter surveys both these forms of innovation, looking at patenting activity in East Asia, as well as broader (firm-level, survey-based) measures of innovation in some of the low- and middle-income economies in the region. It also takes up the two main complementary branches of activity resulting in innovation, that is, on the one hand, indigenous R&D and other domestic innovation activities, and, on the other, the absorption of knowledge from abroad through a variety of channels such as participation in international trade, foreign direct investment (FDI), or crossborder flows of disembodied knowledge often transmitted through telecommunications networks (see map 3.1).

This chapter examines the correlates of innovation, studies the efforts of East Asian economies to absorb ideas from abroad and to encourage innovation at home, and attempts to identify the correlates of success. Among the main findings:

- *Innovation activity is a form of investment* and has many prerequisites in common with general capital investment. Sound fundamentals such as macroeconomic stability, financial sector development, the protection of property rights, and the adequate provision of core public goods are no less important for innovation than for general investment. Knowledge also has distinctive economic features that create specialized preconditions for innovation activity. The partial nonexcludability feature of knowledge (see box 3.1) creates a need for specialized intellectual property rights regimes that allow inventors to recoup the rewards from highly uncertain innovation investments. Public resources are typically needed to fund investments in basic research.

- *Technology from abroad and R&D at home are mutually supporting elements.* It is a mistake to think that poor countries may rely entirely on technology transfer from abroad, while developed countries should switch entirely to domestic R&D. Both are necessary at all levels of income, although the balance between the two may change. Even in poor economies, some indigenous innovation effort increases the country's capacity to absorb knowledge from abroad. As countries approach the global technology frontier, their expanded domestic R&D efforts draw more intensively on the stock of advanced scientific knowledge in the world.

- *Intraregional knowledge flows are small but rising rapidly.* A small number of emerging economies—principally Hong Kong (China), Korea, and Taiwan (China)—are now producing new knowledge at or near the global technology frontiers. Like trade in goods, flows of ideas tend to be greater among neighbors. This chapter provides new evidence that such intraregional knowledge flows are rising rapidly in East Asia.

The next section analyzes knowledge adoption and adaptation in East Asia, looking first at broad measures of innovation among firms from the World Bank's investment climate surveys for low- and middle-income economies, particularly data on the introduction of new product lines and production processes. The investment climate surveys also provide a view into the sources of knowledge that firms in these low- and middle-income economies use to make innovations. By far the largest fraction of firms in all economies (on average over 40 percent) have cited the technology embodied in new machinery or equipment (most of which may be assumed to be imported) as their most important source of technological innovation. These observations provide a good springboard for a more detailed inspection of the methods by which firms absorb knowledge from abroad, for example, imports of advanced capital equipment, industrial upgrading via exports through the global production and marketing networks of foreign multinational companies, technology licensing, and FDI.

The subsequent section takes up trends in indigenous knowledge creation within East Asia, in particular the growth and distribution of R&D. Over the last decade, R&D spending grew much more in East Asia than in any other world region. But already large disparities in R&D spending among economies in the region have also widened. On the one hand, newly industrializing economies (NIEs) such as Korea, Singapore, and Taiwan (China) now devote 2 percent or more of gross domestic product (GDP) to R&D, which is among the most intensive R&D efforts in the world, while the business sector generally performs over two-thirds of the R&D. China has also been rapidly boosting its R&D spending toward an official target of 1.5 percent of GDP. On the other hand, middle-income economies such as Indonesia, the Philippines, and Thailand spend a miniscule 0.1–0.2 percent of GDP on R&D, which is low relative to other economies at similar per capita income levels.

Many studies document high social rates of return to R&D spending in the countries of the Organisation for Economic Co-operation and Development (OECD). Recent World Bank research suggests that the social returns to R&D are even higher in developing countries. Why then are there such large disparities in R&D spending within East Asia and around the world? Part of the answer derives from the peculiar *nonexcludability* characteristic of knowledge, which makes it difficult for investors in business R&D to establish property rights over knowledge under the best of circumstances, but especially so because the legal and institutional framework for protecting intellectual property rights is much weaker in some economies than it is in others (see box 3.1). Since it is a type of investment, business R&D spending is also affected by cross-country differences in many standard factors affecting investment, for example, the extent of financial sector development, macroeconomic volatility, and the cost of capital, as well as by differences in the quality and availability of complementary factors of production, notably, the level of education of the workforce (human capital) and related factors, such as the quality of academic (nonbusiness) R&D.

Using patenting in the United States as an index, the penultimate section of this chapter assesses East Asian prowess in generating innovations that advance the global frontier of knowledge. East Asian patenting per 100,000 population is, in fact, closely related to R&D intensity patterns. It is growing at a pace in the NIEs that is about four times the pace in the developed world and has now reached levels not too distant from developed-country averages. On the other hand, it remains negligible in per 100,000 population terms in most of the middle-income economies in Southeast Asia and practically nonexistent among low-income economies. Patent citation analysis shows that not only the quantity per

---

■ BOX 3.1 **Ideas and Knowledge: Nonexcludability and Nonrival Consumption**

Two features of ideas and knowledge have special economic importance. Because they are generally *nonexcludable* (it is impractical or impossible to stop people from using them once they have become available), ideas and knowledge tend to spill over and benefit many others besides those who have invested in their creation. The private returns to R&D are therefore typically much less substantial than the social returns, and the amount of R&D is often lower than the socially optimal level.

Another feature of ideas and knowledge that is important is the *nonrival* characteristic of their consumption. A piece of knowledge—say, a chemical formula—may require a large fixed cost in R&D to create, but, once it exists, it may be employed by any number of users without reducing the ability of anyone else to use it also. Thus, unlike an apple, for example, consumption by one consumer does not prevent consumption by another consumer. This combination of high fixed or sunk costs and low or zero marginal costs is a potent source of increasing returns to scale among firms; this, in turn, has significant implications for industrial organization and processes of geographical agglomeration.

Arrow (1962), Romer (1990a, 1990b), and Foray (2004) discuss the implications of the nonrival, nonexcludable, and cumulative characteristics of knowledge as an economic good. Baumol (2002) observes that large sunk costs for innovation serve as a barrier to entry and may contribute to a structure of oligopolistic competition among a small number of large firms, whereby innovation is used as a prime instrument for competition. For the role of the increasing returns among firms, of localized technological spillovers, and of pecuniary external economies in fostering geographical agglomeration or clustering, see Fujita and Thisse (1996), Quigley (1998), and Audretsch (1998).

capita but also the quality of patents in the most advanced innovators such as Korea and Taiwan (China) are approaching the levels in developed economies.

The penultimate section also analyzes the technical and scientific citations of East Asian patents so as to trace the international knowledge flows on which this high-level type of domestic knowledge creation rests. As might be expected, East Asian patented innovations continue to draw heavily on knowledge flows from Japan and the United States. But citations to other, compatriot patents in the same East Asian economy or to other East Asian economies are rising quickly, indicating the emergence of East Asian national and regional knowledge stocks that are providing an indigenous or regional foundation for new innovations and crossborder knowledge flows.

The final section discusses the main policy-related findings that might help foster domestic innovation, as well as the absorption of knowledge from abroad. These factors are grouped under three main heads: the overall business environment for innovation, including macroeconomic stability, financial sector development, intellectual property rights, and the quality of the information and communications technology infrastructure; human capital development; and direct government support for innovation activities, including government funding for public sector and university R&D, fiscal subsidies and tax incentives for business R&D, fiscal incentives for FDI, and policies aimed at promoting FDI-related technology transfers.

Acquiring Knowledge From Abroad: Technology Transfers and Spillovers

Most innovation by firms in developing countries does not entail advances on the frontier of global knowledge, but, instead, catching up to the global frontier through the adoption and adaptation of existing products, processes, and methods that are new to the firms though not to the world since they have typically originated in advanced countries. This section takes up such acquisition of existing knowledge from abroad in more detail. The next two sections look at the growing success of some of East Asian economies in carrying out formal R&D and making patentable innovations that advance the global technology frontier.

Innovation Outcomes: A Broad Perspective

Table 3.1 presents information on broad innovation activities among firms in five low- and middle-income East Asian economies. The information is derived from

■ TABLE 3.1 **Indicators of the Dynamism of Firms**
percent of firms in the sample

Outcomes	Cambodia 2002	Indonesia 2003	Philippines 2003	Thailand 2004	Vietnam 2005	Average	Other (34)[a]
Core outcomes							
New product line	0.53	0.38	0.49	0.50	0.44	0.47	0.44
Upgraded product line	0.90	0.68	0.64	0.71	0.66	0.72	0.59
Introduction of new technology[b]	0.60	0.22	0.42	0.52	0.45	0.44	0.38
Other outcomes							
Discontinued product line	0.05	0.22	0.42	0.19	0.19	0.21	0.24
Opened new plant	0.18	0.07	0.13	0.08	—	0.12	0.14
Closed existing plant	0.02	0.08	0.11	0.02	—	0.06	0.10
New foreign joint venture	0.21	0.06	0.06	0.04	0.06	0.08	0.08
New license agreement	0.21	0.08	0.13	0.11	0.10	0.12	0.16
Outsourcing[c]	0.33	0.13	0.21	0.18	0.09	0.18	0.13
Insourcing[c]	0.41	0.10	0.14	0.11	—	0.19	0.12
Core (new product+new technology)	1.14	0.60	0.92	1.02	0.89	0.91	0.82
Dynamism (sum of all)	3.44	2.03	2.76	2.44	—	2.67	2.39

Sources: World Bank investment climate surveys, http://iresearch.worldbank.org/ics/jsp/index.jsp; Ayyagari, Demirgüç-Kunt, and Maksimovic 2006.
Note: — = no data are available.
a. Figures produced on an average among 34 other developing economies.
b. New technology that substantially changes how a main product is produced.
c. Outsourced (insourced) a major production activity previously carried out in house (externally).

World Bank investment climate surveys. The first three rows cover core innovation outcomes and show the proportion of firms that, in the three years preceding the survey, had introduced a new product line, upgraded a product line, or introduced a new technology that substantially changed the method of production. The remaining rows include a number of other activities that Ayyagari, Demirgüç-Kunt, and Maksimovic (2006) propose are indicative of the dynamism of firms. These are activities that promote knowledge transfers, including foreign joint ventures and licensing agreements, and activities that adapt the organization of the production processes of firms, such as opening a new plant or outsourcing a production activity.

Interestingly, even though firms in low-income Cambodia do not do any U.S. patenting at all, they are among the most active in adopting and adapting activities; over half of the firms in the sample introduced or upgraded product lines and production processes. Firms in Thailand are also relatively innovative according to these measures, while those in Indonesia have been laggards. Ayyagari, Demirgüç-Kunt, and Maksimovic (2006) study the correlates of firm innovation and dynamism in a worldwide sample of firms and find:

- Core innovation increases with firm size and with high capacity utilization, understood as indicating significant growth opportunities, while it declines with the age of the firm (that is, younger firms are more innovative).
- These broader measures of innovation are not closely related to per capita income levels, suggesting that, given favorable economic and institutional conditions, firms may be highly innovative and dynamic in this broad sense in even the poorest economies. (As we indicate below, formal R&D and sophisticated innovations that lead to patents are quite different in this respect, tending to rise sharply with per capita income.)
- There is a strong negative association between state ownership and innovation, but there is no discernible difference whether a firm is domestic or foreign and privately owned.
- There is also a strong association between innovation and most types of external financing (equity financing, local or foreign-owned commercial banks, lease finance, investment funds, trade credits, and funds from family and friends), corroborating the importance of financial sector development for innovation revealed in a number of other studies cited in this chapter.[3]
- There is a positive association between innovation and the extent of competition faced by firms.

The World Bank investment climate surveys provide a view into the sources of knowledge that firms in these low- and middle-income economies use to make innovations. Table 3.2 shows the responses of firms to a question about the most important source for the technological innovations they achieved during the preceding three years. By far the largest share of firms in all economies (on average, over 40 percent) cited the technology embodied in new machinery or equipment (most of which may be assumed to be imported). The next two sources of innovation cited most frequently were technology developed in cooperation with client firms and the hiring of key personnel (each cited by 12–13 percent of firms), while innovations developed or adapted within the firm were cited by only 11–12 percent of firms on average, that is, only about one-quarter of the share cited new machinery and equipment. These observations provide a good

■ TABLE 3.2 **Most Important Source of Technological Innovation**
percent of firms

Source	Cambodia 2003	Indonesia 2003	Malaysia 2002	Philippines 2003	Thailand 2004	Average
Embodied in new machinery or equipment	42.1	48.7	49.9	43.0	33.143.4	
Developed in cooperation with client firms	11.9	15.1	8.6	9.7	17.2	12.5
Hiring key personnel	14.5	17.9	11.4	14.2	3.0	12.2
Developed or adapted within the firm locally	16.1	4.7	7.2	8.3	19.4	11.1
Transferred from a parent company	6.0	2.7	11.0	4.3	11.87.2	
Developed with the equipment or machinery supplier	1.6	7.0	5.2	5.0	7.2	5.2
Other	7.8	3.9	6.7	15.5	8.2	8.4

Source: World Bank investment climate surveys, http://iresearch.worldbank.org/ics/jsp/index.jsp.

springboard for a more detailed inspection of the methods by which firms absorb knowledge from abroad (see box 3.2 for a listing of the methods).

Firms and economies at all levels of development rely extensively on knowledge from outside their boundaries. Eaton and Kortum (1996) estimate that, even among developed economies, foreign sources of technology account for 80 percent or more of domestic productivity growth in most OECD countries, the only exceptions being Japan and the United States. Bottazzi and Peri (2005) estimate that a 1 percent increase in R&D in the United States leads to a 0.35 percent rise in knowledge creation (patenting) in other OECD countries within 10 years.

Most obviously, developing-country firms may acquire technology through firms in developed economies by purchasing and importing advanced capital equipment embodying new technologies that could not have been produced at home or could only have been produced at a much higher domestic opportunity cost. The reverse engineering of imported capital equipment has also been an important way that firms in NIEs such as Korea and Taiwan (China) have strengthened their technological understanding and capabilities.

There is a large body of case study literature arguing that East Asian firms also derive significant technological benefits through exportation, especially under longer-term contracts, as part of the global production networks of foreign multi-

■ BOX 3.2 **Channels for Acquiring Technology from Abroad**

Close to 80 percent of world R&D is carried out in developed countries. Knowledge flows from rich nations thus remain the primary mode by which developing countries acquire new ideas. One of the most distinctive features of East Asian economies is their extensive engagement in international trade, reflected in exceptionally high levels of imports and exports. The following are tried and true means of acquiring technology:

■ *Purchases of capital equipment.* Among the various channels for technology transfer from abroad, the importance of advanced capital equipment imports as a source of new technologies has been more clearly documented than any other.

■ *Industrial upgrading through exports.* A rich body of case study literature argues that East Asian firms have also derived significant technological benefits from exports, especially exports under longer-term original equipment manufacturing (OEM) contracts or similar contracts as part of the global production networks of foreign multinationals (a model of technological development sometimes described as supplier-oriented industrial upgrading).[4]

■ *Purchases of technology.* East Asian firms have also generally availed themselves of opportunities to pur-chase disembodied external knowledge, for example, through the acquisition of patents, nonpatented inventions, licenses, disclosures of know-how, trademarks, designs, patterns, and other technological services. This has generated unusually high levels of balance of payments royalty flows.

■ *Foreign direct investment.* Local firms may also learn valuable lessons through interactions with local affiliates established by foreign multinationals using FDI. Some East Asian economies have historically adopted less open FDI policies than others, and yardsticks such as the stock of inward FDI relative to GDP are generally less exceptional than measurement results on other modes of global integration. Technology flows via FDI may occur through so-called horizontal technological spillovers from foreign affiliates competing in the same industry, although the evidence for this is mixed. More convincing is the evidence for technology transfers through vertical relationships when affiliates of multinational corporations undertake to strengthen their suppliers by providing them with training, technical support, and collaboration to solve production and design issues, another form of supplier-oriented industrial upgrading.

nationals, a model of technological development referred to as supplier-oriented industrial upgrading (although the econometric evidence for this is mixed). Certainly, exceptionally high levels of engagement in international trade are a common feature across most East Asian economies, as evidenced by the high ratio of trade to GDP. Figure 3.1 shows that the ratios of imports of machinery and transport equipment to GDP (including much of what is classified as high technology goods) in East Asia are mostly well above the levels associated with countries at similar per capita incomes.[5]

Firms may also purchase disembodied external knowledge, for example, through the acquisition of patents, nonpatented inventions, licenses, disclosures of know-how, trademarks, designs, patterns, and other consultancy and technological services. Royalty payments abroad provide a rough measure of this form of technology transfer. Figure 3.2 indicates that royalty payments abroad by East Asian

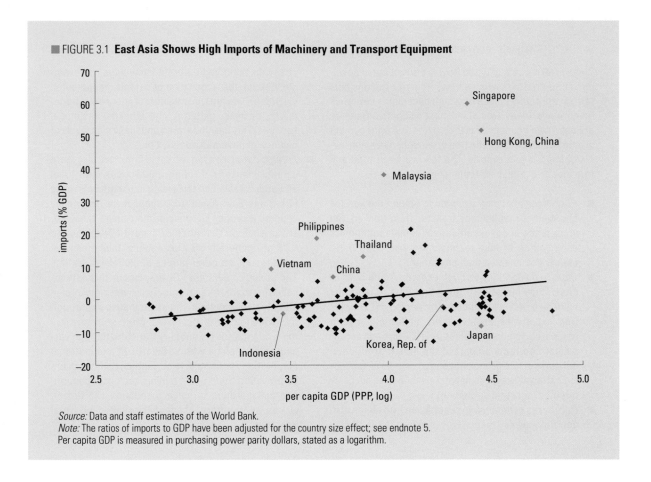

■ FIGURE 3.1 **East Asia Shows High Imports of Machinery and Transport Equipment**

Source: Data and staff estimates of the World Bank.
Note: The ratios of imports to GDP have been adjusted for the country size effect; see endnote 5.
Per capita GDP is measured in purchasing power parity dollars, stated as a logarithm.

economies are generally much higher than those by other economies at similar income levels. Firms may also derive disembodied knowledge flows through technological spillovers, benefiting from a wide range of open source information, for instance, scientific, technical and industry journals, informal contacts, and communications through networks of researchers and specialists, trade and industry associations, and trade fairs.

Local firms may likewise learn valuable lessons through interactions with local affiliates established by foreign multinationals using FDI. This might occur through so-called horizontal technological spillovers from foreign affiliates competing in the same industry, although the evidence for this is mixed. More convincing is the evidence on cooperation in innovation and agreed technology transfers through vertical relationships with customers and suppliers, particularly

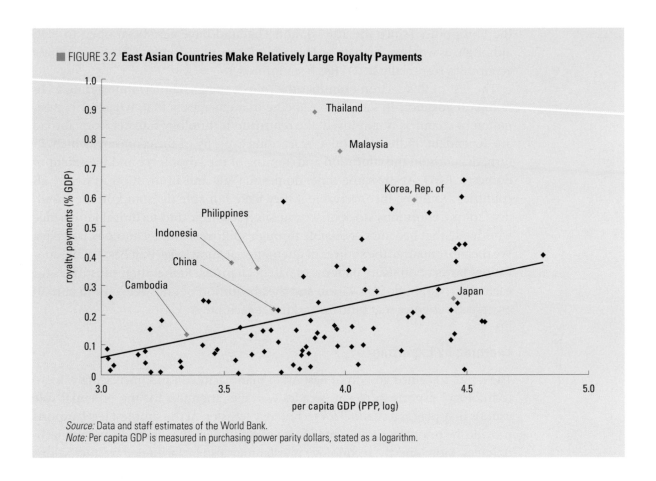

■ FIGURE 3.2 **East Asian Countries Make Relatively Large Royalty Payments**

Source: Data and staff estimates of the World Bank.
Note: Per capita GDP is measured in purchasing power parity dollars, stated as a logarithm.

in the case of developing-country firms that become suppliers to multinational affiliates (another form of supplier-oriented industrial upgrading).

Historically, the differences in the level of reliance of East Asian economies on FDI have been wider than the differences in the level of their reliance on trade or technology licensing, although, in recent years, there has been a convergence toward more openness to FDI. Korea and, to a lesser extent, Taiwan (China) have tended to restrict FDI, while emphasizing the licensing of foreign technology and the upgrading of domestic technological capabilities, including through domestic R&D and the strengthening of technical education and labor force skills. Singapore, on the other hand, has been exceptionally welcoming to FDI, while also fostering domestic technology efforts. China, too, has drawn heavily on FDI inflows, emphasizing joint ventures, while also emphasizing domestic R&D more recently. Middle-income Southeast Asian economies such as Indonesia, Malaysia, the Philippines (since the 1980s), and Thailand have also been open to FDI, although, as we show below, the level of indigenous technological effort in these economies (especially R&D) has been limited.[6]

The rest of this section examines the role of these channels in fostering technological advances in East Asia. A theme that emerges is that, whatever combination of channels is employed, the returns to technology transfer from abroad are dependent on the absorptive or learning capacity of the economy, which, in turn, depends on the education and training of the labor force and the extent of domestic R&D. At the same time, domestic R&D and innovation in nearly all countries would be inconceivable if they were not able to "stand on the shoulders" of the enormous stock of accumulated scientific and technical knowledge worldwide that becomes accessible through spillovers and technology transfers. We therefore analyze the sources of international knowledge that East Asian innovation draws upon using patterns of patent citations. Rather than substitutes for each other, domestic innovation and the absorption of knowledge from abroad emerge as activities that buttress and foster each other.

Learning by Exporting?

The rapid, sustained growth of East Asian manufactured (and, increasingly, high-technology) exports in recent decades warrants attention for the potential role exports may play as a channel for technology transfer. At the simplest level, exports provide the resources for imports of capital equipment that embody modern technologies. More directly, technology transfer may also be facilitated by interactions between developing-country exporters and their developed-country customers, who have an incentive to help suppliers upgrade technical capabilities, productivity, and product quality. East Asian exports of machinery and transport equipment (containing much of what is classified as high-technology products) are generally much higher than those of other economies at similar incomes (see figure 3.3).

The potential for technology transfer through exporting is considered important in the case study literature.[7] Hobday (1995, 2000) stresses the role of the original equipment manufacture (OEM) subcontracting system in fostering industrial exports and technology transfers in the NIEs, particularly in Korea and Taiwan (China) (see box 3.3). Nevertheless, while the case study literature has emphasized the opportunities for technological learning through exports, systematic econometric evidence for this proposition is mixed.[8] There is certainly plenty of evidence that, in general, firms that export exhibit significantly higher productivity than firms that do not export. But this appears to be mainly the result of self-selection by more productive firms, since these are more likely to undertake

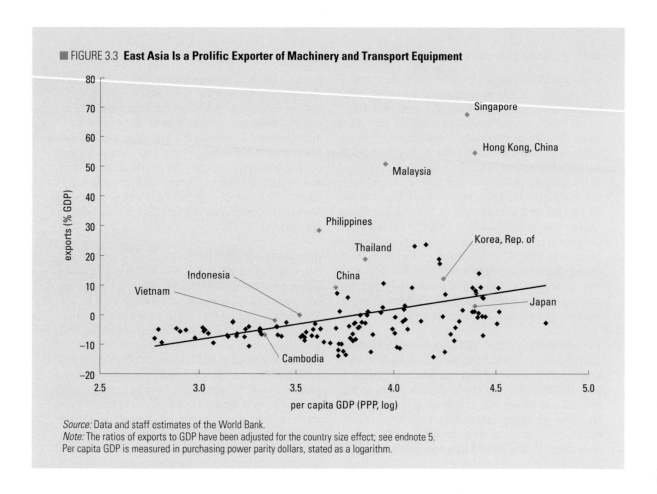

■ FIGURE 3.3 **East Asia Is a Prolific Exporter of Machinery and Transport Equipment**

Source: Data and staff estimates of the World Bank.
Note: The ratios of exports to GDP have been adjusted for the country size effect; see endnote 5.
Per capita GDP is measured in purchasing power parity dollars, stated as a logarithm.

the higher fixed costs and rigors of competing in international markets. Clerides, Lach, and Tybout (1998), for example, discover little evidence for learning effects from exports in plant-level data from Colombia, Mexico, and Morocco. On the other hand, Kraay (2006) and Aw, Chen, and Roberts (1997) do find evidence that experience in exports helps explain the productivity levels of firms in China and Taiwan (China).

Pack (2006) observes that data on exports typically do not separate exports carried out under long-term OEM-type contracts from other types of exports, although it is only the former that are expected to produce learning benefits. Thus, it is perhaps not surprising that econometric studies based on generic export data arrive at only mixed results in explaining export learning effects. There is, however, a good deal of recent econometric evidence for the existence of technology transfers from

■ BOX 3.3 **Scale Economies and the OEM and Design and Brand Manufacturing Sequence**

Under the OEM system, a supplier undertakes production (typically, at thin profit margins) according to the precise design specifications of the foreign buyer, which then markets the product under its own brand name through its international distribution channels. OEM production and exports in the NIEs evolved rapidly during the 1970s and 1980s. Surveys suggest that some 70–80 percent of Korea's electronics exports were occurring under OEM-type contracts by 1990, while over 40 percent of the computer hardware exports from Taiwan (China) took this form. Over the past 15 years, OEM-type contracting has also been central in the enormous expansion of manufactured exports from China. During this time, the OEM model itself has developed into more complex patterns of global production networking in which first-tier suppliers are themselves purchasers from second- and third-tier suppliers.

The potential benefits of OEM-type contracts for developing-country exporters include economies of scale in production that involve less risk and cost relative to firms that attempt to break into global markets on their own, as well as possible assistance in mastering new technologies through technology transfers, services, and training offered by the customer. By building up its technological capabilities in this way, a firm may lay the groundwork for more sophisticated (and profitable) ventures, for example, through original design manufacturing (whereby the firm also takes over responsibility for the postconceptual design and development of products sold under the customer's brand) and original brand manufacturing (whereby the firm produces its own brand after it has mastered the entire product cycle of R&D, innovation, design, development, production, and marketing). This sequential OEM–original design manufacturing–original brand manufacturing pathway has been labeled supplier-oriented industrial upgrading (see above).[9]

Samsung Electronics of Korea is an example of a developing-country firm that has successfully traveled this road, building on OEM and technology licensing deals with advanced multinational corporations such as GTE, Philips, Sony, and Toshiba in the 1980s and then making huge efforts to build up its own design capabilities, R&D, and independent brand in the 1990s. By 2004, it had annual R&D expenditures of US$4 billion–US$5 billion (representing 8–9 percent of sales and employing close to a quarter of the firm's workforce), the largest global market share in sales of dynamic random access memory and static random access memory semiconductor chips, flash memories, televisions, computer monitors, and liquid crystal display panels, as well as the second or third largest market shares in mobile phones and DVD players.

multinational firm affiliates in a host country to local suppliers in the same host country (discussed hereafter). Given this evidence for one form of supplier-oriented industrial upgrading, it may be reasonable to suppose that similar spillovers also exist for another, that is, for crossborder trade carried out under long-term OEM-type contracts between a multinational corporation purchaser abroad and developing-country OEM exporter firms that are part of the purchaser's global production network.

Tybout (2006) also notes that many studies of export learning effects fail to take into account the possibility that future exporters may come into contact with and begin cooperating with potential foreign customers well *before* export flows actually take place. Kim (1997) describes Samsung's efforts to master the production of microwave ovens in the 1970s in response to a prospective order from J. C. Penney in the United States. Here, the prospect of an export market larger than any available at home was the spur to the firm's large investment in mastering microwave technology, and the improvements in its productivity preceded actual export flows.

This and other case studies suggest that the relationship between exports and productivity involves more than a simple choice by firms that are productive for some exogenous reason and that then self-select to become exporters. It seems, rather, that firms make deliberate decisions to improve their productivity so as to serve export markets. Hallward-Driemeier, Iarossi, and Sokoloff (2002) provide firm-level evidence from five East Asian economies for this hypothesis. Domestic firms that begin as exporters have significantly higher levels of productivity than other classes of firms (in particular, firms that only become exporters later), and they also differ systematically in the training of the workforce, the vintage of their capital equipment, the use of outside auditors, and other aspects of production processes and operations. The authors interpret this finding as evidence that the decision to export encourages firms to undertake productivity enhancing improvements, including the technologies applied. They point out that the gap in productivity between firms that begin as exporters and others is largest and most significant in middle-income economies such as Indonesia, the Philippines, and Thailand, less so in Malaysia, and essentially nonexistent in the most developed economy, Korea. They conclude that "to those concerned with policy . . . , the message would be that it is the least developed economies that have the most to gain from measures that would broaden the markets they face" (p. 36).

Nevertheless, while firms in less well developed economies may have the most to gain from taking on the challenges of exporting, they may also be the least well equipped to do so. Nabeshima (2004) observes that, to be selected as an OEM supplier, firms need to possess a certain level of production and technological capabilities that allows them to meet demanding quality, cost, and delivery requirements. Firms have to grapple with even more complex problems in attempting the transition to original design or original brand manufacturing, which helps explain why firms such as Samsung are among only a few East Asian or developing-country firms to have made the transition to primary reliance on internal R&D and their own global brands.

Drawing on extensive interviews with lead firms and suppliers in the electronics and auto parts industries, Sturgeon and Lester (2004) suggest that recent trends are raising significantly the economies of scale and technological competencies required for participation in the global production networks of multinational companies, putting in question the usefulness of the supplier-oriented model for many developing economies. Excellent manufacturing performance and low costs are considered widely available and commodified; moreover, potential suppliers now need to provide the lead firm with value adding capabilities in product and component design, component sourcing, inventory management, testing, packaging, and logistics. Increasingly, suppliers also need to be global in scope so that they are able to support their lead firms all over the world. Besides, lead firms are now less inclined to establish long-term relationships with suppliers who threaten to turn into competitors, preferring to do business with pure play OEM and original design manufacturing suppliers.

Reflecting these trends, since the early 1990s, leading firms in the electronics industry have been outsourcing a larger share of their supplier business to a small group of contract manufacturers that operate extensive global networks of production facilities to support the worldwide operations of their clients, including high-volume production sites in Central and Eastern Europe, East Asia, and Mexico, as well as more specialized sites close to clients in developed economies.[10] As table 3.3 indicates, most of the top contract manufacturers are firms in advanced economies, and only a limited number of firms in Taiwan (China) have broken into the top ranks of this business. The 1990s also saw a huge wave of investment in auto assembly and component supply plants in emerging markets, especially in China and elsewhere in East Asia. As in electronics, the major assemblers are increasingly outsourcing to a small number of component suppliers with global reach, typically advanced economy firms, such as Bosch, Delphi, Denso, and Visteon, that take up the responsibility for the design and supply of

■ TABLE 3.3 **The Top Five Electronic Contract Manufacturers, 1994 and 2004**

Company	1994 revenue (US$ million)	Company	2004 revenue (US$ million)
Sanmina[a]	2,363	Flextronics[c]	15,355
Celestica[b]	1,989	Hon Hai[d]	13,190
Solectron[a]	1,642	Sanmina[a]	12,205
Jabil[a]	404	Solectron[a]	11,638
Flextronics[c]	211	Celestica[b]	8,840

Sources: Sturgeon and Lester 2004; Reed Business Information 2005.
a. United States.
b. Canada.
c. Incorporated in Singapore; managed from the United States.
d. Taiwan (China).

the major component modules going into an automobile and that are able to collocate near the assembler's worldwide operations. Doner, Noble, and Ravenhill (2004, 2006) observe that these assembler strategies are tending to raise barriers to developing-country firms aiming to enter the global auto parts industry.

According to these case studies, growing competitive pressures are raising the technological capability and scale thresholds required of East Asian firms to participate effectively in global production networks. If, in the past, low production costs were an adequate entry ticket for participation in production networks, the price of entry today also increasingly requires firms to possess more sophisticated learning, innovation, and design capabilities. (The final section of this chapter looks at policies that governments may use to further these learning efforts and capabilities.)

Technology Transfer Through Imports

Figure 3.1 above highlighted the exceptionally high levels of imports of capital equipment and components in many East Asian economies. Table 3.2 above showed that three or four times more firms in low- and middle-income economies in East Asia rely on capital equipment imports as a source of technological innovation rather than on any other method. Grossman and Helpman (1991) have analyzed the role of imports of capital equipment as a channel for technology transfer in theoretical models of endogenous growth. Coe and Helpman (1995) have found that the level of total factor productivity in countries is significantly related to the stocks of R&D in trading partners, weighted by overall imports from the trading partners as a share of GDP. In general, the impact of foreign R&D on domestic total factor productivity rises with the openness of the economy, as measured by the level of total imports to GDP. Coe, Helpman, and Hoffmaister (1997) have extended the analysis to developing economies and find that the total factor productivity of these economies is also significantly related to the stock of R&D in developed economies (weighted by imports from developed economies), as well as to the overall share of imports to GDP and the secondary school enrollment rate. Their study finds that East Asian NIEs such as Hong Kong (China), Korea, and Singapore have elasticities of total factor productivity to foreign R&D stocks that are generally higher than the average for developing economies.

Subsequent studies have mainly confirmed these results and elaborated on them in several directions. Keller (2002) offers one of relatively few studies to look at the impact of international trade, FDI, and disembodied knowledge flows (for example, through direct communication) together as channels of knowledge flow.[11] He finds that all three channels are significant for knowledge flows, but that imports are the most important channel, explaining about two-thirds of the estimated impacts, while FDI and disembodied flows (as measured) explain about one-sixth each on average. Xu and Wang (1999) find that imports of capital equipment provide a better index for measuring R&D spillovers than does trade as a whole. Schiff, Wang, and Olarreaga (2002) look not only at the impact on the productivity of developing countries of the R&D stocks accumulated in the North, but also those accumulated in the South, that is, in developing countries.[12] They find that the productivity in developing economies does rise with the R&D in other developing economies (and thus with openness to these economies), but that the elasticity is smaller than it is with respect to the R&D in the North. They find that these kinds of South-South R&D spillovers are mostly important for industries that have a low R&D intensity, but not for industries with a high R&D intensity, which benefit more from R&D in the North (and openness to the North).

Transfers and Spillovers Through FDI

There is a good deal of variation in the levels of FDI in East Asian economies. For these economies, figure 3.4 shows a scatter plot of the accumulated stocks of inward FDI (relative to GDP) versus land area.[13] Economies such as Japan, Korea, and Taiwan (China) have historically exercised relatively restrictive policies on FDI inflows and continue to show low stocks of inward FDI relative to other economies of comparable geographical size (or per capita income). FDI stocks are also low relative to country size and per capita income in Indonesia and the Philippines. On the other hand, FDI stocks in economies such as China, Hong Kong (China), Singapore, and most middle- (and low-) income economies in Southeast Asia are generally at or above the levels predicted by country size or (for the most part) per capita income, partly reflecting more open policies toward FDI. (In a slight exception to these observations, despite the high absolute flows of FDI to China in recent years, the stock of FDI relative to China's GDP remains low compared to the situation in most other economies at a similar per capita income.) Figure 3.5 shows that, while stocks of FDI in manufacturing in East Asia are the highest in the world, FDI in the much larger services sector of these economies is appreciably lower than is the case in other regions.

These results suggest that, broadly, if FDI is indeed a significant source of knowledge transfer and spillovers, then more than a few East Asian economies

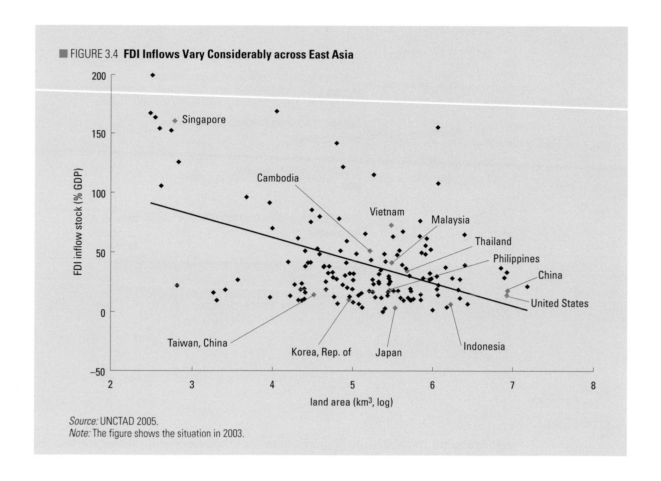

■ FIGURE 3.4 **FDI Inflows Vary Considerably across East Asia**

Source: UNCTAD 2005.
Note: The figure shows the situation in 2003.

may be able to tap greater productivity benefits from greater FDI. Modern theories of the multinational enterprise and FDI emphasize their character as sources of product innovations, new process technologies, managerial expertise, higher quality standards, and export access to global markets. These theories ask why multinationals opt for FDI rather than production technology licensing through arm's-length market transactions. The answer hinges on the existence of the significant externalities or market failures associated with knowledge that prevent firms from protecting or exploiting fully their intangible knowledge assets in arm's-length transactions and lead them to deploy these assets through transactions within the boundaries of the firms through FDI.[14]

FDI is expected to bring a number of benefits. Foreign affiliates of multinational corporations obtain easier access to superior parent company technologies and achieve higher levels of productivity in their operations, which, in a competitive

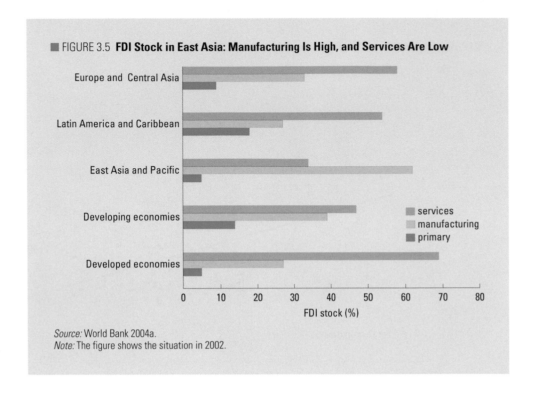

■ FIGURE 3.5 **FDI Stock in East Asia: Manufacturing Is High, and Services Are Low**

Source: World Bank 2004a.
Note: The figure shows the situation in 2002.

environment, translate into higher wages for employees and greater welfare for consumers because higher-quality goods and services become available at lower prices. FDI may also enhance productivity in the rest of the economy by increasing competition or through spillovers of technology and expertise. Some research finds that FDI crowds in domestic investment[15] and may create new export opportunities for domestic firms. Here, we review evidence for two propositions: does foreign ownership convey large productivity benefits for the local firms or operations that are acquired or established by the multinational corporation, and, if these benefits exist, do they spill over to other domestic, unacquired firms?

First, does FDI convey large productivity benefits for the local operations that a multinational corporation acquires? There is much evidence that such operations generally show higher levels of labor productivity, total factor productivity, and wages than do local firms. What has not been clear, however, is whether this superiority is brought about by the restructuring and the infusion of new technology undertaken by the foreign owners or, instead, simply reflects the fact that foreign firms may acquire local firms that were already superior in these respects.

Recent World Bank research addresses some of the difficult econometric problems that bedevil studies of this question. The research uses firm-level data from 1983 to 1996 from the Indonesian census of manufacturing.[16] The analysis shows that Indonesian plants, through foreign acquisition, benefit from a rapid and substantial improvement in total factor productivity, averaging about 46 percent (see figure 3.6). In the first one or two years after acquisition, an acquired plant experiences much more rapid growth in output, employment, investment, and wages than do other local plants. The proportion of skilled workers in the plant labor force increases, and the export orientation of the plant is augmented, as is the plant's use of imported intermediates. All this is consistent with significant restructuring in plant operations after acquisition.

Second, does superior technology among the affiliates of multinational corporations spill over to unacquired local firms? This might happen, for example, if local firms are able to improve their productivity by copying products, technologies,

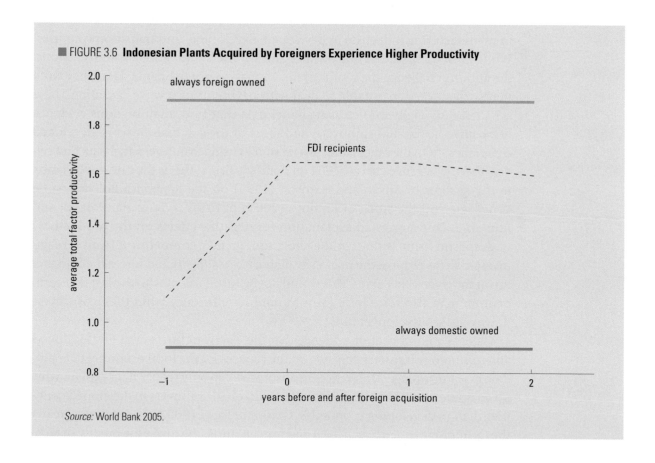

■ FIGURE 3.6 **Indonesian Plants Acquired by Foreigners Experience Higher Productivity**

Source: World Bank 2005.

methods, or strategies from the affiliates of the multinational corporations through observation (*imitation*) or by hiring workers trained by the affiliates (*skill set acquisition*).[17] The entry of multinational corporations might also lead to more *competition* in the host country market, forcing local firms to use their existing resources more efficiently or to search for new technologies.

In evaluating the evidence for spillovers, one should distinguish between horizontal (or intraindustry) and vertical (or interindustry) knowledge transfers or spillovers. Horizontal or intraindustry spillovers refer to a situation wherein local firms benefit from the presence of foreign competition in their own sector. The foreign competitors will, however, have a strong incentive to prevent technology leakages and spillovers. They will try to achieve this through the formal protection of intellectual property, trade secrecy, paying higher wages, or locating in countries or industries where local firms have limited imitative capacity.

Broadly speaking, recent research tends to cast doubt on the existence of horizontal spillovers in developing countries. A recent survey by Görg and Greenaway (2004) takes stock of 40 studies on horizontal productivity spillovers in manufacturing industries in developed, developing, and transition countries. While 22 of these studies find positive and significant horizontal spillover effects, the authors challenge the results of the 14 that do not use panel data. They write that such studies are unable to deal with problems of reverse causality. There are then only eight studies using panel data that find unambiguous evidence of positive horizontal spillovers, and most of these are on firms in developed economies.[18] On the other hand, several studies using firm-level panel data find evidence of the negative effects of FDI on domestic firms. This is the case, for instance, in the analysis of Aitken and Harrison (1999) on the República Bolivariana de Venezuela and the study of Konings (2001) of firms in Bulgaria, Poland, and Romania. One suggested explanation for negative effects on the productivity of domestic firms is that, in the short run, greater competition from foreign-invested firms reduces the market available to local firms and forces them higher up on the given cost curves. This would not be inconsistent with the fact that competition may also force local firms to improve efficiency (shift their cost curves downward) in the longer run.

There is a good deal of evidence that the extent of horizontal FDI spillovers and technology transfers depends on the capacity of the local economy to assimilate new knowledge. Differences in absorptive capacity would help explain why, for example, there is more evidence for horizontal spillovers in developed countries than in developing economies. Glass and Saggi (2002) find that the greater the technology gap between local and foreign firms, the lower the quality of technology transferred and the lower the potential for spillovers. Along the same lines, Kokko, Tansini, and Zejan (1996) find that, in Uruguay, there have been productivity spillovers to domestic firms with moderate technology gaps, but not where the gaps are large. Borensztein, De Gregorio, and Lee (1998) and Lipsey (2000) emphasize the need to improve education in the host economy as a means of strengthening the capacity to incorporate positive spillovers. Kinoshita (2001) finds that, in the Czech Republic, only domestic firms that undertake their own R&D enjoy horizontal FDI spillovers. Furthermore, distinguishing between "the two faces of R&D" analyzed by Cohen and Levinthal (1989), Kinoshita finds that domestic Czech firms performing R&D benefit not only from the innovations produced by the R&D, but also by becoming more able to learn and absorb outside knowledge. The learning effect is several times larger than the innovation effect.

Todo and Miyamoto (2006) observe that the extent of horizontal FDI spillovers to domestic firms is also likely to depend on the level of R&D undertaken in the host country by foreign firms. Local workers and engineers employed in R&D–performing foreign affiliates may be able to gain more knowledge than those working in foreign firms not undertaking local R&D, and this knowledge may diffuse to local firms through job turnover, work-related discussions, and so on. Looking at Indonesian firms in 1994–97, Todo and Miyamoto find that domestic firms received positive spillovers from R&D–performing foreign firms, but not from non-R&D–performing foreign firms. Taken together, the Kinoshita, Todo, and Miyamoto studies suggest that in-country R&D may be important in terms both of foreign affiliates generating spillovers and domestic firms absorbing spillovers.

While foreign investors have an incentive to prevent knowledge leakage to local firms with which they compete, they may gain by transferring knowledge to their local suppliers or customers through vertical input-output links. As in the case of OEM-type supplier-customer relationships, these vertical or interindustry knowledge flows may take place directly through knowledge transfers from foreign firms to local suppliers or customers (for example, through training programs, technical support, and collaboration on production and design issues), indirectly through the movement of workers between customers and suppliers, or simply through higher standards for product quality and on-time delivery that provide an incentive to domestic suppliers to upgrade their production management or technology. Local suppliers may also reap the benefits of economies of scale because of increased demand for intermediate products from new multinational customers, although this is not a knowledge transfer in the strict sense.

There is a good deal of evidence on vertical technology transfers in developing economies. Blalock and Gertler (2005) find strong support for vertical technology transfers from multinational corporation customers to local suppliers in Indonesia, as Javorcik (2004) does in Lithuania. Saggi (2002) finds that Mexican *maquiladoras* (product assembly plants for export), which began as producers of more labor-intensive products, adopted more sophisticated production techniques over time. Many of these techniques were imported from U.S. customers. The size of the effects is generally meaningful. Javorcik (2004) finds, for example, that a 1-standard deviation increase in foreign presence in the purchasing sector of the economy in Lithuania is associated with a 15 percent rise in the output of local firms in supplier sectors. However, as noted in the discussion above on supplier-oriented industrial upgrading through OEM-type contracts, the potential for vertical technology transfers depends, to some extent, on whether domestic firms are chosen as suppliers by the affiliates of multinational corporations, on the technological ability of these firms to meet demanding quality, cost, and delivery requirements, and on the amount of technological learning the firms obtain through vertical spillovers. Blalock and Gertler (2005) find, for example, that, in Indonesia, domestic firms with high levels of human capital are the prime beneficiaries of vertical knowledge transfers.

R&D Efforts in East Asia

Total world spending on R&D reached US$830 billion in 2002 in purchasing power parity terms.[19] Almost by definition, the greater part of world R&D is performed in developed countries: around 78 percent in 2002, much higher than the 59 percent share of these countries in world GDP in purchasing power parity terms. The proportion of R&D done in developed countries has fallen over the last decade, however. Developing economies have been devoting more resources to R&D, and they raised their share in the world total from around 13 percent in 1992 to 22 percent in 2002. East Asia has contributed almost three-quarters of the increase in developing-country R&D over the last decade. In nominal terms, R&D spending in East Asia quintupled over the decade, reaching US$112 billion in 2002, or 13.5 percent of the world total. The R&D intensity in East Asia—the ratio of R&D spending to GDP—also rose, from 0.7 percent in 1992 to 1.2 percent in 2002.

As table 3.4 shows, however, the East Asian economies differ widely in R&D performance. Korea, Singapore, and Taiwan (China) now devote 2.2–2.5 percent of GDP to R&D spending, which is comparable to R&D levels in the United States and at the upper end of the scale among developed economies. Meanwhile, R&D spending in economies such as Indonesia, the Philippines, and Thailand is only 0.1– 0.2 percent of GDP, which is among the lowest levels among all economies

■ TABLE 3.4 **R&D Expenditures**
at purchasing power parity

Region or country	R&D spending, 2002		R&D as % of GDP[a]	
	US$ billions	% of world	1992	2002
East Asia	111.7	13.5	0.7	1.2
NIEs	36.4	4.4	1.6	2.2
Hong Kong, China	1.1	0.1	0.3[b]	0.6
Korea, Rep. of	20.8	2.5	1.9	2.5
Singapore	2.2	0.3	1.2	2.2
Taiwan, China	12.2	1.5	1.8	2.3
Southeast Asia	3.3	0.4	0.1	0.2
Indonesia	0.3	0.0	0.1[c]	0.1[d]
Malaysia	1.5	0.2	0.4	0.7
Philippines	0.4	0.0	0.2	0.1
Thailand	1.1	0.1	0.2	0.2
China	72.0	8.7	0.8	1.2
World	829.9	100.0	1.7	1.7
Developed countries	645.8	77.8	2.3	2.3
Japan	106.4	12.8	2.9	3.1
United States	275.1	33.1	2.6	2.6
Developing countries	184.1	22.1	0.6	0.9
Latin America	21.7	2.6	0.5	0.6
Emerging Europe	30.3	3.7	1.0	1.2

Source: UNESCO 2004, 2006.
a. Regional data are the sum of R&D divided by the sum of GDP.
b. 1995.
c. 1994.
d. 2001.

for which we have data. Between these two extremes is China, where R&D spending rose at 20 percent a year over the last decade to reach 1.4 percent of GDP by 2004, or US$109 billion in purchasing power parity terms.[20] R&D spending in Malaysia also accelerated after the mid-1990s, reaching 0.7 percent of GDP by 2002.

The wide range of R&D intensities in East Asia is of course consistent with the broad cross-country pattern whereby richer countries such as Korea have higher

R&D intensities than poorer ones such as Indonesia. Figure 3.7 shows a scatter plot of available panel data on R&D intensities and per capita GDP for a large number of developed and developing economies between the mid-1970s and the early to mid-2000s. Econometric estimates suggest that R&D intensity not only increases with per capita GDP, but does so at an accelerating pace. As figure 3.7 also indicates, the trajectories of R&D spending in several East Asian economies show significant and sustained deviations from the levels suggested by per capita GDP alone. R&D intensity in economies such as China, Korea, and Taiwan (China) is twice as great as those suggested by per capita income. On the other hand, R&D intensity in Southeast Asian economies such as Indonesia, the Philippines, and Thailand has systematically undershot the estimated average relationship over a long period (both before and after the financial crisis of the late 1990s).

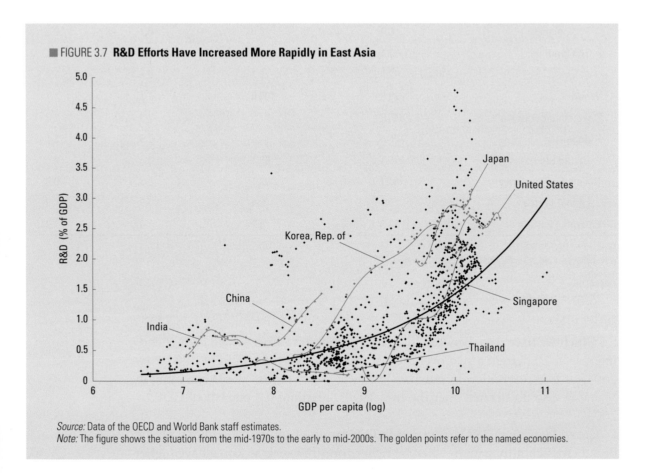

■ FIGURE 3.7 **R&D Efforts Have Increased More Rapidly in East Asia**

Source: Data of the OECD and World Bank staff estimates.
Note: The figure shows the situation from the mid-1970s to the early to mid-2000s. The golden points refer to the named economies.

Research at the World Bank by Lederman and Maloney (2003)—one of only a few studies to examine R&D in developing countries systematically—finds that policies and institutions play an important role in explaining these systematic deviations, while structural differences such as the size of the economy, the size of the labor force, and the relative abundance of natural resources do not. As with other types of investment, the intensity of R&D declines at higher real interest rates and greater macroeconomic volatility. It rises with greater financial depth and stronger intellectual property rights. Subjective measures of the quality of research institutions such as universities and public research centers and the quality of collaboration between these institutions and the private sector also show a positive impact on R&D intensity. The discussion of policy issues at the end of this chapter looks at how East Asian economies rank on these broader aspects of the economic and institutional environment that are relevant for R&D intensity and innovation; it finds marked differences between high- and low-R&D performers.[21]

Are these large differences in R&D performance significant for economic performance? Is formal R&D important only for a few advanced economies such as Korea, while most developing countries need only focus on absorbing advanced knowledge from abroad, for example, through openness to trade and foreign investment? The study by Lederman and Maloney (2003) also estimates the impact of R&D intensity on total factor productivity growth for a sample of developed and developing economies. They find that a 1 percentage point increase in R&D intensity is associated with a 0.78 percent rise in total factor productivity growth: in effect, a 78 percent social rate of return on R&D investment. The term "social" here indicates that the returns measured include not only private returns to the firm making the R&D investment, but also the benefits for others that are generated by R&D spillovers.

The very high social rate of return found here is similar to results in earlier studies for the United States and other OECD countries. Compared to the prevailing costs of capital, these high rates of return imply that actual levels of R&D investment are only a fraction of socially optimal levels. Looking at how returns to R&D in rich countries differ from those in poor ones, the study finds that returns to R&D fall substantially with the level of per capita income; in other words, returns are *higher* in poor countries than they are in rich ones. This result is consistent with the intuition that a dollar of R&D should be more valuable in poor countries that are far from the technology frontier than it is in advanced countries that must focus on cutting-edge innovations that shift the frontier forward. This is likely to be the case especially for the development component of R&D, particularly expenditures devoted to adapting foreign technologies into forms useful in the local environment.

Overall, then, there is at least some evidence that R&D benefits not only rich economies, but may also yield substantial benefits for poor economies. Buttressing a point made above, poor economies may especially benefit from development expenditures that facilitate the absorption of knowledge from abroad (see box 3.4). Although potential returns to R&D in poor countries are high, the levels of R&D in these economies tend to be held back by macroeconomic instability, underdeveloped financial systems, weak intellectual property rights, and low-quality public research institutions.

R&D by Sector of Performance

The business sector in East Asia plays an unusually big role in performing R&D.[22] The median share of national R&D undertaken by the business sector among the main East Asian economies is a little over 60 percent (see table 3.5). That is about

---

■ BOX 3.4 **Foreign Technology and Domestic Innovation May Support Development**

Development experience suggests that domestic knowledge creation and the absorption of knowledge from abroad provide essential support for each other in many ways and in countries at all levels of per capita income, though the balance between the two varies.

On the one hand, it is clear that knowledge absorption from abroad needs a strong domestic technical capacity that is able to adapt and adjust foreign knowledge so as to make it usable and useful under local circumstances. Problems arise because much knowledge cannot be codified, but is tacit; it requires costly face-to-face interactions and learning processes to master. On the other hand, domestic R&D and innovation in nearly all countries would be inconceivable if they were not able to stand on the shoulders of the enormous stock of accumulated scientific and technical knowledge worldwide that they are able to access through spillovers or technology transfers. Openness and close interaction with international scientific, technical, and research communities (firms, universities, and so on) remain fundamental.

Cohen and Levinthal (1989) point out that R&D has two faces: innovation and learning. R&D not only generates new knowledge, but also enhances a firm's ability to assimilate and exploit existing knowledge. For example, developing-country firms are more likely to benefit from FDI spillovers if they conduct R&D themselves. Similarly, being selected as an OEM supplier in a global production chain is increasingly becoming more likely if the developing-country firm already possesses significant in-house design, engineering, and other technical capabilities. The quality of the broader educational and labor force training systems becomes important, as do high-quality national and international telecommunications systems for both the knowledge creation and the knowledge absorption facets of innovation. Telecommunications systems are an important channel for the flow of disembodied knowledge. Elsewhere below, we note evidence that the role of these systems in facilitating knowledge flows may be at least as great as that of trade and FDI. The rapid growth of crossborder intraregional telecommunications flows in recent years suggests that the countries of the region are becoming more integrated through not only trade and financial flows, but also flows of information and ideas.

■ TABLE 3.5 **R&D by Sector of Performance and Funding**

Region or country	Sector of performance			Sector of funding		
	Business	Government	Higher education	Business	Government	Higher education
East Asia	62.2	21.7	14.4	54.3	35.2	2.3
NIEs	63.0	11.7	18.8	58.7	35.9	1.7
Hong Kong, China	33.2	3.1	63.6	35.3	62.8	0.2
Korea, Rep. of	76.1	12.6	10.1	74.0	23.9	1.7
Singapore	63.8	10.9	25.4	54.3	36.6	2.3
Taiwan, China	62.2	24.8	12.3	63.1	35.2	0.0
Southeast Asia	51.3	22.1	15.7	46.6	35.4	6.2
Indonesia	14.3	81.1	4.6	14.7	84.5	0.2
Malaysia	65.3	20.3	14.4	51.5	32.1	4.9
Philippines	58.6	21.7	17.0	59.7	24.6	7.5
Thailand	43.9	22.5	31.0	41.8	38.6	15.1
China	62.4	27.1	10.5	60.1	29.9	. .
Developed (21)	62.9	13.3	27.0	49.2	33.6	2.1
Japan	75.0	9.3	13.7	74.5	17.7	6.3
United States	70.1	12.2	13.6	63.7	31.0	. .
Latin America (11)	29.0	27.2	32.7	32.9	37.3	27.4
Emerging Europe (9)	42.7	29.8	20.1	38.3	54.2	0.5

Source: UNESCO 2006.
Note: The table covers 2002–05 or latest available year and shows medians for regions and subregions.
. . = negligible. The number of countries involved is shown in parentheses.

the same as the median for developed economies, but higher than the share for Latin America (around 30 percent) or emerging Europe (a little over 40 percent). Figure 3.8 indicates that the share of the business sector in R&D generally rises with per capita income. However, several East Asian economies—China, Korea, Malaysia, and the Philippines—are outliers in this regard, showing much higher shares of business R&D than would be expected from the simple cross-country relationship with per capita GDP. Hong Kong (China) is an outlier in the other direction: not only is overall R&D intensity low for an economy at its level of per capita income, but the proportions of R&D performed by the business and government sectors are also low, with the bulk of R&D occurring in institutions of higher education.

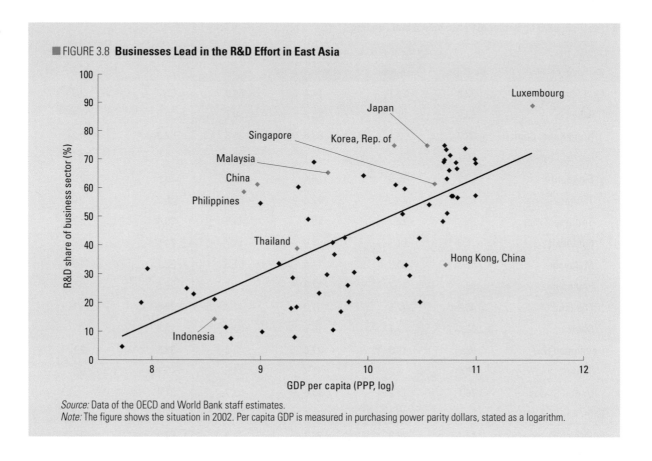

■ FIGURE 3.8 **Businesses Lead in the R&D Effort in East Asia**

Source: Data of the OECD and World Bank staff estimates.
Note: The figure shows the situation in 2002. Per capita GDP is measured in purchasing power parity dollars, stated as a logarithm.

Table 3.5 indicates that, for the East Asia region overall, the median proportion of R&D performed by government—about 22 percent—is much higher than the corresponding figure among developed economies, while the proportion performed by institutions of higher education is lower. This points to a need to strengthen the role of research in East Asian universities, particularly among the NIEs.

R&D by Sector of Funding

Table 3.5 shows that the median share of government funding for R&D in East Asia is about one-third, roughly the same as the share among developed economies. In most cases, the proportion of R&D funded by the business sector is close to the proportion of R&D carried out by business. Two exceptions are Malaysia and Singapore, where the proportion of R&D performed by business is significantly higher than the proportion of R&D financed by business, indicating significant levels of funding support by government for R&D performed in the business sector. Table 3.5 does not include tax incentives for business R&D, a widely used policy instrument.

Does one type of R&D contribute more to growth than another? Most of the work on this question relates to developed economies, but it is informative generally. Guellec and Van Pottelsberghe de la Potterie (2004) look at the long-term impact of business sector R&D, public R&D (defined to include R&D performed by universities), and R&D performed in the outside world on total factor productivity growth in 16 OECD economies. The authors introduced R&D in the outside world to capture the effect of international technology spillovers and transfers. Over the period 1980–98, they find the elasticity of productivity with respect to the stocks of business and public R&D to be the same. Indeed, they find the return to public R&D to be somewhat higher, though the return to business R&D was trending higher, while that to public R&D was declining. Crucially for developing countries, the stock of foreign R&D appears to have an impact two to three times as large as domestic business or public R&D, underlining the importance of openness and of the capacity to absorb international knowledge.

What conditions might affect how much impact each type of R&D stock has on growth? A key finding of Guellec and Van Pottelsberghe de la Potterie is that a higher current flow of business R&D increases the economy's ability to absorb benefits from the accumulated *stocks* of business, public, and foreign R&D. This suggests that a higher flow of current business R&D by domestic firms increases the ability of these firms to absorb the results of R&D carried out past and present by other domestic firms. Similarly, higher business R&D intensity also appears to enhance the ability of firms to access knowledge created by public R&D, raising the impact of public R&D stocks on productivity. Perhaps of most importance for developing countries, higher business R&D intensity also raises the impact of foreign R&D stocks on growth, suggesting that domestic business R&D is important in making firms more capable of absorbing foreign knowledge. Significantly, foreign R&D appears to benefit small economies more than it does large ones.

Advancing the Global Frontier: Patenting in East Asia

Just as R&D expenditures provide a partial measure of the resources an economy devotes to innovation, so do patents and patent citations supply a valuable, though partial, view of an economy's innovation outputs. This view is partial because—at least in theory—patents focus only on those innovations that advance the frontier of global knowledge. A patent gives an inventor a temporary legal monopoly over the exploitation of his invention; it is a device to address some of the problems deriving from the nonexcludability or nonappropriability characteristics of knowledge. To confer this temporary monopoly (in itself a costly economic distortion), an invention must typically satisfy requirements of novelty and nonobviousness, which require that innovations represent a substantial advance over existing knowledge.[23]

Most innovation in developing countries, however, involves the adoption and adaptation of existing knowledge that is mostly derived from abroad. Nevertheless, patentable innovations that, in principle, advance the frontier of global knowledge are growing in importance in East Asia, where a number of economies now generate these kinds of frontier innovations at around the same rate as the advanced economies. This section looks first at patenting activity in East Asia, drawing (in common with many studies in this area) on the database of patents granted by the United States Patent and Trademark Office (USPTO).[24] It then examines at evidence on the factors determining patenting, the distribution of patenting across technology fields, and the quality of patenting in East Asia. Finally, we use patent citations to study flows of knowledge within East Asia and between East Asia and the rest of the world.

Patenting in East Asia

As table 3.6 indicates, the average annual number of patents granted to East Asian economies was at 12,108 per year in 2000–04, more than five times the number a decade earlier, in 1990–94. Over the same period, the number of patents registered by selected Latin American countries rose from 173 to 368. Table 3.6 also shows patents relative to population (patents per 100,000 people). In the early 1990s, the number of patents per 100,000 people in East Asia, at 0.14, was two to three times the number in Latin America and emerging Europe. By 2000–04, East Asian patents per 100,000 had risen to 0.72, six to nine times the levels in the other two regions. The vast majority of patents in the region are generated by the NIEs, particularly Taiwan (China) and Korea, which, by 2004, had become the 4th and 5th biggest recipients of USPTO patents in the world, after the United States, Japan, and Germany.

As with R&D, there is also wide variation in patenting across East Asia. At the head of the league, Taiwan (China) now generates around 30 patents per 100,000 population, about as many as Japan and the United States, the best performers among the developed economies. Another group including Hong Kong (China),

■ TABLE 3.6 **Patents Granted by the USPTO**
annual averages

Region or country	Number of patents		Patents per 100,000 population		
	1990–94	2000–04	1990–94	2000–04	% change
East Asia (9)	2,239	12,108	0.14	0.72	17.6
NIEs	2,159	11,601	2.93	14.74	17.5
Hong Kong, China	184	616	3.15	9.32	11.4
Korea, Rep. of	633	4,009	1.44	8.67	19.7
Singapore	36	382	1.09	9.87	24.6
Taiwan, China	1,307	6,593	6.30	30.17	17.0
Southeast Asia	31	140	0.01	0.04	15.3
Indonesia	6	15	0.00	0.01	8.8
Malaysia	13	64	0.07	0.28	15.3
Philippines	6	18	0.01	0.02	10.4
Thailand	6	43	0.01	0.07	20.9
China	48	368	0.00	0.03	22.9
World	107,361	182,523	1.98	2.95	4.1
Developed (21)	104,170	168,017	12.88	19.58	4.3
Japan	22,647	35,687	18.23	28.54	4.6
United States	59,024	97,104	23.00	33.56	3.9
Developing					
Latin America (11)	173	368	0.04	0.08	6.3
Emerging Europe (9)	205	348	0.07	0.12	5.6

Source: Data of the USPTO.
Note: The number of countries involved is shown in parentheses.

Korea, and Singapore generate around 8–10 patents per 100,000 per year, similar to the performance of the developed OECD countries in the mid-1980s, although only about half the average level in the OECD today. Farther down the scale, Malaysia generates 0.2–0.3 patents per 100,000, similar to Korea in the mid-1980s. Finally, countries such as China, Indonesia, the Philippines, and Thailand bring up the rear with patents per 100,000 in the 0.01–0.07 range, although patenting in China is rising rapidly from a low base. Hu and Jefferson (2005) suggest several reasons for the acceleration in Chinese patenting: (1) the acceleration in China's R&D spending (noted above); (2) the strengthening of

China's patent law in 1992 and 2000; (3) the vast influx of FDI to China, which has greatly increased the market value of intellectual property for foreign and domestic firms; (4) the rapid relative growth in complex industrial sectors, such as electronics and machinery, that involve many separately patentable subproducts and processes; and (5) the acceleration in enterprise reform since the mid-1990s, which has greatly strengthened private property rights with respect to state-owned enterprises.

Figures 3.9 and 3.10 plot patents per 100,000 population versus per capita income (in purchasing power parity terms) using an annual panel data set over the period 1977–2004. (The sample is shown in two figures to permit the display of greater detail at different scales.) As with R&D intensity, patents per 100,000 population tend to rise more than proportionately relative to per capita income, seven to eight times more in this case. Thus, for example, patents per 100,000 population in Singapore are 30 times the corresponding figure for Malaysia, even though

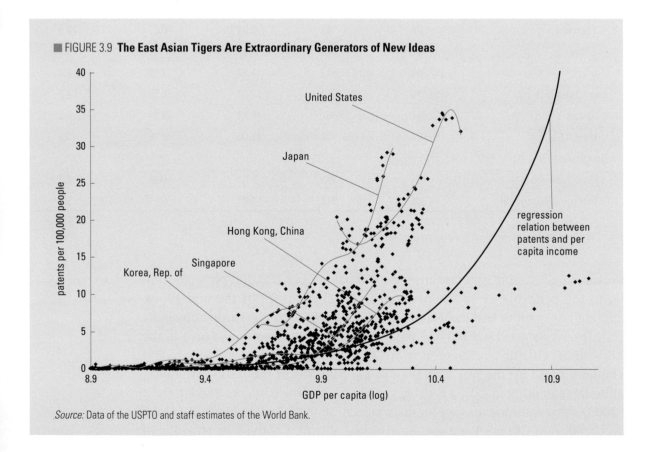

■ FIGURE 3.9 **The East Asian Tigers Are Extraordinary Generators of New Ideas**

Source: Data of the USPTO and staff estimates of the World Bank.

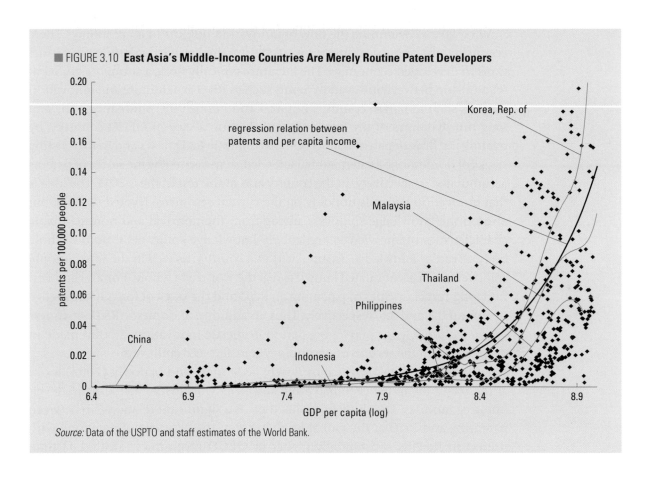

■ FIGURE 3.10 **East Asia's Middle-Income Countries Are Merely Routine Patent Developers**

Source: Data of the USPTO and staff estimates of the World Bank.

Singapore's per capita income (in purchasing power parity terms) is only about three times higher than Malaysia's. The figures pick out the trajectories of patents and income for individual countries over time. Figure 3.9 shows that East Asian NIEs such as Korea and Singapore have generated many more patents per 100,000 population than predicted by the income levels alone, much as the R&D levels in these economies are also much higher than predicted by income. The same is true of Japan and the United States. Interestingly, in recent years patenting in Hong Kong (China) has also exceeded predicted levels, even though R&D there is much lower than the predicted levels. Figure 3.10 shows that China and Malaysia have generally innovated at around the levels predicted by income, although, as noted, China's patenting in recent years has accelerated to levels greater than predicted by income. Indonesia, the Philippines, and Thailand, on the other hand, have performed below the predicted levels, in line with their underperformance in R&D.

What factors determine the flow of innovation outputs in an economy? There is considerable empirical literature estimating the knowledge production functions in developed economies. The literature typically finds a strongly significant relationship between innovation inputs such as R&D expenditure and innovation outputs such as patent counts.[25] Bottazzi and Peri (2005) study the short- and long-run dynamics of the knowledge production sector in OECD countries by relating the flow of patent counts both to domestic R&D flows and to the existing stocks of domestic and international knowledge, measured by the stocks of patents accumulated, respectively, in the country and in the rest of the OECD. The idea is that innovation depends not only on the current resources devoted to R&D, but also on the knowledge spillovers arising from the nonrival and nonexcludable characteristics of knowledge, particularly knowledge spillovers from the whole body of earlier knowledge accumulated in a country, as well as the international spillovers from accumulated knowledge in the world as a whole. Bottazzi and Peri find long-run elasticities of patenting on R&D and the stock of foreign knowledge of around 0.8 and 0.6, respectively. Thus, in addition to domestic R&D, openness to foreign knowledge plays a big part in domestic innovation, a point made in detail above in the section on technology transfers and spillovers.

Recent World Bank research by Bosch, Lederman, and Maloney (2005) looks at the relationship between patenting and R&D worldwide, including in developing economies. The study finds that there is a significant relationship between patenting and R&D at the global level, but that the elasticity of patenting with respect to R&D is substantially higher in OECD economies (around 1) than among developing economies. The lower productivity of R&D spending in developing economies appears to be due to weaknesses in the national innovation systems of these countries. In particular, the study finds that R&D productivity has a significant positive relationship with years of education, the quality of academic institutions, the quality of intellectual property rights, and the level of collaboration between research institutions and the private sector, all factors that, on average, are substantially lower among developing countries than among OECD economies. Among these factors, years of education and intellectual property rights appear to have the most significant impact on R&D efficiency.

Which Technologies Is East Asia Innovating?

Is patenting activity in East Asia diversified, or are there particular sectors in which the region tends to concentrate? The USPTO classifies the patents it grants according to around 480 different categories of technology. Figure 3.11 shows adjusted

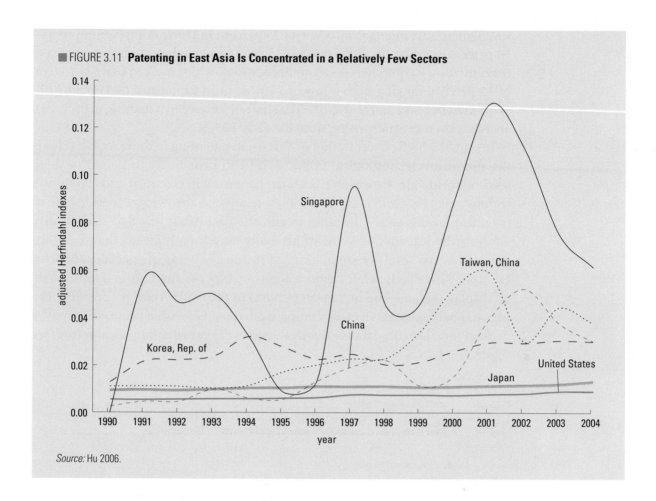

■ FIGURE 3.11 **Patenting in East Asia Is Concentrated in a Relatively Few Sectors**

Source: Hu 2006.

Herfindahl indexes of concentration across these technology classifications. An index level of 1 would indicate complete concentration in only one technology class, while an index of around 0.002 would mean relatively equal distribution across all classes. Figure 3.11 suggests that patenting is considerably more concentrated in East Asian economies than it is in mature developed economies such as Japan and the United States.

In which technologies is East Asian patenting concentrated? Jaffe and Trajtenberg (1999) group the lengthy list of USPTO patent categories into six broad classes: chemicals, computers and communications, drugs and medical technologies, electrical and electronics, mechanical, and all other. A major area of concentration in East Asia is electrical and electronics technologies. The median share of patenting in this technology area among seven East Asian economies in 2002–04 was 38 percent, ranging from a low of 25 percent in Hong Kong (China) to 45–50 percent in Singapore and Taiwan (China). The second most important area of concentration is computers and communications, with a median East Asian share of 15 percent, ranging from a low of 12 percent in China and Malaysia to 25–30 percent in Korea and Singapore. The share of East Asian patenting in these two areas has been generally rising since the early 1990s.

In part, the high concentration of East Asian patenting in these sectors reflects the significant technological opportunity and propensity to patent in these sectors worldwide. However, East Asian patenting in electrical and electronics technologies (in particular) is also high relative to the average world share of patenting in this sector; in other words, the East Asian revealed comparative advantage indexes in this sector are generally substantially greater than 1, reflecting world-class levels of sophistication in specific areas of specialization, for example, Korea in dynamic random access memory technology and liquid crystal display manufacture or Taiwan (China) in the wafer foundry industry, testing, and packaging services. By comparison, most East Asian economies show a distinct revealed comparative disadvantage in the drugs and medical sector (see figure 3.12).

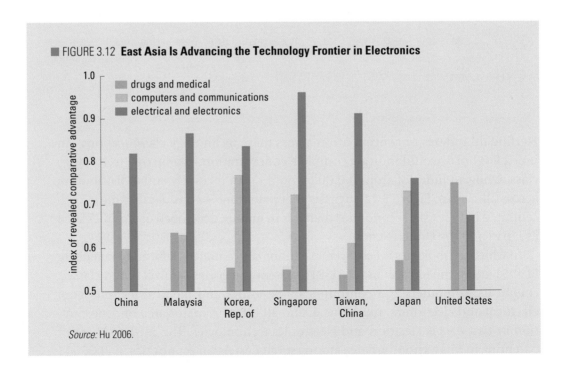

■ FIGURE 3.12 **East Asia Is Advancing the Technology Frontier in Electronics**

Source: Hu 2006.

How Good Is East Asian Patenting?

Although the volume of patenting in economies such as Korea and Taiwan (China) has equaled or exceeded that in most developed economies, is the same also true of the technological quality of their patented innovations? The technological or economic value of patents varies enormously. In fact, the distribution of patent values is highly skewed. A survey of the realized economic value of samples of patents in Germany and the United States, for example, found that the top 10 percent of patents accounted for over 80 percent of the total economic value of all patents (Scherer and Harhoff 2000). Thus, a simple count of patents may not provide an adequate summary of the quality of the underlying innovations.

An especially useful feature of patents for purposes of investigation is the fact that they contain citations to previous patents and the scientific literature, thereby serving to define the "art" to which each patent is making an original contribution. Trajtenberg, Henderson, and Jaffe (1997) have proposed an approach for measuring the quality of patents by constructing indexes of patent generality and patent originality that are based on analyses of patent citations. A patent is deemed to have greater generality and a greater impact if, after assignment of the patent, it is cited more frequently within a wider range of patent technology classifications. Similarly, a patent is deemed more basic or original if it cites a wide range of patent technology classifications.

In a comparison of the quality of patents in the East Asian economies, Japan, and the United States, U.S. patents generally show higher generality and originality indexes across all technology fields. Figures 3.13 and 3.14 show these indexes for Japan, Korea, and Taiwan (China) as a ratio of the index for the United States.[26] Japanese patents generally achieve quality ratings that are 80 to 90 percent or more of the U.S. quality ratings. Korea is close to Japan in most technology areas and even matches or exceeds it in some. Taiwan (China) tends to achieve somewhat lower generality and originality scores than Korea, but is still not too far from Japanese levels, generally scoring at 70–80 percent of U.S. levels.

Knowledge Flows To, From, and Within East Asia: Patent Citations

Knowledge flows from abroad also play a crucial role in domestic R&D and innovation, which would be inconceivable in most economies without access to the accumulated body of knowledge throughout the world. Patent citations provide a unique window into the flows of knowledge between the inventors, firms, and economies upon which the process of innovation draws. This is possible because

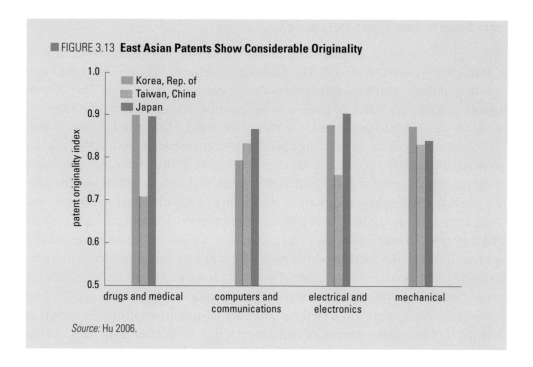

FIGURE 3.13 East Asian Patents Show Considerable Originality

Source: Hu 2006.

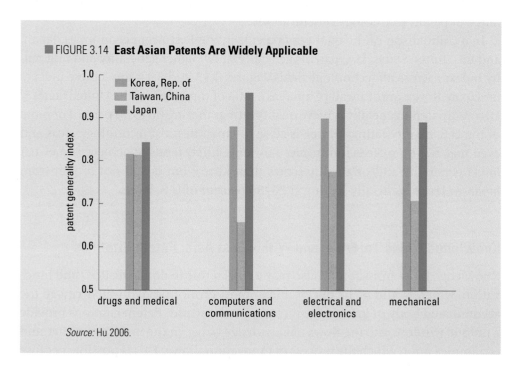

FIGURE 3.14 East Asian Patents Are Widely Applicable

Source: Hu 2006.

patents are required by law to provide citations to previous patents and the scientific literature on which they reside, thereby serving to define the "art" covering the patent.

Figure 3.15 offers an overview of patent citations in seven East Asian economies, showing the average share of various foreign economies as sources for East Asian patent citations. The United States is by far the largest source of citations for East Asian innovators, providing close to 60 percent of the total. This proportion rose slightly between 1992–94 and 2002–04. Japan is the second largest source of citations for East Asia, contributing close to 20 percent, on average. Korea is an interesting exception to this general pattern; its reliance on U.S. citations is substantially lower than the reliance of other East Asian economies, around 45 percent, while its reliance on Japanese knowledge is greater, around 33 percent. The share of G-5 economies, defined here as comprising Canada, France, Germany, Italy, and the United Kingdom, is lower, less than 10 percent, having fallen over the last decade. Perhaps most interesting, the share of citations made by East Asian economies to patents of other East Asian economies, while still low, is rising rapidly; it has picked up from an average 1.7 percent of all citations in 1992–94 to

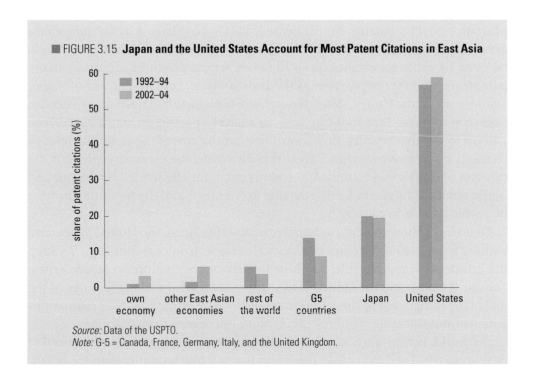

■ FIGURE 3.15 **Japan and the United States Account for Most Patent Citations in East Asia**

Source: Data of the USPTO.
Note: G-5 = Canada, France, Germany, Italy, and the United Kingdom.

5.9 percent in 2002–04. Most of these intra–East Asian patent citations refer to patents held by Korea and Taiwan (China), the two largest innovators in the region. Thus, much as intraregional flows of trade and foreign investment have been rising in relative importance in recent years, so have intraregional knowledge flows, although the size of the intraregional share is much lower at present than the flows for trade and investment. In addition, as figure 3.15 indicates, the share of citations by inventors in one East Asian economy to other patents in the same economy (referred to as compatriot citations) is also rising, reaching 3.3 percent, on average, in 2002–04.

Figure 3.16 supplies a closer look at the rise of intraregional and compatriot knowledge flows for individual East Asian economies. The figure indicates that the share of citations to other East Asian economies (typically to patents of Korea and Taiwan [China]) is highest—around 7–8 percent—in China, Hong Kong (China), Malaysia, and Singapore. On the other hand, the share of own or compatriot patents is highest in Korea (around 6 percent) and Taiwan (China), where it is over 10 percent.

The raw citation shares discussed in the preceding paragraphs provide useful information on the gross or absolute flows of knowledge among economies, but say little about the *intensity* of the various knowledge relationships. For example, it is not too surprising that, in East Asian economies, there should be large shares of citations to U.S. patents, simply because the United States is by far the greatest generator of patents, providing the largest pool of patents that may potentially be cited by other economies. Even in Japan, which produces almost as many patents per 100,000 population as the United States, over 40 percent of patent citations are to the United States. Researchers have therefore developed a *citation frequency* measure that looks at how intensively patents in one country cite patents in another country after controlling for the size of the potential pool of citations in the two countries.[27] In arithmetic terms, the measure represents the number of citations in country A to patents in country B, divided by the product of the potential number of citing patents in country A and the potential number of citable patents in country B.

Figure 3.17 shows patent citation frequencies for Japan, the United States, and various East Asian economies in electrical and electronics technology. To keep the information manageable, we show frequencies of citations to Japan, Korea, Taiwan (China), and the United States. There are several striking features of the data. One is that each of these four main innovating economies cites compatriot patents from the same economy much more intensively than patents in the rest of the world. For instance, after controlling for the fact that the potential pool of citable electrical and electronics patents in Korea is much smaller than the poten-

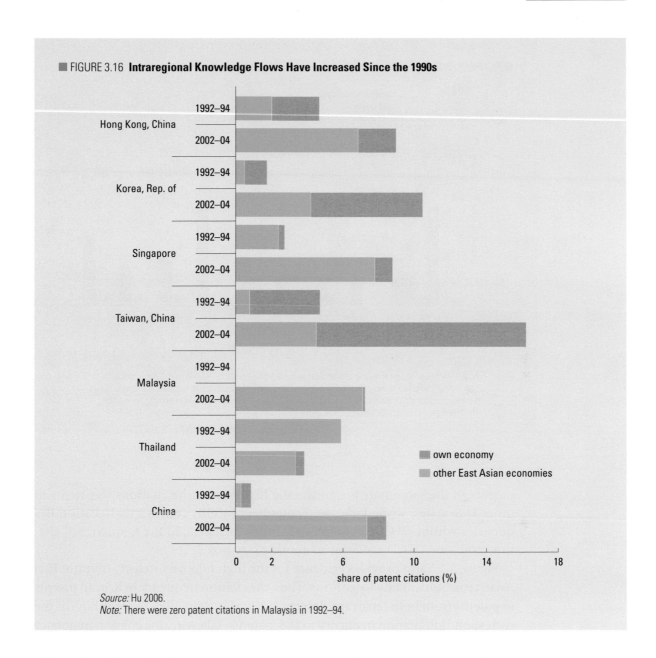

■ FIGURE 3.16 **Intraregional Knowledge Flows Have Increased Since the 1990s**

share of patent citations (%)

own economy
other East Asian economies

Source: Hu 2006.
Note: There were zero patent citations in Malaysia in 1992–94.

tial pool in the United States, Korean patents cite other Korean patents almost five times as intensively as they cite U.S. patents. This finding by Hu (2006) is consistent with earlier findings of *geographical* matters for knowledge spillovers. Thus, Jaffe, Trajtenberg, and Henderson (1993) have found that, even within the United States, the frequency of citation in a patent in one U.S. state to other

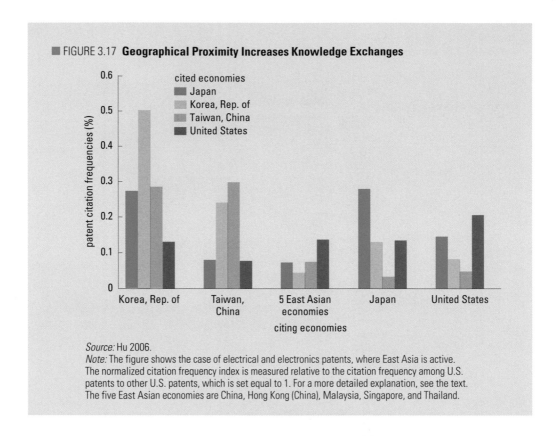

■ FIGURE 3.17 **Geographical Proximity Increases Knowledge Exchanges**

Source: Hu 2006.
Note: The figure shows the case of electrical and electronics patents, where East Asia is active. The normalized citation frequency index is measured relative to the citation frequency among U.S. patents to other U.S. patents, which is set equal to 1. For a more detailed explanation, see the text. The five East Asian economies are China, Hong Kong (China), Malaysia, Singapore, and Thailand.

patents in the same state is significantly higher than the citations to patents in other U.S. states, while Jaffe and Trajtenberg (1998) confirm that citation frequencies within OECD economies are much greater than the frequency of citation from one OECD economy to another (see box 3.5).

Figure 3.17 also provides evidence for the high relative intensity of intra–East Asian crossborder knowledge flows. Thus, the citation frequency in Korean patents to patents from both Japan and Taiwan (China) is more than twice as high as the corresponding citation frequency to U.S. patents. Likewise, the citation frequency in patents in Taiwan (China) is almost as high to Korean patents as to compatriot patents in Taiwan (China), while the citation frequency of patents in Japan is almost as high to patents in Korea as to U.S. patents. These trends confirm the growing regional dimension in East Asian knowledge flows.

Hu (2006) estimates a more rigorous model for the citation frequency data for East Asian economies using the double exponential model of knowledge diffu-

■ BOX 3.5 **Geography and Knowledge Spillovers**

The main reason for the geographical localization of knowledge spillovers is thought to be the *tacitness* of much knowledge. Many types of information, for example, the price of a commodity, may be easily codified and cheaply transmitted across the world by electronic means. Complex scientific and technical knowledge, however, often may not be readily codified or fully captured in a manual or computer file. The accurate and thorough communication of this knowledge often requires face-to-face interaction.

Tacitness and geographical localization provide an important economic advantage to cities and industrial clusters: they facilitate face-to-face interactions and knowledge spillovers. At the national level, they offer more evidence for the value of domestic R&D and innovation efforts: the absorption of knowledge spillovers by local residents is easier from local innovations than it is from foreign innovations.

There is also useful information for policy makers in a study finding that the geographical localization of knowledge spillovers seems to be particularly important for new knowledge and in the early stages of a new industry's life cycle. Jaffe, Trajtenberg, and Henderson (1993) find that the advantage of geographical localization within U.S. states fades gradually. Audretsch and Feldman (1996) find that geographical clustering is greatest in industries with high R&D intensity and high employment of skilled labor, as well as in industries at an early stage of the life cycle, when knowledge about the industry is still located mainly in the minds of staff and workers rather than codified in manuals and protocols.

sion introduced by Caballero and Jaffe (1993). The idea is to derive more refined estimates of citation frequencies among countries after taking into account such factors as the technological proximity between each pair of economies,[28] time lags between citing and cited patents, obsolescence over time, and fixed effects for different technology classes. Table 3.7 shows these estimates, normalized relative to the citation frequency among U.S. patents to other U.S. patents, which is set equal to 1. The results for Japan, Korea, Taiwan (China), and the United States are substantively similar to those for the raw citation frequencies discussed earlier. In the case of other East Asian economies, Singapore shows an exceptionally high citation frequency to patents in Taiwan (China) and also Korea, both of which significantly exceed (also high) citation frequencies to patents in Japan and the United States. Citation frequencies to Korea and Taiwan (China) in China and Malaysia also exceed those to Japan and the United States.

Policy Considerations

This section discusses the policies and institutions that may help foster domestic innovation, as well as the absorption of knowledge from abroad, and briefly reviews differences in the quality of these policies and institutions across East

■ TABLE 3.7 **Citation Frequencies: Estimated Country-Pair Fixed Effects**

Citing economies	Cited economies			
	Japan	Korea, Rep. of	Taiwan, China	United States
China	0.31	0.44	0.41	0.36
Hong Kong, China	0.41	0.42	0.40	0.45
Japan	0.80	0.44	0.23	0.46
Korea, Rep. of	0.70	1.16	0.69	0.46
Malaysia	0.32	0.53	0.57	0.44
Singapore	0.60	0.93	1.63	0.95
Taiwan, China	0.25	0.71	0.83	0.26
Thailand	0.33	0.27	0.10	0.66
United States	0.57	0.38	0.29	1.00

Source: Hu 2006.
Note: The table shows an index whereby U.S. patent citations to U.S. patents = 1.

Asian economies. These factors are grouped under three main heads: the overall business environment for innovation, human capital development, and direct government support for innovation activities.

The Business Environment for Innovation

Given that R&D and other innovation activities by firms are a form of capital investment, it is not surprising that they are influenced by many of the same factors—macroeconomic stability, cost of capital, openness, competition, intellectual property rights regimes, and infrastructure—that affect the overall business investment.

Macroeconomic stability. As is well known, persistent macroeconomic instability is among the factors most adverse to private investment and is also found to have a clear adverse impact on R&D intensity. In one of the few studies of R&D in both developing and developed countries, Lederman and Maloney (2003) find that macroeconomic volatility as measured by the standard deviation of per capita GDP growth has a significant negative relation with R&D intensity. In their study of OECD countries, Jaumotte and Pain (2005a) find that low, stable inflation has a positive influence on the rate of growth of R&D stocks.

Cost of capital and financial development. A second major set of factors in the broad macroeconomic and business environment relates to the cost of capital, the availability of credit, and the level of development of a financial system. Jaumotte and Pain (2005a) find that a measure of the user cost of capital (taking account of the real interest rate, depreciation, and tax allowances) has a significant negative relation with the growth of R&D stocks in OECD countries, while Lederman and Maloney (2003) obtain a similar result for a real interest rate measure with respect to R&D intensity in their broader set of countries. In addition to the cost of capital, the quantity of credit and financial sector depth are also discovered to be important influences on innovation. A well-developed financial sector and capital market help meet the various financing needs of more or less risky short- and long-term innovation projects being undertaken by firms. As noted in the section on technology transfers and spillovers, Ayyagari, Demirgüç-Kunt, and Maksimovic (2006) find that the availability of financing from sources external to the firm shows a strong association with broader measures of firm innovation in developing countries. Jaumotte and Pain (2005a) arrive at similar conclusions for growth in R&D stocks in OECD countries with respect to corporate profits (internal finance for firms), credit to the private sector from financial institutions, and stock market capitalization. Table 3.8 uses credit to the private sector as a rough indicator of financial sector development and shows that financial depth is significantly lower in various middle-income East Asian economies than in the NIEs.

Aghion, Angeletos, et al. (2005) emphasize that credit availability and financial development are particularly important when firms are in a volatile macroeconomic environment. When firms face significant credit constraints, they will be less able to overcome short-term liquidity pressures during economic downturns and so will be less willing to undertake long-term R&D investments. The availability of long-term credit allows firms to look beyond cyclical volatility and liquidity pressures to pursue longer-term innovation objectives. Looking at panel data for OECD countries, the authors find that the interaction term between financial development and volatility has a significantly positive impact on the ratio of R&D to total investment spending. In related work, Aghion, Bacchetta, et al. 2006 demonstrate how financial development may condition the impact of exchange rate volatility on long-run productivity growth; in countries with low financial development, exchange rate volatility has a significant negative impact on productivity growth, while, in financially developed countries, the impact is insignificant.

Openness. The discussion above of imports as a channel for technology transfer suggests that excessively restrictive trade policies may prove a significant barrier to

■ TABLE 3.8 **National Innovation Systems and the Business Environment: Selected Variables**

Region or country	1. Credit market depth, 2000–04[a]	2. Starting a business, days	3. Average years of schooling, 2000	4. Researchers per million population, 2003	5. Quality of scientific research institutions[b]	6. University-industry research collaboration[b]	7. Intellectual property protection[b]	8. Phone subscribers, 2003[c]
East Asia (9)	102	40	7.6	1,375	4.5	4.1	4.3	878
NIEs	125	22	9.2	3,165	5.2	4.7	5.1	1,475
Hong Kong, China	153	11	9.5	1,564	4.9	4.1	5.0	1,640
Korea, Rep. of	98	22	10.5	3,187	5.1	4.8	4.5	1,240
Singapore	115	6	8.1	4,745	5.5	5.0	6.1	1,284
Taiwan, China	135	48	8.5	..	5.2	4.9	4.9	1,735
Southeast Asia	75	66	6.6	210	4.1	3.6	3.8	398
Indonesia	20	151	4.7	207	3.9	3.4	3.2	127
Malaysia	141	30	7.9	299	5.0	4.7	5.1	642
Philippines	38	48	7.6	48	3.3	2.7	2.8	322
Thailand	102	33	6.1	287	4.0	3.6	4.1	499
China	118	48	5.7	663	3.8	3.9	3.2	413
High income (21)	112	20	9.5	3,616	5.1	4.4	5.5	1,392
Japan	100	31	9.7	5,287	5.6	4.6	5.3	1,151
United States	249	5	12.3	4,484	6.4	5.7	6.4	1,175
Latin America (11)	36	67	6.7	300	3.5	3.0	3.1	409
Emerging Europe (9)	29	30	8.7	1,503	4.0	3.1	3.3	850

Sources: 1 and 8: World Development Indicators Database, World Bank, http://www.worldbank.org/data/datapubs/datapubs.html. 2: Doing Business Database, World Bank and International Finance Corporation, http://www.doingbusiness.org/. 3: Barro and Lee 2000. 4: UNESCO 2006. 5, 6, and 7: López-Claros, Porter, and Schwab 2005.

.. = negligible.

a. Credit to the private sector as a % of GDP.

b. This is an index ranging from 1 (weakest) to 7 (strongest).

c. Fixed line and mobile subscribers per 1,000 population. All regional data are simple averages.

international technology transfer. In addition, preferential trading arrangements that create a bias against trade with R&D–rich developed economies will tend to choke off knowledge transfers and spillovers from those economies, which (following the results of Schiff, Wang, and Olarreaga 2002) may be especially detrimental to the development of R&D–intensive industries. Hoekman, Maskus, and Saggi (2005) point out that these arguments for open trade policies are not entirely unconditional, however. If the development of a national industry creates localized knowledge spillovers in the country, there may be a rationale for intervention to foster such development. This was one of the justifications for protectionism and import-substitution-led industrialization strategies in many developing countries in the 1950s and 1960s. Nevertheless, trade restrictions are unlikely to be the most effective or most efficient way of fostering domestic R&D, industrial development, or spillovers, since they create new distortions, reward domestic firms whether they innovate or not, and have a high cost, not least by restricting international knowledge inflows. More direct policies to subsidize domestic R&D, improve the investment climate, and strengthen education are likely to be superior policy instruments.

Competition. As with trade openness, the question whether greater competition in domestic product markets serves to foster innovation does not have an entirely simple answer. A survey of evidence for OECD countries by Ahn (2002) comes to the agnostic conclusion that "empirical evidence does not support the view that market concentration is an independent and significant determinant of innovative behavior and performance" (p. 16). Other studies (for example, Nickell 1996 and Blundell, Griffith, and van Reenen 1999) have pointed to a positive correlation between product market competition and innovation. As usual, the evidence is much thinner for developing economies, but Ayyagari, Demirgüç-Kunt, and Maksimovic (2006) also find a positive relation between several competition indicators and their measure of firm dynamism in low- and middle-income economies (which, as noted above, encompasses the introduction of both new technology and new products).

Aghion, Bloom, et al. (2005) observe that, in theory, greater product market competition between incumbent firms may have two different effects, one discouraging innovation, the other promoting it. Particularly in industries where the existing competition is low and firms have similar levels of technological capability, more competition may promote innovation by giving the innovating firm a competitive advantage over other firms in the industry. On the other hand, in industries where there is already high product market competition and one firm has a large technological lead over others, an increase in competition may discourage innovation by lagging firms because it reduces the rewards for trying to catch up with the leader. The study finds strong evidence for such an inverted-U curve in multi-industry panel data on firms in the United Kingdom: innovation rises as product market competition increases, but, for a minority of firms and industries at already high levels of competition, additional intense competition tends to discourage innovation. In related work, Aghion, Blundell, et al. (2006) argue that the entry of technologically advanced firms into an industry may have a dual-edged effect on innovation among incumbent firms, tending to stimulate innovation when incumbent firms are close to the global technology frontier, but discouraging it when incumbent firms are technological laggards and far from the frontier. They again find evidence for this proposition in multi-industry panel data on firms in the United Kingdom.

Given the limited amount of empirical work available so far, it is probably unwise to draw any strong conclusions for policy in developing countries. A few observations may be ventured, however. First, increased competition has a wide array of potential effects on economic performance other than the impact on innovation. There is a good deal of evidence, for example, of the positive effect of competition on firm efficiency and overall productivity growth.[29] Thus, conclusions about the role of competition policy need to be based on an assessment of all these effects. Second, the balance of the empirical work cited finds a positive association between more competition between incumbent firms and innovation, and, while the study by Aghion, Bloom, et al. (2005) reaches more qualified results, it too suggests that more competition is favorable for innovation if competition is low to start with, that is, when the lack of competition is most likely to be of concern to policy makers.

Turning to new firm entry, the interesting findings by Aghion, Blundell, et al. (2006) for the United Kingdom obviously need to be buttressed by more empirical work across a wider range of countries (including developing countries). Several hypotheses that have relevance for policy emerge from the study and call for more empirical analysis and testing. One hypothesis is that an opening-up to entry by technologically sophisticated competitors may be especially beneficial for innovation through incumbent firms in advanced emerging economies such as Korea, Singapore, and Taiwan (China), where many key sectors now function close to the global technology frontier. It may also be a relevant policy consideration in rapidly moving middle-income economies that are aspiring to follow in the tracks of the advanced emerging economies.

By the same token, the study suggests the possibility that opening-up to technologically sophisticated firms may have a depressing effect on innovation in economies and sectors that are far from the global technology frontier. But a number of other considerations need to be kept in mind in drawing possible policy conclusions from this finding. First, new firm entry may have other, offsetting effects on economic performance, particularly gains in the overall productivity of the economy and in consumer welfare due to the replacement of low-productivity firms by high-productivity firms and the reallocation of resources to more productive uses. Bartelsman, Haltiwanger, and Scarpetta (2004) note that the process of creative destruction—the entry of new firms and the exit of less efficient ones—is important for productivity growth in both developed and developing countries. They find that it contributes from 20 to 50 percent of total labor productivity growth according to a large firm-level panel data set covering 10 developed and 14 developing economies. In contrast to Aghion, Blundell, et al. (2006), they also find a positive relation between the pace of creative destruction (that is, of net entry) and productivity growth in already existing (incumbent) firms. They interpret these results as implying that the increased contestability of markets introduced by new entrants induces incumbent firms to perform more efficiently. A second consideration is that new entry by technologically sophisticated firms is also likely to facilitate vertical technology transfers to local suppliers in upstream sectors. (Evidence for this is presented in the review of FDI elsewhere.) This discussion suggests that, even in less well developed economies, blocking off entry by sophisticated foreign firms is unlikely to be the most efficient way of promoting technological development and productivity growth, especially when looked at from an economy-wide perspective. As with trade, more direct fiscal measures or other measures may provide superior instruments for fostering domestic R&D and innovation. We return to such instruments below in this section.

The intellectual property rights regime. Another factor affecting innovation is the quality of the intellectual property rights regime (for example, patent law). Theoretically, the direction of this effect is ambiguous. On the one hand, a weak regime hampers firms in the appropriation of the returns on their investments in R&D and thus acts as a disincentive to undertaking the investments in the first place. On the other hand, intellectual property rights also create an economic distortion by granting a temporary monopoly to innovators. This may make it more difficult for other firms to access the knowledge they need for their own innovation activities. Intellectual property rights may also dampen innovation if they reduce competition in product markets and if less competition tends to reduce innovation.

Which of these effects prevails is an empirical question. Table 3.8 shows that the quality of the intellectual property rights regime is rated significantly weaker in China and several Southeast Asian economies than it is in the NIEs. Lederman and Maloney (2003) find that stronger rights regimes have a highly significant positive impact on R&D intensity in their sample of developing and developed economies, while Bosch, Lederman, and Maloney (2005) find that the quality of the rights regime has a significant positive impact on the productivity of R&D as measured by patents per dollar of R&D. For OECD countries, Jaumotte and Pain (2005a) find, however, that intellectual property rights have little discernible influence on the growth of R&D stocks, although they do influence the flow of patenting. The authors interpret these results to suggest that, in OECD countries, intellectual property rights influence the propensity to patent within the underlying stream of innovations, but not the flow itself. The lack of influence on R&D in the OECD may reflect the fact that there is much less variation in the quality of the rights regimes across OECD countries than in the world as a whole. The coefficient of variation in the measure of the rights regimes shown for high-income countries in Table 3.8 is only one-third as large as it is for the whole sample of developed and developing countries.

Recent research suggests that rights regimes may influence not only indigenous R&D and innovation, but also the scope of interactions between countries and the outside world, which, as this chapter has stressed, are a primary means of absorbing new knowledge in most developing countries through trade, FDI, the licensing of foreign technologies, or other means. In a survey of this research, Fink and Maskus (2005) note that the potential impact of intellectual property rights on inward technology transfers is also theoretically ambiguous: stronger rights will improve the incentives for a foreign rights-holder to enter the domestic market, but will also increase the market power of that rights-holder, which may lead to restricted sales. Foreign technologies will become more available in the domestic market, but the ability of domestic firms to imitate these technologies is more constrained. The net effect on the volume of international transactions and on domestic productivity growth is an empirical question, the answer to which may differ across countries and sectors.

Fink and Maskus (2005) note a number of recent studies that find a significant positive link between stronger intellectual property rights and international trade. Stronger patent rights in large middle-income economies appear to have the most significant influence on the propensity of multinational companies to export to those economies, given the greater threat of imitation and reverse engineering. The evidence is less conclusive on the impact of intellectual property rights on FDI. However, there is a certain amount of evidence that intellectual property rights are a significant consideration among multinational companies making location decisions in regard to middle-income countries. There is also some evidence that foreign firms may be more likely to invest in local production and R&D facilities rather than in distribution facilities if there are stronger intellectual property rights. Finally, there is clear-cut evidence that stronger rights have a positive impact on international technology licensing (as measured by licensing royalty payments). This kind of technology transfer is sensitive to the reduction in the cost of making and enforcing licensing contracts that is provided by a stronger rights regime.

Information and communications technology infrastructure. The availability of good-quality information and communications infrastructure plays an important role in fostering innovation both by facilitating the cheap circulation of disembodied knowledge flows across and within national boundaries, as well as by reducing the transaction costs of international trade and foreign investment flows. Rapid rates of advance in the availability of information and communications services in developing countries have been driven forward in part by the liberalization of telecommunications markets and regulatory reform in recent decades. Nevertheless, wide disparities remain in information and communications technology development across East Asia. As Table 3.8 indicates, the number of phone subscribers per 1,000 population (to take one example) averages close to 1,500 in the NIEs, but only around 400 among the Southeast Asian economies and in China. The importance of the information and communications infrastructure for innovation and productivity growth is suggested in Wong (2006). This background study for this volume looks at the impact on productivity and growth of various types of crossborder flows, including trade, FDI, and disembodied knowledge flows, the last proxied by international telephone traffic. Telephone traffic is found to have the most robust positive effect on productivity and income.

Human Capital Development

Education and other forms of human capital development clearly provide a fundamental underpinning for domestic innovation activity and the absorptive (learning) capacity of the economy. Table 3.8 shows that populations in Southeast Asian economies and China possess around three fewer average years of schooling relative to those in the NIEs. Higher education is becoming a critical factor for innovation in the region, but the efforts to improve higher education are not uniform across countries. Figure 3.18 shows that the proportion of adults with higher education tends to rise more than proportionately with income. Some countries, such as Korea, have increased higher-education attainment even more rapidly, while others have lagged.

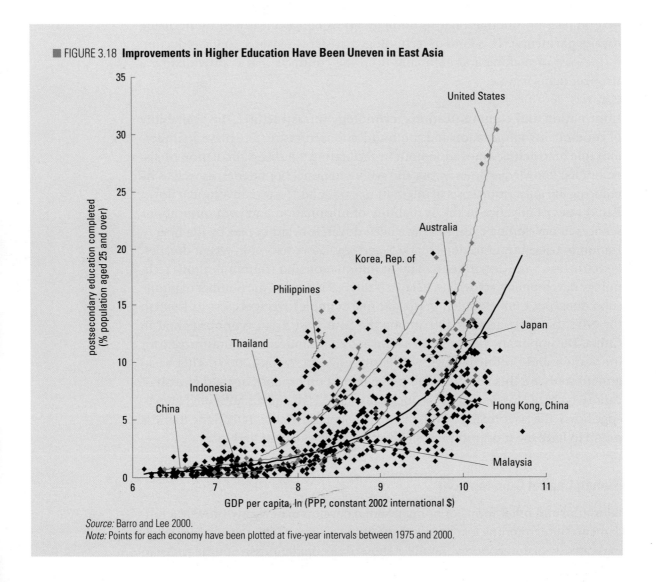

■ FIGURE 3.18 **Improvements in Higher Education Have Been Uneven in East Asia**

Source: Barro and Lee 2000.
Note: Points for each economy have been plotted at five-year intervals between 1975 and 2000.

There are also sharp differences in the quality of education around the region. For example, the four East Asian NIEs achieved the four highest mathematics and science scores among the 45–46 countries and territories participating in the 2003 Trends in International Mathematics and Science Study exercise. On the other hand, the Philippines was among the bottom five countries for both mathematics and science, while Indonesia was among or close to the bottom 10. Similarly, in the 2003 OECD Program for International Student Assessment for mathematics proficiency, Hong Kong (China) and Korea were among the top five in a sample of 40 countries and territories, while Indonesia and Thailand were among the bottom five. There are also wide differences around the region in the extent and quality of tertiary and specialized scientific and technical education, as reflected in the number of researchers per million population shown in Table 3.8. This measure averages over 3,000 in the NIEs and fewer than 10 percent as many, on average, in Southeast Asian economies.

Direct Support for Innovation Activities

So far, this section has mostly covered broad policy areas such as the maintenance of macroeconomic stability, financial sector development, and human capital development, which, while they are expected to promote innovation and technology transfers, are also expected to have other, wider economic and social benefits. This subsection looks briefly at several specific public policies that aim to foster domestic innovation or technology transfer from abroad, typically through targeted fiscal incentives or regulations. The theoretical rationale for direct public interventions of this sort derives from the possibility that they may help offset various types of market failures associated with knowledge, for example, nonexcludability, which makes it difficult for private firms to appropriate all the returns to their R&D investments and which may lead the private sector to fail to undertake adequate innovation activities. The problems of nonexcludability or nonappropriability are likely to be particularly significant in the basic research that provides the foundation for a variety of innovations by many firms or that helps countries gain more access to the global pool of knowledge. Four types of policies are assessed: support for research institutions, incentives for business R&D, fiscal incentives for FDI, and policies to enhance knowledge spillovers.

Support for science and for university and public sector research. As shown in Table 3.5, the public sector in developed countries supplies, on average, about one-third of all R&D funding, amounting to an average 0.6–0.7 percent of GDP, including funding for the basic scientific research undertaken by universities or public sector research laboratories and institutes. In East Asia, public funding for R&D reaches this level of GDP only in a few advanced economies such as Korea, Singapore, and Taiwan (China).

There is a significant body of evidence indicating the positive effect of R&D funded or performed by universities and the public sector on overall productivity and on business R&D. Guellec and van Pottelsberghe de la Potterie (2004) find that the positive impact of university and public R&D stocks on productivity growth in OECD countries is even larger than the impact of business R&D stocks. Jaumotte and Pain (2005b) find that nonbusiness R&D spending has a large and significant impact on growth in business R&D stocks in OECD countries and also offer evidence for two important features of the impact of public and university R&D. First, the impact of public and university R&D is likely to depend on the quality of the links between these sectors and the business R&D sector, which uses the results of more basic research to develop commercially valuable innovations and products. Second, a greater volume of public sector R&D may crowd out business R&D by pushing up the wages of scientific and technical staff. The latter may be a particular concern in developing countries where such specialized skills are in scarce supply. At least in OECD countries, the overall impact of nonbusiness R&D on business R&D remains significantly positive, even after taking crowding-out effects into account.

As regards the evidence on developing countries, Lederman and Maloney (2003) find that the perceived quality of research institutions such as universities and public research institutes has a significant positive impact on overall R&D intensity in developed and developing countries, as does the perceived quality of the interaction between these institutions and the private sector. Bosch, Lederman, and Maloney (2005) find that these two factors also have a significant impact on the productivity of R&D in developed and developing countries. Table 3.8 above shows that there are significant disparities in the quality of scientific and other academic research institutions and the quality of university-industry research collaboration; the NIEs and Malaysia score substantially higher than other Southeast Asian economies and China. To ensure that public research efforts yield good results, policy makers should be concerned about adequate funding and good public-private links, but also see that public funding is allocated among research areas according to transparent, competitive, and merit-based procedures and criteria that strike a proper balance between short-term commercial interests and longer-term needs.

Fiscal subsidies and tax incentives for business R&D. In addition to direct funding of public R&D, many countries also devote significant fiscal resources to subsidies or tax incentives for business R&D. Although, as noted, there is a theoretical rationale for such fiscal measures as a means to counteract market failures related to knowledge, there are also serious informational and incentive problems in implementing such policies, and the limited amount of empirical work has not produced a consensus on the overall effectiveness of these policies.

Among the practical difficulties, two stand out. First, governments are unlikely to possess any special information on which sectors might yield the largest knowledge spillovers from innovation and might therefore merit fiscal incentives. In the face of this severe informational problem, government attempts to pick winners might conceivably lead to outcomes that are worse than those based purely on private decisions about R&D investment that, by definition, remain unconcerned about externalities and market failures.[30] Reviewing research on the effectiveness of preferential industrial policies in Japan, Noland and Pack (2003) conclude that these policies tend to concentrate on declining sectors rather than on industries experiencing rapid technological change or increasing returns and have had no noticeable impact on national or sectoral rates of total factor productivity growth. On reviewing research for Korea, they conclude that the evidence does not support the notion that selective intervention has had a decisive impact on the Korean economy. Outlining principles that should guide the design of a modern or new industrial policy, Rodrik (2004) observes that it should no longer aim to pick winners or sectors; it should be targeted instead at key activities that are likely to be underprovided or underperformed because of specific market failures, for example, through a generalized tax credit that does not discriminate across sectors or through support for the adaptation of foreign technologies to local conditions.

The second major difficulty is that a program of fiscal incentives for innovation may easily become a gateway for corruption and rent seeking. It is thus not clear if the social gains from a fiscal incentives program would offset all the compliance and administrative costs associated with such a program.

Cross-country experience with fiscal incentives for innovation has not been studied well until recently. In a review of the empirical literature, García-Quevado (2004) discovers little consensus on the effectiveness of public R&D subsidies. A number of studies find that such subsidies do have a significant positive impact on business R&D, but that this impact declines after a certain point and even becomes negative, so that subsidies are substituting for private financing sources that would have been used in the absence of the subsidies. Jaumotte and Pain (2005b) find that R&D subsidies have a slightly negative impact on growth in business R&D stocks, evaluated at the mean for a sample of OECD countries. The evidence seems clearer on the effectiveness of R&D tax credits. Bloom, Griffith, and van Reenen (2000) find that changes in R&D tax credits have a large impact on the user cost of capital for R&D and that the long-run elasticity of business R&D with respect to tax incentives may be substantial, on the order of -1. While such analyses suggest that tax incentives are effective in stimulating business R&D, they do not necessarily prove that the incentives would be welfare enhancing overall. A full cost-benefit analysis would also need to account for the alternative uses to which the forgone tax revenues might have been put, the administrative costs of the R&D tax credit system, and the various new distortions the tax scheme might itself introduce.

Fiscal incentives for FDI. This section concludes with a look at the uses and effectiveness of two sets of policies: those to attract FDI to a country and those to enhance the benefits of FDI to a domestic economy. The impact of the policy and institutional environment in host countries on the volume, composition, and benefits of FDI flows has been extensively researched. Recent surveys of this work include Balasubramanyam, Salisu, and Sapsford (2001) and Hanson (2001). A general point is that fundamentals important for encouraging and benefiting from capital investment as such—a market-friendly business climate, macroeconomic stability, political stability, good-quality infrastructure (particularly in communications and transport), a relatively open trade policy regime, and the availability of relatively skilled labor—are also important for FDI.

However, governments around the world also deploy a variety of more well targeted policies to attract FDI, such as tax incentives, import duty exemptions, or land and power subsidies. To the extent that FDI does create positive spillovers (or externalities) for a domestic economy, there is a theoretical economic rationale for such incentives. However, as the preceding discussion indicates, the evidence for horizontal FDI spillovers is mixed, especially in developing economies. There is evidence that domestic firms with good human capital and R&D receive more FDI spillovers and also that foreign firms doing more R&D in host countries tend to generate more spillovers. But this evidence provides a rationale for strengthening education and training and perhaps for more tax incentives for local R&D (whether by local or foreign firms) rather than for subsidizing FDI. Given the stronger evidence for vertical technology transfers between the customers of multinational corporations and developing-country suppliers, it is clear that policies that *discourage* FDI carry a high price tag in forgone technology and, all else being equal, should be avoided. However, this type of vertical technology transfer is internal to supply chain transactions, and the benefits are realized by the supplier and the buyer. By themselves, such technology transfers do not provide a rationale for government intervention.[31]

Overall, the empirical research to date does not provide conclusive evidence that would warrant substantial fiscal incentives to promote FDI on welfare grounds. Nevertheless, more than 100 countries were offering fiscal incentives to attract FDI in the mid-1990s, a pattern that continues. A recent survey of 45 developing countries found that 85 percent offer some kind of tax holiday or reduction of corporate income tax for foreign investment.[32] Given the interest of many governments in FDI promotion, it is worth asking how effective such measures are. A range of econometric studies and survey data over the last few decades show that such incentives are one among a set of fundamental factors, such as market growth, macroeconomic and political stability, the quality of transportation and communications infrastructure, the availability of skilled workers (or at least the available capacity to train workers), and labor market flexibility, including the ability to downsize the labor force or exit an industry without undue complications. Indeed, the World Bank's investment climate surveys show that unreliable power supply, weak contract enforcement, corruption, and crime may impose costs several times greater than taxes. A MIGA (2002) survey of 191 companies with plans to expand operations found that only 18 percent in manufacturing and 9 percent in services considered grants and incentives to be influential in their choice of location. Of 75 Fortune 500 companies surveyed, only four identified grants and incentives as influential.[33]

This, however, does not mean that fiscal incentives are unimportant. When other fundamental considerations have been satisfied, they clearly play a role in the final choice of location on a short list of desirable sites. A growing body of evidence shows that incentives may be influential in a choice of location within regional groupings such as the Association of Southeast Asian Nations, the European Union, or the North American Free Trade Agreement and also in the composition of the kind of FDI that is attracted to a country. However, that incentive packages may be costly for host countries is not in dispute, most obviously through the loss of tax revenue and, hence, of resources for necessary government functions. In Tunisia, the cost of fiscal incentives amounted to almost 20 percent of total private investment in 2001. The package India offered Ford in 1997 was estimated to cost US$200,000–US$420,000 per job. Large incentives are not limited to developing countries. It is estimated that the government of Alabama paid the equivalent of US$150,000 per employee to Mercedes to locate its new plant in the state in 1994.[34] In addition to fiscal costs, fiscal incentives also lead to distortions in resource allocation, for example, by discriminating against local investors or by attracting short-term investors, and they are often costly to administer. Overly discretionary incentive regimes create uncertainty for investors and foster corruption, especially in countries without strong institutions to ensure transparency and accountability over time.

Given these costs and difficulties, there has been a recent trend to eliminate or simplify tax incentives. In general, simple, predictable, and nondiscretionary incentive schemes will be attractive to investors even if they are not excessively generous, while being less costly and distorting for host countries. Fiscal experts are also critical of tax holidays or temporary rebates on corporate income for some types of investments, which tend to attract short-term investments typical of footloose industries, while discouraging investments that rely on long-lived capital, and which also tend to reward the formation of new companies rather than continued investment in new companies. Governments also increasingly try to attract FDI through investment promotion agencies that address possible information failures. There are now at least 160 national and more than 250 subnational investment promotion agencies, compared to only a handful two decades ago. These agencies play a variety of roles: information dissemination, image building, investment facilitation, investment generation, investor monitoring and aftercare, and policy advocacy.

Policies to enhance FDI spillovers. In addition to incentives offered to attract FDI, governments also sometimes use a variety of regulatory, trade-related investment measures to try to enhance the positive spillovers from FDI flows. Domestic content requirements aim to raise the share of inputs that foreign firms buy from local producers on the assumption that this would increase vertical technology transfers. However, it is unlikely that forcing foreign firms to buy inputs from inefficient local firms is the best way to foster vertical transfers. Instead, this may create a disincentive for FDI. Local content requirements in the automobile sectors in Australia and Chile were found to result in large inefficiencies.[35] McKinsey Consultants estimates that local content requirements for Chinese auto parts made cars produced in China 20–30 percent more expensive than those produced in the United States. On the other hand, the lack of local content requirements in the consumer electronics sector in China or the phasing out of such restrictions in the Mexican auto sector has in no way hindered the rapid development of increasingly sophisticated supplier industries in these countries.[36]

Mandated joint ventures or local equity participation regulations also aim to encourage technology spillovers to local partners, but seem mainly to result in rendering foreign firms wary of using their most advanced or sensitive processes, thereby reducing rather than enhancing spillovers. Again, because foreign investors in the automobile sector in China were required to have a local partner, major international firms were reluctant to use the latest processes. As a result, manufacturing methods lagged behind industry standards by about 10 years. Similarly, Kodak was required to have local joint venture partners in its investments in China, but was allowed to have one wholly owned subsidiary. It invested six times more in the wholly owned firm than it did in the average joint venture partner. Its wholly owned subsidiary ended up producing its most advanced film and camera technologies, while the joint ventures produced conventional film under the Kodak label. On the other hand, multinationals are often quite willing to form joint ventures with local partners when this makes economic and strategic sense, even without local equity regulations, as has been the case in the retail sector in Brazil and Mexico. Given the lack of evidence for a link between these kinds of trade-related investment measures and productivity spillovers, countries have also adopted more general strategies to work with foreign affiliates and local firms to overcome information and cultural barriers. These programs are often combined with incentives to help the domestic suppliers meet the production standards demanded by foreign investors. This approach has been followed in economies such as Ireland, Malaysia, Singapore, and Taiwan (China).[37]

Notes

1. See Romer (1990a, 1990b, 1993); Aghion and Howitt (1992, 2005).

2. The *Oslo Manual: Guidelines for Collecting and Interpreting Innovation Data* (OECD and EC 2005) explicitly follows Joseph Schumpeter's pioneering 1934 analysis by defining innovation quite broadly as "the implementation of a new or significantly improved product (good or service), or process, a new marketing method, or a new organisational method in business practices, workplace organisation or external relations" (p. 46). The basic requirement for an innovation in the manual's approach is that it be new to the firm implementing it. Thus, innovations include not only products, processes, or methods originally developed by the firm, but also those adopted from other firms or organizations. They include significant improvements or adaptations of existing product, process, marketing, or organizational methods. Innovation activities are defined as "all scientific, technological, organisational, financial and commercial steps which actually, or are intended to, lead to the implementation of innovations" (p. 47). Innovation activities include not only research and experimental development, but also the acquisition of external knowledge and technology (for example, purchases of patents and nonpatented inventions, licenses, know-how, trademarks, designs, and patterns from other firms), the acquisition of the capital goods, both those embodying improved technological performance and those with no improvement in technological performance, that are required for the implementation of new or improved products or processes, and a

wide range of other activities needed to prepare an innovation, such as industrial design, engineering and setup, trial production, patent and license work, production start-up, and testing.

3. Ayyagari, Demirgüç-Kunt, and Maksimovic (2006) use instrumental variables to control for the obvious possibility of reverse causation (whereby external financing flows to more innovative firms), but find that the instrumented external financing variable remains significant.

4. Although, as indicated elsewhere here, the econometric evidence for technology transfer and productivity gains through exporting is mixed.

5. Small countries (in geographical terms) tend to export and import more per dollar of GDP than do large ones. This is known as the country size effect.

6. Lall (2003) elaborates on the diverse strategies employed by East Asian economies to strengthen industrial competitiveness.

7. For example, Hobday (1995, 2000), Kim (1997), Matthews and Cho (2000), Kim and Lee (2002), and Nabeshima (2004).

8. The relevant literature is surveyed in Hoekman and Javorcik (2006) and Tybout (2006).

9. See Sturgeon and Lester (2004).

10. See Ernst (2004).

11. Keller (2002) proxies disembodied knowledge flows through bilateral language skills (the proportion of the population in the recipient country that speaks the language of the spillover sender country). The study looks at knowledge flows among industries in countries at the world's technology frontier, the G-7 industrialized economies.

12. Schiff, Wang, and Olarreaga (2002) do not measure the R&D actually performed in developing economies. Instead, they construct an indirect measure of the R&D that developing economies have absorbed from the North through trade. They then look at the possible international spillovers through trade of this indirect R&D stock in developing economies.

13. There is a weak and slightly positive correlation between FDI stocks and per capita income across countries, but there is a more significant negative correlation between country size and FDI stocks as a share of GDP.

14. For example, see Caves (1996) and Markusen (2002).

15. Using panel data for 58 developing countries, Bosworth and Collins (2003) show that there is a nearly one-to-one relationship between FDI and domestic investment.

16. See Arnold and Javorcik (2005); World Bank (2005). Arnold and Javorcik (2005) use a nonparametric matching estimator to calculate the causal effect of foreign ownership on plant productivity. This technique creates a missing counterfactual of the acquired firm had it remained under domestic ownership. It does so by pairing up each future acquired plant with a domestic plant from the same sector and year that had observable characteristics similar to the acquisition target prior to the foreign acquisition. The causal effect of foreign ownership is estimated by the average divergence of the total factor productivity growth paths between each acquired plant and its matched control plant, starting from the preacquisition year.

17. Blomström and Kokko (1997) and Glass and Saggi (2002) provide a more detailed exposition on the role of competition; Das (1987) and Wang and Blomström (1992), on imitation; and Haacker (1999), Fosfuri, Motta, and Rønde (2001), and Djankov and Hoekman (2000), on skill set acquisition. For a general literature review of FDI spillover channels, see Görg and Greenaway (2004).

18. For example, Haskel, Pereira, and Slaughter (2002) and Griffith, Redding, and Simpson (2003) find small, but significant effects in the United Kingdom, while Keller and Yeaple (2003) find large and significant effects for the United States. For developing or emerging economies, Javorcik and Spatareanu (2003) find evidence for horizontal spillovers in Romania.

19. See UNESCO (2005, 2006). R&D data are available for a number of economies through 2004 or 2005, but 2002 seems to be the most recent year for which comprehensive data are available for the world as a whole.

20. It is worth noting that the absolute value of China's R&D in purchasing power parity terms is particularly affected by the unusually large disparity between the country's purchasing power parity exchange

rate (as calculated by World Bank staff and other researchers) and its market exchange rate. Thus, China's R&D expenditures in 2004 at market exchange rates were US$23.8 billion, or only 21 percent of the purchasing power parity figure (UNESCO 2006). By comparison, Korea's R&D spending in 2003 was US$22.8 billion in purchasing power parity terms and US$16 billion at market exchange rates, or 70 percent of the purchasing power parity figure. In Malaysia, R&D at market rates was 42 percent of R&D in purchasing power parity terms. Note, however, that, while this issue is relevant for measuring absolute levels of R&D, it does not affect R&D intensity (the ratio of R&D to GDP), since both the numerator and denominator of that ratio rely on the same conversion rate.

21. Jaumotte and Pain (2005a) also provide an extensive analysis of the determinants of business sector R&D in the OECD countries. Among the more important influences on business R&D are economic framework variables such as the user cost of capital, corporate profits, financial development, international trade openness, and product market restrictions (lack of competition). Among significant national innovation system variables are government subsidies for business R&D (although only under some conditions), the level of nonbusiness R&D (largely in universities and nonprofit bodies), business-academic links, and a lagged term for the number of scientists and engineers.

22. The business sector R&D discussed here includes R&D performed by domestic private firms, public sector firms, and foreign affiliates operating in a country. Government R&D refers to organizations not engaged in production, but belonging to the executive branch of government.

23. See the discussion of the definition of innovation in endnote 2. Scotchmer (2004) provides a nontechnical primer on intellectual property law. Issues and pitfalls in the use of patents as innovation indicators are discussed in Hall, Jaffe, and Trajtenberg (2001), Jaffe and Trajtenberg (2002), and Jaffe and Lerner (2004). Apart from the legal requirements for patenting, firms may also make a strategic choice to protect their inventions by means other than patents, for example, secrecy, lead times, first-mover advantages such as moving down the learning curve, and the provision of sales and services that complement the innovation. Levin et al. (1987) and Cohen, Nelson, and Walsh (2002) document the importance of methods other than patents for protecting intellectual property.

24. In particular, the section draws on the NBER Patent Citation Database (http://www.nber.org/patents/), which is described in Hall, Jaffe, and Trajtenberg (2001) and updated through 2002 by Bronwyn Hall (http://elsa.berkeley.edu/~bhhall/bhdata.html) and through 2004 by Albert Hu (Hu 2006). The discussion in this section draws extensively on Hu (2006), a background paper prepared for this report. The paper focuses on patent and citation data on eight East Asian economies: China, Hong Kong (China), Korea, Malaysia, the Philippines, Singapore, Taiwan (China), and Thailand. The use of U.S. patents may be justified by the fact that inventors in other countries have a strong incentive to take out patents in the United States for commercially valuable inventions, given the position of the United States as the largest market in the world. Close to 50 percent of the patents granted by the USPTO in 2000–04 went to foreign inventors. Nevertheless, there is a large home bias in patenting (inventors are much more likely to patent in their home jurisdiction than elsewhere), and inventors in different economies may also face different incentives to patent in the United States (for example, economies that export a great deal to the United States versus those that export little), and this may introduce another source of bias for which adjustment may need to be made.

25. For example, see Hausmann, Hall, and Griliches (1984); Hall, Griliches, and Hausman (1986); Griliches (1990); Blundell, Griffith, and van Reenen (1995); and Jaffe and Trajtenberg (2002).

26. Some East Asian economies have very few if any patents in some technology fields. This means that there are few citations with which to compute generality or originality indexes. In such cases, the indexes may reflect only a few unrepresentative cases rather than the economy's intrinsic inventive capability. To avoid this problem, the discussion focuses on Korea and Taiwan (China). These economies exhibit sufficient patenting activity for meaningful measurement.

27. For additional details, see Jaffe and Trajtenberg (2002) and Hu (2006).

28. Technological proximity is defined as the correlation between the technology vectors of the two economies, wherein each technology vector is defined as the shares of total patents taken out by the economy in all 428 technology classes.

29. For instance, see Ahn (2002).

30. See Pack and Saggi (2006); Klimenko (2004).

31. Blalock and Gertler (2005) argue that there may nevertheless be an externality associated with vertical technology transfers that warrants some public intervention. If a multinational corporation transfers technology to only one supplier, this may enhance the market power of that supplier, which may tend to hold up competition. Thus, the multinational corporation has an incentive to transfer technology to several competing suppliers, leading to a more productive supply base and lower supply prices. However, the multinational corporation is unable to prevent the new supply base from also selling to the competitors of the multinational corporation. These competitors will then be in a position to increase competition and lower prices in the downstream market. The original multinational corporation would not, however, take all these social welfare gains into account and may transfer a less than optimal amount of technology to suppliers.

32. See World Bank (2004b).

33. See World Bank (2004b); MIGA (2002); Morisset (2003); Farrell, Remes, and Schulz (2004); Oman (2000).

34. See Görg (2003).

35. See World Bank (2004b).

36. See Farrell, Remes, and Schulz (2004).

37. See World Bank (2004b).

References

Aghion, Philippe, and Peter Howitt. 1992. "A Model of Growth through Creative Destruction." *Econometrica* 60 (2): 323–51.

———. 2005. "Appropriate Growth Policy: A Unifying Framework." The 2005 Joseph Schumpeter Lecture, delivered to the 20th Annual Congress of the European Economic Association, Amsterdam, August 25. http://post.economics.harvard.edu/faculty/aghion/papers/Appropriate_Growth_Policy.pdf.

Aghion, Philippe, George-Marios Angeletos, Abhijit Banerjee, and Kalina Manova. 2005. "Volatility and Growth: Credit Constraints and Productivity-Enhancing Investment." Draft working paper, April, National Bureau of Economic Research, Cambridge, MA.

Aghion, Philippe, Philippe Bacchetta, Romain Rancière, and Kenneth Rogoff. 2006. "Exchange Rate Volatility and Productivity Growth: The Role of Financial Development." Draft working paper, March, National Bureau of Economic Research, Cambridge, MA.

Aghion, Philippe, Nick Bloom, Richard William Blundell, Rachel Susan Griffith, and Peter Howitt. 2005. "Competition and Innovation: An Inverted-U Relationship." *Quarterly Journal of Economics* 120 (2): 701–28.

Aghion, Philippe, Richard William Blundell, Rachel Susan Griffith, Peter Howitt, and Susanne Prantl. 2006. "The Effects of Entry on Incumbent Innovation and Productivity." Draft working paper, National Bureau of Economic Research, Cambridge, MA.

Ahn, Sanghoon. 2002. "Competition, Innovation, and Productivity Growth: A Review of Theory and Evidence." OECD Economics Department Working Paper 317, Economics Department, Organisation for Economic Co-operation and Development, Paris.

Aitken, Brian J., and Ann E. Harrison. 1999. "Do Domestic Firms Benefit from Direct Foreign Investment?: Evidence from Venezuela." *American Economic Review* 89 (3): 605–18.

Arnold, Jens Matthias, and Beata Smarzynska Javorcik. 2005. "Gifted Kids or Pushy Parents?: Foreign Acquisitions and Plant Performance in Indonesia." CPER Discussion Paper 5065, Center for Econ. Policy Research, London.

Arrow, Kenneth. 1962. "Economic Welfare and the Allocation of Resources for Invention." In *The Rate and Direction of Inventive Activity: Economic and Social Factors*, ed. Richard R. Nelson, 609–26. Princeton, NJ: Princeton University Press.

Audretsch, David B. 1998. "Agglomeration and the Location of Innovative Activity." *Oxford Review of Economic Policy* 14 (2): 18–29.

Audretsch, David B., and Maryann Feldman. 1996. "R&D Spillovers and the Geography of Innovation and Production." *American Economic Review* 86 (3): 630–40.

Aw, Ben Yan, Xiaomin Chen, and Mark J. Roberts. 1997. "Firm-Level Evidence on Productivity Differentials, Turnover, and Exports in Taiwanese Manufacturing." NBER Working Paper 6235, National Bureau of Economic Research, Cambridge, MA.

Ayyagari, Meghana, Asli Demirgüç-Kunt, and Vojislav Maksimovic. 2006. "Firm Innovation in Emerging Markets: Role of Governance and Finance." Unpublished working paper, World Bank, Washington, DC.

Balasubramanyam, V. N., M. A. Salisu, and D. R. Sapsford. 2001. "FDI and Economic Growth in LDCs: Some Further Evidence." In *Creating an Internationally Competitive Economy*, ed. H. Block and P. Kenyon, 233–49. London: Macmillan.

Barro, Robert J., and Jong-Wha Lee. 2000. "International Data on Educational Attainment: Updates and Implications." CID Working Paper 42, Center for International Development, Harvard University, Cambridge, MA.

Bartelsman, Eric, John Haltiwanger, and Stefano Scarpetta. 2004. "Microeconomic Evidence of Creative Destruction in Industrial and Developing Countries." Policy Research Working Paper 3464, World Bank, Washington, DC.

Baumol, William J. 2002. *The Free Market Innovation Machine: Analyzing the Growth Miracle of Capitalism.* Princeton, NJ: Princeton University Press.

Blalock, Garrick, and Paul J. Gertler. 2005. "Foreign Direct Investment and Externalities: The Case for Public Intervention." In *Does Foreign Direct Investment Promote Development?*, ed. Theodore H. Moran, Edward M. Graham, and Magnus Blomström, 73–106. Washington, DC: Institute for International Economics.

Blomström, Magnus, and Ari Kokko. 1997. "How Foreign Investment Affects Host Countries." Policy Research Working Paper 1745, World Bank, Washington, DC.

Bloom, Nick, Rachel Susan Griffith, and John van Reenen. 2000. "Do R&D Tax Credits Work?: Evidence from a Panel of Countries 1979–97." CEPR Discussion Paper 2415, Center for Economic Policy Research, London.

Blundell, Richard William, Rachel Susan Griffith, and John van Reenen. 1995. "Dynamic Count Data Models of Technological Innovation." *Economic Journal* 105 (429): 333–44.

_____. 1999. "Market Share, Market Value, and Innovation in a Panel of British Manufacturing Firms." *Review of Economic Studies* 66 (3): 529–54.

Borensztein, Eduardo, José De Gregorio, and Jong-Wha Lee. 1998. "How Does Foreign Direct Investment Affect Economic Growth?" *Journal of International Economics* 45 (1): 115–35.

Bosch, Mariano, Daniel Lederman, and William F. Maloney. 2005. "Patenting and Research and Development: A Global View." Policy Research Working Paper 3739, World Bank, Washington, DC.

Bosworth, Barry P., and Susan M. Collins. 2003. "The Empirics of Growth: An Update." Brookings Papers on Economic Activities 2003–2, Brookings Institution, Washington, DC.

Bottazzi, Laura, and Giovanni Peri. 2005. "The International Dynamics of R&D and Innovation in the Short and in the Long Run." NBER Working Paper 11524, National Bureau of Economic Research, Cambridge, MA.

Caballero, Ricardo J., and Adam B. Jaffe. 1993. "How High Are the Giants' Shoulders: An Empirical Assessment of Knowledge Spillovers and Creative Destruction in a Model of Economic Growth." In *NBER Macroeconomics Manual*, ed. Olivier Jean Blanchard and Stanley M. Fischer, 15–74. Cambridge, MA: MIT Press.

Caves, Richard. 1996. *Multinational Enterprises and Economic Analysis.* 2nd ed. Cambridge: Cambridge University Press.

Clerides, Sofronis K., Saul Lach, and James R. Tybout. 1998. "Is Learning by Exporting Important?: Micro-Dynamic Evidence from Colombia, Mexico, and Morocco." *Quarterly Journal of Economics* 113 (3): 903–47.

Coe, David T., and Elhanan Helpman. 1995. "International R&D Spillovers." *European Economic Review* 39 (5): 859–87.

Coe, David T., Elhanan Helpman, and Alexander W. Hoffmaister. 1997. "North-South R&D Spillovers." *Economic Journal* 107 (440): 134–49.

Cohen, Wesley M., and Daniel A. Levinthal. 1989. "Innovation and Learning: The Two Faces of R&D." *Economic Journal* 99 (397): 569–96.

Cohen, Wesley M., Richard R. Nelson, and John P. Walsh. 2002. "Links and Impacts: The Influence of Public Research on Industrial R&D." *Management Science* 48 (1): 1–23.

Das, Sanghamitra. 1987. "Externalities and Technology Transfer through Multinational Corporations: A Theoretical Analysis." *Journal of International Economics* 22 (1–2): 171–82.

Djankov, Simeon, and Bernard Hoekman. 2000. "Foreign Investment and Productivity Growth in Czech Enterprises." *World Bank Economic Review* 14 (1): 49–64.

Doner, Richard F., Gregory W. Noble, and John Ravenhill. 2004. "Production Networks in East Asia's Automobile Parts Industry." In *Global Production Networking and Technological Change in East Asia,* ed. Shahid Yusuf, M. Anjum Altaf, and Kaoru Nabeshima, 159–208. Washington, DC: World Bank; New York: Oxford University Press.

———. 2006. "Industrial Competitiveness of the Auto Parts Industries in Four Large Asian Countries: The Role of Government Policy in a Challenging International Environment." Unpublished working paper, World Bank, Washington, DC.

Eaton, Jonathan, and Samuel Kortum. 1996. "Trade in Ideas: Patenting and Productivity in the OECD." *Journal of International Economics* 40 (3/4): 251–78.

Ernst, Dieter. 2004. "Global Production Networks in East Asia's Electronics and Upgrading Perspectives in Malaysia." In *Global Production Networking and Technological Change in East Asia,* ed. Shahid Yusuf, M. Anjum Altaf, and Kaoru Nabeshima, 89–158. Washington, DC: World Bank; New York: Oxford University Press.

Farrell, Diana, Jaana K. Remes, and Heiner Schulz. 2004. "The Truth about Foreign Direct Investment in Emerging Markets." The McKinsey Quarterly 2004–1, 25–35.

Fink, Carsten, and Keith E. Maskus. 2005. *Intellectual Property and Development: Lessons from Recent Economic Research.* Washington, DC: World Bank.

Foray, Dominique. 2004. *The Economics of Knowledge.* Cambridge, MA: MIT Press.

Fosfuri, Andrea, Massimo Motta, and Thomas Rønde. 2001. "Foreign Direct Investment and Spillovers through Workers' Mobility." *Journal of International Economics,* 53 (1): 205–22.

Fujita, Masahisa, and Jacques-François Thisse. 1996. "The Economics of Agglomeration." CEPR Discussion Paper 1344, Center for Economic Policy Research, London.

García-Quevado. José. 2004. "Do Public Subsidies Complement Business R&D?: A Meta-Analysis of the Econometric Evidence." *Kyklos* 57 (1): 87–102.

Glass, Amy Jocelyn, and Kamal Saggi. 2002. "Intellectual Property Rights and Foreign Direct Investment." *Journal of International Economics* 56 (2): 387–410.

Görg, Holger. 2003. "Fancy a Stay at the 'Hotel California': Foreign Direct Investment, Investment Incentives, and Exit Costs." Draft paper, School of Economics, University of Nottingham, Nottingham, United Kingdom.

Görg, Holger, and David Greenaway. 2004. "Much Ado about Nothing?: Do Domestic Firms Benefit from Foreign Direct Investment?" *World Bank Research Observer* 19 (2): 171–97.

Griffith, Rachel Susan, Stephen J. Redding, and Helen Simpson. 2003. "Productivity Convergence and Foreign Ownership at the Establishment Level." CEPR Discussion Paper 3765, Centre for Economic Policy Research, London.

Griliches, Zvi. 1990. "Patent Statistics as Economic Indicators: A Survey." *Journal of Economic Literature* 28 (4): 1661–1707.

———. 1995. "R&D and Productivity: Econometric Results and Measurement Issues." In *Handbook of the Economics of Innovation and Technological Change,* ed. Paul Stoneman, ed., 52–89. Oxford: Blackwell.

Grossman, Gene M., and Elhanan Helpman. 1991. *Innovation and Growth in the Global Economy.* Cambridge, MA: MIT Press.

Guellec, Dominique, and Bruno van Pottelsberghe de la Potterie. 2004. "From R&D to Productivity Growth: Do the Institutional Settings and the Source of Funds of R&D Matter?" *Oxford Bulletin of Economics and Statistics* 66 (3): 353–78.

Haacker, Markus. 1999. "Spillovers from Foreign Direct Investment through Labor Turnover: The Supply of Management Skills." Discussion Paper, Centre for Economic Performance, London School of Economics, London.

Hall, Bronwyn Hughes, Zvi Griliches, and Jerry A. Hausman. 1986. "Patents and R&D: Is There a Lag?" *International Economic Review* 27 (2): 265–84.

Hall, Bronwyn Hughes, Adam B. Jaffe, and Manuel Trajtenberg. 2001. "The NBER Patent Citations Data File: Lessons, Insights, and Methodological Tools." CEPR Discussion Paper 3094, Center for Economic Policy Research, London.

Hallward-Driemeier, Mary, Giuseppe Iarossi, and Kenneth L. Sokoloff. 2002. "Exports and Manufacturing Productivity in East Asia: A Comparative Analysis with Firm-Level Data." NBER Working Paper 8894, National Bureau of Economic Research, Cambridge, MA.

Hanson, Gordon H. 2001. "Should Countries Promote Foreign Direct Investment?" G-24 Discussion Paper 9, United Nations, Geneva.

Haskel, Jonathan E., Sonia C. Pereira, and Matthew J. Slaughter. 2002. "Does Inward Foreign Direct Investment Boost the Productivity of Firms?" NBER Working Paper 8724, National Bureau of Economic Research, Cambridge, MA.

Hausman, Jerry A., Bronwyn Hughes Hall, and Zvi Griliches. 1984. "Econometric Models for Country Data with an Application to the Patents-R&D Relationship." *Econometrica* 52 (4): 909–38.

Hausmann, Ricardo, and Dani Rodrik. 2002. "Economic Development as Self-Discovery." NBER Working Paper 8952, National Bureau of Economic Research, Cambridge, MA.

Hobday, Michael. 1995. *Innovation in East Asia: The Challenge to Japan.* Cheltenham, UK: Edward Elgar.

———. 2000. "East Versus Southeast Asian Innovations: Comparing OEM- and TNC-Led Growth in Electronics." In *Technology, Learning, and Innovation: Experiences of Newly Industrializing Economies,* ed. Linsu Kim and Richard R. Nelson, 129–69. Cambridge: Cambridge University Press.

Hoekman, Bernard M., and Beata Smarzynska Javorcik, eds. 2006. *Global Integration and Technology Transfer.* Trade and Development Series. Washington, DC: World Bank; Basingstoke, Hampshire, United Kingdom: Palgrave Macmillan.

Hoekman, Bernard M., Keith E. Maskus, and Kamal Saggi. 2005. "Transfer of Technology to Developing Countries: Unilateral and Multilateral Policy Options." *World Development* 33 (10): 1587–1602.

Hu, Albert Guangzhou. 2006. "Knowledge Flow in East Asia and Beyond." Background paper, World Bank, Washington, DC.

Hu, Albert Guangzhou, and Gary H. Jefferson. 2005. "A Great Wall of Patents: What Is behind China's Recent Patent Explosion?" Paper presented at the joint conference of the School of Economics, Shanghai University of Finance and Economics, Shanghai, and the Department of Economics, Örebro University, Örebro, Sweden, "Globalization and Economic Growth: The Role of Openness, Innovation, and Human Capital, Evidence from Micro Data," Shanghai, November 4–6.

Jaffe, Adam B., and Josh Lerner. 2004. *Innovation and Its Discontents.* Princeton, NJ: Princeton University Press.

Jaffe, Adam B., and Manuel Trajtenberg. 1998. "International Knowledge Flows: Evidence from Patent Citations." NBER Working Paper 6507, National Bureau of Economic Research, Cambridge, MA.

———. 1999. "International Knowledge Flows: Evidence from Patent Citations." *Economics of Innovation and New Technology* 8 (1–2): 105–36.

———. 2002. *Patents, Citations, and Innovations: A Window on the Knowledge Economy.* Cambridge, MA: MIT Press.

Jaffe, Adam B., Manuel Trajtenberg, and Rebecca Henderson. 1993. "Geographic Localization of Knowledge Spillovers as Evidenced by Patent Citations." *Quarterly Journal of Economics* 108 (3): 577–98.

Jaumotte, Florence, and Nigel Pain. 2005a. "From Ideas to Development: The Determinants of R&D and Patenting." OECD Economics Department Working Paper 457, Economics Department, Organisation for Economic Co-operation and Development, Paris.

_____. 2005b. "An Overview of Public Policies to Support Innovation." OECD Economics Department Working Paper 456, Economics Department, Organisation for Economic Co-operation and Development, Paris.

Javorcik, Beata Smarzynska. 2004. "Does Foreign Direct Investment Increase the Productivity of Domestic Firms?: In Search of Spillovers through Backward Linkages." *American Economic Review* 94 (3): 605–27.

Javorcik, Beata Smarzynska, and Mariana Spatareanu. 2003. "To Share or Not to Share: Does Local Participation Matter for Spillovers from Foreign Direct Investment?" Policy Research Working Paper 3118, World Bank, Washington, DC.

Jones, Charles I., and John C. Williams. 1997. "Measuring the Social Return to R&D." *Quarterly Journal of Economics* 113 (4): 1119–35.

Keller, Wolfgang. 2002. "Knowledge Spillovers at the World's Technology Frontier." CEPR Discussion Paper 2815, Center for Economic Policy Research, London.

_____. 2004. "International Technology Diffusion." *Journal of Economic Literature* 42 (3): 752–82.

Keller, Wolfgang, and Stephen R. Yeaple. 2003. "Multinational Enterprises, International Trade, and Productivity Growth: Firm-Level Evidence from the United States." Working Papers 2003–06, Department of Economics, Brown University, Providence, RI.

Kim, Linsu. 1997. *From Imitation to Innovation: Dynamics of Korea's Technological Learning.* Boston: Harvard Business School Press.

Kim, Linsu, and Richard R. Nelson. 2000. *Technology, Learning, and Innovation: Experiences of Newly Industrializing Economies.* Cambridge: Cambridge University Press.

Kim, Youngbae, and Byungheon Lee. 2002. "Patterns of Technological Learning among the Strategic Groups in the Korean Electronic Parts Industry." *Research Policy* 31 (4): 543–67.

Kinoshita, Yuko. 2001. "R&D and Technology Spillovers via FDI: Innovation and Absorptive Capacity." CEPR Discussion Paper 2775. Center for Economic Policy Research, London.

Klimenko, Mikhail M. 2004. "Industrial Targeting, Experimentation, and Long-Run Specialization." *Journal of Development Economics* 73 (1): 75–105.

Kokko, Ari, Ruben Tansini, and Mario C. Zejan. 1996. "Local Technological Capability and Productivity Spillovers from FDI in the Uruguayan Manufacturing Sector." *Journal of Development Studies* 32 (4): 602–11.

Konings, Josef. 2001. "The Effects of Foreign Direct Investment on Domestic Firms." *Economics of Transition* 9 (3): 619–33.

Kraay, Aart. 2006. "Exports and Economic Performance: Evidence from a Panel of Chinese Enterprises." In *Global Integration and Technology Transfer*, ed. Bernard M. Hoekman and Beata Smarzynska Javorcik, 139–61. Trade and Development Series. Washington, DC: World Bank; Basingstoke, Hampshire, United Kingdom: Palgrave Macmillan.

Lall, Sanjay. 2003. "Foreign Direct Investment, Technology Development and Competitiveness: Issues and Evidence." In *Competitiveness, FDI and Technological Activity in East Asia*, ed. Sanjay Lall and Shujiro Urata, Chapter 2. Cheltenham, United Kingdom: Edward Elgar.

Lall, Sanjay, and Shujiro Urata, eds. 2003. *Competitiveness, FDI and Technological Activity in East Asia.* Cheltenham, United Kingdom: Edward Elgar.

Lederman, Daniel, and William F. Maloney. 2003. "Research and Development (R&D) and Development." Policy Research Working Paper 3024, World Bank, Washington, DC.

Levin, Richard C., Alvin K. Klevorick, Richard R. Nelson, and Sidney G. Winter. 1987. "Appropriating the Returns from Industrial Research and Development." Brookings Papers on Economic Activity 1987–03, Brookings Institution, Washington, DC.

Lipsey, Robert E. 2000. "Interpreting Developed Countries' Foreign Direct Investment." NBER Working Paper 7810, National Bureau of Economic Research, Cambridge, MA.

López-Claros, Augusto, Michael E. Porter, and Klaus Schwab. 2005. *Global Competitiveness Report 2005–2006: Policies Underpinning Rising Prosperity.* Geneva: World Economic Forum; Basingstoke, Hampshire, United Kingdom: Palgrave Macmillan.

Markusen, James. 2002. *Multinational Firms and the Theory of International Trade.* Cambridge, MA: MIT Press.

Matthews, John A., and Dong-Sung Cho. 2000. *Tiger Technology: The Creation of a Semiconductor Industry in East Asia.* Cambridge: Cambridge University Press.

MIGA (Multilateral Investment Guarantee Agency). 2002. *Foreign Direct Investment Survey.* Multilateral Investment Guarantee Agency, World Bank Group, Washington, DC. http://www.ipanet.net/fdisurvey/.

Moran, Theodore H., Edward M. Graham, and Magnus Blomström, eds. 2005. *Does Foreign Direct Investment Promote Development?* Washington, DC: Institute for International Economics.

Morisset, Jacques. 2003. "Tax Incentives." Viewpoint Note 25, World Bank, Washington, DC.

Nabeshima, Kaoru. 2004. "Technology Transfer in East Asia: A Survey." In *Global Production Networking and Technological Change in East Asia,* ed. Shahid Yusuf, M. Anjum Altaf, and Kaoru Nabeshima, 395–434. Washington, DC: World Bank; New York: Oxford University Press.

Nickell, Stephen J. 1996. "Competition and Corporate Performance." *Journal of Political Economy* 104 (4): 724–46.

Noland, Marcus, and Howard Pack. 2003. *Industrial Policy in an Era of Globalization: Lessons from Asia.* Washington, DC: Institute for International Economics.

OECD (Organisation for Economic Co-operation and Development). 2000. "Policy Brief: Science, Technology and Innovation in the New Economy." OECD Observer, September, Organisation for Economic Co-operation and Development, Paris.

———. 2003. *Frascati Manual. Proposed Standard Practice for Surveys on Research and Experimental Development.* Measurement of Scientific and Technological Activities Series. Paris: Organisation for Economic Co-operation and Development.

OECD (Organisation for Economic Co-operation and Development) and EC (European Commission). 1997. *Proposed Guidelines for Collecting and Interpreting Technological Innovation Data: Oslo Manual.* 2nd ed. Measurement of Scientific and Technological Activities Series. Paris: Organisation for Economic Co-operation and Development.

———. 2005. *Oslo Manual: Guidelines for Collecting and Interpreting Innovation Data.* 3rd ed. Measurement of Scientific and Technological Activities Series. Paris: Organisation for Economic Co-operation and Development.

Oman, Charles P. 2000. *Policy Competition for Foreign Direct Investment: A Study of Competition among Governments to Attract FDI.* Development Center Studies Series. Paris: Organisation for Economic Co-operation and Development.

Pack, Howard. 2006. "Econometric Versus Case Study Approaches to Technology Transfer." In *Global Integration and Technology Transfer,* ed. Bernard M. Hoekman and Beata Smarzynska Javorcik, 29–50. Trade and Development Series. Washington, DC: World Bank; Basingstoke, Hampshire, United Kingdom: Palgrave Macmillan.

Pack, Howard, and Kamal Saggi. 2006. "The Case for Industrial Policy: A Critical Survey." Unpublished working paper, World Bank, Washington, DC.

Quigley, John M. 1998. "Urban Diversity and Economic Growth." *Journal of Economic Perspectives* 12 (2): 127–38.

Reed Business Information. 2005. *Electronic Business,* September 1. http://www.edn.com/article/CA6252391.html?partner=eb&pubdate=9%2F1%2F2005.

Rodrik, Dani. 2004. "Industrial Policy for the 21st Century." Unpublished working paper, September, John F. Kennedy School of Government, Harvard University, Cambridge, MA.

Romer, Paul M. 1990a. "Are Nonconvexities Important for Understanding Growth?" NBER Working Paper 3271, National Bureau of Economic Research, Cambridge, MA.

———. 1990b. "Endogenous Technological Change." *Journal of Political Economy* 98 (5): 71–102.

———. 1993. "Idea Gaps and Object Gaps in Economic Development." *Journal of Monetary Economics* 32 (3): 543–73.

Saggi, Kamal. 2002. "Trade, Foreign Direct Investment, and International Technology Transfer: A Survey." *World Bank Research Observer* 17 (2): 191–235.

Scherer, F. M., and Dietmar Harhoff. 2000. "Technology Policy for a World of Skew-Distributed Outcomes." *Research Policy* 29 (4–5): 559–66.

Schiff, Maurice, and Yanling Wang. 2006. "On the Quantity and Quality of Knowledge: The Impact of Openness and Foreign R&D on North-North and North-South Technology Spillovers." In *Global Integration and Technology Transfer*, ed. Bernard M. Hoekman and Beata Smarzynska Javorcik, 99–112. Trade and Development Series. Washington, DC: World Bank; Basingstoke, Hampshire, United Kingdom: Palgrave Macmillan.

Schiff, Maurice, Yanling Wang, and Maurice Olarreaga. 2002. "Trade-Related Technology Diffusion and the Dynamics of North-South and South-South Integration." Policy Research Working Paper 2861, World Bank, Washington, DC.

Schumpeter, Joseph. 1934. *The Theory of Economic Development*. Cambridge, MA: Harvard University Press.

Scotchmer, Suzanne. 2004. *Incentives and Innovation*. Cambridge, MA: MIT Press.

Sturgeon, Timothy J., and Richard K. Lester. 2004. "The New Global Supply Base: New Challenges for Local Suppliers in East Asia." In *Global Production Networking and Technological Change in East Asia*, ed. Shahid Yusuf, M. Anjum Altaf, and Kaoru Nabeshima, 35–88. Washington, DC: World Bank; New York: Oxford University Press.

TeleGeography Research. 2006. *TeleGeography Report*. Washington, DC: TeleGeography Research. http://www.telegeography.com/products/tg/report.php.

Todo, Yasuyuki, and Koji Miyamoto. 2006. "Knowledge Spillovers from Foreign Direct Investment and the Role of Local R&D Activities: Evidence from Indonesia." *Economic Development and Cultural Change* 55 (1): 173–200.

Trajtenberg, Manuel, Rebecca Henderson, and Adam B. Jaffe. 1997. "University versus Corporate Patents: A Window on the Basicness of Invention." *Economics of Innovation and New Technology* 5 (1): 19–50.

Tybout, James R. 2006. "Plant- and Firm-Level Evidence on 'New' Trade Theories." In *Global Integration and Technology Transfer*, ed. Bernard M. Hoekman and Beata Smarzynska Javorcik, 67–98. Trade and Development Series. Washington, DC: World Bank; Basingstoke, Hampshire, United Kingdom: Palgrave Macmillan.

UNCTAD (United Nations Conference on Trade and Development). 2005. *World Investment Report 2005: Transnational Corporations and the Internationalization of R&D*. Geneva: United Nations.

UNESCO (United Nations Educational, Scientific, and Cultural Organization). 2004. "A Decade of Investment in Research and Development (R&D): 1990–2000." *USI Bulletin on Science and Technology Statistics* 1 (April). Montreal: Institute for Statistics, United Nations Educational, Scientific, and Cultural Organization.

———. 2005. *UNESCO Science Report 2005*. Paris: UNESCO Publishing.

———. 2006. "Statistics on Research and Development." Data table, updated on May 3. Montreal: Institute for Statistics, United Nations Educational, Scientific, and Cultural Organization. http://www.uis.unesco.org/ev.php?ID=5182_201&ID2=DO_TOPIC.

Wang, Jian-Ye, and Magnus Blomström. 1992. "Foreign Investment and Technology Transfer: A Simple Model." *European Economic Review* 36 (1): 137–55.

Wong, Wei-Kang. 2006. "Do Crossborder Flows Raise Income and Productivity?" Background paper, World Bank, Washington, DC.

World Bank. 2004a. *Global Development Finance 2004: Harnessing Cyclical Gains for Development*. Washington, DC: World Bank.

_____. 2004b. *World Development Report 2005: A Better Investment Climate for Everyone.* Washington, DC: World Bank; New York: Oxford University Press.

_____. 2005. "Raising Investment in Indonesia: A Second Generation of Reforms." Report, World Bank, Washington, DC.

World Bank, the International Finance Corporation, and OUP (Oxford University Press). 2005. *Doing Business in 2005: Removing Obstacles to Growth.* Washington, DC: World Bank; New York: Oxford University Press.

Xu, Bin, and Jianmao Wang. 1999. "Capital Goods Trade and R&D Spillovers in the OECD." *Canadian Journal of Economics* 32 (5): 1258–74.

Yusuf, Shahid, M. Anjum Altaf, and Kaoru Nabeshima, eds. 2004. *Global Production Networking and Technological Change in East Asia.* Washington, DC: World Bank; New York: Oxford University Press.

Map 4.1 **Investment Flows within East Asia Are Important**

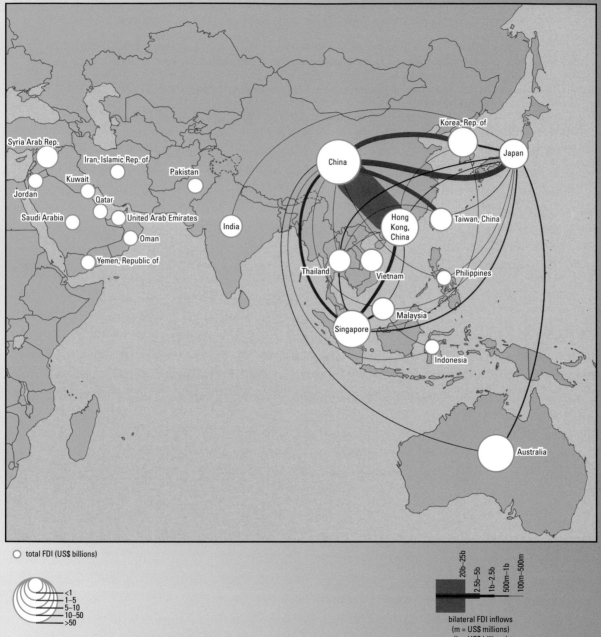

total FDI (US$ billions)

<1
1–5
5–10
10–50
>50

The area of each circle is proportional to the annual average FDI inflows
from the entire world into each country, in the 2000–04 period.

Source: World Bank staff estimates.

20b–25b
2.5b–5b
1b–2.5b
500m–1b
100m–500m

bilateral FDI inflows
(m = US$ millions)
(b = US$ billions)

Each band is proportional to the annual average FDI inflows
in both directions for each pair of countries, in the
2000–04 period (or available years within that period).

CHAPTER 4

FINANCE

The challenge of stability is being met as financial sources diversify, but financial structures are better suited to financing trade, not innovation. Corporate bond markets are underdeveloped.

From Breakdown to Buildup

The financial structure underpinning the rapid economic growth and the trade in East Asia failed in 1997–98. The massive economic dislocation and loss of market value among firms highlighted the necessity of developing a more robust regional financial architecture to support trade and investment. Whereas, prior to the crisis, one could say that the focus of attention was on mobilizing finance, the focus has shifted since the crisis to the efficiency of resource allocation, the diversification of supply, and the reduction of systemic risk. The structure of the financial system has become more important. At the same time, because of the considerable integration of financial markets both globally and within the region, policy makers have recognized that stability depends not only on each country's efforts and financial structures, but also on how the financial links between countries operate.[1] This chapter looks at how the structure of finance in the region is changing and considers the remaining challenges for the establishment of a system that is able to support the sort of trade and innovation that are necessary for continued rapid growth in the middle-income and rich countries of the region.

Map 4.1 shows that the economies in the region are increasingly becoming linked by foreign direct investment (FDI). Hong Kong (China), Japan, the Republic of Korea, Singapore, and Taiwan (China) all have links with each other, as well as with China. China is, of course, the dominant recipient of FDI from the region, which is to be expected given the size of its economy, but Malaysia, the Philippines, and Thailand also have strong FDI links across the region. Only Indonesia, which was a main target for Japanese FDI before the crisis, appears to be less well integrated. While some FDI is now moving to India from Japan, the amounts are still low in absolute terms.

The growing regional ties through FDI and the resilience of these flows contrast with the falling share of FDI from Europe and the United States. At the same time, crossborder bank loans and portfolio flows have oscillated, while foreign exchange reserves have soared, reaching US$1.6 trillion (excluding Japan) by the end of 2005. East Asia has become a significant net exporter of capital to the rest of the world. Meanwhile, the value of domestic financial assets—bonds, equities, and bank deposits—has surged since the crisis, reaching US$9.6 trillion. This raises the two related questions that we explore in this chapter:

■ Has there been a shift in the manner in which the East Asian economies are engaging with global and regional capital markets, and, if so, what has motivated this shift?
■ How have East Asian domestic financial markets changed since the crisis?

How Finance Supported Production Networks Before the 1997–98 Crisis

Within East Asia, finance has always been viewed as a mechanism to support the real economy. To understand how and why financial structures have changed in the region, it is therefore important to examine how the needs of the real economy have changed, particularly the financial requirements of production networks.

Production networks require low-cost, long-term financing for capital investment and the expansion of facilities. They require short-term working capital to finance trade and more patient capital to finance innovation and research. Thus, production networks call for specialized financial products.

As production chains become more complex, the potential risks within the system also become more complex. Global or regional production networks operate internationally and therefore rely on a broad array of crossborder financial services. They are exposed to currency risk when the cost structures of different components are dependent on local currency wages. Because most trade is denominated in U.S. dollars and because the United States is the most important end consumer of the output of Asian production networks, financing throughout the network is best undertaken in U.S. dollars. When it is not, a currency risk arises. A movement in local currencies against the U.S. dollar may affect the cost of inputs relative to product prices and thereby directly affect profits.

In addition to international operations, production networks encompass a large and diverse number of companies governed by different contractual agreements between one another. Affiliates, subsidiaries, original equipment manufacturers, and other types of related companies, some big and some small, may all be engaged in a network. Each transaction within this chain of producers carries a credit risk.

As became abundantly clear in 1997–98, currency risk and credit risk may combine and accumulate.

The production networks in East Asia developed rapidly after the Plaza Accord in 1985. This sharp realignment appreciated the Japanese yen against European currencies and the U.S. dollar. It encouraged Japanese firms to relocate abroad. It also provided Japanese banks with a larger capital base from which to make loans denominated in U.S. dollars to their domestic multinational clients and client affiliates. Japan became one of the first countries to embrace offshoring and develop the organizational systems needed to establish production networks. Japanese banks and Japanese foreign investors therefore played an important role in the early development of East Asian production networks.

The interlinked system of FDI and international bank lending proved adequate so that production networks could be expanded throughout East Asia. FDI provided the equity capital required to build new plants and fund innovation where needed. It was used primarily in middle-income countries such as Indonesia, Malaysia, and Thailand, where domestic capabilities were less strong. In Korea and Taiwan (China), which had more restrictive foreign exchange regimes, offshoring took place through commercial arrangements. Japanese multinationals used their own credit standing to mobilize the resources to invest abroad, mostly relying on banks in their home country.

Bank credit, on the other hand, was used to provide short-term trade finance. Because a major multinational was the central organizer of the production network, banks were happy to take on the credit risk represented by the suppliers in the chain since they knew that the credit of the buyer was sound. Traditional commercial banking products such as letters of credit acted as the mechanisms for such transactions. International banks could minimize their risk by intermediating their funds through local banks, which had better information on the credit standing of suppliers and which might more easily monitor management in the diverse companies within the supply chain.

This system of financing depended heavily on the absence of significant currency or credit risk. Governments were relied on to minimize the currency risk, and local banks were relied on to minimize the credit risk.

When Thailand was forced to devalue the baht in July 1997 following a series of speculative attacks on the Thai currency, the assumptions on which the production networks had been organized were shattered.

The 1997–98 Crisis

There have been many descriptions of the East Asian crisis, and many factors came into play. Here, it is useful to mention a few facts. First, East Asia suffered from a major capital reversal during the crisis. As Sheng (2006) notes, roughly US$200 billion flowed into emerging East Asia in the five years prior to 1997.[2] Over the next two years, about US$160 billion left the region. Much of this outflow may be attributed to Japanese banks, which withdrew about US$65 billion from the region, part of a global exposure reduction of US$170 billion between 1996 and 2000. The retrenchment of credit coincided with a depreciation of the Japanese yen against the U.S. dollar from ¥85 to ¥135 per dollar between 1995 and 1997. This movement, combined with a fall in the Nikkei stock index, increased the loan-capital ratio of major Japanese banks. Because almost 80 percent of the international loans of these banks booked to Asian borrowers, it is not surprising that the bulk of the adjustment fell on East Asian economies.

Second, the crisis period coincided with growth in international capital markets. In addition to bank lending, portfolio flows from abroad had risen steeply in the mid-1990s in response to rising local equity markets. Equity financing was attractive to many firms in the region because it freed them from the surveillance of banks and multinational firms. With less scrutiny by lenders, local firms were able to venture into areas other than production networking, including more speculative real estate development. This reaction was not limited to firms. Local banks, too, used the opportunity offered by the available foreign financing to shift to the financing of nontradables. Agency problems proliferated.

Portfolio flows are traditionally more volatile than bank credits. But they may also increase the possibility of bank credit reversals. When banks provide both short-term and long-term credits, they are more likely to be patient and roll over short-term credit lines in difficult times so as to protect the value of their medium-term claims. When portfolio flows replace medium-term bank credits, then the incentive for banks to exit at the first sign of trouble grows. Thus, the probability of capital flow reversals and sudden stops rises as the structure of finance becomes more varied.[3]

A third important observation is that, at the time of the crisis, the supervision of local banks was weak, and the credit culture in economies that were hit the most severely by the crisis was generally considered poor. The leverage of corporate borrowers had risen to high levels, and the exposure to firms with interest coverage ratios at less than 1 was significant. The monitoring and oversight function that is supposed to be associated with bank credits was absent in many East Asian economies.

It would be an overstatement to claim that these factors caused the East Asian financial crisis. There are too many other factors that also played a role. But it is not too farfetched to claim that the crisis revealed:

- A need for a more reliable mechanism to ensure foreign exchange predictability
- A need for more effective mechanisms to price credit risk
- A need for more thorough corporate governance so as to reduce agency problems

East Asian policy makers discovered to their cost what theoretical economists had already foreseen. They tried to shift toward capital account convertibility to ease the flow of capital and dividends and grease production networks. They tried to fix the exchange rate to minimize foreign exchange risk. And they tried to pursue an easy monetary policy to encourage investment in their countries and maintain growth. These three desirable goals cannot be simultaneously achieved. Frankel (1999) refers to them as the "impossible trinity." A balance has to be struck. That balance required changes in the way in which financial systems were integrated globally and regionally and in the way in which they developed domestically.

The Pattern of Global and Regional Financial Integration

Since the crisis, the nature of international capital flows in East Asia has changed perceptibly. The levels of FDI, in aggregate, have been relatively stable, but the composition has shifted markedly. Much more FDI now originates within East Asia than was the case prior to the crisis. At the same time, the number of FDI sources has grown, with Hong Kong (China), Japan, Korea, and Taiwan (China) all playing important roles. Recognizing the value of FDI, countries in the region have liberalized their foreign investment regimes. An index of foreign investment openness—defined as the sum of the stock of FDI inflows, plus the stock of FDI outflows, divided by gross domestic product (GDP)—shows that foreign investment is more significant in the region today: the index rose from 10 percent in 1990 to 28 percent in 2004.

Other flows to the region have been more volatile, especially those going to China. These flows have been pulled into countries by their internal policies and performance and pushed out of developed countries by broader global factors such as interest costs and liquidity. Recent research suggests that pull and push factors may be complementary: the push factors determine the timing and magnitude of capital flows to emerging economies, and the pull factors determine the geographical distribution of the flows.[4]

The biggest change in the region's financial integration, however, revolves around the accumulation of foreign exchange reserves and the management of foreign exchange risk. The stock of reserves had increased to over US$1.6 trillion by the end of 2005, and there was every indication of a continuing upward trend despite the fact that countries had moved to more flexible exchange rates, at least de jure. But, at the same time, East Asian economies have begun to cooperate regionally on financial matters under the auspices of the Association of Southeast Asian Nations, plus China, Japan, and Korea (ASEAN+3), in a way that reflects a determination to integrate regional financial markets. Yet, if shocks in the region are correlated, as they would be if a production network were affected, then risk sharing with the rest of the world would be more efficient than risk sharing only within the region. Table 4.1 shows these trends in foreign capital flows.

■ TABLE 4.1 **Trends in Capital Flows to Emerging East Asia, 1990–2005**
US$ billions

Emerging East Asia	Average, 1990–95	1996	1997	1998	1999	2000	2001	2002	2003	2004	2005
Net direct investment	27.0	51.9	54.7	54.4	64.0	58.3	43.6	42.3	59.7	50.5	74.0
Net portfolio flows	7.8	17.0	0.4	4.0	31.8	11.6	−68.1	−72.4	−16.9	−14.2	−16.2
Other net capital flows	17.4	37.6	−75.3	−134.5	−101.7	−81.1	14.3	7.2	−49.8	33.8	−22.0
Change in reserves	40.7	61.5	18.8	60.7	74.4	45.7	69.4	154.8	236.2	337.1	243.1
Memo items											
Stock of FDI	229.2	417.2	625.2	658.3	888.9	962.9	945.0	887.8	984.5	1,111.9	1,243.5
Stock of foreign exchange reserves	289.5	466.4	485.1	545.9	620.2	666.0	735.3	890.1	1,126.4	1,463.5	1,706.7

Sources: International Financial Statistics Database, International Monetary Fund, http://ifs.apdi.net/imf/; UNCTAD 2005; World Bank staff calculations.
Note: For a definition of emerging East Asia, see endnote 2.

Foreign Direct Investment

FDI has been important for capital formation and upgrading technology across East Asia. Most foreign investment has been vertical, that is, associated with production networks and supply chain networks organized to minimize cost. This kind of FDI is closely linked to higher trade between countries. Horizontal FDI, on the other hand, describes a process whereby foreign producers jump trade barriers so as to reduce their costs of accessing a domestic market. These costs may arise from a variety of trade frictions, such as tariffs, distance and transport costs, time to market, or the costs of providing customer services. Horizontal FDI is trade reducing.

Figure 4.1 shows the level of gross FDI inflows across East Asia. Like trade, both inflows and outflows of FDI may yield benefits. Gross inflows show the degree to which foreign management and technology are being imported. Gross outflows show the degree to which local firms are able to reduce costs by moving production abroad. Thus, the impact of FDI does not depend on the net levels of FDI, as given in balance of payments statistics, but on the gross levels.

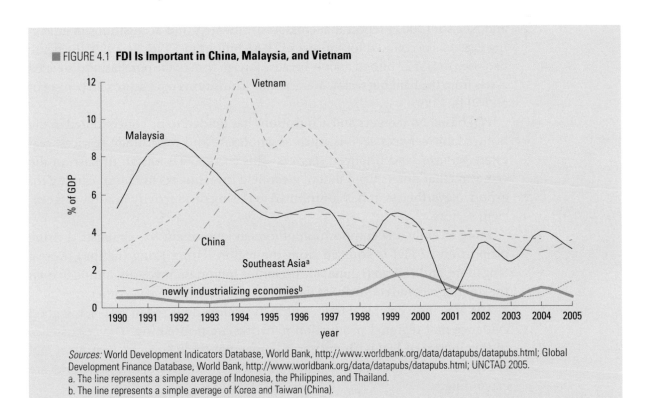

■ FIGURE 4.1 **FDI Is Important in China, Malaysia, and Vietnam**

Sources: World Development Indicators Database, World Bank, http://www.worldbank.org/data/datapubs/datapubs.html; Global Development Finance Database, World Bank, http://www.worldbank.org/data/datapubs/datapubs.html; UNCTAD 2005.
a. The line represents a simple average of Indonesia, the Philippines, and Thailand.
b. The line represents a simple average of Korea and Taiwan (China).

Figure 4.1 shows a high level of FDI across East Asia, averaging 4 percent of GDP. The latecomer middle-income economies have relied particularly heavily on FDI. Malaysia showed inflows reaching above 8 percent of GDP in the early 1990s before seeing FDI taper off. China and Vietnam are currently the largest destinations for FDI relative to the size of their economies. Korea and Taiwan (China), on the other hand, historically implemented strategies that did not rely on FDI. The trailing off of FDI in Indonesia, the Philippines, and Thailand is of more concern. These economies had FDI inflows of 2–3 percent of GDP before the crisis, but show much lower levels now.

In aggregate, FDI flows were not materially affected by the 1997–98 crisis, although they did decline in absolute value in some economies as the level of GDP and trade fell. FDI collapsed only in Indonesia, where a radically new business environment caused investors to rethink their long-term strategies and their exposure. Indonesia received 25 percent of Japanese FDI to emerging Asia in 1992, but only 3 percent in 2004. In some countries, such as Korea and Thailand, the level of FDI actually increased shortly after the crisis as a result of a wave of mergers and acquisitions triggered by economic reform in these countries. Mody and Negishi (2001) report that crossborder mergers and acquisitions in emerging East Asia accounted for inflows of US$3 billion in 1996. By 1999, the figure had risen to US$22 billion mainly because foreign firms were purchasing distressed assets from the banking sector. Mergers and acquisitions represented 30 percent of all FDI in 1999.

FDI based on mergers and acquisitions has tended to be concentrated in the nontradable services sectors, such as wholesale and retail trade services, real estate services, and financial services. This sort of FDI has an impact on the economy that differs from that of greenfield investments in manufacturing for export. Nevertheless, it has contributed to raising productivity in some less efficient sectors.

More recently, the composition of foreign investment has changed. A rising proportion of FDI is sourced from the region. Hong Kong (China), Korea, Singapore, and Taiwan (China) are becoming important investors, although even the middle-income countries of the region are investing in each other.

The growing web of FDI flows within the region, depicted in map 4.1, is good evidence that regional production networks are flourishing. The coexistence of this increased FDI with greater intraregional trade suggests that most FDI is vertical.[5] This provides additional evidence that production networks are expanding.

Production networks may be global in principle, but, within East Asia in practice, they are regional. Geographical proximity appears to be a significant determinant of FDI location, other things being equal. Market size also appears as significant. A survey of Japanese investors discussed in a 2005 white paper on trade and the international economy by the Japanese Ministry of Economy, Trade, and Industry (METI 2005) shows that Japanese firms are concerned about the quality of the bureaucracies in host countries and about macroeconomic risk.

FDI is emphasized because it has long been considered a source of technology transfer, as well as capital. One study, based on surveys among firms and controlling for other factors such as firm age, sector, and size, finds that total factor productivity is significantly higher in Indonesia, Korea, the Philippines, and Thailand when a firm is foreign owned.[6] Furthermore, when foreign ownership is in a majority, the productivity gains are highest, suggesting that management control provides greater incentives and enhances the ability to invest in technology improvements. The reported productivity differentials are large: around 40 percent in Indonesia and the Philippines and 10–20 percent in Korea and Thailand.

In general, the policy environment facilitating FDI is similar to the broader policy environment for investment in a country. The World Bank has conducted surveys of several thousand firms across the region since 2003, asking firms about the key constraints they face. In general, the results show that key concerns relate to policy. Macroeconomic risk remains at the top of the agenda both for exporters and for domestically oriented firms. Regulatory and policy risk (especially in decentralized economies), the availability of skills, infrastructure quality, and corruption are other key concerns. There is much that can be done on these fronts to improve business conditions in the region, and the relevant reforms are important if the middle-income countries are to continue to be competitive with lower-cost producers such as China and Vietnam (see figure 4.2.).

It is worth emphasizing that management in about 20 percent of firms in East Asia feels that access to finance is a major or very severe obstacle. In China, Indonesia, and Thailand, the proportion is somewhat higher among exporters than it is among nonexporters. However, these perception data should be interpreted with caution. The fact that a small fraction of firms in Cambodia report major obstacles in obtaining access to finance is probably more telling about the serious nature of other problems facing Cambodian firms than about ready access to finance (see figure 4.3).

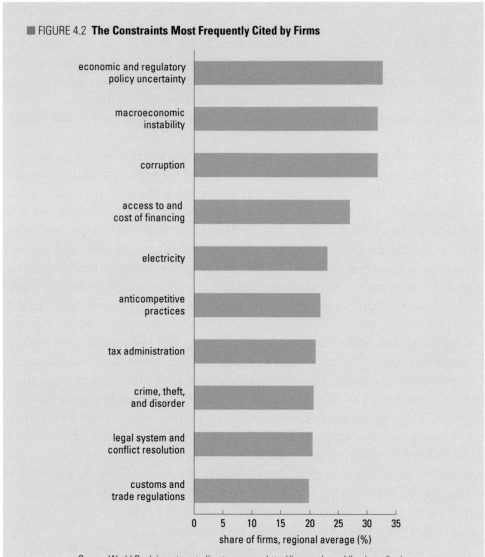

■ FIGURE 4.2 **The Constraints Most Frequently Cited by Firms**

share of firms, regional average (%)

Source: World Bank investment climate surveys, http://iresearch.worldbank.org/ics/jsp/index.jsp.
Note: The figure shows the percent of firms identifying a problem as "major" or "very severe." The following investment climate surveys have been used in composing the figure: Cambodia (2003), China (2002, 2003), Indonesia (2003), the Philippines (2003), Thailand (2004), and Vietnam (2005).

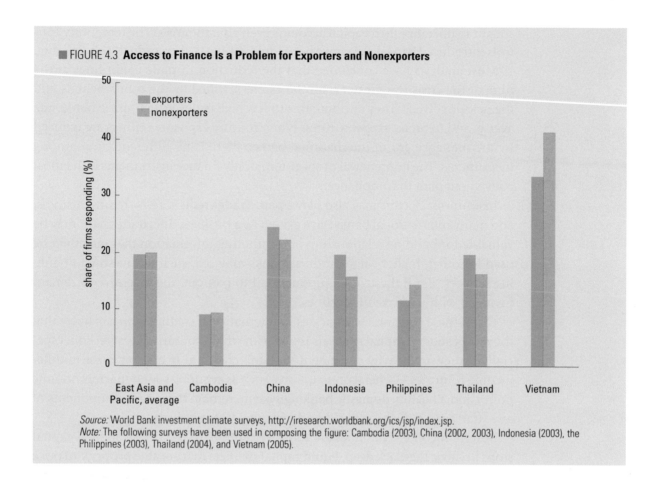

■ FIGURE 4.3 **Access to Finance Is a Problem for Exporters and Nonexporters**

Source: World Bank investment climate surveys, http://iresearch.worldbank.org/ics/jsp/index.jsp.
Note: The following surveys have been used in composing the figure: Cambodia (2003), China (2002, 2003), Indonesia (2003), the Philippines (2003), Thailand (2004), and Vietnam (2005).

Other Capital Flows

While international bank credit naturally followed the trends in FDI during the early stages of the development of production networks, it has become less important today. This is partly a consequence of greater financial openness. It is not surprising that countries with high levels of trade should also move toward greater financial openness. Capital controls become difficult to enforce when trade flows are large: export underinvoicing and import overinvoicing are expensive to monitor. Some analysts have put weight on the effect of the political economy.[7] Closed, repressed domestic financial sectors may act as a mechanism to protect domestic players against new entrants and competition. But, in an open trade regime, there is already competition from abroad; so, protection against domestic entrants is less a concern. In such an environment, most countries in East Asia sought to liberalize their capital accounts even after the crisis. The temporary controls introduced by Malaysia have been lifted. China is also gradually liberalizing.

Most analysts have concluded that the reduction in trade credit lines at the time of the crisis was greater than the extent justified by the fundamentals and the risks involved.[8] They attribute this to leverage issues, which make banks risk averse, and to broad exposure rules. When country exposure ceilings are reduced by the management of international banks, there is no differentiation among instruments. The nonrenewal of short-term trade finance instruments is the most convenient path to compliance.

Institutional factors may also play a part. Trade credit is a low-return business, and many international banks have exited. As a business line, trade credit may be valuable for building relationships and gathering information that may then be used for other, higher-value products banks may sell, such as investment banking services. But if these other products fail to pan out, the incentive to remain involved with trade credits declines.

Given these structural weaknesses in international credit, it appears likely that the risk of sudden capital reversals is one with which countries must reckon, especially if they are heavily dependent on bank credit, as is true for most middle-income countries.[9] General prescriptions, such as ensuring sound macroeconomic policy and a healthy domestic banking system, remain important components of any strategy to reduce the likelihood of capital flow reversals.

Middle-income economies are most susceptible to the risk of sudden capital stops because they lack deep, liquid capital markets that are able properly to price risk. As a result, risk management takes the form of changes in the volume of the credit extended. This line of argument suggests that a more effective integration of domestic capital markets would be beneficial. But should this integration be global, regional, or both?

As a practical matter, regional integration is more likely to occur than global integration. Portes and Rey (1999) point to the importance of information asymmetries in capital market integration and note the related effect of geographical distance, as in the case of trade models. They argue that both trade in goods and investments in foreign assets generate valuable information that reduces transaction costs. The implication is that countries with more trade will also tend to experience more crossborder asset flows. This has been confirmed econometrically by Aviat and Coeurdacier (2005) and Aizenman and Noy (2005).

There is also direct evidence that intraregional foreign portfolio investment is increasing. According to the coordinated portfolio investment survey of the International Monetary Fund, the value of the foreign portfolio investment in

■ TABLE 4.2 **East Asia NIEs Have Replaced Japan as the Regional Source of Portfolio Finance**
percent

Portfolio Investor	1997	2001	2002	2003
United States	41.4	37.0	37.4	37.0
European Union	27.3	34.2	28.5	30.9
Japan	12.7	6.3	6.6	4.3
East Asia NIEs	6.1	13.8	17.4	15.2
Developing East Asia	0.5	0.4	0.4	0.3
Others	15.0	13.4	13.6	15.8
Total	100.0	100.0	100.0	100.0

Source: World Bank staff estimates based on the Coordinated Portfolio Investment Survey Database, International Monetary Fund, http://www.imf.org/external/np/sta/pi/cpis.htm.

stocks and bonds that is coming into East Asia rose from 9 percent of the region's GDP in 1997 to 14 percent in 2003. Notably, the share of the portfolio investment originating from newly industrializing economies (NIEs) in East Asia more than doubled between 1997 and 2003 (see table 4.2).

By 2004, the East Asian NIEs held a larger share in absolute value terms in the equity and bonds in developing East Asian countries than did the European Union, Japan, or the United States. Unlike the developed countries, a much greater share of the portfolio investments of the NIEs are tied up in the developing countries of the region (see table 4.3).

■ TABLE 4.3 **NIEs Are the Most Important Portfolio Investors in Developing East Asia**
US$ billions

Investor	1997	2004
Equity, total	32.6	122.0
NIEs	6.0	37.9
European Union	8.1	36.7
United States	14.4	32.4
Japan	2.0	4.9
Bonds, total	40.2	67.0
European Union	7.9	19.2
United States	17.2	10.8
Japan	10.0	3.7

Source: Ghosh 2006.

Another way of looking at integration is to estimate econometrically the movement of equity returns in a country with equity movements in another country or region. The closer the movements, the more one may claim that equity markets are integrated. This is the approach used by Beale et al. (2004) for Europe and by Kharas, Aldaz-Carroll, and Rahardja (2007) for East Asia. Kharas, Aldaz-Carroll, and Rahardja look at how equity returns in middle-income countries in East Asia compare to a regional average of equity returns (excluding the dependent country), equity returns in Japan, and equity returns in the United States. Using weekly data, they do this for two periods: before the 1997–98 crisis and after the crisis. They find that some East Asian countries are closely integrated with regional markets and that the degree of integration is approximately the same as that found by Beale et al. for the euro area. On average, postcrisis, the equity markets in East Asia are showing greater integration with the region, as well as with Japan and the United States.[10] Figure 4.4 shows the correlations.

Foreign Exchange Reserve Accumulation

Emerging East Asia has over US$1.6 trillion dollars in foreign exchange reserves; almost all of it has been accumulated since the crisis. This has occurred despite an ostensible move in the region toward more flexible exchange rates. The pattern of accumulation is the same across most countries, including Japan (see figure 4.5). The region as a whole accounts for about one-half of global reserve accumulation in the world.[11] While China and Japan have been the drivers behind this trend, the reserves of Korea and the other NIEs have also swelled significantly since the crisis.[12] In Korea and other economies that were hit by the crisis, policy makers have decided to amass reserves as a precaution and for self-insurance against future financial crises.[13]

The precautionary or financial safeguard motive for the accumulation of reserves is consistent with modern, second-generation models of currency crises, such as those developed by Obstfeld (1986, 1994). These models emphasize the possibility of multiple equilibriums in a world of substantial capital mobility, whereby a country's underlying payments position is neither strong nor hopelessly weak, that is, where it is vulnerable. In such circumstances, the level of reserves not only influences a country's ability to finance speculative runs on its currency, but may also have a bearing on the probability that runs will occur. Large levels of own liquidity may be especially necessary in the absence of acceptable programs of international lenders of last resort, such as those developed by the International Monetary Fund, or in the face of untested regional programs of monetary cooperation.[14]

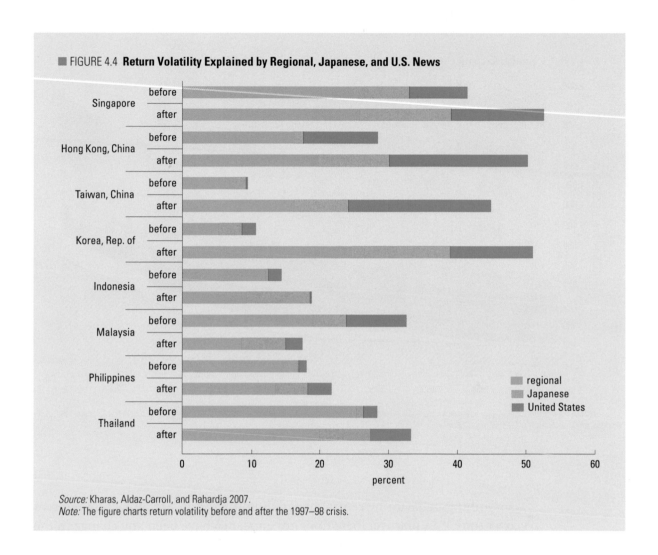

■ FIGURE 4.4 **Return Volatility Explained by Regional, Japanese, and U.S. News**

Source: Kharas, Aldaz-Carroll, and Rahardja 2007.
Note: The figure charts return volatility before and after the 1997–98 crisis.

Other authors who promote the precautionary motive note that the differences in the reserve accumulation levels in emerging markets are closely related to the degree of capital market liberalization and global integration. Empirically, the higher the level of capital account liberalization (relative to 1980), the higher the ratio of reserves to GDP.

Reserves have also been building up as a side effect of exchange rate objectives. Some have argued that the reserve growth in Asia is a by-product of a desire by regional central banks to smooth exchange rate movements. While concerns about excessive volatility in trade and FDI may be well founded,

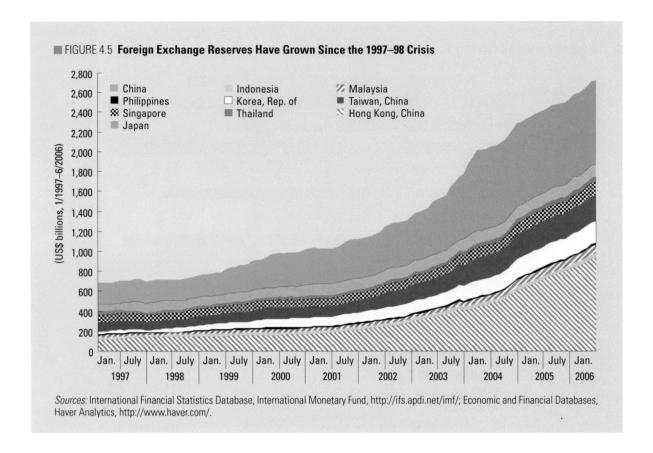

■ FIGURE 4.5 **Foreign Exchange Reserves Have Grown Since the 1997–98 Crisis**

Legend:
- China
- Philippines
- Singapore
- Japan
- Indonesia
- Korea, Rep. of
- Thailand
- Malaysia
- Taiwan, China
- Hong Kong, China

y-axis: (US$ billions, 1/1997–6/2006)

Sources: International Financial Statistics Database, International Monetary Fund, http://ifs.apdi.net/imf/; Economic and Financial Databases, Haver Analytics, http://www.haver.com/.

smoothing behavior by central banks should have no net impact on reserves over time.[15] In practice, there does not appear to have been any change in the volatility of Asian exchange rates against the U.S. dollar before or since the crisis, although the crisis period itself was characterized by high volatility. Interestingly, there is also little difference between the extent of the volatility of Asian currencies and that of Latin American currencies after 2003, with the exception of Brazil and the República Bolivariana de Venezuela, which show abnormally high volatilities.

An alternative explanation for Asia's accumulation of reserves is that it stems from a desire to maintain relatively stable and competitive exchange rates so as to export aggressively as a solution to the crisis and deep recession of 1997–98.[16] This argument, however, may only explain part of the story. If it were true, one would expect the accumulation of reserves to be closely related to current account surpluses. The evidence does not support this. There is no direct correlation between reserve stockpiling and current account surpluses in East Asia. In fact, East Asia had a long history of rapid export growth without large reserve accumulation prior to the 1997–98 crisis. In addition, the argument suggests that countries should target the real effective exchange rate, not the nominal bilateral rate against the U.S. dollar, to account for the fact that they trade with countries other than the United States.[17] And real effective rates in the region, including the rates in China, have been variable (see figure 4.6).

East Asian businesses do not seem to put much faith in the ability of their governments to stabilize nominal exchange rates either. There has been a boom in the global growth of foreign exchange derivatives that are traded largely over the counter. East Asia is thought to be responsible for about 15 percent of this trade, mostly in Hong Kong (China), Korea, and Singapore.

Since 2002, while the current account surplus still represents much of the increase in reserves, the private capital account surplus in East Asia has taken up a growing share of the region's accumulation in reserves, especially for China (see table 4.4).[18]

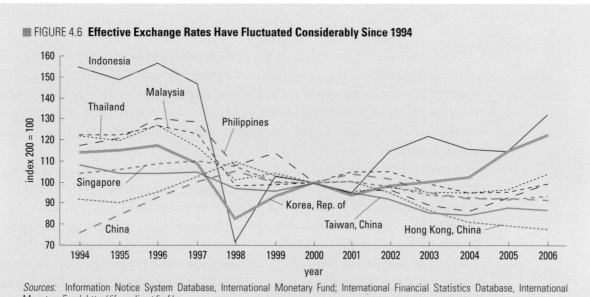

■ FIGURE 4.6 **Effective Exchange Rates Have Fluctuated Considerably Since 1994**

Sources: Information Notice System Database, International Monetary Fund; International Financial Statistics Database, International Monetary Fund, http://ifs.apdi.net/imf/.

■ TABLE 4.4 **Current and Capital Account Surpluses, 2002–05**
US$ billions

Economy	Current account balance				Net capital inflows[a]			
	2002	2003	2004	2005	2002	2003	2004	2005
East Asia	125.0	161.2	184.4	268.8	29.3	72.9	151.3	−27.6
China	35.4	45.9	68.7	160.8	40.1	71.1	137.7	46.2
Southeast Asia	27.2	30.8	27.1	21.8	−13.9	−12.8	1.8	−14.7
Indonesia	7.8	8.1	3.1	3.0	−3.8	−3.8	−3.1	−4.6
Malaysia	8.0	13.3	14.9	20.0	−4.3	−2.9	6.9	−16.2
Philippines	4.4	1.4	2.2	2.5	−4.5	−1.0	−2.8	0.3
Thailand	7.0	8.0	6.9	−3.7	−1.3	−4.9	0.7	5.7
NIEs	62.3	84.6	88.7	86.3	3.1	14.5	11.8	−59.1
Hong Kong, China	12.4	16.5	15.7	20.3	−11.7	−10.0	−10.5	−19.6
Korea, Rep. of	5.4	12.0	28.2	16.6	13.2	22.0	15.5	−5.2
Singapore	18.9	26.9	26.3	33.2	−12.3	−13.2	−9.8	−29.6
Taiwan, China	25.6	29.3	18.5	16.2	13.8	15.7	16.6	−4.7

Sources: International Financial Statistics Database, International Monetary Fund, http://ifs.apdi.net/imf/; Economic and Financial Databases, Haver Analytics, http://www.haver.com/.
a. Sum of all capital account flows, plus errors and omissions; derived as change in reserves, less the current account.

These various explanations of the accumulation of reserves have different policy implications. The precautionary approach links the accumulation of reserves directly to the exposure to sudden stops, capital flight, and volatility, whereas the mercantilist approach views the accumulation of reserves as a residual of an industrial policy that may impose negative externalities on other trading partners.

A third explanation focuses on the risk properties of foreign exchange reserves, which are held largely in liquid, safe investments, and the risk properties of foreign portfolio capital, which is risk bearing. As noted by McCauley (2003: 46), "East Asian economies are grossing up their balance sheets systematically to transfer risk to the rest of the world and to build up liquidity." Some attribute this to a strategic positioning whereby countries with weak property rights, such as China, hold foreign exchange reserves as collateral to minimize concerns about expropriation.[19] But this view has been widely criticized largely because of the mismatch between the location of reserves (in U.S. Treasury bonds) and the sources of FDI (mainly regional).[20]

Significant costs accrue to regional economies because of the accumulation of such large reserves. These costs include the opportunity costs of capital, the quasi-fiscal costs of monetary sterilization, and the possible capital losses from exchange rate fluctuations. But there are also benefits from transferring risk to the rest of the world. As noted above, large reserves may substantially reduce the risk of capital reversals, and, if a reversal were to occur, large reserves would offer some protection by reducing the impact. One implication of this explanation is that, once the desired level of risk sharing has been achieved, then reserves will even out or grow in line with trade or other risk factors.

In an environment in which capital account liberalization is only beginning, it is difficult to comment on whether foreign exchange reserves are excessive or not. If the ratio of all foreign assets (public and private) to GDP is compared across countries, developing East Asia does not appear to have any excess despite its relatively large public foreign exchange reserves. The inference is that East Asia's private sector is holding much less in foreign exchange than one might expect for countries at similar incomes. This is perhaps because of regulations that have restricted the set of institutional investors in the region, such as insurance companies and pension funds. This implies that the issue in the region may have more to do with the balance of foreign asset holdings between the public and private sectors than with the size of the foreign exchange reserves themselves. The policy implication is that high foreign exchange reserves might reflect an underdeveloped institutional investor base; foreign assets will shift from the central bank to the private sector, where they will be managed from a different risk-return perspective (see figure 4.7).

Regional Financial Cooperation

Foreign exchange reserves provide a mechanism for reducing the risk of a sudden capital flow reversal, but may be an expensive way to achieve this goal. The region is looking for other options.

One significant development is the Chiang Mai Initiative established in May 2000 under the auspices of ASEAN+3.[21] Through this agreement, the central banks of the 13 ASEAN+3 countries have agreed to make lines of credit available to each other in the event of a crisis. Some 17 agreements have already been

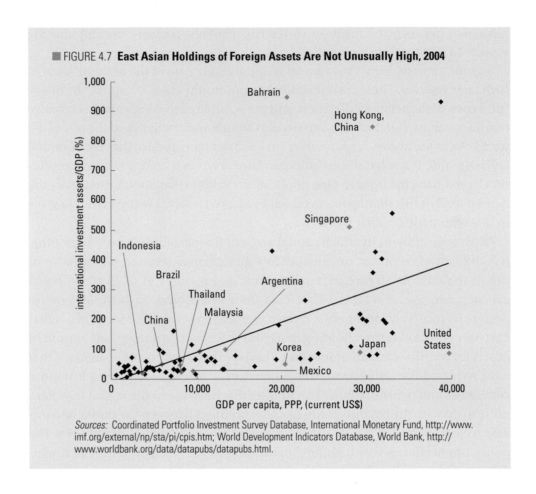

■ FIGURE 4.7 **East Asian Holdings of Foreign Assets Are Not Unusually High, 2004**

Sources: Coordinated Portfolio Investment Survey Database, International Monetary Fund, http://www.imf.org/external/np/sta/pi/cpis.htm; World Development Indicators Database, World Bank, http://www.worldbank.org/data/datapubs/datapubs.html.

signed, valued at over US$40 billion. But the Chiang Mai Initiative is broader than simply a line of credit. It now also provides for timely data provision and regional surveillance through regular exchanges, the monitoring of capital flows, and the training of key personnel. It represents the clear statement of a desire to reduce the need for individual country self-insurance by creating a regional reserve-pooling mechanism (albeit for comparatively small amounts) and an early warning mechanism to guard against financial contagion.

The development of a regional bond fund is another area of regional cooperation. Bond financing is considered more stable relative to bank financing. The diversification of funding sources to include international bond markets also adds to the stability of flows. Through the Executives' Meetings of East Asia–Pacific Central Banks, concrete measures have been taken to address weaknesses in Asian bond markets from the investor perspective, as well as weaknesses in the process of issuance.

The first Asian Bond Fund involved voluntary contributions by the 11 member governments of the Executives' Meetings of East Asia–Pacific Central Banks. Each government provided about 1 percent of its reserves to a fund dedicated to purchasing U.S. dollar sovereign and semi-sovereign bonds of eight of the member economies. (Australia, Japan, and New Zealand do not supply bonds for the fund.) The initial size of the fund was about US$1 billion, and the fund has been passively managed by the investment management unit of the Swiss-based Bank for International Settlements.

In a noteworthy next step, a second Asian Bond Fund was established in December 2004. The resources were doubled (US$2 billion), and the mandate of the new fund is to invest in selected domestic-currency sovereign and quasi-sovereign bonds of the eight economies.

The second fund comprises two components valued at US$1 billion each: the Pan-Asian Bond Index Fund and the Fund of Bond Funds. The first is a single bond fund, while the second is a two-layered structure consisting of a parent fund that invests in eight single-market subfunds.[22] The funds are passively managed to match the benchmark indexes. The seed money for single bond funds has been divided according to predetermined criteria, and local fund managers have been appointed to oversee the respective funds. The specific criteria for market weights in each subfund (and the distribution within the Pan-Asian Bond Index Fund) are based on (1) the size of the local market, (2) the turnover ratio in that market, (3) the sovereign credit rating, and (4) a market openness factor. The market weights are reviewed annually, and market openness is a particularly important factor in the allocation of weights. The parent fund is limited to investments by central banks that are members of the Executives' Meetings of East Asia–Pacific Central Banks. While the initial phase of the Pan-Asian Bond Index Fund was confined to investments only by member central banks (US$1 billion), it has been opened up to investments by other retail investors during the second phase.

The Asian Bond Fund should help the region diversify from bank lending to bond financing by reducing constraints and introducing low-cost products on the supply side and by raising investor awareness and broadening the investor base on the demand side.[23]

Beyond the potential for recycling regional funds intraregionally and obtaining a superior risk-return trade-off, the Asian Bond Fund initiative might also help lessen the extent of currency and maturity mismatches. Insofar as a narrow investor base is one of the reasons for the "original sin" problem that has afflicted developing East Asia, regional integration measures like the Asian Bond Fund that enhance the investor base should help moderate this problem.[24]

The combination of regional cooperation, self-insurance through the accumulation of foreign exchange reserves, and greater access to international capital markets, as well as syndicated bank credits, suggests that East Asia is on its way to integrating more deeply with regional and global financial markets. But, while regional cooperation may provide an impetus to diversification, most of the needed policy measures will have to be implemented in domestic financial systems. The next section discusses recent developments in these systems.

Toward More Robust Domestic Financial Markets

Financial markets in East Asia have grown rapidly since the crisis. The sum of bank assets, equity markets, and bond markets has surpassed US$10 trillion equivalent (see table 4.5). In most international comparisons, the financial depth in East Asian financial markets is above the average relative to other

■ TABLE 4.5 **Financial Markets, Especially Securities Markets, Have Surged Since 1997**

| | Bank assets | | | | Equity market capitalization | | | | Bonds outstanding | | | |
| | US$ billions | | % of GDP | | US$ billions | | % of GDP | | US$ billions | | % of GDP | |
Economy	1997	2005	1997	2005	1997	2005	1997	2005	1997	2005	1997	2005
China	1,125.7	3,692.2	124.6	163.1	101.4	401.9	11.2	17.8	116.4	552.0	12.9	24.4
Indonesia	74.1	140.0	31.1	49.8	29.1	81.4	12.2	28.9	4.5	55.2	1.9	19.6
Korea, Rep. of	196.4	736.1	37.9	93.5	41.9	718.0	8.1	91.2	130.3	599.8	25.2	76.2
Malaysia	100.9	208.5	100.9	159.4	93.2	180.5	93.2	138.0	57.0	115.1	57.0	88.0
Philippines	46.5	62.2	56.1	63.2	31.2	39.8	37.7	40.4	18.5	36.1	22.4	36.7
Thailand	120.3	183.0	79.7	103.6	22.8	123.9	15.1	70.1	10.7	72.1	7.1	40.8
Hong Kong, China	361.6	790.1	205.1	444.6	413.3	1,055.0	234.5	593.6	45.8	82.9	26.0	46.6
Singapore	117.0	216.4	122.0	185.4	106.3	257.3	110.8	220.4	23.7	79.8	24.7	68.2
Total	2,142.5	6,028.5	94.6	149.5	839.2	2,857.8	37.0	70.9	406.9	1,593.0	18.0	39.5

Sources: International Financial Statistics Database, International Monetary Fund, http://ifs.apdi.net/imf/; World Federation of Exchanges (http://www.world-exchanges.org/WFE/home.Asp); Bank for International Settlements (http://www.bis.org/); Asian Bond Indicators Database, Asian Development Bank, http://asianbondsonline.adb.org/asiabondindicators/; World Development Indicators Database, World Bank, http://www.worldbank.org/data/datapubs/datapubs.html; World Bank staff calculations.

countries at similar income levels. This applies to banking, equity, and even bond markets.[25]

Significant financial market reforms have already been undertaken. Banks have been restructured and recapitalized and are now much sounder. Prudential regulations and supervision have been strengthened, although areas remain that need strengthening, including on-site examination. Businesses are also showing healthier balance sheets; they have deleveraged substantially since the crisis. At the same time, banks have expanded into consumer lending, thereby adding to their revenue base.

Yet, there is still more to be done, particularly in the development of corporate bond markets. Banks are healthy precisely because they have reduced their lending to corporates lacking adequate credit ratings. And local capital markets are better suited to provide the patient capital that innovators require. A healthy corporate bond market would manage risk through higher pricing rather than just through lower volumes, and this would help bring to the market a more diversified set of investors, including institutional investors that have yet to play a major role in capital market deepening in the region.

Banking

The banking sector in East Asia is considerably healthier today than it was in 1997. There has been a trend toward consolidation in the sector, and, with the exception of the case of China, the number of banks in each middle-income country has fallen, even as GDP has recovered. There has thus been an appreciable increase in the median size of banks since the crisis. The size of the average bank is larger in several economies in the region (Hong Kong [China], Korea, and Thailand), than in Germany, the United Kingdom, or the United States. Despite this, the industry is not more concentrated than before: there is no marked trend in the share of assets held by the top three banks. Another positive sign is that the average level of state ownership in the top 10 banks has fallen, while the average foreign ownership has risen.

Because of these changes, the efficiency of the system has improved. One measure of efficiency is the ratio of operating costs to total assets. This ranges between 1 and 2 percent for most countries in the region. Hong Kong (China) banks show the lowest operating costs. Indonesia and the Philippines are exceptions; there, bank operating costs correspond to close to 3 percent of assets. The figures for the region are comparable to those on banks in Europe and Japan and are significantly lower than those on banks in the United States, where the average is around 3 percent of assets.

Low operating costs have permitted banks to improve their financial stability and soundness. The average share of nonperforming loans has fallen to around 11 percent, although the share continues to display considerable variation across the region. Both Indonesia and Thailand, which had peak nonperforming loan ratios of 48 and 45 percent, respectively, in 1998, had brought the ratios down to single digits by the end of 2005 (7.6 percent and 8.3 percent, respectively). In Korea, the ratio has fallen to only 1.2 percent. At the same time, all banks (except those in China) have rebuilt their capital base, and capital adequacy ratios in the region stand at around 14 percent, which is comparable to the ratios of banks in emerging Europe and in Latin America (see figures 4.8 and 4.9).

On the other side of the ledger, the corporate customers of banks are also showing much healthier balance sheets than they did before the crisis. The most extreme example is Korea. Before the crisis, the average corporate borrower in Korea had a debt-equity ratio of 181, three times higher than an average borrower in the United States. Indonesia and Thailand were other countries in which leverage was high (71 and 94 percent, respectively). By 2004, these leverage ratios had declined to 49 percent (Korea) and 47 percent (Thailand), though the ratio remained high in Indonesia (68 percent).

Obviously, firms with very high debt levels tend to be risky customers. But here, too, the trend is toward better balance sheets. The proportion of firms with debt-equity ratios greater than 200 percent has been halved in Indonesia, Korea, and Thailand since 2000.

Sound banks and healthy corporate balance sheets should be a recipe for solid credit expansion, but the reverse has happened in East Asia. Banks have been improving their balance sheets by cutting back on credit except to the best borrowers. Credit to the private sector is generally lower in the region, and an increasing share of this credit is going to consumers rather than to corporates. Thus, in 2004, consumer lending accounted for 53 percent of total credit in Malaysia, 49 percent in Korea, 40–50 percent in Hong Kong (China) and Singapore, 30 percent in Indonesia, 17 percent in Thailand, 15 percent in China, and 10 percent in the Philippines.

Clearly, the nature of the banking system is changing in East Asia. The provision of credit to the corporate sector is no longer the principal activity of banks. Banks have diversified by lending to households. They have also engaged in a number of investment activities through which they earn fees and trading income. While this makes for sounder banks, it suggests that the era of easy credit

■ FIGURE 4.8 **The Share of Nonperforming Loans Has Shrunk Since 1997**

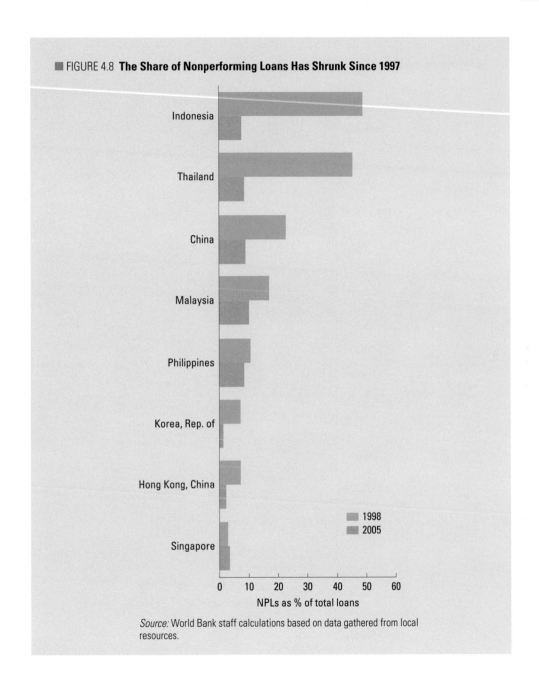

NPLs as % of total loans

1998
2005

Source: World Bank staff calculations based on data gathered from local resources.

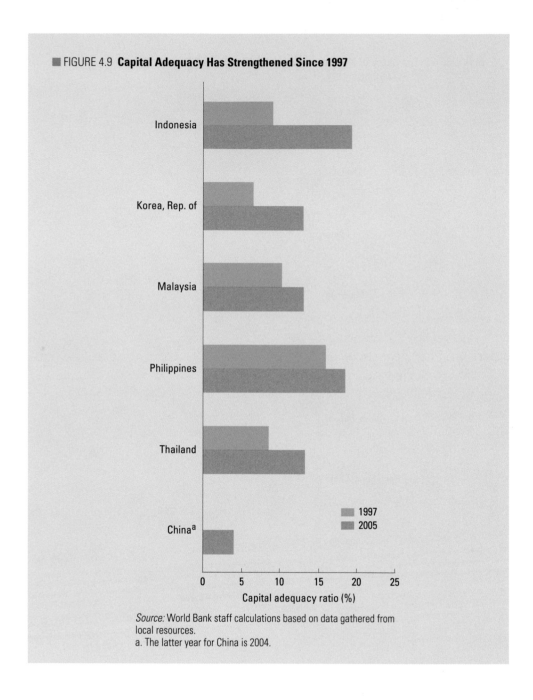

■ FIGURE 4.9 **Capital Adequacy Has Strengthened Since 1997**

Capital adequacy ratio (%)

Source: World Bank staff calculations based on data gathered from local resources.
a. The latter year for China is 2004.

to the firms making up the production networks has passed. Firms must meet a more stringent test of financial market discipline.

Securities Markets

Securities markets—equities and bonds—have grown appreciably in the region since 1997. Stock market capitalization had almost tripled, to US$2.3 trillion, by 2004. Bond markets have added another US$1.5 trillion. Measured as a share of GDP, the region's capital markets appear to be sizable.

This impression is reinforced by the amount of capital that has been raised. In 2004, US$66.6 billion in new equity was raised, half through initial public offerings. By contrast, only US$4.6 billion was raised in emerging Europe and US$660 million in Latin America.

These aggregates disguise the varying performance of securities markets across the region. At one end, Hong Kong (China) and Singapore have well-developed markets. In the middle, Korea and Malaysia have also deepened their markets and now have relatively large bond markets as well. In its bond markets, Thailand has experienced one of the most rapid growth rates in the region, but much of this growth reflects the issuance of government and financial institution bonds to meet the costs associated with recapitalizing banks following the crisis. China, Indonesia, and the Philippines have significantly weaker systems that do not provide adequate finance to the corporate sectors.[26]

Part of the problem is that the tolerance of investors for risk appears to be low in the region. Even in countries with large bond markets, such as Korea and Malaysia, most issuers have excellent credit ratings. In Malaysia, 80 percent of issuances have AA or better credit ratings. In Korea, 80 percent of issues are rated A or better. Many issuers are quasi-government firms that enjoy explicit or implicit guarantees and therefore have the highest credit quality available domestically.

The result for smaller corporates is that they cannot access securities markets effectively. Because of their small size, liquidity in their paper is low. Transaction costs may also mount as a fraction of the amount of capital being raised. Firms must pay management fees to structure the transaction, credit rating agency fees, registration fees, and other documentation fees associated with disclosure rules, as well as underwriting fees, legal fees, and taxes. Not surprisingly, many firms find themselves squeezed out of the market.

Measures of the efficiency of equity markets in the region against the situation in other countries show that Hong Kong (China), Korea, Malaysia, and Singapore fare reasonably well in global terms, while China, Indonesia, the Philippines, and Thailand do poorly.

The efficiency measure captures transaction costs, as well as the extent to which the price of the equity reflects firm fundamentals rather than general market sentiment. It therefore provides a measure of the effectiveness of the market in generating useful information based on a large number of perceptions. If transaction costs are high, then trading is reduced and small changes in information will be ignored, reducing the efficiency of the market.

The key determinant of efficiency is liquidity. Liquidity shrinks the gap between bid prices and offer prices. It permits most trading to occur without a worry that prices will be affected by the trade itself, giving investors confidence that they may buy or sell at a specified market price. And it ensures that the market will return to normalcy if it becomes disrupted by an imbalance in orders or other shocks. Without liquidity, the market is unable to develop.

It is common to describe East Asia as a region with high liquidity because of the sizable amount of domestic savings that are generated. But this does not translate into better performance in securities markets because of the deficiencies in information for pricing accurately, the high transaction costs, including underdeveloped market infrastructure in some places, and the lack of a diversified investor base, especially among the insurance companies, pension funds, and mutual funds that manage large amounts of the long-term capital that is best suited for securities markets.

Conclusions

Looking ahead, the development of the corporate bond market remains the priority for policy makers in attempting to create a more diversified, robust capital market in the region.

Financial Structure and Firm Performance

The development of securities markets so as to diversify East Asia's financial markets is important because the structure of finance exerts an influence on firm performance. Firms tend to behave differently when they fund themselves through bank credits than through securities markets. There is increasing evidence that more innovative firms prefer to finance themselves through securities markets.

Innovative activity requires a high degree of trust on the part of financial investors. Innovations take time to implement, and returns accrue far in the future.

They are risky and imply venturing into uncharted waters. Many innovations fail, but the ones that succeed show high returns. Firms that are successful innovators must understand when it is appropriate to admit to failure and cease spending money on a project and when to keep going. Managers cannot be trusted to make these decisions because the incentives they face are different from those of share-holders. Shareholders bear the costs of failure, while managers reap many of the benefits of success.

Bank credits typically involve significant monitoring by banks of the managers of their client borrowers. This type of relationship lending is founded on the theory that banks know the business in which their customers are operating and, because of this expertise, are able to make sound judgments about the business prospects of their clients. The willingness of banks to extend credit is tied to this steady updating of their views on the health of the borrower firms.

For small incremental innovations, bank lending may be efficient. The bank is able to appraise the new technology adequately. It monitors the timeliness of the research and the process of application, and, if the project appears to be moving too slowly, jeopardizing future benefits, the bank may pull back its credit and force the firm to stop the project. Because banks adapt quickly to changes in the prospects of firms, they can afford to lend greater sums. Higher debt-equity ratios for firms mean, in turn, that free cash flow is reduced and that managers must constantly seek approval before moving forward with new projects.

But, when innovations are more significant, banks may become too conserva-tive. They may not have the skills to properly evaluate whether a new technology is likely to be successful. They might terminate projects prematurely because they do not wish to take on too much risk by extending more credit to firms. In these circumstances, arm's-length financing in capital markets is preferred.

Capital markets bring together a range of investors who may express substan-tial differences in their opinions on the likely success or failure of an innovation. This increases the likelihood that a firm will find a group of investors who believe in the new technology. Capital markets provide more long-term capital, and they permit greater management discretion. If equity is raised, rather than public debt, then there is greater cash flow, and the firm has more time to prove the value of its innovation.

Thus, bank credits may support incremental innovation, while capital markets are better suited to support more radical technological change.

These arguments are confirmed by empirical evidence from developed countries. In the United States, firms that rely more on public financing receive a larger num-ber of patents. These patents tend to be more valuable, as indicated by the frequency with which they are cited by others.[27] Changes in the financing structure of firms appear to be related to large changes in the value of the firms because of the impact on the rate of innovation.

In general, a broader financial structure supports the financing of a broader array of new innovations and so supports technological progress. Because constant innovation is critical for members of a production network, a broad, diversified financial system is desirable.

Financial Markets Must Manage Risk

Financial markets mobilize resources and allocate risks. In the East Asian context, the focus has shifted to the process of risk allocation. As the real economies in the region become more integrated, there has been a premium on stability. The region seems less vulnerable now than it once was to sudden shifts in investor sentiment because the structure of financing has shifted toward FDI, the maturities of liabilities have lengthened, and financing sources have become more diversified to include important regional economies.

As noted in IMF (2006), regional economies are now more resilient to a sudden reversal of inflows than they were a decade ago because their economic fundamentals have improved and because exchange rates in the majority of economies are more flexible. Furthermore, risks to the banking systems in the region have diminished because only a small portion of the flows have been intermediated this time through banks, leaving banking balance-sheets largely unaffected. However, not all economies have moved at the same pace in reducing domestic and external vulnerabilities. Some economies still possess underlying weaknesses, which leave them vulnerable to a sudden reversal of capital flows that may be brought by changes in sentiment and international financial conditions.[28]

But these successes have had costs. Countries in the region have moved rapidly to build up their defenses against major foreign exchange movements and conquer the "fear of floating." In some instances, they may even have moved too far. Rodrik (2006) has concluded that "developing countries have responded to financial globalization in a highly unbalanced and far from optimal manner. They have overinvested in the costly strategy of reserve accumulation and underinvested in capital account management policies" (p. 12). The region is trying to address this imbalance through enhanced regional cooperation. It does appear, however, that the foreign exchange risks that might undermine regional production networks have been lessened.

Credit risk remains a major obstacle in the region. Banks have cleaned up their balance sheets by reducing their exposure to the corporate sector, especially small firms. Capital markets have not developed rapidly enough to offer a viable alternative source of funding. Lack of public capital may be especially detrimental to innovation. The priority for the region is to develop equity and bond markets to permit more effective risk sharing at home and abroad.

Notes

1. See Sheng (2006) on the Asian network economy.

2. East Asia refers to the member countries of the Association of Southeast Asian Nations (Brunei Darussalam, Cambodia, Indonesia, the Lao People's Democratic Republic, Malaysia, Myanmar, the Philippines, Singapore, Thailand, and Vietnam), plus China, Hong Kong (China), Japan, the Republic of Korea, Mongolia, and Taiwan (China). Emerging East Asia refers to East Asia, minus Japan. Developing East Asia refers to emerging East Asia, minus Hong Kong (China), Korea, and Singapore.

3. The sudden stop was first suggested in Dornbusch, Goldfajn, and Valdés (1995). See also Calvo (1998).

4. See Carlson and Hernandez (2002), Dasgupta and Ratha (2000), and Montiel and Reinhart (1999).

5. See Gopinath and Echeverria (2004) and Blonigen (2005).

6. See Hallward-Driemeier, Iarossi, and Sokoloff (2002).

7. See Rajan and Zingales (2004).

8. See IMF (2003).

9. For instance, see Ito and Park (2004) and Eichengreen and Luengnaruemitchai (2004).

10. Malaysia shows up as an exception perhaps because it has exercised capital controls during much of the postcrisis period.

11. See Aizenman and Siregar (2006) for more detailed descriptive data on reserve stockpiling in East Asia.

12. Outside East Asia, India has also shown a sharp increase in reserves, from US$1 billion in 1990–91 to US$150 billion by early 2006.

13. See Aizenman and Marion (2003) and Bird and Rajan (2003). There is a growing body of literature exploring various aspects of the precautionary motive for reserve hoarding. See Aizenman and Lee (2005), García and Soto (2004), Jeanne and Rancière (2006), Kim et al. (2004), and Li and Rajan (2005).

14. See Bird and Rajan (2002) and Rajan (2003).

15. See Calvo and Reinhart (2002), Rajan (2002), and the references cited therein.

16. In addition, part of the change in reserves in U.S. dollar terms arises from revaluation gains caused by the depreciation of the U.S. dollar against the major currencies in which reserves might be held, especially the euro.

While Aizenman and Lee (2005) argue against the mercantilist rationale for the accumulation of reserves in East Asia, Ghosh (2005) has observed that:

> Intervention was initially motivated by a desire to build up a buffer stock after the Asian crisis had depleted levels of reserves . . . However, rapid reserve accumulation . . . continued through late 2004, as countries sought to limit the impact of heavy capital inflows on external competitiveness, at a time when domestic demand generally remained subdued. (p. 29)

Similarly, the IMF (2004) has noted that:

> Monetary authorities seem to have been driven by a desire to prevent nominal exchange rate appreciation in the pursuit of export-led growth policies, especially in Asia and after the increase in inflows in 2003–04. (p. 148)

17. See Goldstein and Lardy (2005).

18. A substantial portion of the balance of payments surplus is, of course, driven by China. See Ouyang, Rajan, and Willett (2006) and Prasad and Wei (2005) for details on the dynamics of the capital and current account balances in China.

19. See Dooley, Folkerts-Landau, and Garber (2004).

20. See Kamin (2005); Prasad and Wei (2005); Eichengreen (2005).

21. See Rajan (2006) and Rana (2002).

22. The International Index Company, which is owned by ABN Amro, JP Morgan, Morgan Stanley, and other international banks and global financial firms, has created the benchmark indexes for all nine funds.

23. Hamada, Jeon, and Ryou (2004), Leung (2005), and Ma and Remolona (2005) elaborate on this.

24. See Mehl and Reynaud (2005).

25. This section draws on Ghosh (2006).

26. See Gyntelberg, Ma, and Remolana (2006).

27. See Atanassov, Nanda, and Seru (2005).

28. In addition, while there has been better matching in the current composition of assets and liabilities in the developing East Asia region, this is largely due to an accumulation of reserves in foreign currency terms. It is important to ensure that individual corporates and financial institutions take appropriate care to manage the risks associated with these currency mismatch risks.

References

Aizenman, Joshua, and Jaewoo Lee. 2005. "International Reserves: Precautionary Versus Mercantilist Views, Theory and Evidence." NBER Working Paper 11366, National Bureau of Economic Research, Cambridge, MA.

Aizenman, Joshua, and Nancy Marion. 2003. "The High Demand for International Reserves in the Far East: What Is Going On?" *Journal of the Japanese and International Economies* 17 (3): 370–400.

Aizenman, Joshua, and Ilan Noy. 2005. "FDI and Trade: Two Way Linkages?" NBER Working Paper 11403, National Bureau of Economic Research, Cambridge, MA.

Aizenman, Joshua, and Reza Siregar. 2006. "Finance and Economic Integration in East Asia." Background paper, World Bank, Washington, DC.

Atanassov, Julian, Vikram K. Nanda, and Amit Seru. 2005. "Finance and Innovation: The Case of Publicly Traded Firms." Ross School of Business Paper 970 (October), Stephen M. Ross School of Business, University of Michigan, Ann Arbor, MI.

Aviat, Antonin, and Nicolas Coeurdacier. 2005. "The Geography of Trade in Goods and Asset Holdings." DELTA Working Paper 2004-10, Department and Laboratory of Applied and Theoretical Economics, Ecole Normale Supérieure, Paris.

Beale, Lieven, Annalisa Ferrando, Peter Hördahl, Elizaveta Krylova, and Cyril Monnet. 2004. "Measuring Financial Integration in the Euro Area." Occasional Paper 14, European Central Bank, Frankfurt am Main.

Bird, Graham, and Ramkishen S. Rajan. 2002. "The Evolving Asian Financial Architecture." Princeton Essays in International Economics 226 (February), Princeton University, Princeton, NJ.

_____. 2003. "Too Much of a Good Thing?: The Adequacy of International Reserves in the Aftermath of Crises." *World Economy* 26 (6): 873–91.

Blonigen, Bruce A. 2005. "A Review of the Empirical Literature on FDI Determinants." NBER Working Paper 11299, National Bureau of Economic Research, Cambridge, MA.

Calvo, Guillermo A. 1998. "Capital Flows and Capital-Market Crises: The Simple Economics of Sudden Stops." *Journal of Applied Economics* 1 (1): 35–54.

Calvo, Guillermo A., and Carmen M. Reinhart. 2002. "Fear of Floating." *Quarterly Journal of Economics* 117 (2): 379–408.

Carlson, Mark, and Leonardo Hernandez. 2002. "Determinants and Repercussions of the Composition of Capital Inflows." International Finance Discussion Paper 717, Board of Governors of the Federal Reserve System, Washington, DC.

Dasgupta, Dipak, and Dilip Ratha. 2000. "What Factors Appear to Drive Capital Flows to Developing Countries? And How Does Official Lending Respond?" Policy Research Working Paper 2392, World Bank, Washington, DC.

Dooley, Michael P., David Folkerts-Landau, and Peter M. Garber. 2004. "The U.S. Current Account Deficit and Economic Development: Collateral for a Total Return Swap." NBER Working Paper 10727, National Bureau of Economic Research, Cambridge, MA.

Dornbusch, Rudiger, Ilan Goldfajn, and Rodrigo O. Valdés. 1995. "Currency Crises and Collapses." Brookings Papers on Economic Activity 2: 219–93.

Eichengreen, Barry. 2005. "The Blind Men and the Elephant." Paper presented at the Tokyo Club Foundation's "Macroeconomic Research Conference on the Future of International Capital Flows," Kyoto, November 21–22.

Eichengreen, Barry, and Pipat Luengnaruemitchai. 2004. "Why Doesn't Asia Have Bigger Bond Markets?" NBER Working Paper 10576, National Bureau of Economic Research, Cambridge, MA.

Frankel, Jeffrey A. 1999. "No Single Currency Regime Is Right for All Countries or at All Times." NBER Working Paper 7338, National Bureau of Economic Research, Cambridge, MA.

García, Pablo, and Claudio Soto. 2004. "Large Hoardings of International Reserves: Are They Worth It?" Central Bank of Chile Working Paper 299, Central Bank of Chile, Santiago, Chile.

Ghosh, Swati R. 2005. "East Asian Finance: The Road to Robust Markets." Draft report, World Bank, Washington, DC.

———. 2006. East Asian Finance: The Road to Robust Markets. Washington, DC: World Bank.

Goldstein, Morris, and Nicholas Lardy. 2005. "China's Role in the Revived Bretton Woods System: A Case of Mistaken Identity." IIE Working Paper 05–2, Institute for International Economics, Washington, DC.

Gopinath, Munisamy, and Rodrigo Echeverria. 2004. "Does Economic Development Impact the Foreign Direct Investment–Trade Relationship?: A Gravity Model Approach." American Journal of Agricultural Economics 86 (3): 778–83.

Gruber, Joseph W., and Steven B. Kamin. 2005. "Explaining the Global Pattern of Current Account Imbalances." International Finance Discussion Paper 846, Board of Governors of the Federal Reserve System, Washington, DC.

Gyntelberg, Jacob, Guonan Ma, and Eli M. Remolana. 2006. "Developing Corporate Bond Markets in Asia." BIS Paper 26 (February): 13–21, Bank for International Settlements, Basel.

Hallward-Driemeier, Mary, Giuseppe Iarossi, and Kenneth L. Sokoloff. 2002. "Exports and Manufacturing Productivity in East Asia: A Comparative Analysis with Firm-Level Data." NBER Working Paper 8894, National Bureau of Economic Research, Cambridge, MA.

Hamada, Koichi, Seung-Cheol Jeon, and Jai-Won Ryou. 2004. "Asian Bonds Market: Issues, Prospects, and Tasks for Cooperation." Paper presented at the Association of Korean Economic Studies, University of Washington Research Center for International Economics, and Korea Development Institute Conference, "Korea and the World Economy III," Sungkyunkwan University, Seoul, July 3–4.

IMF (International Monetary Fund). 2003. "Trade Finance in Financial Crises: Assessment of Key Issues." Policy Development and Review Department, International Monetary Fund, Washington, DC. http://www.imf.org/external/np/pdr/cr/2003/eng/120903.pdf.

———. 2004. Global Financial Stability Report: Market Developments and Issues, September. Washington, DC: International Monetary Fund.

———. 2006. "Regional Economic Outlook: Asia and Pacific." World Economic and Financial Surveys, May, International Monetary Fund, Washington, DC.

Ito, Takatoshi, and Yung-Chul Park, eds. 2004. Developing Asian Bondmarkets: Challenges and Strategies. Canberra: Asia Pacific Press.

Jeanne, Olivier, and Romain Rancière. 2006. "The Optimal Level of International Reserves for Emerging Market Countries: Formulas and Applications." IMF Working Paper 229, International Monetary Fund, Washington, DC.

Kamin, Steven B. 2005. "The Revived Bretton Woods System: Does It Explain Developments in Non-China Developing Asia?" Paper presented at the Federal Reserve Bank of San Francisco Symposium on "The Revived Bretton Woods System: A New Paradigm for Asian Development?" February 4.

Kharas, Homi, Enrique Aldaz-Carroll, and Sjamsu Rahardja. 2007. "East Asia: Regional Integration among Open Economies." In *Economic Integration in Asia and India*, ed. Masahisa Fujita. Basingstoke, United Kingdom: Palgrave Macmillan.

Kim, Jung Sik, Jie Li, Ramkishen S. Rajan, Ozan Sula, and Thomas D. Willett. 2004. "Reserve Adequacy in Asia Revisited: New Benchmarks Based on the Size and Composition of Capital Flows." Paper presented at Claremont Graduate University, Claremont McKenna College, and Korea Institute of International Economic Policy "Conference on Monetary and Exchange Rate Arrangements in East Asia," Seoul, August 26–27.

Leung, Julia. 2005. "Developing Bond Markets in Asia: Experience with ABF2." Paper presented at the Bank for International Settlements, People's Bank of China Seminar, "Developing Corporate Bond Markets in Asia," Kunming, China, November 17–18.

Li, Jie, and Ramkishen S. Rajan. 2005. "Can High Reserves Offset Weak Fundamentals?: A Simple Model of Precautionary Demand for Reserves." CIES Discussion Paper 0509, Center for International Economic Studies, University of Adelaide, Adelaide, Australia.

Ma, Guonan, and Eli M. Remolona. 2005. "Opening Markets through a Regional Bond Fund: Lessons from ABF2." *BIS Quarterly Review* June: 81–92.

McCauley, Robert N. 2003. "Capital Flows in East Asia since the 1997 Crisis." *BIS Quarterly Review* June: 41–55.

Mehl, Arnaud, and Julien Reynaud. 2005. "The Determinants of 'Domestic' Original Sin in Emerging Market Economies." Working Paper 560, European Central Bank, Frankfurt am Main.

METI (Japan, Ministry of Economy, Trade, and Industry). 2005. *White Paper on International Economy and Trade 2005: Towards a New Dimension of Economic Prosperity in Japan and East Asia.* Tokyo: Ministry of Economy, Trade, and Industry.

Mody, Ashoka, and Shoko Negishi. 2001. "The Role of Cross-Border Mergers and Acquisitions in Asian Restructuring." In *Resolution of Financial Distress: An International Perspective on the Design of Bankruptcy Laws*, ed. Stijn Claessens, Simeon Djankov, and Ashoka Mody, 305–39. Washington, DC: World Bank.

Montiel, Peter J., and Carmen M. Reinhart. 1999. "Do Capital Controls and Macroeconomic Policies Influence the Volume and Composition of Capital Flows?: Evidence from the 1990s." *Journal of Money and International Finance* 18 (4): 619–35.

Obstfeld, Maurice. 1986. "Rational and Self-Fulfilling Balance-of-Payments Crises." *American Economic Review* 76 (1): 72–81.

———. 1994. "The Logic of Currency Crises." *Cahiers économiques et monetaires* 43: 189–213, Banque de France, Paris.

Ouyang, Alice Y., and Ramkishen S. Rajan. 2005. "Monetary Sterilization in China since the 1990s: How Much and How Effective?" CIES Discussion Paper 0507, Center for International Economic Studies, University of Adelaide, Adelaide, Australia.

Ouyang, Alice Y., Ramkishen S. Rajan, and Thomas D. Willett. 2006. "Monetary Sterilization in Asia." Draft working paper, School of Public Policy, George Mason University, Arlington, VA.

Portes, Richard, and Helene Rey. 1999. "The Determinants of Cross-Border Equity Flows." NBER Working Paper 7336, National Bureau of Economic Research, Cambridge, MA.

Prasad, Eswar, and Shang-Jin Wei. 2005. "The Chinese Approach to Capital Inflows: Patterns and Possible Explanations." NBER Working Paper 11306, National Bureau of Economic Research, Cambridge, MA.

Rajan, Ramkishen S. 2002. "Exchange Rate Policy Options for Southeast Asia: Is There a Case for Currency Baskets?" *World Economy* 25 (1): 137–63.

_____. 2003. "Safeguarding against Capital Account Crises: Unilateral, Regional, and Multilateral Options for East Asia." In *Financial Governance in East Asia: Policy Dialogue, Surveillance and Cooperation*, ed. Gordon de Brouwer and Yunjong Wang, 239–63. London: Routledge.

_____. 2006. "Monetary and Financial Cooperation in Asia: Taking Stock of Recent On-Goings." RIS Discussion Paper 107, Research and Information System for Developing Countries, New Delhi.

Rajan, Raghuram G., and Luigi Zingales. 2004. *Saving Capitalism from the Capitalists: Unleashing the Power of Financial Markets to Create Wealth and Spread Opportunity*. Princeton, NJ: Princeton University Press.

Rana, Pradumna B. 2002. "Monetary and Financial Cooperation in East Asia: The Chiang Mai Initiative and Beyond." ERD Working Paper 6 (February), Economics and Research Department, Asian Development Bank, Manila.

Rodrik, Dani. 2006. "The Social Cost of Foreign Exchange Reserves." *International Economic Journal* 20 (3): 253–66.

Sheng, Andrew. 2006. "The Asian Network Economy in the 21st Century." In *East Asian Visions: Perspectives on Economic Development*, ed. Indermit S. Gill, Yukon Huang, and Homi Kharas, chap. 15. Washington, DC: World Bank.

UNCTAD (United Nations Conference on Trade and Development). 2005. *World Investment Report 2005: Transnational Corporations and the Internationalization of R&D*. Geneva: United Nations.

MAP 5.1 East Asian Cities of All Sizes Will Expand Rapidly during the Next Decade

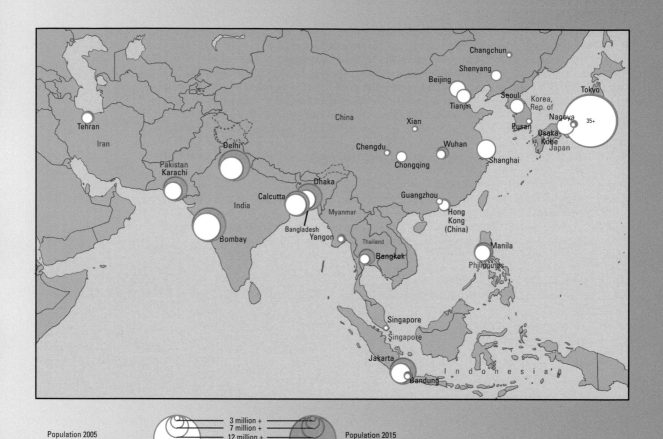

Population 2005
(represented by lighter shades)

3 million +
7 million +
12 million +
25 million +

Population 2015
(represented by darker shades)

The area of each circle is proportional to the estimated total population in the years 2005 and 2015 respectively.

Source: United Nations 2003.

CHAPTER 5

CITIES

East Asian cities have been a source of agglomeration economies, but there are big differences in economic management. A rapid urbanization is under way that will strain cities of all sizes.

Scale Economies, Cities, and Economic Growth

In the most compelling formulations of modern growth theory, new ideas and the benefits of human capital are shared with others who are nearby and equipped to take advantage of them.[1] In aggregate, these externalities or knowledge spillovers allow economies to defy the law of diminishing returns: bigger, richer economies may continue to grow more rapidly than smaller, poorer ones. Geography is almost always important in determining who—besides those who create or possess them—benefits from these ideas and skills. Put another way, the spillovers of knowledge tend to decline with distance both within and across countries. These phenomena therefore encourage people to live in close proximity to one another to become wealthier, and the phenomena encourage firms in a single industry to locate close to each other to become more innovative and competitive. The result is the growth of towns and cities.

Cities are perhaps the most important and most visible manifestation of economies of scale, and they play a central role in economic growth. By facilitating geographical proximity, cities enable people to benefit from the ideas that others create. By bringing together pools of entrepreneurs with similar economic interests, cities facilitate both the creation of new ideas and the translation of ideas into production. Besides these knowledge spillovers, by creating thick markets for labor, capital, and intermediate and final goods, cities enable cost savings and efficiency. Economists call all these effects agglomeration economies (see box 5.1). By enabling connections to the outside world, towns and cities allow entrepreneurs to access ideas and markets in other countries. Some cities grow ever bigger and become megacities. The most dynamic cities do all these things—generating ideas, exchanging them internationally, and growing bigger and more vibrant— and come to be known as world cities. Small, medium, large, or mega, cities are at the center of specialization, innovation, trade, and growth. Map 5.1 shows the principal Asian cities and their expected growth during the next decade.

It is difficult to understand a country's economic growth without understanding its urban centers. In Vietnam, for example, while the share of the urban population in total population is less than 30 percent, the contribution of towns and

---

■ BOX 5.1 **Agglomeration Economies**

Three reasons are usually given to explain why firms in a particular industry may locate close to each other. Spatial concentration helps in:

- *Sharing:* broadening the market for input suppliers, thereby allowing them to exploit internal economies of scale in production (average costs decline as the scale of production rises). This sharing of inputs also permits suppliers to provide highly specialized goods and services that are tailored to the needs of their buyers. The result is higher profits for all, accompanied by easier access to a broader range of inputs.
- *Matching:* expanding the availability of the range of skills required by employers to facilitate better matching to their distinctive needs. At the same time, workers find it less risky to be in locations where there are many possible employers.
- *Learning:* accelerating spillovers of (rivalrous and nonrival, explicit and tacit) knowledge, allowing workers and entrepreneurs to learn from each other.

The ability to go beyond industry-specific sharing, matching, and learning (localization economies) to citywide processes (urbanization economies) requires the recognition that additional mechanisms are active in the growth of metropolitan areas. These include, for example, the

effects of cumulative causation and the interpenetration of production and trade across industries. They also include gains from the cross-fertilization of ideas, the notion that concentrations of workers and suppliers lead to a concentration of consumer demands (possibly reflecting specific consumption patterns in the home market), and economies on the consumption side choices of individuals.

If economies of scale are large and unexhausted and if firms are able to compete not only on price, but also through product differentiation, the new framework of economic geography posits that strong centripetal forces come into play and that these may explain the formation of cities. In addition, by formally introducing the concept of distance (the cost of shipping inputs and outputs), the framework is able to provide useful insights into the centrifugal forces that explain spatial dispersion or urban agglomeration in a country. Generally speaking, the dominance (primacy) of one or a handful of metropolitan areas in a country increases if the benefits from economies of scale are great in relation to transportation costs. Many regional development policies in East Asia have been focused on attempts to assess and work with this particular trade-off.

cities to national output is 70 percent.[2] In China, 120 cities account for about three-quarters of the country's gross domestic product (GDP) in a year. In the Philippines, urban areas account for over 80 percent of economic growth; by themselves, the national capital region and adjoining areas account for more than 60 percent of GDP growth.[3] In richer countries, this share is even higher. For example, metropolitan areas today contribute more than 85 percent of the GDP of the United States.[4] Little wonder then that economic growth and urbanization have increased in lockstep. The transformation of economies from agricultural to industrial is generally equated with urbanization, but the key factor is that non-agricultural activities require agglomerations that farming does not. Indeed, the most parsimonious and most insightful formulations of an economy that recognize the importance of space start with a two-sector economy in which agriculture displays returns to scale that are constant and industry is characterized by returns to scale that are increasing.[5] The central feature is the importance of scale economies and cities in economic development.

While simplifying an economy so as to make it consist of two sectors, these economic formulations explicitly recognize links between them. Urbanization in a well-functioning economy is not a one-way process; urbanites do not abandon the countryside forever and sever their connections with rural areas. Adam Smith (1776) pointed out that:

> The increase and riches of commercial and manufacturing towns contributed to the improvement and cultivation of the countries to which they belonged in three different ways.
>
> First, by affording a great and ready market for the rude produce of the country, they gave encouragement to its cultivation and further improvement. This benefit was not even confined to the countries in which they were situated, but extended more or less to all those with which they had any dealings. . . .
>
> Secondly, the wealth acquired by the inhabitants of cities was frequently employed in purchasing such lands as were to be sold, of which a great part would frequently be uncultivated. . . .
>
> Thirdly, and lastly, commerce and manufactures gradually introduced order and good government, and with them, the liberty and security of individuals, among the inhabitants of the country . . . (pp. 384–85).

That is, well-integrated economies have thriving cities that grow themselves, but also spur growth in the rest of the economy through product and factor market connections and through beneficial political intercourse.

The power of economic geography is seen in different ways in East Asian countries. As in other parts of the world, there is a positive correlation between per capita income and the level of urbanization.[6] This association is far from close because the large differences in income levels should imply heterogeneous outcomes (see table 5.1). The region contains two of the least urbanized countries in the world (Cambodia and Papua New Guinea) and one (Singapore) that is among the most urbanized. Consistent with theories of economic geography, the variations in physical features, economic performance, industrial structure, and openness of a country also generate dissimilar contexts for the evolution of the country's metropolitan areas. In East Asia, per capita incomes vary between US$400

■ TABLE 5.1 **Urban Populations Have Grown at Twice the Rate of Total Populations**

Economy or region	GNI per capita (US$, 2005)[a]	Population		Urban population	
		Total (millions, 2004)	Growth rate (%, 2000–05)	Share of total (%)	Growth rate (%, 2000–05)
Cambodia	380	14.5	2.4	19	5.5
China	1,740	1,313.3	0.7	39	3.2
Indonesia	1,270	222.6	1.3	46	3.9
Lao PDR	440	5.8	2.3	21	4.6
Malaysia	4,960	24.9	1.9	64	3.0
Mongolia	670	2.6	1.3	57	1.4
Myanmar	—	50.1	1.1	30	3.1
Papua New Guinea	660	5.8	2.2	13	2.3
Philippines	1,250	81.4	1.8	61	3.1
Thailand	2,750	63.5	1.0	32	1.9
Vietnam	620	82.5	1.3	26	3.2
East Asia and Pacific	1,610	1,869.5	0.8	41	3.1
Hong Kong, China	26,810	7.1	1.1	100	1.1
Korea, Rep. of	15,810	48.0	0.6	80	0.9
Singapore	24,220	4.3	1.7	100	1.7
Developing East Asia	1,680	5,360.8	1.3	43	2.5
Australia	27,100	19.9	1.0	92	1.4
Japan	37,210	127.8	0.1	65	0.3
World	6,329	6,365.0	1.2	49	2.1

Sources: United Nations 2003; World Bank staff calculations.
Note: — = no data are available.
a. GNI = gross national income.

and US$5,000, industrial production ranges from 27 to 50 percent of GDP, and external trade from 35 to 196 percent of GDP. Accordingly, urbanization rates and patterns differ across countries.

This chapter therefore examines the role cities are playing in East Asia's economic growth. It discusses the priorities for easing the stresses and strains that economic and demographic changes are exerting on cities in the region and briefly assesses how effective East Asian national and subnational governments have been in dealing with these pressures. The main conclusions are as follows:

- First, because of rapid economic growth, East Asian countries have reached levels of industrialization and per capita income that are generally associated with higher levels of urbanization. A side effect is a heavy reliance on megacities both for external economies associated with agglomeration and for connections with regional and global markets. In some countries, these growth patterns have led to lopsided urbanization that is reflected in the dominance of primate cities, which, in countries such as the Philippines and Thailand, account for close to half of the total urban population and an even larger share of national economic output. As the middle-income countries of the region attempt to grow to high-income levels, megacities will play a central role in deepening international integration and fostering innovation. The livability of these cities will become even more important than it has been in the past.
- Second, over the next 25 years, more than 550 million people are expected to join the approximately 750 million currently living in East Asia's towns and cities. With many cities already straining to stay livable and business friendly, this implies a challenge for policy makers. The magnitude of this challenge has historically never been confronted in middle-income countries. It will require unprecedented efforts at the national, provincial, and municipal levels of government.
- Third, it is widely held among urban specialists that a big part of the response to this impending urbanization will lie in the growth of small (less than 500,000 residents) and midsize cities (between 500,000 and 2 million residents). These cities must be well managed to enable the exploitation of scale economies; they must be livable and, perhaps even more importantly, they must be well connected to larger cities. While their livability will depend on city governments, their connectedness to other, especially larger cities will depend mainly on national and provincial governments. Success will require good planning and economic management at the city level and good planning and sound infrastructural investments at the provincial and national levels.

Challenges Confronting East Asia's Cities

After a brief setback during the financial crisis of 1997–98, a rapid rise in incomes and the resumption of intense global activity have accompanied an acceleration in urbanization in East Asia. The metropolitan population has risen by 3.1 percent per year over the past five years, compared to an overall population increase of only 0.8 percent. In other words, while total population has risen by about 59 million people, the number of people living in urban areas has increased by 88 million.

This is to be expected. The simple correlation between (the log of) income per person and the level of urbanization is 0.61 in East Asia. But, while urbanization has quickened, the distribution of urban inhabitants among settlements of various sizes has been uneven. Metropolitan areas with fewer than 500,000 inhabitants have grown most rapidly. Although megacities continue to expand in population and size (see table 5.2), the number of settlements with between 500,000 and 5 million inhabitants has risen only slowly in parts of East Asia, while the shares of these settlements in total populations may even have fallen.[7]

Over the next 25 years, there will be three related developments in East Asia: the size of urban populations will grow rapidly; the livability of large cities will come under stress; and the connectedness of small and medium cities will become even more necessary. More than 200 million of the projected 555 million increase in urban populations will be in large- and medium-sized cities; about 300 million, or close to 60 percent, will settle in small cities of fewer than a million inhabitants. As this massive shift of population occurs, large cities will experience greater stresses. At the same time, the size, economic contribution, and global links of large cities will increase.[8] Large cities will continue to generate more than half of all exports and more than three-quarters of economic growth.[9] However, population projections make clear that planning for the expansion of small and medium cities will become equally, if not more essential for rapid and sustainable economic growth.

The Accelerating Urbanization in East Asia

Today, roughly 50 percent of the world's population is urban. Only Africa and Asia, each with urbanization rates of about 39 percent, may still expect the most significant urbanization in their histories to occur in the future. Among all regions, the largest rural-to-urban shift will occur in East Asia both because of the size of the shift and because of the anticipated high rate of economic transformation and growth. Projections suggest that, among the middle-income regions

■ TABLE 5.2 **East Asia Has Mega, Primate, Capital, and Gateway Cities**

City type	2003				2015		
	Primacy indicator (%)[a]	World rank	Population (millions)	National population share (%)	World rank	Population (millions)	National population share (%)
Megacities							
Tokyo	42.1	1	35.0	27.4	1	36.2	28.5
Shanghai	2.5	9	12.8	1.0	15	12.7	0.9
Jakarta	12.0	10	12.3	5.5	8	17.5	7.0
Seoul	31.8	11	12.2	25.4	18	12.0	24.2
Osaka	13.5	14	11.2	8.8	19	11.4	9.0
Beijing	2.1	17	10.8	0.8	21	11.1	0.8
Manila	20.9	20	10.4	12.7	16	12.6	13.1
Primate cities							
Taipei[b]	32.0	43	6.9	30.1	—	6.8	29.0
Bangkok	32.0	46	6,5	10.2	—	7.5	10.7
Yangon	26.6	68	4.0	8.0	—	5.3	9.4
Kuala Lumpur	14.4	73	2.3	8.8	—	2.7	9.2
Phnom Penh	43.6	311	1.2	7.8	—	1.5	8.1
Ulaanbaatar	54.0	—	0.8	31.4	—	1.0	32.7
Vientiane	65.7	—	0.8	13.0	—	1.2	16.0
Port Moresby	39.8	—	0.3	4.8	—	0.4	5.3
Capital cities							
Hanoi[c]	19.1	67	4.1	4.9	—	5.3	5.6
Gateway cities							
Hong Kong, China	100.0	38	7.1	100.0	—	7.9	100.0
Singapore	100.0	65	4.3	100.0	—	4.7	100.0

Sources: United Nations 2003; World Gazetteer Database, http://www.world-gazetteer.com/; The Principal Agglomerations of the World Database, Thomas Brinkhoff, http://www.citypopulation.de; World Bank staff calculations.
Note: Metropolitan areas with 10 million inhabitants or more are classified as megacities. Such agglomerations include a central city and neighboring communities linked to it by continuous built-up areas or commuters, inhabited at urban-density levels. Some metropolitan areas have more than one central city (for example, Kuala Lumpur–Petaling Jaya, Osaka-Kobe, and Tokyo-Yokohama-Kawasaki). Primate cities in this table are those that are at least twice as large as the next largest city in the country. Gateway cities function as important points of entry or exit for regional trade and investment.— = no data are available.
a. Percentage of urban population.
b. Refers to the share of the population of Taiwan Province, China.
c. Does not meet the definition of a primate city. Ho Chi Minh City is larger than Hanoi.

of the world, East Asia's urban population growth rates will be the highest (see figure 5.1).

In the region's middle income countries, urbanization will be a major force. Over the next 25 years, urban populations will rise from 536 million to 878 million in China, from 108 million to 189 million in Indonesia, from 52 million to 87 million in the Philippines, from 22 million to 47 million in Vietnam, and from 21 million to 35 million in Thailand. In many of these countries, urbanization in the past has generally meant an increase in the size of the largest metropolitan areas. It is an open question whether these cities, which today house about 740 million people, can expand sufficiently to accommodate 500 million more people without seriously compromising their potential to contribute to economic growth.

The experience around the world shows that government policies are generally ineffective in changing the rate of overall migration. Furthermore, given the importance of the large East Asian cities as growth poles, it is unlikely that policy

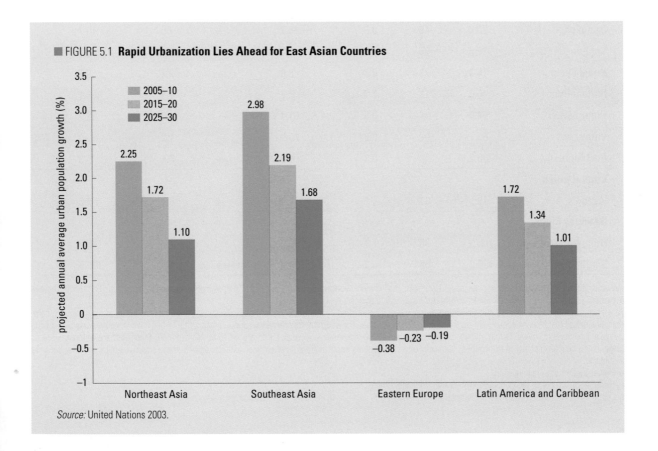

■ FIGURE 5.1 **Rapid Urbanization Lies Ahead for East Asian Countries**

Source: United Nations 2003.

makers will be able to resist the future economic development of these cities. Practically speaking, therefore, the role of public policy will be to manage the distribution of settlement sizes within a country, while harnessing the dynamism and improving the livability of major metropolitan areas.[10]

The Growing Congestion in Large Cities

Because of the large rise in urban populations in East Asia, the problem of metropolitan congestion—the costs associated with big city grime, crime, and time—may thwart efforts to exploit agglomeration economies. While urban crime does not appear to be a pressing problem in much of East Asia, the growing pollution and congestion in the region's cities have the potential of becoming the most important factors compromising economic growth. (See table 5.3 for a comparison of China's urban pollution and congestion with the situation in developed countries.)

National governments have been active in competing for global investors and tourists through megaurban projects and developments that have been concentrated largely in capital and major cities. Driving the rate of urbanization, as well as the dynamism of urban areas, has been the capacity of the largest cities, such as Tokyo, to command a central position first in the national economy, then the regional economy, and, ultimately, the global economy. In the 1960s, Tokyo was a capital city that attracted local business investments, and it was a destination for migrants from other parts of Japan. By the 1970s, it had become the financial, telecommunications, and transnational corporate center of the country. Full integration into the world economy came in the 1980s. Such a metropolitan

■ TABLE 5.3 **Chinese Cities Compare Poorly to Cities in the G-7 in Grime and Time Costs**

Indicator	China	G-7
Congestion		
Average travel time to work (minutes)	47	25
Transport-related injuries and deaths (per 1,000 vehicles)	31	12
Pollution		
Particulate matter in the air (mg per m^3)	320	45
Sulphur dioxide (mg per m^3)	82	19
Nitrous oxide (mg per m^3)	88	56

Source: Zhou 2006.

development process appears to have influenced equally the dynamics of growth in Seoul and Taipei, as well as other cities in Southeast Asia and, more recently, along coastal China and Vietnam. There is every indication that cities are powering both economic growth and human development in much of East Asia.

The contribution of metropolitan areas to national economies and the pace of urbanization (the increase in the number of people) and urban expansion (the increase in the amount of land occupied) have diverged.[11] For example, envelopment—metropolitan areas spreading to absorb areas previously designated as rural—is almost as important in explaining urbanization in some East Asian countries (for example, China, Indonesia, and Vietnam) as are natural increases in city populations and migration.[12] Furthermore, the conditions that will sustain East Asia's metropolitan areas—consisting mainly of good management (governance), the quality of the physical environment, and efficient and sufficient financing—differ markedly from country to country, as well as from the corresponding conditions in other regions of the world. For example, seven of the world's 21 megacities are in East Asia, compared to only two in the (outside-Asia) group of countries in the Organisation for Economic Co-operation and Development. The challenges involved in sustaining megacities—dealing with the problems of grime, crime, and time—are often of a significantly higher order than the challenges in smaller-sized metropolitan areas. Therefore, given such considerations, while some generalizations about public policies for raising employment and incomes in East Asia's urban areas are possible, policies will have to be customized to the particular circumstances in each country.

The Growing Importance of Small and Midsized Cities

East Asian policy makers and analysts in most of the countries are giving exceptional attention to the growth, contribution, and sustainability of the 15 to 20 capital, primate, and megacities. Over the next decade, half of the increase in urban populations in the countries of the region will be in cities of less than 500,000 people (see table 5.4). If these cities need to enable economic growth at the pace of the last decade, they will have to be both well managed and well connected.

Services tend to be poorer in smaller cities because capital is frequently captured by large cities. But capital-output ratios are higher in large cities, indicating lower efficiency. Nonetheless, from a settlement perspective, big cities are more efficient. The efficiencies may lead to overconcentration (see box 5.2). With new communications and transport technologies, however, it is possible to obtain the benefits of livability *and* reap productivity gains from investments in small cities.

■ TABLE 5.4 **About 60 Percent of the Urban Population Lives in Cities of Less Than a Million**
millions of people

City population	2005	2010	2015	Increase, 2005–10	2015 (%)
10 million or more	96	101	117	21	10.1
5–10 million	64	69	90	26	7.8
1–5 million	233	279	299	66	25.8
500,000 to 1 million	99	103	105	6	9.1
Fewer than 500,000	429	489	549	120	47.3
Total urban	921	1,041	1,160	239	100.1

Source: United Nations 2006.
Note: The table covers Brunei, Cambodia, China (including Hong Kong [China] and Macao [China]), Indonesia, Japan, the Democratic People's Republic of Korea, the Republic of Korea, the Lao People's Democratic Republic, Malaysia, Mongolia, Myanmar, the Philippines, Singapore, Thailand, Timor-Leste, and Vietnam.

■ BOX 5.2 **Optimal Urban Concentration?**

The literature on city size in developing countries has three strands, all of which point toward the tendency of these countries to overconcentrate and, hence, to pay a price in terms of reduced economic growth. The first is a theoretical strand, which argues that cities are either only efficiently sized or oversized since both types of city will pull resources from undersized cities that are not exploiting scale economies sufficiently. The second strand is empirical; it tries to estimate the costs and benefits of expanding city size and concludes that the marginal social costs of expansion in large cities exceed the marginal benefits. The third strand points to governments that favor capital cities or business center cities over other types of cities in terms of access to public services or public officials; it encourages overconcentration.

Henderson (2000) addresses these questions for a panel of between 80 to 100 countries during 1960–95 and finds that: (1) there is an optimal degree of concentration for given levels of development; the rise is up to a per capita income of US$5,000 (in 1995 purchasing power parity dollars) before a modest decline; (2) the optimal concentration becomes lower as a country grows larger;

(3) several countries in East Asia (notably, the Republic of Korea and Thailand) are overly concentrated relative to their level of development; the region that exhibits the most systematic overconcentration is Latin America; (4) the main policy variable affecting concentration is investment in interregional transport infrastructure; and (5) the growth losses of excessive concentration rise with income, so that the growth effects of investment are higher among middle-income countries than they are among low-income countries.

Au and Henderson (2006) ask whether China's cities are too small. They develop and test a model of the scale economies and diseconomies internal to a city and the effects of intercity trade costs following the new economic geography. They conclude that migration restrictions may have caused between half and two-thirds of Chinese cities to remain too small. In contrast, less than 5 percent of the cities are too large. For the typical city, being too small implies a loss of about 17 percent in terms of net output per worker. But, for at least a quarter of the cities, these losses may range between 25 and 70 percent. Their recommendation is the liberalization of domestic migration policies.

Good economic management is required to achieve this outcome. Yet, good economic management has generally proved a challenge for the governments of small and medium cities.

There are large differences in livability among all cities, not merely among the main cities of East Asia. Within each country, we find significant variations between core and secondary urban areas. Despite such heterogeneity, there are common issues. The principal one is connectivity. Large cities have generally been successful in becoming connected. This is often an important reason why these cities grew in the first place. For small cities, connectivity is a challenge still to be met.

China is facing all these tests—large rural-to-urban shifts, rising congestion in large cities, the mushrooming of small cities, and heterogeneity in the economic and administrative performance of cities—at the same time. In this sense, it is therefore essentially a microcosm of the East Asia region. However, China seems to have realized the enormity of the task ahead and has moved farther than other middle-income countries of the region in addressing some of this complexity. The next section analyzes the forces of the economic geography of China in which cities play a central role.

Economic Geography in East Asia: Illustrations from China

The new economic geography is one of the more exciting developments in economic analysis. It permits a consideration of economic structure and behavior within a framework of interconnected markets (general equilibrium) in explaining the spatial formation of economic activity. It therefore has the potential to explain critical (though not all) underpinnings of metropolitan growth. However, there are few empirical studies supporting the main hypotheses. The gap is especially noticeable for developing countries. So, it is useful to consider insights provided by the application of several simple propositions of the new economic geography to developments in East Asia.

In the new economic geography, the primary reason for city formation and growth is external economies of scale or agglomeration economies (see box 5.1). The basic observation is that spatial concentrations of production, trading, and creative activity have a propensity to feed off themselves and to generate environments that promote the additional clustering of economic activity.[13] This also means that there is greater path-dependence than conventionally assumed by development theorists and practitioners: the set of opportunities available to a metropolitan area is shaped powerfully by the economic activities the area has already established.[14] The initial set of activities might arise from a variety of factors, including happenstance (for example, Hong Kong [China], Macau [China], and Singapore), endowments (Melaka, Malaysia), or policy (Bandung, Indonesia), but, once established, agglomeration tends to lock into specific locations. Both labor and capital (including new technologies, creative centers, and links to other countries) are heavily concentrated in metropolitan areas, regardless of the level of development of a country. This section discusses some aspects of economic geography in China, where recent work has been done.

Transport Costs, International Integration, and Specialization

The interaction of economic geography with international integration is illustrated by two examples from China. The first of these is shown in table 5.5, which uses simplified costs for containerized garment exports from China to the western coast of the United States. At the same input costs, but a different transport burden, the maximum possible value added in Lanzhou (a city in the interior of China) only reaches 60 percent of that in Shanghai. The return to labor in the interior province reaches only 43 percent of that in the coastal area and only 33 percent of the international wage. Geography has a strong impact on wages and per capita incomes and, therefore, on the size and scope of urban agglomerations. As the experience of most countries suggests, offsetting such effects is costly, takes time, and requires a multipronged strategy.

■ TABLE 5.5 **Geography Influences the Returns to Labor in China**
percent

Cost, price component	Seattle, WA	Shanghai, China	Lanzhou, China
Output sale price c.i.f.[a]	100	n.a.	n.a.
Output transport cost	0	5	15
Output sale price f.o.b.[b]	n.a.	95	85
Input cost	40	40	40
Input transport	0	5	15
Value added	60	50	30
Capital	15	15	15
Labor	45	35	15

Source: Compiled by the authors.
Note: As in most garment processing for export from China, the inputs are imported; the output price is determined in the competitive U.S. market. Overland access to the port from China's interior typically accounts for two-thirds of the total transport costs. n.a. = not applicable.
a. The output sale price in Seattle includes the cost, plus insurance and freight.
b. The output sale price in Lanzhou and Shanghai is the price free on board.

This point may be seen in a more generalized manner in table 5.6, which compares returns to land and labor in interior cities with those at the access points (all seaports) through which the output of the interior cities reaches other markets. In all cases, labor costs are lower in the interior cities than in the coastal cities. Moreover, the price of real estate is generally 25 to 50 percent less in the interior cities than in the major seaports.[15] The link with competitiveness may also be deduced in the survey upon which the table is based and which covered 12,400 firms in 120 Chinese cities that account for between 70 and 80 percent of China's GDP.[16]

Because of the interaction among the various types of lower factor costs, especially labor, and the higher transport costs, interior cities tend to be more suitable for bulk production (for example, coal, which is shipped by slower means of transport such as railways) or high-value goods (for example, computer chips, which are valuable enough to be shipped by air). High transport costs tend to affect medium-value, high-volume goods that are too valuable to ship by rail, but not worth shipping by air. By and large, this is the spatial pattern of production found in China's industrial structure.

■ TABLE 5.6 **China: Representative Factor and Transport Costs for Typical City-Pairs, 2005**
yuan

Interior city	Land	Labor	Transport	Designated seaport	Land	Labor	Transport[a]
Changchun	5,240	10,491	3,948	Dalian	10,556	14,061	400
Harbin	12,341	9,080	5,244	Dalian	10,556	14,061	400
Taiyuan	16,539	8,666	3,342	Tianjin	19,274	14,429	400
Huhehaote	8,014	7,983	4,176	Tianjin	19,274	14,429	400
Xi'an[b]	10,188	10,786	6,684	Shanghai	24,603	21,095	400
Lanzhou[b]	5,899	8,695	11,016	Shanghai	24,603	21,095	400
Wulumuqi[b]	13,930	9,937	22,710	Shanghai	24,603	21,095	400
Chengdu	19,049	10,618	15,048	Shanghai	24,603	21,095	400
Changsha	8,911	9,917	4,770	Guangzhou	6,760	20,772	400
Guiyang[c]	8,824	8,987	5,058	Guangzhou	6,760	20,772	400
Kunming[c]	11,850	10,967	6,432	Guangzhou	6,760	20,772	400

Source: World Bank 2006b.
Note: Land cost is the average monthly rent for 1,000 square meters. Labor is the monthly wages for 10 workers, assumed to include six full-time and four part-time workers. Unless otherwise indicated, transport costs are assumed to be Y6 per kilometer to truck a 20-foot container to the relevant seaport.
a. Transport costs are negligible; the analysis assumes Y400 for handling costs within each seaside city.
b. Transport costs are to Lianyungang.
c. Transport costs are to Fancheng.

The relative lack of success of the export processing model in the interior cities of China is explained by the fact that transport costs are much higher for interior cities that import low- or medium-value inputs from the coastal cities or from overseas.[17] Because export-led growth, often through joint ventures with foreign investors, has played a dominant role in the early successes of the rapidly growing coastal cities of China, the combined effects of geographical distance and cumulative causation from agglomeration economies go a long way toward explaining the lagging status and smaller sizes of interior cities in China.

Economic Geography and Spatial Income Differentials

Geography has major consequences for the welfare of individuals and communities. Agglomeration effects, while powerful levers for growth, are also a source of significant spatial inequality. As seen in figure 5.2, spatial disparities in average incomes across China's metropolitan regions may be related to a single dominant factor: distance from a port. These income differences are also reflected in provincial wage disparities: cities in coastal regions gain a wage premium due to their location advantage.[18]

In fact, analysis of the survey results for Chinese cities shows that city characteristics (per capita income, economic growth, and transport costs) explain more than one-third of the observed differences in the productivity of firms in various locations in the country. Especially in cases where globalization is leading to more-or-less uniform worldwide prices for products and material inputs, high transport costs are unequivocally depressing returns to labor in interior cities. Enhancing competitiveness, raising incomes in interior cities, and reducing spatial inequalities through cumulative processes therefore require nationwide logistics initiatives that increase access to markets and lower the costs of this access.

Space, Industry, and Policy in China

The Chinese economy has grown rapidly since the reforms in the late 1970s. However, selective policies and the incremental extension of liberalization from the coast to the west have biased regional growth in favor of the coastal areas beyond their natural advantages. Double-digit annual growth in many coastal provinces has resulted in the appearance of wide regional disparities. A quarter century after the reforms started, all provinces in the rich cluster are coastal, while all provinces in the poor cluster are remote or western.[19]

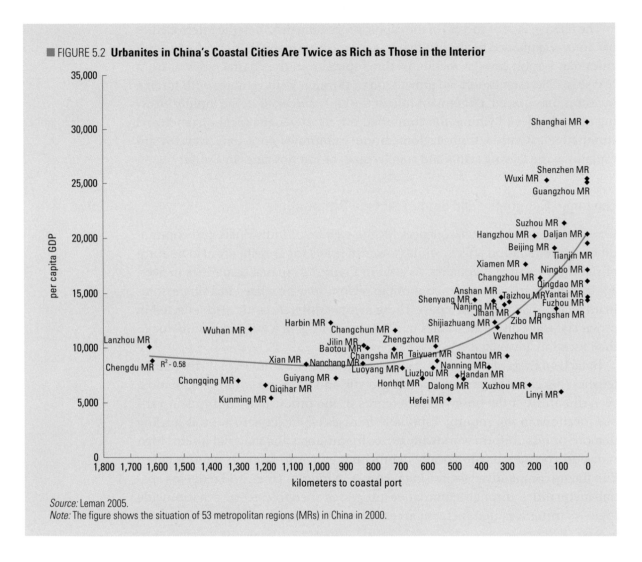

■ FIGURE 5.2 **Urbanites in China's Coastal Cities Are Twice as Rich as Those in the Interior**

Source: Leman 2005.
Note: The figure shows the situation of 53 metropolitan regions (MRs) in China in 2000.

Agglomeration effects are self-reinforcing. Firms located in coastal provinces have benefited from a liberal investment climate and, eventually, from economies of scale. High population densities, the geographical concentration of activities, the development of export sectors, and the large inflows of foreign direct investment in coastal provinces have increased productivity and attracted more firms. The coastal regions have developed as economic centers thanks to their advantageous geographical position, but also because of favorable effects in the agglomeration process tied to the fact that they were first movers. Technology and labor-intensive industries have concentrated in different provinces. High-technology industries have tended to locate in the most developed coastal clusters; labor-intensive industries have gradually deconcentrated and moved from these clusters to the less well developed coastal provinces, but almost entirely to those provinces with relatively easier access to domestic and international markets.

Nevertheless, the diffusion of activities has been limited. Only a few industries have relocated to inland provinces adjacent to dynamic coastal neighbors. To some extent, the industrialization of the coastal region has been fueled by the inflow of labor and capital. Slower urbanization in the inland regions, which are less advanced, has limited the potential of these regions to benefit from economies of scale. Inadequate regional integration has restricted the spillover effects from the coast to entire territories, especially to remote inland areas.[20] Rapid economic growth has led to a surging demand for infrastructure. The shortage of transport facilities has become a development bottleneck and has aggravated the fragmentation of regional economies. In the 1990s, investments in infrastructure became a national priority. However, a large part of these investments is still concentrated in coastal provinces. Consequently, remote inland provinces labor under a heavy economic and geographical handicap.

As China has become more market oriented, economic geography has played an increasingly important role in development. High transport costs have lowered profit margins or even eliminated the potential for trade. Remoteness is associated with slower growth. The attractiveness of a region depends on its effective distance to economic centers, which is conditioned by distance and by the availability of transport facilities.[21] Better infrastructure would reduce not only the transport costs of the receiving province, but also those of the provinces that serve as transit points. To improve access to the markets of a province, the province's own infrastructure network and that of the transit provinces linking the province to economic centers are all important. Similar amounts of investment in infrastructure in different locations will have varying impacts in modifying the effective distances between provinces and economic centers. Investment that targets location is able to change relative regional geographical and economic attractiveness, thereby contributing to wider growth.[22] In this context, the following points are worthy of note:

- Infrastructure in coastal provinces is estimated to have the largest impact on national growth, but the positive effects are likely to be limited mainly to coastal areas due to the significant cumulative effects of infrastructure investment on local development and the importance of intracoastal trade. The increased regional inequalities that might result from such a policy are inconsistent with China's long-term development goals.

■ The uncoordinated construction of infrastructure in remote and western provinces will produce unsatisfactory growth results not only for China generally, but also for the western provinces. In the absence of better interregional transport facilities, it is likely that only the receiving provinces will benefit. If western provinces are not appropriately linked to markets, improvements in the intraprovincial transport network may lead merely to an inward-looking production structure. In some cases, the limited size of the local market may not be able to trigger or support economies of scale.

■ Building infrastructure in central transport hubs such as Henan, Hubei, and Hunan will most effectively encourage the growth of inland provinces by modifying the economic geography of the entire territory in favor of the inland region. On the one hand, improvement in transport facilities in central hubs reduces transport costs from the west to economic centers; on the other, the large multiplier effects of investment in infrastructure on local development favor the emergence of central hubs as future growth centers.

Access to neighboring markets also plays an important role in regional development thanks to nonnegligible growth spillover effects through backward and forward links. In China, although regional inequality has widened, positive regional growth spillover effects are dominating over the negative shadow effects: the growth of one province encourages rather than eclipses the growth of others.[23] The rapid take-off of the coastal region following the reforms maximized aggregate growth at the national level. In this sense, the regional development pattern has been effective. Some second-tier coastal provinces such as Fujian, Guangdong, Hebei, Jiangsu, Shandong, and Zhejiang have emerged as growth locomotives. On one side, their rapid acceleration provided a growth push in the most developed poles, such as Shanghai. On the other, it propelled a growth pull so that less well developed inland neighbors, such as Henan, Hubei, and Hunan, might catch up.

Thus, as in the case of choice of location of infrastructure, if the objective is to maximize national growth, this analysis would suggest that investment in these second-tier coastal provinces would be most effective in optimizing regional growth spillovers. However, the distribution of this additional investment and its spillover effects would disproportionately favor coastal regions, and this would result in a widening in regional inequality. If the objective is to achieve balanced growth without compromising spillovers at the national level, targeting investments in *central regional hubs* that facilitate interregional exchanges between the coast and inland areas might be the most effective strategy.

Reducing domestic transport costs is important, but reducing differences in the quality of city management also represents a sound way to offset some of the disadvantages of unfavorable location. Box 5.3 shows that differences in city management appear to reinforce the power of economic geography in China.

Meeting the Urban Challenge

International links, the fragmentation of production and service processes, and the mobility of workers are compelling policy makers to reappraise conventional policies. Natural forces and public policy instruments are powerful tools for restructuring urban hierarchies so as to offset the current biases against secondary and small metropolitan areas. Nationwide and regional economic policies (including those needed to eliminate biases), together with accelerated programs for the provision of interurban connective infrastructure, have the potential to generate relatively more well balanced urban outcomes.

■ BOX 5.3 **Differentials in City Performance in China**

A 2005 World Bank survey of 120 cities in China documents that the quality of the investment climate varies widely. Since basic business laws and many regulations are essentially the same across provinces, the differences must often reflect variations in the implementation of the laws and regulations and, more broadly, variations in city management. Taxes and fees range from 3 percent of sales revenue to almost 7 percent; firm interactions with the bureaucracy vary from 36 days annually to 87 days, and times for customs clearances may range from about 5 days to 20 days across cities. There appears to be regional differences in ratings. The best is the southeast (well connected to foreign and domestic markets), and the worst is the most remote northwest. The survey report estimates that cities at the bottom of the investment quality ladder might expect 30 percentage point increases in firm productivity and foreign ownership if they are able to improve government efficiency and labor flex-

ibility to the levels of the top-performing cities in the southeast.

The share of university-educated workers also varies widely across cities, from about 11 percent at the lower end to almost 29 percent at the upper end. The survey finds that firms in more populated cities are more productive, indicating the presence of agglomeration economies. But the report also suggests that infrastructure investments are able to improve the attractiveness of smaller, remote cities. The data indicate, for example, that a 30 percent reduction in overland transport costs might raise foreign ownership in firms by 5 to 10 percent. The report's recommendations include improvement in the management of China Rail, the development of national trucking companies, more regular air cargo services, and regulatory reforms to encourage domestic and international integrated logistics providers to expand services to the interior.

Source: World Bank 2006b.

As emphasized in the previous section, it is important to conceive of the development of cities in parallel with the development of regions and subregions, rather than as isolated nodes in economic space. For example, the Singapore-Johore-Riau growth triangle and the Hong Kong–Zhujiang Delta are experiencing the kind of urban expansion and interconnections that reflect the emerging links between city growth and new patterns of economic activity. It is difficult in these areas to conceive of city development without embedding plans on settlements, business districts, and infrastructure links within broader plans for regional development.[24] Coordination, especially in the provision of infrastructure such as access roads and common spaces for nodal activity such as tourism and logistics, will help exploit synergies within a broader set of economic activities. At the same time, the application of effective incentives and monitoring mechanisms, together with performance-oriented measures of success and governance, will allow countries to harness decentralized local government efforts more effectively so as to address income and employment needs.

The management of cities *within* discrete regions presents a special set of problems for East Asian policy makers. Nodal cities within regional development belts have economic importance far beyond their individual contribution to national output and growth. So, it is vital that metropolitan, regional, and sometimes even national planners work together. Several elements of such coordinated planning need attention. Vertical functional mandates within large cities need to be clear to enhance the productivity of metropolitan investment, as well as the efficiency with which firms operate in a city. At the same time, jurisdictional boundaries and functional responsibilities between the nodal city and the local governments in an associated region need to be sufficiently flexible to accommodate urban expansion and promote an efficient trunk infrastructure and regional spatial structure. In China, especially, but also in Indonesia, the Philippines, and Thailand, horizontal fiscal disparities between nodal cities and adjoining local governments have emerged from the pattern of existing economic specializations (for example, manufacturing) or government policy. Better regional spatial planning often requires dispersing specific urban functions (such as solid waste treatment, airports, and skills and training centers) within a contiguous region, rather than crowding them in a large city. Mechanisms to transfer fiscal resources among urban governments in a region are essential to achieve such efficiencies.

Governments should also continue efforts to develop the potential of the megacities and larger metropolitan areas of East Asia and enhance their competitiveness so they serve as growth drivers for national economies. Typically, this involves careful attention to labor costs and the quality and availability of human capital (see box 5.4). More broadly, there is a need to focus on the provision of a world-class business environment, taking guidance from the numerous city rankings that provide benchmarks and assistance to investors in their location decisions. However, market potential, infrastructure (especially power, telecommunications, and transport), transparency in the real estate market, and certainty and predictability in transactions will play an equal, if not more important part in enhancing competitiveness.[25]

Keeping Large Cities Livable

A mixture of mainstream national, regional, and urban economic policies discussed extensively by urban planners in recent years is likely to generate high levels of income growth in most East Asian cities.[26] A major issue confronting the larger metropolitan areas of East Asia, especially the megacities, is whether this growth is sustainable. Limits to agglomeration operate through the costs of grime, time, and crime mentioned above, which operate not only by raising the costs of production and service links, but also by reducing the livability of cities.

Figure 5.3 plots measures of livability of large cities in East Asia, Eastern Europe, and Latin America against per capita incomes. The scatter plot indicates that East Asian cities do not do any better or worse than expected for their levels of national per capita income. The potential problem, of course, is that urban populations are expected to grow much more rapidly in the countries of the region than they are in Latin America (where they are expected to rise mainly due to population growth in cities) or Eastern Europe (where urban populations are likely to shrink).

■ BOX 5.4 **Human Capital Externalities in Cities**

Cities may help societies obtain more out of their stock of educated workers because human capital spillovers might increase aggregate productivity beyond the direct effect of human capital on individual productivity.[27] Increases in the concentration of educated workers may also improve governance and reduce crime.

Moretti (2003) examines these effects for the United States. Virtually all cities experienced an increase in the ratio of educated workers between 1980 and 2000. But cities that initially showed high ratios of educated workers experienced larger increases than cities with low ratios. Other studies report that per capita incomes have grown more rapidly in cities with initially high levels of education. Still others estimate that rising average levels of education in a city raise average wages over and above the private return to education.

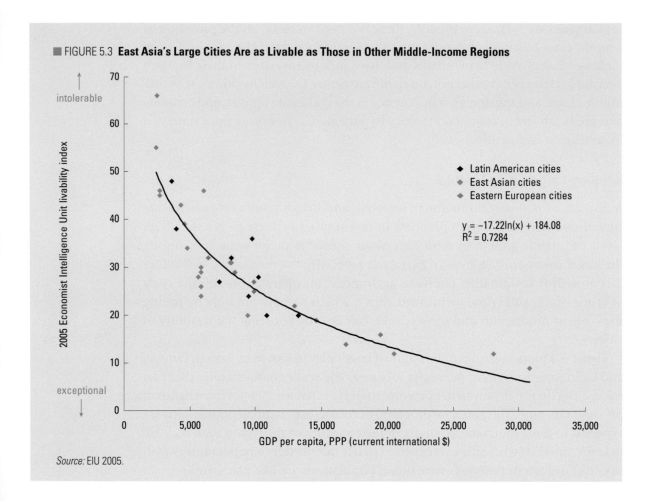

■ FIGURE 5.3 **East Asia's Large Cities Are as Livable as Those in Other Middle-Income Regions**

Source: EIU 2005.

Such indicators by themselves do not provide a good basis for assessing the efficiency of East Asian cities as population settlements. The proof would have to be in the physical living conditions of the populations in these cities. To take one example, urban transport is an essential aspect of infrastructure provision to ensure mobility in East Asian cities by supplying connectivity for urban residents between their homes, places of work, and social or business engagements. Not all the cities in developing East Asia are opting for sustainable modes of urban transport and mobility, at least in terms of the indicators shown in table 5.7 (for example, passenger car ownership compared to total public transport vehicles per million people in the population). Not surprisingly, indicators such as road safety measured through total transport deaths per million people are worse in cities

■ TABLE 5.7 **Urban Transport and Road Safety Indicators**

City	Roads (per 1,000 persons)	Public transport lines (miles per 1,000 persons)	Passenger cars (per 1,000 persons)	Public transport investment (% of city GDP)	Average road network speed (km/hour)	Public transport vehicles (per million persons)	Transport deaths (per million persons)
Bangkok	584.1	642.3	249.1	1.59	15.0	1,890.4	192.1
Beijing	323.6	556.0	42.9	0.63	18.0	657.4	38.2
Ho Chi Minh City	266.9	347.5	7.9	0.00	25.2	671.8	114.5
Hong Kong, China	276.2	2,139.9	46.5	0.37	28.3	1,807.6	38.4
Jakarta	664.5	1,104.8	90.9	0.83	18.6	2,044.6	227.1
Kuala Lumpur	1,518.3	1,196.1	208.7	1.08	28.1	428.5	282.7
Manila	519.7	745.1	82.4	0.38	18.0	13,375.4	80.5
Osaka	3,901.2	498.0	264.5	0.37	33.0	951.1	67.6
Seoul	945.8	2,724.2	160.1	0.90	23.8	1,122.3	170.3
Shanghai	314.3	2,852.8	15.2	0.55	20.0	738.0	82.3
Singapore	979.1	1,200.1	116.3	0.44	35.2	1,304.2	78.7
Taipei	848.6	2,435.8	175.2	1.32	16.6	1,113.1	184.0
Tokyo	4,013.9	417.0	306.8	0.30	26.1	976.1	53.1

Source: Ooi 2006.

where passenger car ownership in relation to the total availability of roads is relatively higher.

Other indicators of livability may also be assessed to determine whether the rapid growth rate of major metropolitan areas has necessarily improved the sustainability of cities as settlements. Table 5.3 elsewhere above presents a comparison of transport-related indicators of livability in metropolitan areas in China and the leading developed countries. It suggests that, on average, city residents in China have a significantly lower quality of life compared to residents in developed countries. Moreover, the high motor vehicle emissions, which are high not only in Chinese cities, but also in other East Asian cities, degrade the environment more generally within countries and across borders.

The results of a potentially useful attempt at constructing an urban sustainability index are presented in table 5.8. The table shows an equally weighted index that encompasses several variables at the city level. The variables include economy (for example, metropolitan GDP per person), urban transport and road safety (for instance, road network speed), air quality (carbon emissions, for example), health (such as infant mortality), crime (homicides, rapes, thefts, and so

■ TABLE 5.8 **Hong Kong (China) Leads the Region in Sustainable City Development**

City	Composite score	Index
Ho Chi Minh City	976	33.5
Bangkok	874	40.7
Jakarta	822	44.4
Manila	806	45.5
Kuala Lumpur	805	45.6
Beijing	724	51.3
Taipei	702	52.9
Seoul	640	57.2
Shanghai	619	58.7
Singapore	616	58.9
Osaka	534	64.7
Tokyo	515	66.0
Hong Kong, China	442	71.2

Source: Ooi 2006.
Note: Data are for 2000–01.

on), housing and environmental infrastructure (water and electricity connections, for instance), and waste management (such as solid waste disposal through landfills, incineration, and recycling).

An index of this sort is indicative of some of the parameters that might determine the sustainability of a metropolitan area. Decisions regarding the location of economic activity are tied closely to judgments about how easy or difficult it is to live in specific metropolitan areas. Urban planners and national authorities in places such as Bangkok, Ho Chi Minh City, and Jakarta, among others, therefore need to pay attention to basic social, economic, and physical infrastructure that would enhance sustainability.

Traffic congestion is a major problem in many megacities in East Asia. In order to ameliorate this problem, policy makers have attempted various solutions, ranging from building additional road capacity and promoting public transportation to introducing various taxes and quotas on the number of cars allowed on a certain road. Seoul provides an example of how local authorities are attempting to solve traffic congestion, while trying to make the city more livable. A major motorway carrying over 160,000 cars per day was perpetually jammed. Local authorities decided to tear it down, restore the Cheonggyecheon River, which had once flowed underneath the motorway, and create a five-mile long, 800-yard wide, 1,000-acre park where the river previously flowed in the middle of the city. Surprisingly, traffic congestion has fallen despite the demolition of the motorway. This paradox has been observed in cities such as New York and Stuttgart as well.[28] Megacities such as Shanghai have also shown an interest in implementing similar projects to improve livability and reduce congestion.

Managing Development on the Urban Fringe

In China, Indonesia, Thailand, and Vietnam, because of the high rural densities around cities, rural settlements are being transformed into urban areas. In Indonesia, for example, about a third of the urbanization in the cities in Java is due to urban expansion into formerly rural areas; about a third is due to rural-urban migration; and the remaining third is the result of the natural increase in urban populations.

High population densities are a feature of most East Asian cities, and city planners have highlighted the smaller territorial footprint of these cities relative to cities in developed countries (see table 5.9). Typically twice as dense as their developed-country comparators, cities in East Asia are potentially efficient nodes of economic activity and settlement. Often, however, there is great divergence

■ TABLE 5.9 **Kuala Lumpur Has the Lowest Density Indicators among Metropolises, 2000–01**

Metropolitan area	Urban density (persons/ha)	Job density (jobs/ha)	Jobs in central business districts (% of total)	Metropolitan GNI per capita (US$)[a]
Ho Chi Minh City	355.7	139.1	10.3	1,029
Beijing	123.1	95.9	25.3	1,829
Jakarta	173.4	66.6	22.8	1,861
Manila	206.4	91.8	18.4	2,217
Shanghai	196.3	114.9	75.2	2,474
Bangkok	138.7	73.5	10.5	6,317
Kuala Lumpur	57.9	24.4	20.0	6,991
Seoul	230.4	109.4	7.5	10,305
Taipei	230.1	96.4	14.3	13,036
Hong Kong, China	320.4	151.3	6.4	22,969
Singapore	93.5	53.3	16.4	28,578
Osaka	98.1	40.0	15.9	39,937
Tokyo	87.7	47.5	14.3	45,425

Source: Ooi 2006.
a. GNI = gross national income.

between the employment and population densities of urban areas. With the exception of Shanghai, central business districts account for only a small share of urban employment. In the absence of adequate data, we may only speculate that there are large efficiency gains—for example, through a reduction in service link costs—that would accrue to East Asia's largest metropolitan areas through improved urban planning.

A visible effect of inadequate planning is the growth of slums. A third of East Asia's urban population lives in slums, a ratio that is already higher than the ratio in other middle-income regions such as the Middle East and Latin America (see figure 5.4). Given that urban populations are expected to grow at a more rapid rate over the next two decades, city managers in East Asia face a stiff challenge. There is perhaps nothing more important for keeping the growth prospects of countries in the region bright than proper urban management as cities expand. The way to ensure this is through better city and land use planning; the improved exploitation of green spaces; the optimization of utility assets, energy conservation, enhanced urban water and sanitation management; and solid waste management.

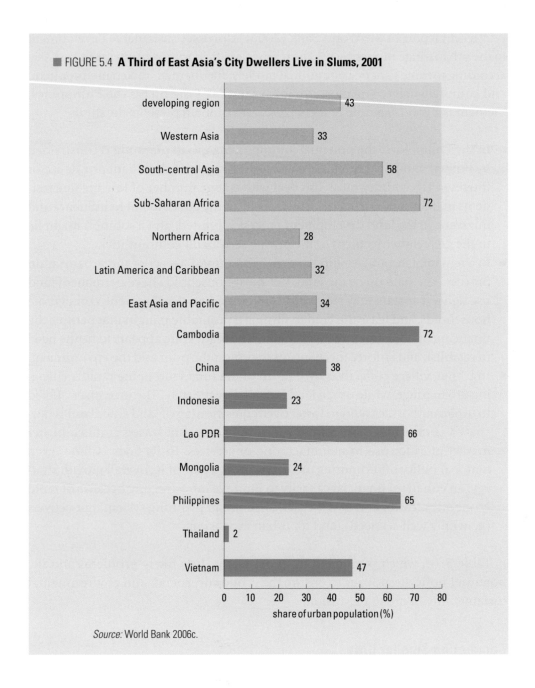

■ FIGURE 5.4 **A Third of East Asia's City Dwellers Live in Slums, 2001**

Region/Country	share of urban population (%)
developing region	43
Western Asia	33
South-central Asia	58
Sub-Saharan Africa	72
Northern Africa	28
Latin America and Caribbean	32
East Asia and Pacific	34
Cambodia	72
China	38
Indonesia	23
Lao PDR	66
Mongolia	24
Philippines	65
Thailand	2
Vietnam	47

Source: World Bank 2006c.

A recent report of the World Bank (2006c) discusses sustainable development in the urban fringe in East Asia.[29] The report classifies city governments in East Asia according to three generic institutional models: fragmented, mixed metropolitan, and comprehensive. The most notable example of the first is the Philippines, Vietnam is a good example of the second, and China represents the third:

- In the Philippines, the potential for improving urban planning is constrained by limited municipal revenues, weak institutions, and dominant private sector interests. The country must also deal with a large number of low-income residents in informal settlements. The capacity of the government to influence and intervene in the land development process is limited, and a solution might lie in the greater involvement of the private sector and communities.
- In Vietnam, land ownership patterns are a central aspect of the urbanization process. The state owns the land, but most households have permanent land use rights. The state may requisition land for urban development, compensate households, and lease the land to firms at a profitable margin that permits the financing of infrastructure investments. The main issue appears to be the need to establish and enforce mechanisms to protect the poor and the environment.
- In China, village collectives own much of the rural land in the rapidly changing urban fringe, while urban land is owned by the state. The incentives offered to urban authorities tend to foster overrequisitioning of land since land is purchased at rates based on current agricultural uses, but leased at much higher market rates for use in manufacturing or services. In its favor, China has a national policy of promoting urbanization as a part of its overall growth strategy, an enhanced financial capacity to improve infrastructure because of rapid economic growth, and a well-established urban planning system that delivers (generally well-serviced) land for urban expansion.

Table 5.10, which is adapted from the report, lists likely problems and the potential policy responses to ensure the economic, social, and environmental sustainability of urban expansion.

Connecting Smaller Cities

The results presented in the section on economic geography in East Asia provide some guidance for a country such as China because of its vast distances. But they are valid as well for other, more compact East Asian metropolitan systems.

■ TABLE 5.10 **Urbanization Problems and Policy Responses**

Problems	Policy responses
Economic	
Economic enterprises are inappropriately located	Land use planning and financial incentives
Agricultural land is lost to less valuable urban uses or is retained despite more valuable urban uses	Regulatory land use or land conversion policies
Excessive service and transportation costs due to inadequate infrastructure	Regulatory land use policies to increase densities and concentrate development
	Imposition of development impact fees to obtain developer contributions for offsite infrastructure
Social	
Development leaves existing residents less well off	Improvements in the compensation rates, employment measures, and financial stake in ensuing development
Unserviced informal settlements	Tenure regularization, upgrading, relocation
	Low-cost housing construction, land management, land pooling, appropriate planning and construction standards, direct and indirect subsidies
	Improved municipal finances for infrastructure in low-income areas
	Requirements that developers provide quotas of affordable housing
Environmental	
Excessive pollution	Regulatory measures, including standards for pollution discharges and market-based instruments
	Conditions regarding antipollution measures are included as part of the development approval process
Encroachment on land that is better left undeveloped	Regulatory land use and environmental controls
	Community-based projects to reduce the adverse impact of encroachment

Source: Adapted from World Bank 2006c.

Differences in factor returns and a negative correlation of those with access to larger markets and transport costs are also found in Cambodia, Indonesia, Malaysia, the Philippines, Thailand, and Vietnam.[30] It is evident to policy makers in East Asia that metropolitan areas account for the high, often spectacular national growth rates, but also that this performance is unevenly distributed within each country. The cumulative effect of such variations is to exacerbate income inequality, a major source of friction across East Asia today.

A balanced pattern of growth is therefore desirable. However, the achievement of this balance is checked by the strong imperative to build on the success of existing metropolitan areas. Given the restricted development budgets, weak financial markets, and limited opportunities available in each country, the solution will require a careful weighing of the trade-offs involved in a strategy that attempts to disperse the spatial locus of new growth.

At the center of this trade-off is the debate over large *versus* small cities. Initially, development efforts focused on the largest metropolitan areas, while financially strapped East Asian governments adopted incremental approaches to resolving the perceived binding constraints on economic growth.[31] Subsequently, however, most countries have tried actively to affect the pattern of settlement size to promote regional development through the creation of new growth poles or to deconcentrate overgrown metropolitan areas.

Typically, governments have employed a range of instruments toward these ends. The instruments have included, for example, the promotion of out-migration from Java and restrictions on migration into the larger metropolitan areas of China. Governments have provided investment incentives or relocated social and educational facilities to lagging areas, such as Thailand's northeastern cities. They have financed urban infrastructure investment in Davao (the Philippines), built satellite towns for Shanghai and Tokyo, and even attempted to relocate capital cities in Korea (Yeongi-Kongju), Malaysia (Putrajaya), and Myanmar (Pyinmana). The record is mixed.[32] Regional development efforts of this kind have been very costly. Where government intervention has made a difference, it has usually depended on market forces and natural geographical advantages, that is, on a reactive mode.[33]

What is clear is that infrastructure plays the most critical role in ensuring that small, medium, and large cities are both livable and well linked domestically. A recent report has estimated East Asia's infrastructure needs (including urban-, rural-, connectivity-, and energy-related needs) at about US$150 billion a year, more than three-quarters of which is represented by China (see figure 5.5). Electricity and roads account for more than two-thirds of the required outlays.

Iimi (2005) points out that, in East Asia today, public service infrastructure in small and medium-sized cities is weak compared to that in large cities, and this infrastructure is needed to prevent overconcentration in large cities. To this, one should perhaps add that better connections between large and small cities will also help to prevent congestion in East Asia's metropolitan areas.

■ FIGURE 5.5 **East Asia's Infrastructure Needs Are Increasing, 1996–2010**

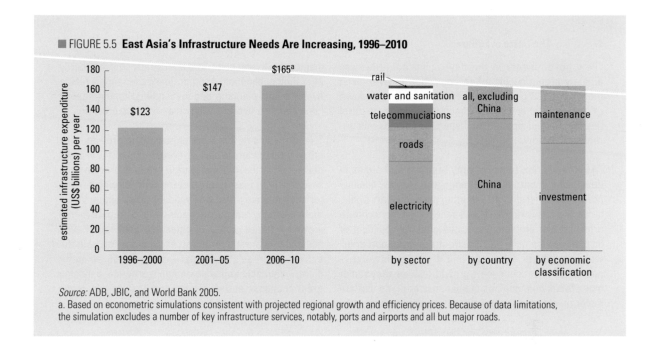

Source: ADB, JBIC, and World Bank 2005.
a. Based on econometric simulations consistent with projected regional growth and efficiency prices. Because of data limitations, the simulation excludes a number of key infrastructure services, notably, ports and airports and all but major roads.

Financing Livable and Connected Cities

While there is adequate global knowledge and experience to improve urban policies and institutions, the financial constraints on doing so are severe. In the transition to better cities, both remedial—giving attention to distressed areas, filling housing and other infrastructure gaps, dealing with social problems—and proactive approaches to improving competitiveness and livability require much greater amounts of financing than are currently being allocated. Because urbanization is arguably the most important dynamic factor in East Asia today, identifying the magnitude of the financing problem in building urban infrastructure and fixing the problem are urgent issues. Urbanization and urban expansion are ubiquitous, and, in most of developing East Asia, the rural-urban transition is still under way. Even if economic growth slows or stalls in the region, this is sufficient reason to expect that large demands will continue to be placed on urban infrastructure. If, as described in the first part of this chapter, there will be 555 million new city residents over the next 25 years and if each one will need between 100 and 200 square meters of urban space, the demand for serviced land will rise by 56 billion to 111 billion square meters.[34] Anticipating this need is vital; yet, steps to do so have generally been inadequate (see box 5.5).

■ BOX 5.5 **The Costs of Failure**

"Few governments in the developing countries are actively preparing for urban population growth, even though it is now generally accepted that slowing it down or reversing the tide of urbanization—through rural development or population dispersion policies—is unrealistic and unworkable. . . .

"As a result, the large majority of urban authorities in developing countries do not engage in realistic minimal preparations for growth: securing the necessary public lands and public rights-of-way necessary to serve future urban growth, protecting sensitive lands from building, or investing in the minimal infrastructure—transport grids, water supply, or sewerage and drainage networks—necessary to accommodate growth. Instead, they sometimes focus on ambitious utopian master-plans that are never meant to guide development on the ground, take

many years to complete, and are usually shelved shortly after their publication. At other times, they simply refuse even minimal planning and investment, hoping against hope that their overcrowded cities will stop growing. . . .

"Needless to say, it is more expensive to provide trunk urban infrastructure in built-up areas—especially in areas developed by the informal sector—than to provide such services, or at least to protect the right-of-way needed for such services—before building takes place. While there are many reasons for neglecting to prepare for the inevitable future growth of cities, the absence of even minimal preparation for urban expansion—on both the activist and regulatory fronts—is, no doubt, an inefficient, inequitable and unsustainable practice, imposing great economic and environmental costs on societies that can ill afford them."

Source: Angel, Sheppard, and Civco 2005: 101–02.

A detailed investigation of urban financing issues is beyond the scope of this chapter. However, a few basic points may be highlighted with respect to the problems in financing city development in East Asia.

Currently, public sector expenditures on infrastructure range from about 2 percent of GDP in the Philippines to about 9 percent of GDP in Thailand; China is an outlier at the high end. Taxes and user fees constitute the two major sources of urban infrastructure funding under the control of different levels of government. As a result of the decentralization wave witnessed in East Asia over the past decade, revenue and expenditure assignments for urban infrastructure have been pushed downward toward local governments, without a comprehensive alignment of other fiscal responsibilities, spending accountabilities, or supportive transfer mechanisms. Consequently, given the peculiar nature of the cash flows associated with infrastructure projects (costs are frontloaded, while returns come later), most municipalities underinvest because they face chronic public funding shortfalls in the wake of burgeoning demand for urban infrastructure. Lately, the rise in property values across cities in the region has offered a brief respite since revenues have increased from standard property taxes and land transactions taxes (geared toward sharing in the capital gains that would otherwise accrue only to sellers). User fees have proven to be less buoyant sources of revenue, and there are both practical and distributional concerns that constrain the potential take from this source. In a decentralized framework, cross-subsidization between urban spaces and projects offers a highly restricted solution to meeting financing needs.

The financial challenge is therefore to create adequate fiscal space for an expansion of urban and associated catalytic infrastructure to support a metropolitan hierarchy that addresses growth and spatial inequality concerns. Obviously, there are macroeconomic constraints on the expansion of overall public spending. The question that arises is whether private financing is capable of filling the gap in urban infrastructure funding in the region. There are two main issues:

- First, if nonurban investment funded through private sources is excluded, the total funding for regional projects during 1994–2004 is estimated at US$90 billion, an average of only US$9 billion per year. By contrast, Indonesia alone is estimated to require an additional 2 percent of GDP per year in urban financing (US$5 billion per year).
- Second, the returns necessary to attract private capital into urban infrastructure even in middle-income developing countries are much higher than those required in developed countries.[35] Moreover, with few exceptions, private finance requires additional government guarantees, which add to the high level of contingent fiscal liabilities at various levels of government. Therefore, while partnerships with the private sector are necessary, they should not be viewed as sufficient.

In developing East Asia, it appears that China, Lao PDR, Thailand, and Vietnam have begun to act aggressively to meet these challenges. Table 5.11 lists the expenditure on infrastructure in 1998 and 2003. These four countries have ratcheted up their infrastructure spending threefold as a share of GDP, while Vietnam has maintained a high level of investment. Conversely, infrastructure spending as a share of output fell between 1998 and 2003 in Cambodia, Indonesia, and the Philippines.

Conclusions

Perhaps the most important test facing policy makers in cities in East Asia involves responding simultaneously to two challenges: first, keeping cities livable since this is central to the role of cities as conduits for international trade, investment,

■ TABLE 5.11 **China, Thailand, and Vietnam Have Raised Infrastructure Spending**
share of GDP, percent

Country	Expenditure on infrastructure		Investment
	1998	2003	2003
Cambodia	2.9	2.3	22
Indonesia	3.1	2.7	16
Philippines	5.6	3.6	19
Lao PDR	1.7	4.7	20
China	2.6	7.3	44
Vietnam	9.8	9.9	35
Thailand	5.3	15.4	25

Sources: ADB, JBIC, and World Bank 2005; World Bank 2005, 2006a.

and technology flows and, indeed, as centers of innovation; second, at the same time, absorbing the massive influx of populations from rural areas as rapid structural transformation occurs. The East Asian economies are unique in that they combine an advanced stage of openness today with a potential for future urbanization on an unprecedented scale.

This combination of global imperatives and local pressures puts East Asian cities at the center of development and ensures that sustained growth in living standards in these countries will require commensurately bold measures by policy makers. The main conclusions of this chapter are as follows:

■ *Pent-up urbanization.* Because of rapid economic growth, the East Asian countries have reached levels of industrialization and per capita income that are generally associated with higher levels of urbanization. Over the next 25 years, East Asian cities will be filling this urbanization gap through the largest rural-to-urban population shift in human history. This extraordinary shift will require an equally extraordinary response from policy makers in national, provincial, and municipal governments.

■ *A threat to the livability of large cities.* As elsewhere, East Asia's growth is based on exploiting unexhausted scale economies in industry and services, which relies on large cities. Because many megacities are already straining to stay livable, this represents a challenge for policy makers, the magnitude of which has never before been confronted in middle-income countries. For these high-performing economies to become high-income countries, East Asia's large cities will have to continue to serve as the conduits for global commerce in goods, finance, and ideas and become centers of innovation. The challenge has to be met in large part by city governments.

- *A need for well-managed and well-connected small and midsized cities.* A big part of the solution lies in the growth of small and midsized cities of less than 2 million residents. To enable the exploitation of scale economies, these cities will have to be well managed and well connected to larger cities. The connectedness will depend mainly on national and provincial governments. The fate of small, medium, and large cities and national economies is therefore interlinked. Evidence on China's cities shows that improved city management and infrastructural links produce large payoffs for smaller, more remote, and generally less well managed cities.

From the available data, we know that substantial and often widening rural-urban household inequality is a characteristic of both low- and middle-income countries in East Asia. In some places, rural-to-urban migration and improved terms of trade for rural households have slowed or reversed the trends in overall inequality. Migration has been the more significant factor by far, as households have shifted from lower-valued rural occupations to higher-valued urban jobs. Adam Smith (1776) pointed out long ago the inevitability and, indeed, the desirability of rural-to-urban population movements:

> That the industry which is carried on in towns is, everywhere in Europe, more advantageous than that which is carried on in the country, without entering into any very nice computations, we may satisfy ourselves by one very simple and obvious observation. In every country of Europe we find, at least, a hundred people who have acquired great fortunes from small beginnings by trade and manufactures, the industry which properly belongs to towns, for one who has done so by that which properly belongs to the country . . . Industry, therefore, must be better rewarded, the wages of labour and the profits of stock [capital] must evidently be greater in the one situation than in the other. But stock and labour naturally seek the most advantageous employment. They naturally, therefore, resort as much as they can to the town, and desert the country (pp. 125–26).

Clearly, if a sufficient number of households were to do this, overall inequality will decline at some point. Therefore, one key question is: what is needed to continue or even accelerate the creation of productive employment in the metropolitan areas of East Asia? Furthermore, because most East Asian governments have introduced a range of measures to decentralize decision making on local economic development, a related question is: what is the role of government in establishing dynamic metropolitan areas that will help these countries arrive at a stage at which national spatial inequalities begin to narrow? This chapter provided a general assessment of these issues. Chapter 6 takes up issues of inequality in more detail.

Notes

1. For example, see Lucas (1988) and Romer (1990).

2. See World Bank (2006a).

3. See World Bank (2004).

4. See Global Insight (2006).

5. For example, see Krugman (1991) and Fujita, Krugman, and Venables (1999).

6. Definitions of urban vary among the countries of East Asia, but are usually based on administrative boundaries or on the size and density of populations living in a contiguous physical area connected by roads, frequent transport, commuters, and common production, trade, and cultural facilities (called metropolitan areas in this chapter). *World Urbanization Prospects* (United Nations 2006) collects comprehensive data on such areas, but these data must be interpreted with care as they rely on statistics supplied by national governments based on different definitions.

7. These are preliminary estimates based on comparisons of the data available in United Nations (2006) and information contained in national gazetteers and other compilations.

8. Already, East Asia (excluding Japan) contains 16 of the largest seaports in the world, 14 of the largest container ports, 7 of the largest cargo airports, and 4 of the largest passenger airports.

9. The World Bank recently estimated the contribution of large cities at about 70 percent of annual economic growth (in 2004) and between 50 and 60 percent of exports.

10. The role of alternative policy regimes is discussed in David and Henderson (2003).

11. Urbanization refers to the share of a national population living in urban areas (cities and towns), while urban expansion refers to the physical size (spatial dimension) of urban areas.

12. This is also different from the early experience of cities in the developed countries. In China, the issue of rural land acquisition and compensation have become socially explosive. The government has acted this year to improve processes and increase surveillance.

13. The core principles can be traced back to Marshall (1920), although a more recent nontechnical exposition of the processes that foster the growth of specialization and interdependence within and among cities is contained in Jacobs (1970). Useful technical surveys are found in Henderson and Thisse (2004). This section draws on the concepts and terminology presented in that volume, especially chapters 48, 49, and 58.

14. This goes beyond the more common, though still important observation that urban infrastructure investment—given its lumpiness and long life—is an example of the reasons why sunk costs matter, because they determine, to some extent, the pace and growth of future metropolitan development.

15. Land rents are sometimes fixed at low administrative rates by local governments so as to promote investment. This is evident for Guangzhou in the table. There, artificially low rents in development zones affect the city average.

16. See World Bank (2006b).

17. The econometric analysis of these survey results shows that transport costs, in particular, affect foreign investment and also have an effect on the productivity of firms in different cities.

18. See Lin (2005).

19. This section summarizes recent work at the World Bank on regional development and infrastructure policy in China. The main papers are Luo (2004, 2005), Catin, Luo, and Van Huffel (2005), and other studies referenced in those papers.

20. See Catin, Luo, and van Huffel (2005).

21. See Luo (2001a).

22. See Luo (2001b, 2004).

23. See Luo (2005).

24. The policy content of this observation is that specific points of entry for this sort of coordination have proved successful in parts of East Asia. These points include building on existing technology and industrial strengths, facilitating innovation and cluster development, promoting institutions of higher education, improving social and fiscal cohesion, and increasing the attractiveness and sustainability of cities and subregions.

25. See Jones Lang LaSalle (2004) for a concise description of location factors that matter to global investors.

26. There is a vast amount of literature on such policies. Three useful references are: National Research Council (2003), UN-Habitat (2004), and World Bank (2004).

27. See Moretti (2003).

28. The Braess paradox states that taking away space in an urban area may actually improve the flow of traffic. Conversely, adding capacity to a road network may reduce overall performance. The paradox is named after Dietrich Braess, who, in 1968, noted that, in a network the utilization of which is optimized by users, not administrators, the change in equilibrium flows may result in a higher cost when a new link is added, implying that the users were more well served without the link. See Vidal (2006).

29. The report defines the urban fringe as areas subject to urban expansion on the edge of cities, as well as environmentally fragile urban areas that are unstable and unfit for occupation. It is estimated that about half of the projected urban population growth in East Asia will occur on the urban fringe, and the rest will take place through increased population densities in areas that are already built up.

30. There are theoretical reasons for the correlation of these differences with the degree of openness of a metropolitan area. The Balassa-Samuelson hypothesis suggests that the relative price of nontradable goods and services (for example, land rents) is positively correlated with openness, given their relatively inelastic supply and the effect of higher productivity growth in the traded goods sector.

31. Some examples are the development of enclaves in China, Korea, Malaysia, and Singapore to promote exports and foreign investment. More recently, encouragement for specialized (for example, electronics, biotechnology) and general industrial clusters has relied on compromises among various perspectives on agglomeration economics and the spread and demonstration effects of growth poles.

32. There has been some success in changing the global connectivity of cities, such as the rise of Kuala Lumpur as opposed to Penang and the rise of Beijing as opposed to Shanghai.

33. Conversely, as described in Pernia, Paderanga, and Hermoso (1983), policies adopted during the post-1948 import-substitution phase in the Philippines led to a heavy concentration of manufacturing and urban population growth in metropolitan Manila and its periphery. The introduction of export promotion and regional development policies (for example, export processing zones and industrial estates at other locations) failed to prevent or significantly reduce the heavy concentration of manufacturing in this large metropolitan area.

34. See Angel, Sheppard, and Civco (2005), chap. 6.

35. See Estache and Pinglo (2005) and Sirtaine et al. (2005).

References

ADB (Asian Development Bank), JBIC (Japan Bank for International Cooperation), and World Bank. 2005. *Connecting East Asia: A New Framework for Infrastructure.* Washington, DC: World Bank.

Angel, Shlomo, Stephen C. Sheppard, and Daniel L. Civco. 2005. *The Dynamics of Global Urban Expansion.* With Robert Buckley, Anna Chabaeva, Lucy Gitlin, Alison Kraley, Jason Parent, and Micah Perlin. Transport and Urban Development Department, World Bank: Washington, DC.

Au, Chun-Chung, and J. Vernon Henderson. 2006. "Are Chinese Cities too Small?" *Review of Economic Studies* 73 (3): 549–76.

Catin Maurice, Luo Xubei, and Christophe van Huffel. 2005. "Openness, Industrialization, and Geographic Concentration of Activities in China." Policy Research Working Paper 3706, World Bank, Washington, DC.

David, James C., and J. Vernon Henderson. 2003. "Evidence on the Political Economy of the Urbanization Process." *Journal of Urban Economics* 53 (1): 98–125.

Diechmann, Uwe, Kai Kaiser, Somik V. Lall, and Zmarak Shalizi. 2005. "Agglomeration, Transport and Regional Development in Indonesia." Policy Research Working Paper 3477, World Bank, Washington, DC.

EIU (Economist Intelligence Unit). 2005. *Economist Intelligence Unit Global Liveability Rankings.* London: Economist Intelligence Unit. http://www.eiu.com/.

Estache, Antonio, and Maria Elena Pinglo. 2005. "Are Returns to Private Infrastructure in Developing Countries Consistent with Risks since the Asian Crisis?" *Journal of Network Industries* 6 (1): 47–71.

Fujita, Masahisa, Paul R. Krugman, and Anthony J. Venables. 1999. *The Spatial Economy: Cities, Regions, and International Trade.* Cambridge, MA: MIT Press.

Global Insight. 2006. "The Role of Metro Areas in the U.S. Economy." Report prepared for the United States Conference of Mayors, Global Insight, Lexington, MA.

Henderson, J. Vernon. 2000. "The Effects of Urban Concentration on Economic Growth." NBER Working Paper 7503, National Bureau of Economic Research, Cambridge, MA.

———. 2003. "Marshall's Scale Economies." *Journal of Urban Economics* 53 (1): 1–28.

Henderson, J. Vernon, and Jacques-François Thisse. 2004. *Cities and Geography.* Vol. 4 of *Handbook of Regional and Urban Economics.* Amsterdam: Elsevier B. V.

Iimi, Atsushi. 2005. "Urbanization and Development of Infrastructure in the East Asian Region." JBICI Review 10 (March): 88–109, Japan Bank for International Cooperation Institute.

Jacobs, Jane. 1970. *The Economy of Cities.* New York: Vintage Books.

Jones Lang LaSalle. 2004. "Global Offshoring Index: Deciding Where to Offshore." Research report, September, Jones Lang LaSalle, Chicago. http://www.joneslanglasalle.com/en-GB/.

Krugman, Paul R. 1991. "Increasing Returns and Economic Geography." *Journal of Political Economy* 99 (3): 483–99.

Leman, Edward. 2005. "Metropolitan Regions: New Challenges for an Urbanizing China." Paper presented at the World Bank and Institute of Applied Economic Research "Urban Research Symposium," Brasilia, April 4.

Lin, Songhua. 2005. "International Trade, Location, and Wage Inequality in China." In *Spatial Inequality and Development,* ed. Ravi Kanbur and Anthony J. Venables, 260–91. WIDER Studies in Development Economics Series. New York: Oxford University Press.

Lucas, Robert E. 1988. "On the Mechanics of Economic Development." *Journal of Monetary Economics* 22 (1): 3–42.

Luo Xubei. 2001a. "La mesure de la distance dans le modèle de gravité: une application au commerce des provinces chinoises avec le Japon." (The Measurement of Distance in the Gravity Model: An Application to the Trade between Chinese Provinces and Japan). *Revue Région et Développement* 13–2001.

———. 2001b. "L'accessibilité au marché des provinces chinoises: le rôle des 'hubs' de transport." (Access to Markets in Chinese Provinces: The Role of Transport Hubs). *Revue Région et Développement* 14–2001.

———. 2004. "The Role of Infrastructure Investment Location in China's Western Development." Policy Research Working Paper 3345, World Bank, Washington, DC.

———. 2005. "Growth Spillover Effects and Regional Development Patterns: The Case of Chinese Provinces." Policy Research Working Paper 3652, World Bank, Washington, DC.

Marshall, Alfred. 1920. *Principles of Economics.* 8th ed. London: Macmillan and Co., Ltd. http://www.econlib.org/library/Marshall/marP.html.

Moretti, Enrico. 2003. "Human Capital Externalities in Cities." NBER Working Paper 9641, National Bureau of Economic Research, Cambridge, MA.

National Research Council. 2003. *Cities Transformed: Demographic Change and Its Implications in the Developing World.* Washington, DC: National Academies Press.

Ooi Giok Ling. 2006. "The Dynamism of East Asian Cities: Challenges for Urban Governance and Public Policy." Background paper, World Bank, Washington, DC.

Pernia, Ernesto M., Cayetano Paderanga, and Victoria P. Hermoso. 1983. *The Spatial and Urban Dimensions of Development in the Philippines.* Manila: Philippines Institute for Development Studies.

Romer, Paul M. 1990. "Endogenous Technological Change." *Journal of Political Economy* 98 (5): 71–102.

Sirtaine, Sophie, Maria Elena Pinglo, J. Luis Guasch, and Vivien Foster. 2005. "How Profitable are Private Infrastructure Concessions in Latin America?: Empirical Evidence and Regulatory Implications." *Quarterly Review of Economics and Finance* 45 (2–3): 380–402.

Smith, Adam. 1776. *An Inquiry into the Nature and Causes of the Wealth of Nations.* London: Adam Smith Institute. http://www.adamsmith.org/.

UN-Habitat (United Nations Human Settlements Programme). 2004. *The State of the World's Cities 2004/ 2005: Globalization and Urban Culture.* London: Earthscan.

United Nations. 2003. "World Urbanization Prospects: The 2003 Revision Population Database." Department of Economic and Social Affairs, Population Division, United Nations, New York.

_____. 2006. "World Urbanization Prospects: The 2005 Revision Population Database." Department of Economic and Social Affairs, Population Division, United Nations, New York. http://esa.un.org/unup/.

Vidal, John. 2006. "Heart and Soul of the City." *The Guardian,* November 1.

World Bank. 2004. "Urbanization Dynamics and Policy Frameworks in Developing East Asia." Urban Development Working Paper 32535, East Asia Infrastructure Department, East Asia and Pacific Region, World Bank, Washington, DC.

_____. 2005. *World Development Indicators 2005.* Washington, DC: World Bank. http://devdata. worldbank.org/wdi2005/Cover.htm.

_____. 2006a. "Infrastructure Strategy: Cross-Sectoral Issues." Report, World Bank, Hanoi.

_____. 2006b. *Governance, Investment Climate, and Harmonious Society: Competitiveness Enhancements for 120 Cities in China.* Report Series 37759-CN. Washington, DC: Poverty Reduction and Economic Management Unit, Financial and Private Sector Development Unit, East Asia and Pacific Region, World Bank.

_____. 2006c. "EAP Sustainable Development on the Urban Fringe." Draft report, East Asia and Pacific Regional Office, World Bank, Washington, DC.

Zhou Jiangping. 2006. "China's Urban Transportation since 1978: Challenge, Publication, and Policy." *Projections,* Department of Urban Studies and Planning, MIT, Cambridge, MA.

MAP 6.1 **Within-Country Differences in Poverty Are Considerable in East Asia**

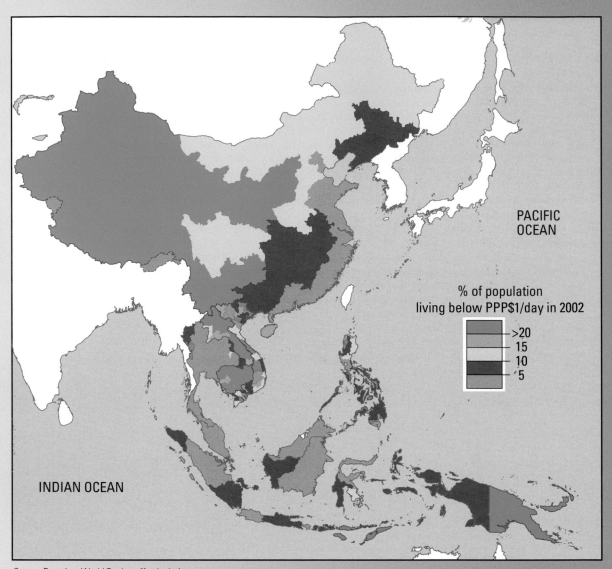

% of population
living below PPP$1/day in 2002

- >20
- 15
- 10
- 5

PACIFIC
OCEAN

INDIAN OCEAN

Source: Based on World Bank staff calculations.
Note: In purchasing power parity dollars.

CHAPTER 6

COHESION

Convergence is occurring among countries, but within-country inequality is rising because of widening spatial and social gaps. Inequality is a natural consequence of scale-centered growth.

Much has been written about East Asia's stellar growth performance over the last two decades or so. The record is well known. As Chapter 1 notes, in terms of per capita growth in gross domestic product (GDP), East Asia has been the most rapidly growing region in the world by a good margin. The massive improvement in living standards is reflected in the fact that, between 1980 and 2004, average GDP per capita levels in the region rose by a factor of 4.5, while world GDP per capita increased by a factor of only 0.5. Per capita GDP in the region is now beginning to approach the levels Latin America and the Caribbean attained in the 1980s. Regional GDP per capita in 2004 was about three-quarters of the per capita GDP in Latin America and the Caribbean in 1980.[1] In hindsight, even the Asian crisis of 1997–98 appears to have been a hiccup in the unfolding of an overall robust growth experience.[2]

While this record is both impressive and uncontroversial, concerns remain about how well this growth has successfully delivered on enhancing the lives of the 1.9 billion people who inhabit the region. Beyond the averages are questions on how widely the benefits have been shared and whether the region has also appreciably improved the economic and social opportunities for the vast majority of the citizenry. Underlying some of these concerns are questions about whether socioeconomic disparities can threaten economic growth aspects. This chapter is an attempt to assess these concerns and the emerging implications for public policy.

A review of East Asia's development experience since the 1990s from this perspective reveals the following significant facts:

- Absolute poverty in terms of both the percentage and the absolute number of poor people has declined dramatically since the 1990s.
- The reduction of income poverty has been accompanied by progress in overall human development indicators on the countries in the region.
- However, looking beyond extreme poverty, a large proportion of the region's population continues to subsist at fairly low levels in terms of living standards.
- Inequality in income or consumption has risen significantly since the 1990s, and most of this rise is driven by the increase in inequality within countries.
- Even where relative inequalities do not show a trend, absolute disparities have been growing rapidly.
- Two fault lines of inequality within countries are of particular concern: the urban-rural divide and the regional-ethnic divide. These divisions are apparent in both the income and nonincome indicators of welfare.
- Vulnerability expressed as the ex ante risk of falling into poverty is emerging as a concern.

The next section documents these trends in greater detail. The rest of the chapter discusses some of the underlying forces driving these trends (the subsequent section), why we should care about rising disparities (the penultimate section), and some emerging implications for public policy (the final section).

The Main Trends

Poverty

Table 6.1 sets out the record of poverty reduction in the region since the 1990s. The progress has been dramatic and historically unprecedented. During the 1990s, the proportion of populations living on less than US$1 a day declined from 29 to 14 percent; in absolute terms, the number of poor declined from 457 million to 248 million. Projections (based on macroeconomic and sectoral growth patterns and the most recent available household survey data) indicate that the current levels of US$1-a-day poverty are around 8 percent, while the number of poor is down to about 150 million. The region has already attained and surpassed the Millennium Development Goal target of halving the 1990 absolute poverty rate by 2015.

■ TABLE 6.1 **East Asia's Progress in Poverty Reduction Since 1990**

Indicator	East Asia and Pacific	Cambodia	China	Indonesia	Korea, Rep. of	Lao PDR	Malaysia	Philippines	Thailand	Vietnam
Population (millions)										
1990	1,585.4	10.3	1,143.3	178.2	42.9	4.2	18.2	62.6	55.6	66.2
2000	1,789.6	12.7	1,267.4	210.5	47.0	5.4	23.3	76.3	61.9	79.9
2005	1,868.5	14.1	1,307.7	226.1	48.3	6.1	25.5	83.7	65.1	86.1
Mean consumption (1993 purchasing power parity US$ per person per day)										
1990	2.24	1.84	1.88	2.02	9.90	1.29	6.42	2.97	3.38	1.37
2000	3.73	2.32	3.47	2.38	16.31	1.75	10.00	3.52	4.12	2.41
2005	5.32	2.61	5.43	3.05	18.21	2.11	12.06	3.76	5.16	2.97
Headcount index (% of population living on less than US$1 a day)										
1990	28.8	32.5	31.5	20.6	<0.5	53.0	2.0	19.1	12.5	50.8
2000	13.8	22.6	15.4	9.9	<0.5	33.9	<0.5	13.5	5.2	15.2
2005	8.0	17.3	8.9	4.4	<0.5	20.0	<0.5	10.8	1.7	7.9
Number of poor (millions living on less than US$1 a day)										
1990	456.9	3.4	360.6	36.7	—	2.2	0.4	12.0	7.0	33.6
2000	247.8	2.9	194.8	20.9	—	1.8	—	10.3	3.2	12.1
2005	149.7	2.4	117.0	9.9	—	1.2	—	9.0	1.1	6.8

Source: World Bank 2006a.
Note: — = no data are available.

While the regional aggregate numbers are dominated by the dramatic decline in poverty in China (from 361 million people to 117 million people living on less than US$1 a day during 1990–2005), it is evident from Table 6.1 that progress has been rapid in most countries. Average consumption in the region and in most countries is now at a level suggesting that the virtual elimination of extreme poverty (less than US$1 a day) is a potentially realizable objective.

The progress is also reflected in the human development index, which is a composite measure of development that aggregates three indexes: an index of life expectancy at birth, an education index (itself a combination of the adult literacy rate and the gross enrollment ratio), and an index for GDP per capita in purchasing power parity dollars. As shown in figure 6.1, most countries in the region have recorded significant improvements in the human development index during

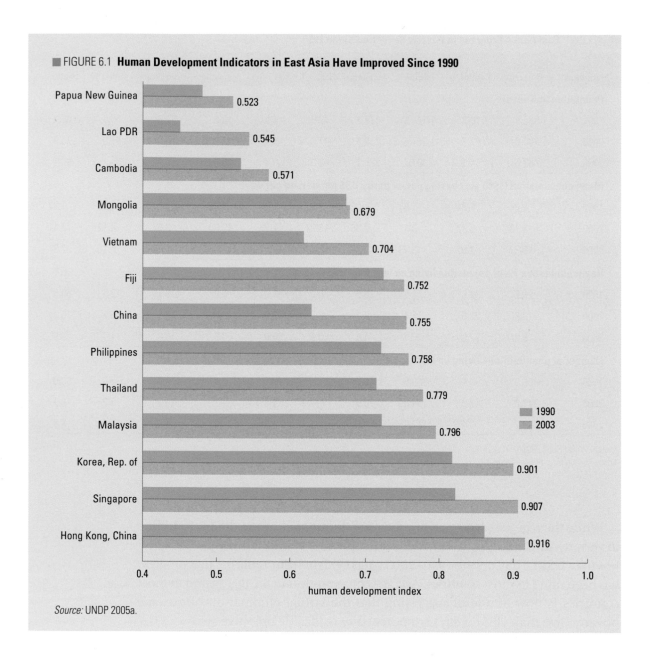

■ FIGURE 6.1 **Human Development Indicators in East Asia Have Improved Since 1990**

Source: UNDP 2005a.

this period. Improvements are especially noteworthy in China, the Lao People's Democratic Republic, and Vietnam. However, the disparities across countries are also striking; despite the improvement in the human development index across all countries, the countries nevertheless remain at quite different stages of economic and social development.

The extreme-poverty goalpost of a dollar-per-day is important. However, even the threshold of US$1.08 a day adjusted to purchasing power parity dollars does not offer much in terms of the standard of living it affords.[3] It is hardly surprising that most countries have chosen to set their national poverty lines (typically based on a threshold of the cost to provide about 2,100 calories per person per day, with some allowance for basic nonfood expenditure) well above US$1 a day in purchasing power parity dollars. Going beyond US$1 a day, there is a dramatic rise in the numbers at the relevant thresholds. For instance, it is estimated that nearly a quarter of East Asia's population currently has consumption levels at between US$1 and US$2 a day. Altogether, almost 585 million persons in the region, including large proportions of the population in many countries, are living below a US$2-a-day benchmark (see table 6.2).

Inequality Across and Within Countries

While poverty has declined and human development indexes have improved, inequality within the region has grown. As shown in table 6.3, the Theil index of inequality of per capita consumption for the region as a whole increased from 34.5 percent in 1990 to 42.6 percent in 2002, a rise of about 24 percent.[4] A decomposition of the overall inequality into between-country and within-country components indicates that most—about three-quarters—of the current inequality in the region is attributable to inequality within countries. In other words, even if all countries showed an identical level of mean consumption, but relative disparities in consumption persisted within countries, the overall inequality in the region would only decline by about a quarter.

There has been a limited decline in inequality across countries, but a key feature of the evolution of inequality in the region is the sharp increase in within-country inequality. In terms of changes during 1990–2002, the between-country component declined by a modest 1.5 percentage points owing to more rapid growth in mean consumption in relatively poorer countries. However, within-country inequality increased sharply by 9.6 percentage points, and this resulted in a rise in overall inequality by about 8 percentage points.

■ TABLE 6.2 Progress in Reducing US$2-a-Day Poverty Since 1990

Indicator	East Asia and Pacific	Cambodia	China	Indonesia	Korea, Rep. of	Lao PDR	Malaysia	Philippines	Thailand	Vietnam
Headcount index (% of population living on less than US$2 a day)										
1990	66.9	76.3	69.9	71.1	<0.5	89.6	18.5	53.5	47.0	87.0
2000	45.8	67.8	44.8	59.5	<0.5	79.4	9.7	47.2	35.6	63.5
2005	31.3	62.1	28.6	44.4	<0.5	68.6	5.5	41.9	22.8	49.1
Number of poor (millions living on less than US$2 a day)										
1990	1,060.8	7.9	799.6	126.7	—	3.7	3.4	33.5	26.1	57.6
2000	819.9	8.6	567.4	125.3	—	4.3	2.3	36.0	22.0	50.7
2005	584.5	8.7	373.5	100.5	—	4.2	1.4	35.1	14.8	42.3

Source: World Bank 2006a.
Note: — = no data are available.

■ TABLE 6.3 **Evolution of Inequality in East Asia, 1990-2002: The Theil Index**

Index	Around 1990		Around 2002		1990–2002	
	Theil index	Contribution to Theil index, %	Theil index	Contribution to Theil index, %	Change in index, %	Contribution to change, %
Total	34.5	100.0	42.6	100.0	23.6	100.0
Between country	12.0	34.8	10.0	23.6	−16.3	−17.7
Within country	22.5	65.2	32.6	76.4	44.8	117.7
Within Theil index	22.5	100.0	32.6	100.0	44.8	100.0
China	21.1	57.2	35.8	74.9	69.7	93.7
Indonesia	20.6	9.4	23.8	5.4	15.5	3.4
Korea, Rep. of	17.0	9.1	17.5	6.0	2.9	0.6
Lao PDR	19.8	0.1	23.1	0.1	16.7	0.1
Malaysia	35.2	5.2	36.7	3.5	4.2	0.5
Philippines	30.1	7.1	36.8	4.1	22.3	3.7
Thailand	39.2	9.3	34.2	3.9	−12.8	−2.8
Vietnam	22.4	2.6	25.4	2.1	13.4	0.8

Source: Calculations of the authors based on household survey data for these countries.

As table 6.3 also shows, inequality appears to have risen over this period in seven of the eight countries, the only exception being Thailand. Increases have been especially pronounced in China, but they have also been significant in Indonesia, Lao PDR, the Philippines, and Vietnam.

Changes in China are a big part of the story. The within-country component of regional inequality is a (consumption-share) weighted sum of inequality within individual countries. Given its large size, China contributed 57 percent to overall within-country inequality in the region even in 1990. However, due to the sharp growth in inequality in China (its own Theil index increased from 21.1 percent to 35.8 percent), as well as its growing prominence in the regional economy (reflected in its rising share in aggregate consumption from 61 to 68 percent), China's contribution to the within-country component of regional inequality had climbed to nearly 75 percent by 2002.

Figure 6.2 presents a decomposition of inequality within China in components relating to rural inequality, urban inequality, and intersectoral inequality. During 1990–2002, all three components contributed to the rise in inequality. Inequality within rural and urban areas increased, and intersectoral disparities rose sharply.

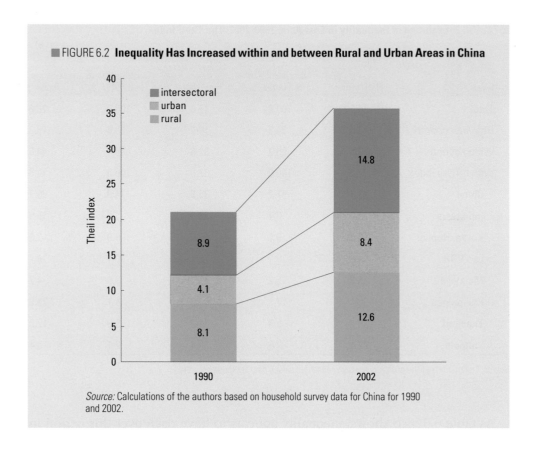

■ FIGURE 6.2 **Inequality Has Increased within and between Rural and Urban Areas in China**

Source: Calculations of the authors based on household survey data for China for 1990 and 2002.

Of the total increase in the Theil index between 1990 and 2002, the rise in rural and urban inequality contributed in equal measure, about 30 percent each, while widening intersectoral disparities contributed the remaining 40 percent.

The Rural-Urban Divide

As the rising contribution of intersectoral disparity to overall inequality in China illustrates, the rural-urban divide is emerging as a key focal point of inequity in the region. This is obvious in economic and social indicators. As illustrated in figure 6.3, average real consumption levels in urban areas are often about twice as large as those in rural areas. In countries such as China and the Philippines, the gaps have been rising.

The differences in mean consumption levels are magnified in the rural-urban poverty rates (see figure 6.3). While poverty declined in rural and urban areas over the 1990s, there are no signs of a significant narrowing of the poverty dif-

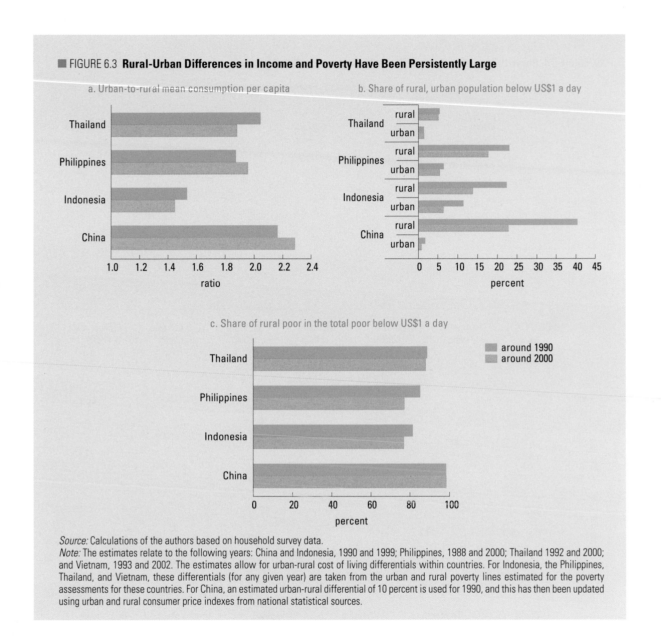

■ FIGURE 6.3 **Rural-Urban Differences in Income and Poverty Have Been Persistently Large**

a. Urban-to-rural mean consumption per capita

b. Share of rural, urban population below US$1 a day

c. Share of rural poor in the total poor below US$1 a day

around 1990
around 2000

Source: Calculations of the authors based on household survey data.
Note: The estimates relate to the following years: China and Indonesia, 1990 and 1999; Philippines, 1988 and 2000; Thailand 1992 and 2000; and Vietnam, 1993 and 2002. The estimates allow for urban-rural cost of living differentials within countries. For Indonesia, the Philippines, Thailand, and Vietnam, these differentials (for any given year) are taken from the urban and rural poverty lines estimated for the poverty assessments for these countries. For China, an estimated urban-rural differential of 10 percent is used for 1990, and this has then been updated using urban and rural consumer price indexes from national statistical sources.

ferences between cities or towns and the countryside. As a result, poverty in the region continues to be an overwhelmingly rural phenomenon.

Nor are the disparities limited to income and consumption. For instance, the mean number of years of schooling of adults who are likely to have completed their participation in education is between two and four years greater in urban areas relative to rural areas (see figure 6.4). The average adult in rural areas in

■ FIGURE 6.4 **Rural-Urban Differences in Social Indicators Are Considerable**

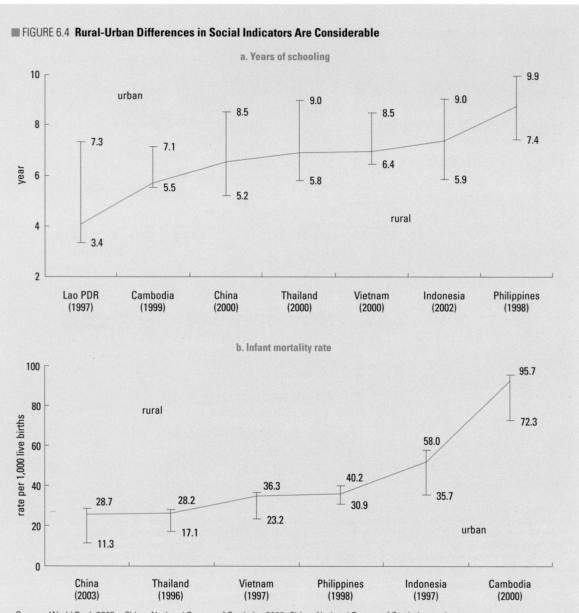

Sources: World Bank 2005a; China, National Bureau of Statistics 2003; China, National Bureau of Statistics, various years.

Note: The orange lines show national mean values for the indicator.

many countries still has six or fewer years of lifetime schooling, and the average adult woman has fewer still. Similarly, infant mortality rates in rural areas remain well above those in urban areas throughout the region. With the available data, it is difficult to be conclusive about trends in these nonincome aspects of rural-urban disparities, but there is no denying that substantial gaps remain a continuing source of friction in the region.

Evidence for China does, however, indicate some worsening of rural-urban disparities in education and health indicators. For instance, while illiteracy and infant mortality rates declined in rural and urban areas, the ratio of the rural to the urban illiteracy rates rose from 2.1 to 2.3 between 1981 and 2000, and, similarly, the ratio of rural to urban infant mortality rates increased from 1.7 to 2.8 over the same period.[5]

The Regional and Ethnic Divide

Another important element of inequality within countries is regional disparity. Map 6.1 presents a province-level picture of poverty in the region in 2002. For each subregion, it indicates the proportion of the population living on less than US$1 a day.

The provincial map illustrates three features of the geography of poverty in the region:

- First, national averages hide large differences within countries. Low-income countries include provinces with low poverty incidence, and middle-income countries include provinces with high poverty incidence. There are some regularities across the region. Poverty incidence tends to be higher in remote rural upland areas (for example, in China's Yunnan Province and in Lao PDR and Vietnam), in areas with a weak natural resource base (as in the northeast of Thailand), and in areas distant from major urban centers. Conversely, poverty headcount ratios are generally lower in urban agglomerations and surrounding areas. Poverty incidence also tends to be higher in provinces in the interior relative to coastal areas.
- Second, poverty incidence tends to be spatially clustered, and the clustering may transcend national borders. This suggests that there is an important role for geography in determining poverty over and above the influence of national history, policies, and institutions. The subregion with the most significant crossborder spillovers of poverty incidence is the Greater Mekong subregion,

which includes Cambodia, Yunnan Province in China, Lao PDR, Thailand, and Vietnam.

■ Third, poor areas are generally sparsely populated. Areas exhibiting high poverty incidence and low population density include the western provinces of China (Xinjiang and Tibet), the upland areas of Lao PDR, the eastern provinces of Indonesia and Papua New Guinea, and the northern mountain areas of Vietnam. Low-incidence and high-density areas include the plain of Vientiane and the Mekong River corridor in Lao PDR, Luzon Island in the Philippines, and the Mekong River and Red River deltas in Vietnam. Nonetheless, some areas here show high poverty incidence and a large number of poor: for instance, Yunnan Province in China, Java Island in Indonesia, the eastern provinces of the Philippines, and the northeast region of Thailand.

Regional disparities are also notable in human development indexes across provinces. Based on the national *Human Development Reports* for seven countries in the region, figure 6.5 presents the range of human development indexes across provinces within each country. The provinces with low (high) indexes are often the ones with high (low) poverty rates, although the correlation is not perfect.

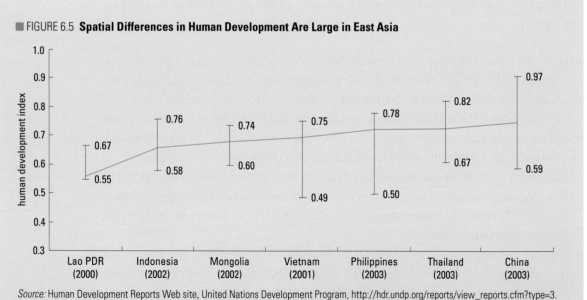

■ FIGURE 6.5 **Spatial Differences in Human Development Are Large in East Asia**

Source: Human Development Reports Web site, United Nations Development Program, http://hdr.undp.org/reports/view_reports.cfm?type=3.
Note: The numbers and solid vertical lines indicate ranges of the human development index in provinces of the countries shown. The intersections of the orange line with the vertical lines indicate the nationwide value of the index for each country.

For instance, in the Philippines in 2003, seven of the 10 most and least well performing provinces in terms of poverty incidence were also among the 10 most and least well performing provinces in terms of the indexes.[6]

There is also a significant ethnic dimension to inequality within countries that often also overlaps with the spatial disparities discussed above. For instance, compared with the majority community (Lao-Tai) in Lao PDR, ethnic minority groups exhibit higher poverty and child malnutrition rates, lower net primary enrollment rates, and lower values for agricultural assets per capita, thus compounding any deprivations because of their minority status in multiple ways (see table 6.4). It is notable that the Lao-Tai mostly live along the busy Mekong corridor, while the ethnic minorities live mainly in more remote upland areas in the north and center-south.

Similarly, in rural China, poverty rates among the non-Han ethnic minorities are two to three times higher than those among the Han population (see figure 6.6). Remoteness in terms of mountainous residence accentuates the poverty among minority communities. Thus, while only about a fifth of the Han population is located in mountainous areas, the proportion of minorities living in such areas is around two-thirds.

The story is similar in Vietnam, where, relative to the Kinh and Chinese majority, the ethnic minorities are much poorer in terms of consumption levels, access to clean water, and school enrollment, especially at the lower secondary and post-secondary levels (see table 6.5).

There is also evidence of increasing regional disparities in some countries, for instance, China. Using data on per capita consumption expenditure in rural and urban areas in 28 provinces, Kanbur and Zhang (2005) report that measures of

■ TABLE 6.4 **The Ethnic Dimension of Disparities in Lao PDR, 2002–03**

Population segment	Share of population, %	Poor, %	Underweight children under 5, %	Net primary enrollment, %	Value of agricultural assets per capita, KN millions
Majority group					
Lao-Tai	66	25	34	76	4.5
Minority groups					
Mon-Khmer	24	54	43	49	2.0
Hmong-lu Mien	3	46	41	35	2.0
Chine-Tibet	8	40	37	47	3.8

Source: Lao PDR, Committee for Planning and Investment et al. 2006.

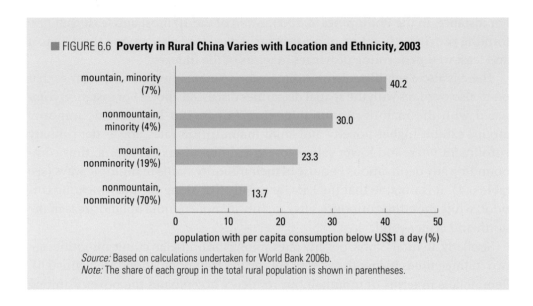

■ FIGURE 6.6 **Poverty in Rural China Varies with Location and Ethnicity, 2003**

Source: Based on calculations undertaken for World Bank 2006b.
Note: The share of each group in the total rural population is shown in parentheses.

regional inequality have been increasing significantly since the postreform period; the Gini and Theil indexes rose from about 26 percent and 11 percent, respectively, in 1984 to 37 percent and 25 percent in 2000.

Evidence on trends over time in ethnic disparities is often not readily available. One exception is Vietnam, where the data clearly indicate that improvements among ethnic minorities have not kept pace with those among the majority pop-

■ TABLE 6.5 **The Ethnic Dimension of Disparities in Vietnam, 1993, 1998, and 2002**
percent

Population segment	1993	1998	2002
Share who are poor			
Kinh and Chinese	53.9	31.1	23.1
Ethnic minorities	86.4	75.2	69.3
Lower secondary enrollment rate			
Kinh and Chinese	33.6	66.2	75.9
Ethnic minorities	6.6	36.5	48.0
Share with access to clean water			
Kinh and Chinese	29.0	44.9	52.6
Ethnic minorities	5.3	9.9	12.8

Source: World Bank 2003.
Note: Ethnic minorities had a 13 percent share in the Vietnamese population in 2002.

ulation in most cases (see table 6.5). This widening ethnic gap cannot be generalized for other countries, but the reality of the large gaps is undeniable. Evidence such as that presented above for China and Lao PDR illustrates that, despite the growth and poverty reduction of the 1990s, ethnicity continues to be a significant axis of disparity in the region.

Vulnerability

The cross-sectional data that underlie the evidence presented above are, however, limited in one important respect: they do not tell us how the living standards of the same households have changed over time. Poverty reduction would be an easier problem to solve if the remaining poor at any given time were a fixed group of households. Instead, there is considerable income and consumption mobility and, especially, movements of people into and out of poverty. This has an important implication: the number of people who are at risk of poverty may be appreciably larger than the number who are observed to be poor. This is illustrated by recent longitudinal data on rural China showing that, as against 18 percent of the population who were observed to be poor, on average, during 2001–04, about 31 percent of the population were poor during at least one of the three years examined (see figure 6.7). Thus, for every poor person, there is another person who faces a one-third or higher probability of entering poverty during the same period.

It is difficult to determine if the relative risk of poverty has been increasing in China or, more generally, within the East Asia region. However, subnational-level evidence on China does indicate that, as the incidence of poverty declines, the share of transient poverty tends to rise.[7] If that is any guide, then the issue of transient poverty is likely to become more important as East Asia reduces poverty.

Understanding Disparities

The uneven spread of economic growth within countries has thus been as compelling a feature of the growth experience in East Asia over the last two decades as has been the rapid pace of growth itself. Put differently, growth has been accompanied by friction, understood here as the widening or at least the persistence of disparities across space, sectors, or groups and, ultimately, across individuals. The two features are not unrelated, of course. As argued below, many of the same forces that have contributed to rapid growth have also shaped this unevenness in growth. This section looks at five major drivers of friction in the region that have, to varying degrees, influenced the emerging trends in different countries: (1) trade and globalization, (2) labor market reform, (3) the formation

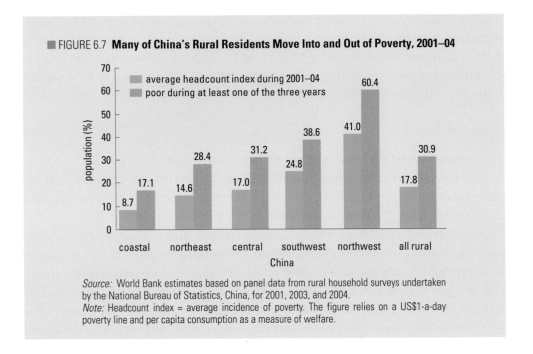

■ FIGURE 6.7 **Many of China's Rural Residents Move Into and Out of Poverty, 2001–04**

Source: World Bank estimates based on panel data from rural household surveys undertaken by the National Bureau of Statistics, China, for 2001, 2003, and 2004.
Note: Headcount index = average incidence of poverty. The figure relies on a US$1-a-day poverty line and per capita consumption as a measure of welfare.

of clusters and agglomeration effects, (4) the ongoing process of fiscal decentralization, and (5) impediments to the process of internal migration within countries, which is otherwise an equalizing force.

While the first two factors appear to have contributed to rising skill premiums in East Asian labor markets, the third factor underlies much of the observed spatial concentration of economic activity, and the fourth factor has had significant implications for the equitable distribution of public spending, especially in education and health. Given the centrality of China to both the level of and trends in inequality in the region, the following discussion pays particular attention to developments in China.

The "China Price" Is Not Only Cheap, Unskilled Labor

A key factor underlying the rise in inequality within the region has been the expansion in wage inequality.[8] There has been a significant increasing trend in the returns to education in several countries, which reflects rising skill premiums in labor markets. For instance, in urban China, returns to the completion of educational levels above senior high school rose sharply during 1988–2001 (see figure 6.8). Those completing technical school earned 3 percent more than did

■ FIGURE 6.8 **Well-Educated Workers Are Earning More in High-Growth Countries**

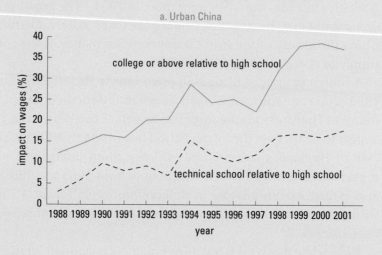

a. Urban China

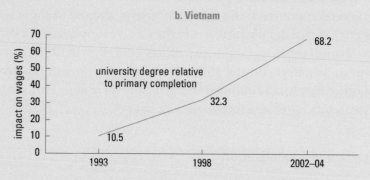

b. Vietnam

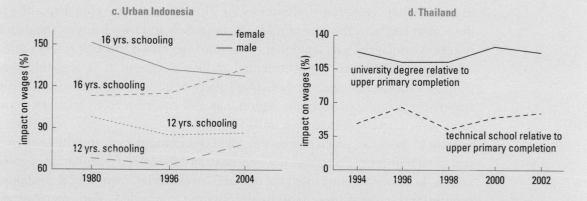

c. Urban Indonesia   d. Thailand

Sources: China: Zhang et al. 2005; Vietnam: World Bank 2005b; Indonesia: Alatas and Bourguignon 2005 and World Bank 2006c; Thailand: Blunch 2004.

senior high school graduates in 1988; by 2001, this had increased to 18 percent. Similarly, college graduates earned 12 percent more than did senior high school graduates in 1988, but 37 percent more in 2001.[9] The growing returns to education suggest that the so-called China price that has been instrumental in making China the factory of the world is not merely a matter of the country's abundant supply of cheap, unskilled labor.

A similar pattern of rising skill premiums is also notable for Vietnam during 1993–2004 and for men workers in urban Indonesia during 1980–2004, while trends in Thailand indicate some increase since the 1998 crisis, though the trends appear to be flat over the longer period from 1994 to 2002 (see figure 6.8). In the case of Thailand, there is some evidence of an increase in relative returns to higher education during an earlier period, from 1985 to 1998. Similarly, there is also evidence of an increase in skill premiums for Taiwan (China) in 1979–94, while rates of return to different levels of education remained stable for Malaysia over 1989–97.[10]

Thus, while the trend is not universal, there is evidence of rising returns to skills in several countries in the region. Moreover, the rise in these wage premiums has often occurred despite increases in the relative supply of skilled labor. For instance, the share of urban workers with a college education in China increased from 13 percent to 28 percent during 1988–2001;[11] growth rates in postsecondary education in other East Asian countries also generally increased. This suggests that demand-side factors have been important (see below).

Trade and Globalization

The sources of the East Asian growth miracle have been extensively studied.[12] One key factor that is especially relevant to the discussion of emerging disparities in the region has been the role of trade liberalization and the ability of the region to take advantage of greater global economic integration through foreign direct investment (FDI) and export-oriented industrialization. It is arguable that, through various channels, the particular pattern of trade and globalization, while stimulating rapid growth in the region, has also contributed to relatively more rapid growth in the demand for skilled labor.

First, in most East Asian economies, rapid economic growth and the associated structural transformations have not only expanded the traded manufactured goods sectors, but have also increased the demand for financial, commercial, and other services and boosted these (still predominantly nontraded) skill-intensive sectors. Skilled labor supply is in less elastic supply in the short to medium term because of the costs and the time required for acquiring education. Hence, even skill-neutral growth in labor demand (arising from economic growth) may widen wage dispersion for a while if supply elasticities differ across skill categories. As a result, in rapidly growing economies such as China and Vietnam, we may reasonably expect to see some widening of wage disparities even if no other forces are at work.

Second, the pattern of trade and globalization in the region has not conformed to the stylized Heckscher-Ohlin framework, which predicts reduced wage dispersion in countries relatively abundant in unskilled labor. In this framework, trade liberalization leads countries to expand the production of goods that are intensive in the factor in which the countries are relatively abundant, thereby increasing the returns to that abundant factor. Since unskilled labor is the relatively abundant factor in developing countries, trade liberalization might be expected to reduce the relative returns to skilled labor in these countries. However, as noted above, skill premiums have, on the contrary, increased in several countries in the region. This points to the role of other factors affecting such premiums (for instance, labor market reform, as discussed below), but also to some important ways in which the simple Heckscher-Ohlin framework fails to capture the particular features of trade and globalization in the region. Two of these features are notable, as follows.

International capital flows. Contrary to the assumption in the standard Heckscher-Ohlin model that there is no international factor mobility, the capacity to attract large amounts of FDI has been a distinguishing feature of the development success of East Asia. The FDI-trade nexus in East Asia has contributed substantially to narrowing the technology gap with the developed world, a by-product of which has also been the increasing demand for (and wages of) relatively skilled labor through a number of channels. FDI has tended to be concentrated in relatively skill-intensive sectors in East Asian economies.[13] FDI has also induced skill-biased technological change through the technology directly brought in by foreign firms, as well as through horizontal and vertical transmission to existing and new local firms.[14] Foreign-owned enterprises have likewise tended to pay relatively more to (relatively scarce) skilled labor than have local firms.[15]

Production networks. Another significant development in the region has been the growth of production and distribution networks, whereby firms in East Asia have become increasingly integrated into global supply chains. The process of production has been deverticalized and fragmented such that lead firms in developed countries have sought to outsource the noncore fragments of the value chain to external suppliers. The phenomenon—greatly facilitated by the spread of recent advances in information and communications technology and logistics—is particularly developed in the manufacturing sector, but is by no means confined to manufacturing. A measure of the increasing importance of production networks in the region is the growing importance of the trade in parts and components.[16] The development of production networks and outsourcing have tended to boost the demand for skilled labor in both home and host countries because the outsourced activities, while less skill intensive in the home country, are nonetheless more skill intensive relative to the host country average.[17] Theoretical models that explicitly incorporate intermediate goods and product fragmentation generate results suggesting that trade liberalization and globalization may increase skill premiums and widen wage dispersion.[18] While the mechanisms that link wage dispersion to higher levels of product fragmentation differ across various theoretical models, the complementarity of skilled labor with particular types of capital often emerges as an important mechanism.

Direct econometric evidence of the contribution of increasing trade and globalization to widening wage dispersion in East Asian economies remains sparse, but the above theoretical insights and empirical observations are highly suggestive of such an effect, and the limited direct evidence is also consistent with this view. For instance, in a study of five East Asian economies—Hong Kong (China), the Republic of Korea, the Philippines, Singapore, and Thailand—during 1985–98, Te Velde and Morrissey (2004) find that trade and FDI tend to raise wage inequality.[19] Similarly, Kanbur and Zhang (2005) find that greater trade openness has contributed appreciably to the rise in spatial income inequality in China over the postreform period.

Labor Market Reform

A factor that has been particularly important in transition economies such as China and Vietnam is the implementation of labor market reforms, which have been associated with a progressive reduction in the share of the state sector in the economy and the accompanying fall in state sector employment. Since the early 1990s, the de facto deregulation of labor markets in both China and Vietnam has progressed briskly, and market forces play the dominant role in wage setting within the greatly expanded private sector. For example, in China, the share of the state-owned and collective sector in urban employment had declined from over 85 percent in 1980 to less than 30 percent by 2004.[20] Similarly, in Vietnam, the number of state-owned enterprises had declined from about 12,000 at the end of

1989 to less than 2,600 by early 2006.[21] The share of private domestic and foreign enterprises in total employment rose from 11 percent in 1993 to over 18 percent in 2004, while state-owned enterprises and the government sector only accounted for about 8 percent of total employment in 2004.[22]

The effects of economic restructuring and labor market reform on wage and income inequality may emerge through a number of channels, as illustrated in the Chinese case. First, as wages begin to reflect skill-related productivity differences, wage dispersion across workers increases. The evidence for China indicates that returns to education rose in the private sector, as well as state and collective sector enterprises, indicating that increasing wage dispersion was not merely the result of a rising share of the private sector in overall employment, but wider labor market reforms involving a shift from a system of wages set by the government along a compressed wage scale to a more market-determined system.[23]

Second, the massive layoffs associated with economic restructuring meant that many (especially older) workers opted out of the labor force, and many others remained unemployed for long periods. Giles, Park, and Cai (2006), using data for five cities in China, estimate that, of all those people experiencing job separation during 1996–2001, only about 35 percent were employed again within 12 months, and about 55 percent were still unemployed in November 2001. The limited public support available (through subsidies for laid-off workers, pensions, unemployment insurance, and a minimum income support program) failed to compensate for the income losses among those who were not reemployed.[24]

Third, there is also evidence of greater wage disparity among those people who were sufficiently fortunate to find reemployment. For instance, Giles, Park, and Cai (2006) estimate that, among those who were reemployed, workers under 40 experienced an increase in their average wage, while those over 40 saw their average wage decline.

Fourth, a parallel process has been the rising share of employment in the urban informal sector. The share of such employment in urban China is estimated to have grown from about 14 percent in 1990 to about 39 percent in 2003.[25] While part of this increase may be statistical in that it reflects some previously unrecorded economic activity, especially in the tertiary sector,[26] most seems to have occurred on account of the rapid growth in the unregistered and imperfectly monitored private sector, among unreported migrant workers, and through the significant share of informal employment carried out among urban residents employed in the state and collective sector.[27] The share of informal employment is higher among women, among the youngest and oldest workers, among migrants, and among less well edu-cated workers.[28] Workers in the informal sector not only show relatively lower wage earnings,[29] but, because they are largely uncovered by protective regulation and social insurance programs, they are also the most vulnerable segment in the labor market.[30]

Agglomeration Effects and Clusters

The emergence and growth of industrial and services clusters around large cities and the persistent and, in many instances, widening disparities between dynamic growth regions and underdeveloped lagging regions is the most visible aspect of uneven growth in East Asia.[31] Spatial concentration or the clustering of economic activities reflects the influence of location and agglomeration economies. Transport costs and factor availability provide incentives for locating close to input suppli-ers and output markets, and increasing returns to scale magnify the advantages of locating in such clusters. Forward and backward links generate centripetal forces toward agglomeration, and distance (which influences market access) and market size begin to matter in decisions on industry location. Firms that locate in a cluster enjoy access to thicker labor pools and more component suppliers. Because agglomeration processes are path dependent, an existing industry con-centration may exert a powerful gravitational pull on new industries. These forces often complement rather than conflict with classical comparative-advantage-based locational factors that attract industries to locate and expand in particular cities or regions.

While such agglomeration effects are powerful levers for growth, they may also be a source of significant spatial inequality. Spatial disparities in average incomes across China's metropolitan regions may be related to one dominant factor: dis-tance from a port. The income differences are also reflected in provincial wage disparities: provinces in coastal regions gain a wage premium due to their loca-tion advantage.[32]

While first-nature geography (the proximity to coasts, rivers, or borders) is often an instigating factor in the development of clusters and spatial concentration, the role of trade and foreign investment on the one hand and public policy on the other is being increasingly recognized.[33] For instance, about 80 percent of FDI in China during 1989–2003 was concentrated in the coastal provinces, and the three provinces of Dong Nai, Hanoi, and Ho Chi Minh City accounted for almost 61 per-cent of FDI in Vietnam during 1988–2003 (see figure 6.9).[34] Analysis reveals that the entry decisions of foreign firms with respect to China are influenced by the access to

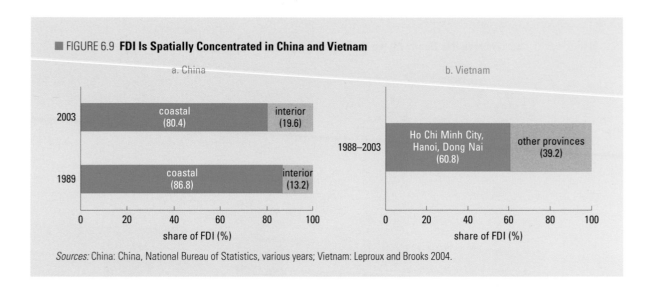

■ FIGURE 6.9 **FDI Is Spatially Concentrated in China and Vietnam**

a. China

b. Vietnam

Sources: China: China, National Bureau of Statistics, various years; Vietnam: Leproux and Brooks 2004.

international markets and suppliers, such that provinces with good access to sea and river berths and open to international trade attract more foreign entry.[35]

These trends in FDI are also highly correlated with foreign trade. For instance, the top four provinces attracting FDI in China (Guandong, Jiangsu, Shandong, and Shanghai) accounted for about 56 percent of total FDI in 2003 and about 66 percent of the country's total trade (exports, plus imports).[36] As shown in figure 6.10, the persistently high shares of coastal (relative to inland) provinces in trade and FDI are also reflected in growth in incomes. During 1989–2004, while the share of coastal provinces in total population remained stable, their share in GDP increased from 47 to 54 percent, indicating significantly more rapid growth in per capita incomes in the coastal region.

Domestic public and private investments have favored the same regions. For instance, in 2004, coastal provinces in China accounted for 55 percent of total domestic investment in fixed assets.[37] The locational advantages are thus magnified over time as a result of investments in superior infrastructure and facilities, all of which, in turn, contribute to a growing geographical concentration of economic activity.[38]

It is not surprising then that growth has also been spatially concentrated. For China, it is estimated that about 19 percent of the increase in regional inequality (log variance of GDP per worker across provinces) during 1986–98 is explained by regional differences in trade and foreign capital, while nearly three-quarters is explained by domestic capital.[39]

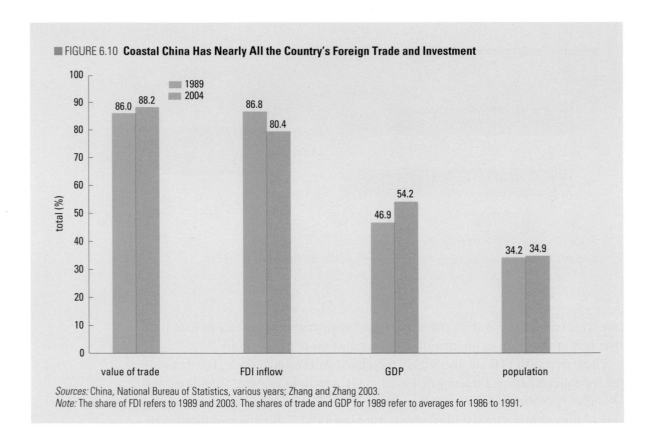

■FIGURE 6.10 **Coastal China Has Nearly All the Country's Foreign Trade and Investment**

Sources: China, National Bureau of Statistics, various years; Zhang and Zhang 2003.
Note: The share of FDI refers to 1989 and 2003. The shares of trade and GDP for 1989 refer to averages for 1986 to 1991.

Fiscal Decentralization

Another significant trend in East Asia that gained momentum during the 1990s is the move toward greater fiscal decentralization. Various structural and political imperatives have propelled the process in different countries, ranging from the end of authoritarian regimes in Indonesia and the Philippines to the transition to a market economy in China and Vietnam. The share of subnational government spending has risen in several countries in the region to significant, though varying levels (see figure 6.11).

However, while fiscal decentralization has progressed, subnational fiscal disparities remain persistently large. There are big differences in revenue capacity across local governments. These reflect the underlying and substantial variations in the economic and resource base of the local governments, which seek to fill the vertical imbalances between subnational revenues and expenditures through transfers from the central government. However, the transfers have not been suf-

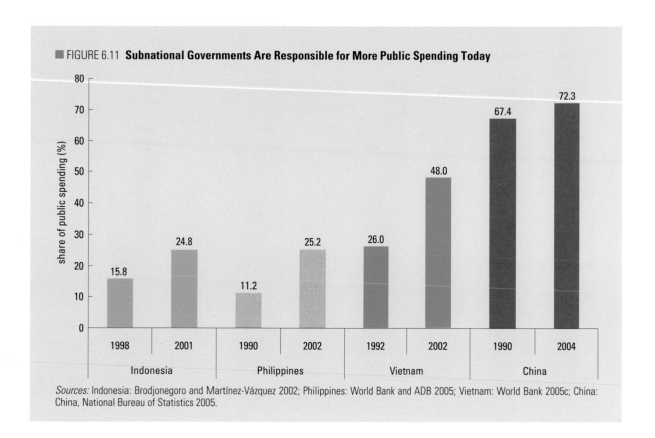

■ FIGURE 6.11 **Subnational Governments Are Responsible for More Public Spending Today**

Sources: Indonesia: Brodjonegoro and Martínez-Vázquez 2002; Philippines: World Bank and ADB 2005; Vietnam: World Bank 2005c; China: China, National Bureau of Statistics 2005.

ficient to address the horizontal inequality. Central government transfers reduce the disparities in per capita revenues, but often not by much (see figure 6.12).

As a consequence, there are large disparities in per capita local government spending across lower levels of government. For instance, Shanghai Province in China spends eight times as much per capita as Henan Province.[40] Differences at the subprovincial level are much larger still; the county with the highest per capita expenditure spends 48 times as much as the one with the lowest.[41]

As may be expected, the differences in per capita spending are closely related to the level of per capita income, as illustrated for China in figure 6.13. As the figure shows, the positive relationship between per capita GDP and provincial expenditures is equally strong for total provincial spending and for spending on education and health care. In public health and education, there is an increasing reliance on user charges such that the share of out-of-pocket expenses in total sectoral spending has grown rapidly.[42] While this may have filled some of the

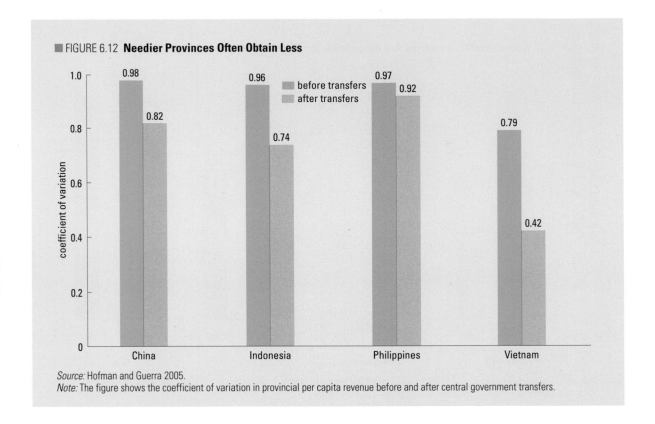

■ FIGURE 6.12 **Needier Provinces Often Obtain Less**

Source: Hofman and Guerra 2005.
Note: The figure shows the coefficient of variation in provincial per capita revenue before and after central government transfers.

financing gap, out-of-pocket spending is often regressive, discourages the utilization of services by the poor, and, in the case of health shocks, exposes households to financial risks.

These fiscal disparities are reflected in the widely varying coverage (and quality) of the public services supplied across regions. Hofman and Guerra (2005) provide some evidence of how spending disparities are related to education and health outputs and outcomes in China, Indonesia, and Vietnam. Other evidence for China suggests that, during the postreform period, fiscal decentralization has contributed to the increase in inequality of per capita consumption expenditures across provinces, rural and urban areas, and coastal and inland regions.[43]

Impediments to Internal Migration

Over the past few decades, massive internal migration, especially from the rural agricultural sector to urban secondary and tertiary industries, has been observed

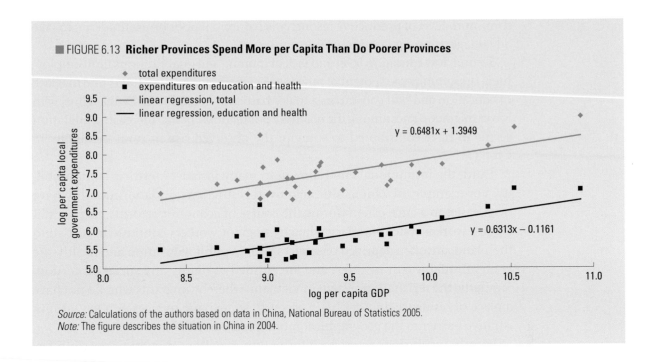

■ FIGURE 6.13 **Richer Provinces Spend More per Capita Than Do Poorer Provinces**

Source: Calculations of the authors based on data in China, National Bureau of Statistics 2005.
Note: The figure describes the situation in China in 2004.

in a number of East Asian countries. For instance, household survey data for China suggest that the total population of rural migrant labor was nearly 120 million in 2004.[44] For Vietnam, it is projected that the flow of migrants to urban areas may reach almost 1 million every year over the next two decades.[45] More generally, the level of urbanization has increased rapidly in all countries.

Labor mobility may be a powerful equalizing force through its effect on reducing wage and income differentials across regions and sectors. However, the persistence of disparities noted above within many countries suggests that the equalizing role of migration has been more limited than may have been believed. In practice, a number of factors have inhibited the process of migration and its effect on reducing inequalities.

First, studies have suggested that the poorest households, constrained by their limited endowments, may be unable to make use of migration opportunities. Du, Park, and Wang (2005) and McKenzie and Rapoport (2004) find an inverted-U-shaped relationship between household endowments and the likelihood of migration. Specifically, Du, Park, and Wang (2005) find that households near the poverty line are most likely to migrate, while, for those households at lower or higher incomes, the probability of migration is lower. This suggests that a minimum level of productive resources is required if poor households are to take advantage of new migration opportunities.

Second, low education level and lack of training and qualifications limit employment opportunities for potential migrants. Du, Park, and Wang (2005) find that lack of education and skill constitutes a major barrier to migration in China. Thus, with lower migration rates among the relatively poorer households, increasing migration seems to have contributed to some of the observed rise in rural inequality in China.[46]

Third, the institutional environment in many instances restricts labor mobility. For example, in China, although overt restrictions on labor mobility have been eased to a large extent during the course of economic reforms, there is still a guest worker system in place whereby migrant workers continue to be tied to their land, are often deprived of services such as public education and health care at an affordable cost in cities, and are entitled to hardly any social protection. Similarly, the registration system in Vietnam, whereby migrants who do not have a place of residence do not obtain access to some basic services, is a key administrative barrier to the geographical mobility of labor.[47]

Fourth, insufficient access to information may limit migration possibilities. The available evidence suggests that there is a heavy reliance on informal networks in migration. For instance, Sheng and Peng (2005) find that the primary source of migrant employment information in China is families, relatives, and friends from the same province of origin of the migrants. Those who migrate through the channel of government organizations account for less than 2 percent of all migrants. This highlights a significant inadequacy in the formally organized sources of information that facilitate and assist migration processes.

Should We Care about Disparities?

Since rapid growth in East Asia has also been associated with rapid poverty reduction, one may wonder if the persistence or the increase of inequalities, as documented above, should be particularly worrisome. One might indeed take the view that, since some of the factors that have been responsible for rising disparities are the same ones that have contributed to growth, the observed higher inequality is merely the price to be paid for rapid growth. Alternatively, rising disparities might be viewed as transitional within a Lewisian model of development whereby recent economic growth is seen as characterized by the development of the modern sector. According to this view, as the modern sector continues to grow and absorb ever-larger proportions of low-productivity labor from other sectors, the disparities will eventually decline. Migration is seen as an essential part of this process. While there is an element of truth to each of these viewpoints, several reasons remain for concern about the level and the trends in economic and social disparities in the region.[48]

The first and perhaps most basic reason is that people care about inequalities. For example, according to a 2002 household survey in urban China, more than 80 percent of the respondents considered the income distribution to be "either not so equitable" (48 percent) or "very inequitable" (34 percent).[49] Related evidence from the World Values Survey for East Asia is more mixed. On the particular question of whether large income differences are needed as incentives for individual effort, the majority of respondents in all seven countries participating in the survey favored such differences.[50] On the broader issue of market capitalism, however, while there is majority support in Japan, Korea, and Singapore, only minority support is indicated for China, Indonesia, the Philippines, and Vietnam.[51] Two other considerations are relevant in this context. First, inequality is generally more easily tolerated in an environment of rapid growth. If there were to be a slowdown in the rapid growth that East Asia has recently experienced, the current levels of inequality would likely find less acceptance in the region. Second, even if relative inequalities remain unchanged, absolute disparities widen with economic growth. For instance, Ravallion and Chen (2006) estimate that absolute Gini indexes in urban and rural China increased much more rapidly during 1981–2001 than did the conventional relative-income Gini indexes.[52] Because this translates into large differences in absolute standards of living, it may be an additional source of discontent and friction.

The second main reason for concern about the level and the trends in economic and social disparities in the region is that inequality in income and wealth may become inequality of opportunity across generations. Estimates of intergenerational mobility are low even for developed countries.[53] For developing countries in East Asia, with their weaker credit markets, the estimates are likely to be lower still, meaning that inequalities will probably be reproduced over time.[54] Thus, given the presence of credit market imperfections, even merit-based or incentive-promoting income differentials may turn into inherited advantages or drawbacks, and inequality at one date may become reinforced or even widen as time passes.

A third and related concern arises from the growing evidence that inequality may hamper productive investments, especially in human capital.[55] Because investments in human and physical capital are a crucial factor in determining household incomes, differential ability to invest in such capital affects the degree of income inequality.[56] In an environment of highly imperfect credit and factor markets, individual investments are often limited by individual endowments. Thus, the resource- and income-poor tend to underinvest, which, in turn, limits their future income growth. This is consistent with the evidence that higher inequality tends to make growth less pro-poor.[57]

Fourth, high levels of inequality (especially when they overlap with ethnic or religious divisions) may be a source of political instability. As figure 6.14 shows, countries with more (less) equal income distributions tend to exhibit greater (less) political stability. There are indications of growing social unrest in some parts of East Asia. Thus, estimates cited by Gill (2006) indicate that the number of incidents of social unrest in China grew from 8,300 in 1993 to over 80,000 in 2005. While there are many underlying reasons for such unrest, spatial and other

■ FIGURE 6.14 **Political Stability Tends to Decline with Rising Inequality**

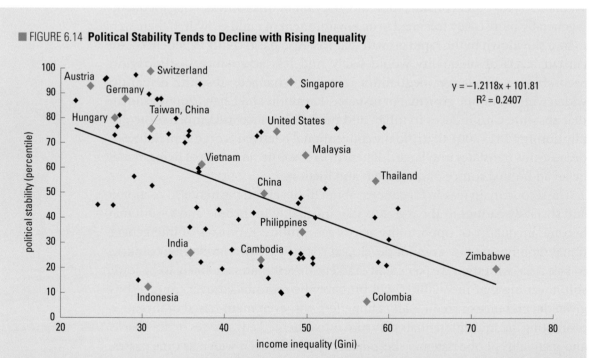

Sources: World Income Inequality Database, United Nations University–World Institute for Development Economics Research, http://www.wider.unu.edu/wiid/wiid.htm (version 2.0a, June 2005); Kaufmann, Kraay, and Mastruzzi 2005.
Note: The figure is based on a sample of 76 countries during 1996–2004. The gold diamonds indicate the countries identified by name in the figure.

disparities related to the economic reform process appear to be a factor.[58] Similarly, the rise of ethnic-based (Malay-Muslim) violence in Thailand's southernmost provinces (Narathiwat, Pattani, and Yala) since 2001 appears to be grounded in part on the absolute and relative deprivation of the local populations.[59] In the Philippines, while the Moro and communist insurgencies have been mostly concentrated in the Mindanao region, their effects have been felt throughout the country (in 91 percent of the provinces during 1986–2004). A recent analysis suggests that a contributing factor to the incidence of armed conflict in the country during 1986–2004 was the disparity in access to basic infrastructure and services, especially a reliable water supply, electricity, and education.[60] Such incidents of social unrest, in addition to their direct human cost, also have the potential of eroding popular support for economic reforms and, more generally, disrupting the process of economic growth.

To summarize, the existence of a certain degree of inequality is consistent with economic systems (increasingly typical of East Asian countries) that aim to reward higher individual effort, productivity, and innovation. As the data of the World Values Survey show, there is a fair degree of social support in the region for such incentive-promoting inequality. However, from a normative perspective, the primary concern is with the equality of opportunity and, hence, with the need to ensure that income and wealth differences do not translate into highly unequal opportunities across society. At a more pragmatic level, a key concern is that high or rising levels of inequality do not threaten social and political stability, which is not only important in its own right, but is also necessary for sustaining growth.

Addressing Spatial and Social Disparities

While East Asia's record of poverty reduction over the past two decades has been enviable, the foregoing discussion indicates that the issue of disparities across people, sectors, and regions is becoming more important. Large disparities persist in terms of income and human development, and, in many instances, they have grown. This chapter discusses several underlying forces contributing to the observed patterns, including the role of trade and globalization, labor market reform, the growth of clusters and agglomeration economies, fiscal decentralization, and internal migration. Because many of these underlying forces are likely to endure during the next phase of growth, equity in the countries of the region is a mounting concern. As the discussion highlights, many of the same forces that have helped augment growth in the region have also contributed to these disparities.

It is reasonable to expect that these forces will continue to unfold in the foreseeable future. Greater openness to trade and investment, international production and distribution networks, dynamic urban clusters building on agglomeration economies, the reform of labor markets in transitional countries, migration and the process of decentralization: these trends are all well established in the region and are unlikely to be reversed. Hence, looking ahead, the policy challenge for the region involves determining how these processes may be managed so as to reap the benefits in terms of growth (and poverty reduction), while keeping disparities in check so as to maintain the overall social cohesion that is necessary (though not sufficient) for sustaining the growth process itself. From this perspective, this concluding section draws out the emerging implications for public policy in the region in the following areas.

- *Investments in human capital.* Increasing rates of return to education and rising skill premiums raise the private incentives to acquire higher education. Hence, some of the increase in wage dispersion may be viewed as transitional and may be reversed as people invest more in their human capital, enabling them to make better use of the opportunities created by economic growth. However, in an environment of imperfect credit markets, individual investments are typically constrained by individual endowments, and this points to an important role for public policy. Moreover, the social return to human capital investment is even higher than the private return because there are significant spillover effects of human capital in improving the absorption of new ideas and technology, enhancing the adaptability to the changing configuration of new opportunities, and promoting systems for innovation. While East Asia has made big strides in primary education over the last two decades, enrollments at the secondary and tertiary levels remain relatively low in many countries, and there are large disparities within countries. Policies to promote wider and more equal access to higher education, which will almost certainly require greater public investment, will be critical not only for the next phase of growth in the region, but also for ensuring that this growth is more equitably distributed.
- *Facilitating migration.* Internal migration has the potential to become a major equalizing force within countries, in addition to its contribution to growth, which is already being realized in several countries in the region. However, the large differences existing in rural-urban and cross-regional wage and income levels indicate that impediments to labor mobility remain. These include the low human capital base of potential migrants, the de facto restric-

tions on the movement of people across regions, and the poor access to basic services (education of children, housing, and health) for migrants in destination areas. Public policy to alleviate such impediments will be important in realizing the potential of migration in contributing to more equitable growth.

- *Investments in lagging regions.* Moving people to where the jobs are will not be enough, however. In the medium term, this effort will need to be supplemented through policies to support greater job creation in lagging areas through investments in physical and social infrastructure and measures to improve the investment climate in smaller cities, so that growth clusters beyond the current set of dynamic urban agglomerations may be developed that offer off-farm employment opportunities to rural populations. This will require some rethinking of the role of industrial policy during the next phase of growth in the region.

- *The development of credit markets.* An additional policy area relevant to physical and human capital investment, as well as migration, is credit market development. The financial constraints faced by poor households often inhibit these households from taking advantage of the income-generating opportunities offered by the process of economic growth. Thus, lessening the impediments to access to credit by the poor may be a major step in supplementing public investments and promoting a more equitable distribution of the benefits of economic growth.

- *The development of social protection systems.* Greater economic integration has tied the fate of people in East Asia to changes in the world and regional economies, thus exposing populations to new sources of vulnerability. The coverage of formal social protection systems is limited in most countries, while the demands on the systems have risen because of expanding urbanization and migration and the aging populations in several countries. Improving the coverage and performance of unemployment insurance, health insurance, and pension systems, as well as targeted income-transfer programs, is likely to assume more importance in the future. East Asian countries should strive to develop systems that do not unduly weaken the incentives to work, save, and maintain strong family ties.

- *The promotion of greater fiscal equalization.* While the ongoing process of decentralization faces many challenges, addressing large fiscal disparities in the system will be important for ensuring a more equitable distribution of public services, especially in education, health care, and the upgrading of local infrastructure. Current intergovernmental transfer systems will need to rebalance greater horizontal equalization against the goal of maintaining optimal fiscal incentives for local governments. However, the provision of greater resources to poorer areas in itself will not be sufficient, and building adequate channels of accountability at different levels of government will continue to be a key challenge.

These observations are inevitably rather general in character. The region comprises a diverse group of countries which—despite their shared experience of rapid growth over the last decade or more—remain at very different stages of development. And, hence, the nature of specific policy challenges and options for addressing these priorities in different countries will vary with the level of development of the countries. The discussion above nonetheless suggests that there may be some short-term trade-offs between promoting greater growth and more equity. However, keeping equity considerations in mind while designing and implementing public policies is likely to be good for long-term growth. This will likely require clearer and more transparent governments than in the past.

Notes

1. In 1980, per capita GDP in East Asia and the Pacific was about 30 percent of that in Latin America and the Caribbean. Growth in Latin America and the Caribbean languished, while East Asia and the Pacific prospered, and the ratio was 64 percent by 2004 (World Development Indicators Database, World Bank, http://www.worldbank.org/data/datapubs/datapubs.html).

2. As Joseph Stiglitz noted, "What is remarkable about East Asia is not that it experienced a crisis in 1997 but that it had experienced so few crises over the preceding three decades—two of the countries had not had one year of downturn and two had had one year of recession, a better record than any of the supposedly advanced and well-managed Organization for Economic Co-operation and Development (OECD) countries" (Stiglitz 2001: 510).

3. The dollar-a-day line actually refers to a threshold of US$32.74 per person per month, or about US$1.08 per person per day, in 1993 purchasing power parity dollars (World Bank 2005a).

4. The Theil index provides a measure of the discrepancy between the structure of the distribution of income across groups and the structure of the distribution of individuals across those same groups. Groups that receive their fair share of income contribute nothing to the Theil index. If all groups receive the fair share of income, the Theil index attains its minimum value of zero. See Conceição and Ferreira (2000).

5. See Zhang and Kanbur (2005).

6. See HDN (2005).

7. See World Bank (2006b).

8. Benjamin et al. (2005) estimate that, on decomposing income inequality by source of income, wage income was shown to be the largest contributor to overall income inequality in both urban and rural China in 2000–01. It was also the biggest contributor to the increase in inequality during 1987–2001.

9. For further evidence of increasing returns to education in urban China and the growing concentration of urban wages during 1995–2002, see Khan and Riskin (2005).

10. See Hawley (2004) on Thailand; Bourguignon, Fournier, and Gurgand (2005) on Taiwan (China); Fields and Soares (2005) on Malaysia.

11. See Zhang et al. (2005).

12. The literature on this is too voluminous to be referenced or summarized adequately. For a detailed review of the East Asian growth experience following the crisis of 1997–98 and the subsequent recovery, see Stiglitz and Yusuf (2001).

13. See Te Velde and Morrissey (2004).

14. See Hu and Jefferson (2002); Keller (2002).

15. For instance, Zhao (2001, 2002), using data for 1996 on China, finds that, even accounting for nonwage benefits (pensions, housing, and health care) for state sector employees, skilled workers earn more and unskilled workers earn less in foreign-invested enterprises than in state-owned enterprises. For related evidence, see Lipsey and Sjoholm (2001) on Indonesia; Matsuoka (2001) on Thailand; Ramstetter (2000) on Hong Kong (China), Malaysia, Singapore, and Taiwan (China).

16. See Athukorala and Yamashita (2005), who report that, while the trade in parts and components has grown more rapidly than total world trade in manufacturing, East Asia's dependence on this form of trade is larger, and the growth in this trade relative to overall manufacturing trade is more rapid in East Asia than in the rest of the world. Also see Okamoto (2005) for similar evidence on the changing spatial pattern and structure of trade in East Asia.

17. See Feenstra and Hanson (1996).

18. See Ethier (2002), for instance.

19. The positive effect of the trade ratio was significant in the authors' pooled regression; the effect of FDI was insignificant in the pooled regression, but significant for Thailand.

20. See Park, Cai, and Zhao (2006).

21. See World Bank (2006d).

22. See World Bank (2005b).

23. See Zhang et al. (2005).

24. See Meng (2004) for similar evidence.

25. See Park, Cai, and Zhao (2006). The phenomenon of the high and rising share of informal employment in labor markets is not limited to China. For parallel evidence on Indonesia and the Philippines, see ADB (2005).

26. Based on the economic census of 2005, the National Bureau of Statistics made a 50 percent upward revision in GDP related to the tertiary sector in 2004 (with corresponding adjustments going back to 1994), raising the share of the tertiary sector in GDP from 32 to 41 percent (Park, Cai, and Zhao 2006).

27. Cai and Wu (2006) use ninefold criteria to determine informal employment. The most important categories include self-employed workers, people working on a temporary or hourly basis, and people without labor contracts and not considered officially registered workers. Cai and Wu estimate that 23 percent of employment in the state and collective sector in 2002 was informal, while the share of informal employment was as high as 84 percent in other sectors.

28. See Park, Cai, and Zhao (2006); Cai and Wu (2006).

29. There is evidence of a significant, even growing, segmentation in the Chinese urban labor market. A large share of the difference in wage earnings during 1995–2002 between private domestic enterprises and state-owned or foreign-invested enterprises was not caused by differences in worker endowments, but by higher wage premiums in the latter sectors (Démurger et al. 2006).

30. For instance, in 2002, the proportions of informal workers in urban China covered by pensions, unemployment insurance, and health insurance were 34, 21, and 14 percent, respectively, against 85, 73, and 62 percent among formal workers (Park, Cai, and Zhao 2006).

31. For a detailed survey of clusters in East Asia, see Yusuf (2003).

32. See Lin (2005).

33. See Yusuf (2003); Kanbur and Venables (2005).

34. Altogether, five provinces, containing 15 percent of the total population of Vietnam, accounted for 74 percent of total FDI in the country (Leproux and Brooks 2004).

35. See Amiti and Javorcik (2005).

36. Calculated from data reported in China, National Bureau of Statistics (2005).

37. See China, National Bureau of Statistics (2005).

38. See Wen (2004) for evidence on the growing regional concentration of manufacturing activity in China during 1980–95.

39. See Zhang and Zhang (2003).

40. Similar fiscal disparities have also been found in other countries in the region. For evidence on Indonesia, the Philippines, and Vietnam, see Hofman and Guerra (2005). See King and Guerra (2005) for evidence on disparities in per capita education spending across districts in Indonesia and in per pupil spending through the special education fund across municipalities in the Philippines.

41. See Dollar and Hofman (2006). For related evidence on the growth of fiscal disparities in China, see Wong and Bird (2005).

42. See World Bank (2006b).

43. See Kanbur and Zhang (2005).

44. See Sheng and Peng (2005).

45. See World Bank (2003).

46. It is important to note that migrant workers are included in rural (not urban) household surveys in China. Thus, rises in the incomes of migrant workers are reflected in rural rather than urban poverty and inequality measures. Benjamin et al. (2005) point out that the failure of nonfarm labor markets to provide sufficient income opportunities (mostly through migration outside the village) to offset the declining share of crop incomes was a significant cause of the increase in rural inequality during 1987–2001.

47. See World Bank (2003).

48. The empirical evidence on the relationship between growth and inequality remains rather inconclusive in terms of the direction of causality—is the relationship positive, negative, or nonmonotonic?—and the mechanisms underlying the relationship. For a range of differing results, see, for instance, Barro (2000), Banerjee and Duflo (2003), and Voitchovsky (2005).

49. See UNDP (2005a). Similarly, Han and Whyte (2006) report that 72 percent of over 3,000 Chinese adults surveyed in 2004 either "strongly agreed" (40 percent) or "agreed somewhat" (32 percent) that inequality in the country as a whole is "too large."

50. See Shin and Dalton (2006).

51. See Shin (2005), who describes market capitalism as norms relating to (1) the private ownership of business and industry, (2) competition in the marketplace, (3) the unequal distribution of income as an incentive for individual striving, and (4) the responsibility of individuals for their own welfare.

52. Absolute Gini indexes are calculated by normalizing income differences by a fixed mean income at a particular date.

53. See World Bank (2005a).

54. From a theoretical perspective, Fender and Wang (2003) present an overlapping-generations model wherein credit constraints contribute to a rise in inequality between the skilled and the unskilled through the channel of human capital accumulation. Empirically, using a measure of financial depth and inequality in the distribution of land as proxies for capital market development, Li, Squire, and Zou (1998) find that capital market imperfection is an important determinant of international and intertemporal inequality across 49 countries spanning the period 1947 to 1994.

55. See World Bank (2005a), especially chapter 5, for a review of this evidence.

56. For instance, Wan and Zhou (2005) identify capital input as an increasingly significant determinant of income inequality in rural China. For similar evidence on urban and rural China as a whole, see Zhang and Zhang (2003).

57. For international evidence, see World Bank (2005a); for evidence on China during 1981–2001, see Ravallion and Chen (2006).

58. See Keidel (2005).

59. See Croissant (2005).

60. See Edillon (2005).

References

ADB (Asian Development Bank). 2005. *Key Indicators 2005: Labor Markets in Asia, Promoting Full, Productive, and Decent Employment.* Key Indicators of Developing Asian and Pacific Countries Series. Manila: Asian Development Bank.

Alatas, Vivi, and François Bourguignon. 2005. "The Evolution of Income Distribution during Indonesia's Fast Growth, 1980–96." In *The Microeconomics of Income Distribution Dynamics in East Asia and Latin America,* ed. François Bourguignon, Francisco H. G. Ferreira, and Nora Lustig, 175–218. Washington, DC: World Bank; New York: Oxford University Press.

Amiti, Mary, and Beata Smarzynska Javorcik. 2005. "Trade Costs and Location of Foreign Firms in China." Policy Research Working Paper 3564, World Bank, Washington, DC.

Athukorala, Prema-chandra, and Nobuaki Yamashita. 2005. "Production Fragmentation and Trade Integration: East Asia in a Global Context." Working Papers in Trade and Development 2005–07, Research School of Pacific and Asian Studies, Australian National University, Canberra.

Banerjee, Abhijit V., and Esther Duflo. 2003. "Inequality and Growth: What Can the Data Say?" *Journal of Economic Growth* 8 (3): 267–299.

Barro, Robert. 2000. "Inequality and Growth in a Panel of Countries." *Journal of Economic Growth* 5 (1): 5–32.

Benjamin, Dwayne, Loren Brandt, John Giles, and Sangui Wang. 2005. "Income Inequality during China's Economic Transition." Draft working paper, Department of Economics, University of Toronto, Toronto.

Blunch, Niels-Hugo. 2004. "Returns to Education in Thailand, 1994–2002." Unpublished background paper, East Asia and Pacific Region, World Bank, Washington, DC.

Bourguignon, François, Martin Fournier, and Marc Gurgand. 2005. "Distribution, Development, and Education in Taiwan, China, 1979–94." In *The Microeconomics of Income Distribution Dynamics in East Asia and Latin America,* ed. François Bourguignon, Francisco H. G. Ferreira, and Nora Lustig, 313–56. Washington, DC: World Bank; New York: Oxford University Press.

Brodjonegoro, Bambang, and Jorge Martínez-Vázquez. 2002. "An Analysis of Indonesia's Transfer System: Recent Performance and Future Prospects." International Studies Program Working Paper 02–13, Andrew Young School of Policy Studies, Georgia State University, Atlanta.

Cai, Fang, and Yaowu Wu. 2006. "China's Urban Informal Employment: Scale and Characteristics." Unpublished working paper.

Cai, Fang, Yaohui Zhao, and Albert Park. 2006. "The Chinese Labor Market in the Reform Era." In *China's Economic Transition: Origins, Mechanism, and Consequences,* ed. Loren Brandt and Thomas Rawski, forthcoming.

China, National Bureau of Statistics. Various years. *State Statistical Yearbook.* Beijing: China Statistics Publishing House.

China, National Bureau of Statistics. 2003. *State Statistical Yearbook 2003.* Beijing: China Statistics Publishing House.

China, National Bureau of Statistics. 2005. *State Statistical Yearbook 2005.* Beijing: China Statistics Publishing House.

Conceição, Pedro, and Pedro Ferreira. 2000. "The Young Person's Guide to the Theil Index: Suggesting Intuitive Interpretations and Exploring Analytical Applications." UTIP Working Paper 14, University of Texas Inequality Project, University of Texas at Austin, Austin, Texas. http://utip.gov.utexas.edu/papers/utip_14.pdf.

Croissant, Aurel. 2005. "Unrest in South Thailand: Contours, Causes, and Consequences since 2001." *Contemporary Southeast Asia* 27 (1): 21–43.

Démurger, Sylvie, Martin Fournier, Li Shi, and Wei Zhong. 2006. "Economic Liberalization with Rising Segmentation on China's Urban Labor Market." Draft working paper, Society for the Study of Economic Inequality, Palma de Mallorca, Spain.

Dollar, David, and Bert Hofman. 2006. "Intergovernmental Fiscal Reforms, Expenditure Assignment, and Governance." Unpublished working paper, World Bank, Washington, DC.

Du, Yang, Albert Park, and Sangui Wang. 2005. "Migration and Rural Poverty in China." *Journal of Comparative Economics* 33 (4): 688–709.

Edillon, Rosemarie G. 2005. "Ideologically Motivated Conflicts in the Philippines: In Search of Underlying Causes." Background paper, United Nations Development Program, Manila.

Ethier, Wilfred J. 2002. "Globalization, Globalisation: Trade, Technology, and Wages." PIER Working Paper 02–031, Department of Economics, Penn Institute for Economic Research, University of Pennsylvania, Philadelphia.

Feenstra, Robert C., and Gordon H. Hanson. 1996. "Globalization, Outsourcing, and Wage Inequality." *American Economic Review* 86 (2): 240–45.

Fender, John, and Ping Wang. 2003. "Educational Policy in a Credit Constrained Economy with Skill Heterogeneity." *International Economic Review* 44 (3): 939–64.

Fields, Gary S., and Sergei Soares. 2005. "The Microeconomics of Changing Income Distribution in Malaysia." In *The Microeconomics of Income Distribution Dynamics in East Asia and Latin America*, ed. François Bourguignon, Francisco H. G. Ferreira, and Nora Lustig, 219–74. Washington, DC: World Bank; New York: Oxford University Press.

Giles, John T., Albert Park, and Fang Cai. 2006. "How Has Economic Restructuring Affected China's Urban Workers?" *China Quarterly* 185 (March): 61–95.

Gill, Bates. 2006. "China's Domestic Transformation: Democratization or Disorder?" In *China: The Balance Sheet: What the World Needs to Know Now about the Emerging Superpower*, ed. C. Fred Bergesten, Bates Gill, Nicholas R. Lardy, and Derek Mitchell, 40–72. New York: Public Affairs.

Han, Chunping, and Martin King Whyte. 2006. "The Social Contours of Distributive Injustice Feelings in Contemporary China." Unpublished working paper, Harvard University, Cambridge, MA.

Hawley, Joshua D. 2004. "Changing Returns to Education in Times of Prosperity and Crisis, Thailand 1985–1998." *Economics of Education Review* 23 (3): 273–86.

HDN (Human Development Network). 2005. *Philippine Human Development Report 2005: Peace, Human Security, and Human Development in the Philippines.* 2nd ed. Manila: Human Development Network.

Hofman, Bert, and Susana Cordeiro Guerra. 2005. "Fiscal Disparities in East Asia: How Large and Do They Matter?" In *East Asia Decentralizes: Making Local Government Work*, ed. World Bank, 67–83. Washington, DC: World Bank.

Hu, Albert Guangzhou, and Gary H. Jefferson. 2002. "FDI Impact and Spillover: Evidence from China's Electronic and Textile Industries." *World Economy* 25 (8): 1063–76.

Kanbur, Ravi, and Anthony J. Venables. 2005. "Spatial Inequality and Development." In *Spatial Inequality and Development*, ed. Ravi Kanbur and Anthony J. Venables, 3–13. WIDER Studies in Development Economics Series. New York: Oxford University Press.

Kanbur, Ravi, and Xiaobo Zhang. 2005. "Fifty Years of Regional Inequality in China: A Journey through Central Planning, Reform, and Openness." *Review of Development Economics* 9 (1): 87–106.

Kaufmann, Daniel, Aart Kraay, and Massimo Mastruzzi. 2005. "Governance Matters IV: Governance Indicators for 1996–2004." Policy Research Working Paper 3630, World Bank, Washington, DC.

Keidel, Albert. 2005. "The Economic Basis for Social Unrest in China." Paper presented at the Third European-American Dialogue on China, George Washington University, Washington, DC, May 26–27.

Keller, Wolfgang. 2002. "Geographic Location of International Technology Diffusion." *American Economic Review* 92 (1): 120–42.

Khan, Azizur Rahman, and Carl Riskin. 2005. "China's Household Income and Its Distribution, 1995 and 2002." *The China Quarterly* 182 (June): 356–84.

King, Elizabeth M., and Susana Cordeiro Guerra. 2005. "Education Reforms in East Asia: Policy, Process, and Impact." In *East Asia Decentralizes: Making Local Government Work*, ed. World Bank, 179–207. Washington, DC: World Bank.

Lao PDR, Committee for Planning and Investment, National Statistics Center; Asian Development Bank; Swedish International Development Cooperation Agency; and World Bank. 2006. "From Valleys to

Hilltops: 15 Years of Poverty Reduction, Lao PDR Poverty Assessment." Joint report, World Bank, Washington, DC.

Leman, Edward. 2005. "Metropolitan Regions: New Challenges for an Urbanizing China." Paper presented at the World Bank and Institute of Applied Economic Research "Urban Research Symposium," Brasilia, April 4.

Leproux, Vittorio, and Douglas H. Brooks. 2004. "Viet Nam: Foreign Direct Investment and Postcrisis Regional Integration." ERD Working Paper 56, Economics and Research Department, Asian Development Bank, Manila.

Li, Hongyi, Lyn Squire, and Heng-fu Zou. 1998. "Explaining International and Intertemporal Variations in Income Inequality." *Economic Journal* 108 (446): 26–43.

Lin, Songhua. 2005. "International Trade, Location, and Wage Inequality in China." In *Spatial Inequality and Development*, ed. Ravi Kanbur and Anthony J. Venables, 260–91. WIDER Studies in Development Economics Series. New York: Oxford University Press.

Lipsey, Robert E., and Fredrik Sjoholm. 2001. "Foreign Direct Investment and Wages in Indonesian Manufacturing." NBER Working Paper 8299, National Bureau of Economic Research, Cambridge, MA.

Matsuoka, Atsuko. 2001. "Wage Differentials among Local Plants and Foreign Multinationals by Foreign Ownership Share and Nationality in Thai Manufacturing." ICSEAD Working Paper 2001–25, International Center for the Study of East Asian Development, Kitakyushu, Japan.

McKenzie, David, and Hillel Rapoport. 2004. "Network Effects and the Dynamics of Migration and Inequality: Theory and Evidence from Mexico." BREAD Working Paper 063, Bureau for Research and Economic Analysis of Development, Harvard College, Cambridge, MA.

Meng, Xin. 2004. "Economic Restructuring and Income Inequality in Urban China." *Review of Income and Wealth* 50 (3): 357–79.

NCSSH (National Center for Social Sciences and Humanities) and UNDP (United Nations Development Program). 2001. *National Human Development Report 2001: Doi Moi and Human Development in Vietnam.* Hanoi: Political Publishing House.

Okamoto, Susumu. 2005. "The Spatial Pattern of Development and the Triangular Trade Structure as a Regional Manufacturing Platform." Unpublished discussion paper, Research Institute of Economy, Trade, and Industry, Tokyo.

Park, Albert, Fang Cai, and Yaohui Zhao. 2006. "The Informalization of the Chinese Labor Market." Background paper for the China Poverty Assessment, World Bank, Washington, DC.

Ramstetter, Eric D. 2000. "Recent Trends in Foreign Direct Investment in Asia: The Aftermath of the Crisis to Late 1999." ICSEAD Working Paper 2000–02, International Center for the Study of East Asian Development, Kitakyushu, Japan.

Ravallion, Martin, and Shaohua Chen. 2006. "China's (Uneven) Progress against Poverty." *Journal of Development Economics* 82 (1): 1–42 (forthcoming).

Sheng, Laiyun, and Liquan Peng. 2005. "The Population, Structure, and Characteristics of Rural Migrant Workers." In *Research on Rural Labor of China 2005*, 75–81. Beijing: Department of Rural Surveys, National Bureau of Statistics.

Shin, Doh Chull. 2005. "The Parallel Development of Democracy and Markets." CSD Paper 05–04, Center for the Study of Democracy, University of California, Irvine, CA.

Shin, Doh Chull, and Russell J. Dalton. 2006. "Exploring Weber's Theory of Capitalism in Confucian East Asia." In *Citizens, Democracy, and Markets around the Pacific Rim: Congruence Theory and Political Culture*, ed. Russell J. Dalton and Doh Chull Shin, 159–80. New York: Oxford University Press.

Stiglitz, Joseph E. 2001. "From Miracle to Crisis to Recovery: Lessons from Four Decades of East Asian Experience." In *Rethinking the East Asian Miracle*, ed. Joseph E. Stiglitz and Shahid Yusuf, 509–26. Washington, DC: World Bank; New York: Oxford University Press.

Stiglitz, Joseph E., and Shahid Yusuf, eds. 2001. *Rethinking the East Asian Miracle.* Washington, DC: World Bank; New York: Oxford University Press.

Te Velde, Dirk Willem, and Oliver Morrissey. 2004. "Foreign Direct Investment, Skills, and Wage Inequality in East Asia." *Journal of the Asia Pacific Economy* 9 (3): 348–69.

UNDP (United Nations Development Program). 2001. *National Human Development Report Lao PDR 2001: Advancing Rural Development.* Vientiane, Lao PDR: United Nations Development Program.

_____. 2003a. *Human Development Report Mongolia 2003: Urban-Rural Disparity in Mongolia.* Ulaanbaatar, Mongolia: Government of Mongolia and United Nations Development Program.

_____. 2003b. *Thailand Human Development Report 2003.* Bangkok: United Nations Development Program.

_____. 2004. *Indonesia Human Development Report 2004: The Economics of Democracy, Financing Human Development in Indonesia.* Jakarta: BPS-Statistics Indonesia, National Development Planning Agency, and United Nations Development Program.

_____. 2005a. *Human Development Report 2005: International Cooperation at a Crossroads: Aid, Trade and Security in an Unequal World.* New York: United Nations Development Program.

_____. 2005b. *China Human Development Report 2005: Development with Equity.* Beijing: China Development Research Foundation and United Nations Development Program.

Voitchovsky, Sarah. 2005. "Does the Profile of Income Inequality Matter for Economic Growth?: Distinguishing Between the Effects of Inequality in Different Parts of the Income Distribution." *Journal of Economic Growth* 10 (3): 273–96.

Wan, Guanghua, and Zhangyue Zhou. 2005. "Income Inequality in Rural China: Regression-Based Decomposition Using Household Data." *Review of Development Economics* 9 (1): 107–20.

Wen, Mei. 2004. "Relocation and Agglomeration of Chinese Industry." *Journal of Development Economics* 73 (1): 329–47.

Wong, Christine C. P., and Richard M. Bird. 2005. "China's Fiscal System: A Work in Progress." International Studies Program Working Paper 05–20, Andrew Young School of Policy Studies, Georgia State University, Atlanta.

World Bank. 2003. *Vietnam Development Report 2004: Poverty.* Report Series 27130-VN. Washington, DC: Poverty Reduction and Economic Management Unit, East Asia and Pacific Region, World Bank.

_____. 2004. "East Asia Update: Strong Fundamentals to the Fore, Regional Overview." Report, April, East Asia and Pacific Region, World Bank, Washington, DC.

_____. 2005a. *World Development Report 2006: Equity and Development.* Washington, DC: World Bank; New York: Oxford University Press.

_____. 2005b. *Vietnam Business: Vietnam Development Report 2006.* Report Series 34474-VN. Washington, DC: Poverty Reduction and Economic Management Unit, East Asia and Pacific Region, World Bank.

_____. 2005c. "Vietnam: Managing Public Expenditure for Poverty Reduction and Growth, Public Expenditure Review and Integrated Fiduciary Assessment." Draft report, World Bank, Washington, DC.

_____. 2005d. *World Development Indicators 2005.* Washington, DC: World Bank. http://devdata.worldbank.org/wdi2005/Cover.htm.

_____. 2006a. "East Asia Update: Solid Growth, New Challenges." Report, March, East Asia and Pacific Region, World Bank, Washington, DC.

_____. 2006b. "China Poverty Assessment." Draft report, World Bank, Washington, DC.

_____. 2006c. "Indonesia Poverty Assessment." Draft report, World Bank, Washington, DC.

_____. 2006d. "Taking Stock: An Update on Vietnam's Economic Developments and Reforms." Paper prepared by the World Bank Vietnam Mid-Year Consultative Group Meeting for Vietnam, Nha Trang, June 9–10.

World Bank and ADB (Asian Development Bank). 2005. "Decentralization in the Philippines: Strengthening Local Government Financing and Resource Management in the Short Term." Joint document, Poverty Reduction and Economic Management Unit, East Asia and Pacific Region, World Bank, Washington, DC; Philippines Country Office, South East Asia Region, Asian Development Bank, Manila.

Yusuf, Shahid. 2003. *Innovative East Asia: The Future of Growth.* Washington, DC: World Bank; New York: Oxford University Press.

Zhang, Junsen, Yaohui Zhao, Albert Park, and Xiaoqing Song. 2005. "Economic Returns to Schooling in Urban China, 1988 to 2001." *Journal of Comparative Economics* 33 (4): 730–52.

Zhang, Xiaobo, and Ravi Kanbur. 2005. "Spatial Inequality in Education and Health Care in China." *China Economic Review* 16 (2): 189–204.

Zhang, Xiaobo, and Kevin H. Zhang. 2003. "How Does Globalization Affect Regional Inequality within a Developing Country?: Evidence from China." *Journal of Development Studies* 39 (4): 47–67.

Zhao, Yaohui. 2001. "Foreign Direct Investment and Relative Wages: The Case of China." *China Economic Review* 12 (1): 40–57.

_____. 2002. "Earnings Differentials between State and Non-State Enterprises in Urban China." *Pacific Economic Review* 7 (1): 181–97.

MAP 7.1 The Quality of the Rule of Law Varies Considerably across East Asia

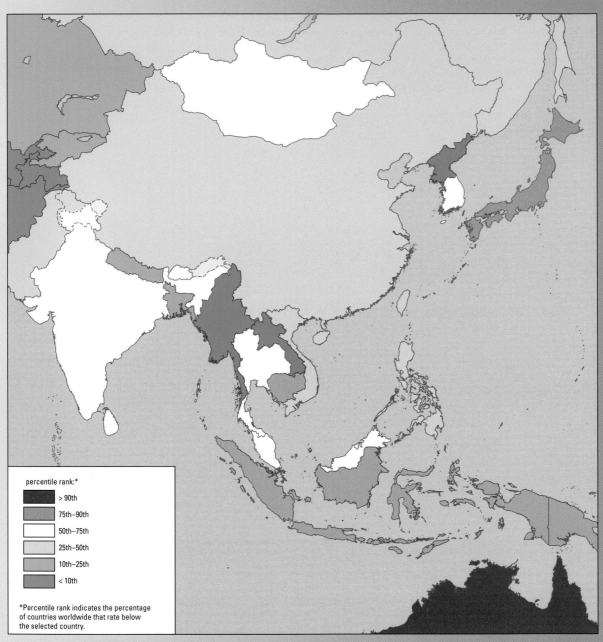

percentile rank:*

- > 90th
- 75th–90th
- 50th–75th
- 25th–50th
- 10th–25th
- < 10th

*Percentile rank indicates the percentage of countries worldwide that rate below the selected country.

Source: Based on Kaufmann, Kraay, and Mastruzzi 2005.
Note: The rule of law indicator encompasses several indicators that measure the extent to which agents have confidence in and abide by the rules of society. These include perceptions of the incidence of crime, the effectiveness and predictability of the judiciary, and the enforceability of contracts. Together, these indicators measure the success of a society in developing an environment in which fair and predictable rules form the basis for economic and social interactions and, importantly, the extent to which property rights are protected. The map depicts the percentile rank of the indicator, subject to a margin of error. The percentile rank shows the percentage of countries worldwide that rate below the selected country. Each color follows a simple quartile distribution for illustrative purposes (see the map label). For the top quartile, the top 10 economies worldwide are a dark gray (for instance, Australia on the map), while, for the bottom quartile, the bottom 10 economies worldwide are a dark orange (for instance, Myanmar on the map).

CHAPTER 7

CORRUPTION

The rule of man is being swept away, but the rule of law has not been fully instituted. Because of lagging anti-corruption efforts, East Asian economies may pay a high price in economic growth.

From the Rule of Man to the Rule of Law

East Asia is widely perceived as one of the world's most corrupt regions. Since the 1997–98 financial crisis there, corruption scandals have been frequently reported in the regional and international media. The relationship between government and business in East Asia is often described as crony capitalism. East Asia certainly includes many economies in which corruption is widespread, but, after examining the issue, this chapter challenges the idea that corruption is endemic to East Asia and that there is any characteristically East Asian level of corruption.

Corruption in East Asia presents a paradox. In some economies, high levels of corruption have coexisted for extended periods with rapid economic growth and development.[1] Clearly, this runs against the conventional wisdom according to which corruption impedes economic and social progress. The chapter explores the various hypotheses put forward to explain this paradox and assesses their empirical foundation. It investigates the nature of corruption in East Asia and the extent to which the autocratic mode of governance in many East Asian countries in the postwar period may have enabled an East Asian model of corruption that is less damaging to growth and development.

Before the crisis, commentators were quick to point to Asian values to explain East Asia's remarkable postwar success. Postcrisis, the same people were equally quick to say that Asian values explained the crisis and were, in some way, more conducive to corruption than were the values of the West. The chapter suggests that attitudes toward corruption may be evolving as part of the economic and social transformations sweeping the region. Democracy and decentralization have clearly made significant advances across East Asia. The chapter shows that demands for new modes of governance and more effective action to tackle corruption have grown and may continue to grow during East Asia's renaissance. Economic, political, and social transformations have already rendered the East Asian model of organizing and constraining corruption unsustainable.

Countries in the region will move away from traditional modes of governance based on the "rule of man" to modern modes of governance based on the "rule of law" or, as the Chinese say, from *renzhi* to *fazhi*.[2] This chapter notes the evidence that, in the longer term, this may result in more effective governance and less corruption. However, the legal, political, and administrative institutions needed to make democracy and decentralization work will take time to build. In the short term, there is a risk that the challenges of corruption will intensify across the region. For many countries, the road from *renzhi* to *fazhi* may not be an easy one (see map 7.1).

Is There an East Asian Level of Corruption?

Defining Corruption

In English, the term corruption is colorful but vague. In its simplest sense, it refers to a process of decay, rot, or perversion. Beyond this, it is at best a shorthand reference for a large range of illicit and illegal activities.[3] In its broadest usages, it may refer to the act or the process of corrupting and the state of being corrupt. It may refer to such processes in public office, private business, or personal life.

In the context of public sector governance, corruption is often succinctly defined as the misuse of public office for private gain.[4] Even within the limited context of the public sector, however, corruption comes in too many forms to permit easy generalization.

Activities frequently identified as corrupt include bribery; the stealing, misappropriation, or other misuse of public funds or assets; illegal fines, duties, taxes, or charges; vote rigging; the abuse of privileged information; misprocurement; the manipulation of regulatory and licensing authority; campaign financing abuses; influence peddling and favor-brokering; the acceptance of improper gifts; cronyism; and nepotism. However, societal norms may vary about the inappropriateness of each form of corruption or even about whether some of these actions are corruption at all.[5]

Nevertheless, a number of distinctions are often drawn. There is grand corruption (the theft of billions of dollars by a Marcos or a Suharto) and petty corruption (for example, the demand for small bribes by public service providers). There is administrative corruption (perpetrated by lower-ranking bureaucrats and officials), and there is political corruption (sometimes called clientelism or state capture: the misuse of public power by elected officials to shape the rules of the game to the advantage of themselves and those who pay them, at the expense of the rest of society). A distinction is sometimes drawn between corruption of the deviant variety, whereby officials accept inducements to undertake actions they are not supposed to perform, and grease money corruption, whereby officials accept inducements to do what they are supposed to do anyway or to do it more quickly. Finally and arguably of particular relevance in the East Asian context, there is syndicated corruption, whereby elaborate systems are devised for receiving and disseminating bribes, and nonsyndicated corruption, whereby individual officials seek to compete for bribes in an ad hoc, uncoordinated fashion.

Although most people would consider corruption undesirable almost by definition, it seems very likely that these diverse forms of corruption will have impacts that differ significantly in extent and incidence.

The Level of Corruption

Measuring corruption is complicated by its very nature. Not only is corruption typically secretive, but, as discussed above, it takes many forms.

Identifying and applying objective measures of corruption are difficult. Financial measures of corruption are "extremely approximate"[6] and typically available only for the worst cases of grand corruption. The *Global Corruption Report 2004* of Transparency International (2004), for example, includes some estimates of the funds allegedly embezzled by 10 leaders who have been notorious for corruption within the last 20 years. According to these estimates, Mohammad Suharto, president of Indonesia between 1967 and 1998, embezzled from US$15 billion to US$35 billion; Ferdinand Marcos, president of the Philippines between 1972 and 1986, US$5 billion to US$10 billion; and Joseph Estrada, president of the Philippines between 1998 and 2001, between US$78 million and US$80 million.[7]

Among households and firms, corruption levels are often measured by the monetary cost of bribes. The investment climate surveys sponsored by the World Bank have recently been attempting to collect such data among firms. However, firms (and households) may be unwilling to admit to paying bribes, and, so, the estimates of the frequency and value of the bribes paid may be distorted.

Because of the difficulties of obtaining objective information about corruption, the dominant empirical approach to examining the determinants of corruption is the use of perception-based data. Perceptions of corruption may vary from the actual level of corruption, thereby affecting the conclusions of empirical studies. Kaufmann, Kraay, and Mastruzzi (2006) argue that measuring perceptions may nonetheless have direct relevance: "when citizens view the courts and police as corrupt, they will not want to use their services, regardless of what the 'objective' reality is" (p. 2).

Most indicators of corruption that are widely cited are cross-country perception-based indexes such as the corruption perceptions index of Transparency International and the Kaufmann-Kraay control of corruption index. As with all governance indicators, both of these indexes are subject to measurement errors.[8]

The corruption perceptions index of Transparency International, an international civil society organization, is a composite index that reflects the perceptions of business people and country analysts both resident and nonresident.[9] The 2005 survey ranks 159 countries and draws on 16 polls by 10 independent institutions. A country is included only if it has been featured in at least three polls. (Most major East Asian economies are included; the Democratic People's Republic of Korea is not included.) The corruption perceptions index has been produced annually since 1995, although Lambsdorff (2005) describes it as "a snapshot of the views of businesspeople and country analysts, with less of a focus on year-to-year trends" (p. 3). The corruption perceptions index ranks countries in terms of the degree to which corruption is perceived to exist. The surveys used in compiling the corruption perceptions index ask questions relating to the misuse of public power for private benefit, but do not make any other distinctions, such as, for example, between administrative and political corruption or between petty and grand corruption. Figure 7.1, chart a, illustrates the corruption perceptions index for East Asian economies in 1995, 2000, and 2005.

The control of corruption index is a complementary measure. It has been prepared biennially since 1996 with the support of the World Bank and is based mostly on non–World Bank sources.[10] Like the corruption perceptions index, the control of corruption index is a composite indicator drawing on multiple primary indicators of perceptions of corruption to produce country rankings. Also like the corruption perceptions index, the control of corruption index focuses on public corruption, though it otherwise treats corruption as a single, homogenous phenomenon. Whereas the corruption perceptions index is stand-alone, the control of

■ FIGURE 7.1 **Indexes of Corruption Vary Widely across East Asia**

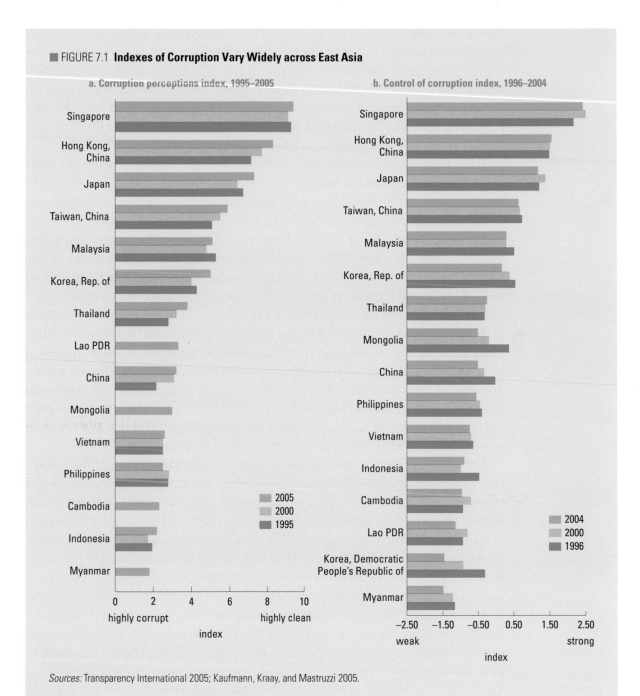

a. Corruption perceptions index, 1995–2005

b. Control of corruption index, 1996–2004

Sources: Transparency International 2005; Kaufmann, Kraay, and Mastruzzi 2005.

corruption index is one of six Kaufmann-Kraay governance indicators; the others are voice and accountability, political stability and absence of violence, government effectiveness, regulatory quality, and rule of law. The Kaufmann-Kraay indicators have a slightly larger coverage than the corruption perceptions index and draw on a wider range of surveys (209 countries and 352 variables culled from 37 data sources produced by 31 organizations). Figure 7.1, chart b, illustrates the control of corruption index for East Asian economies in 1996, 2000, and 2004.[11]

These two perception-based indicators offer broadly similar conclusions as far as East Asia is concerned. A first observation is that there is an enormous range in the indicators. Some East Asian economies rank among the least corrupt in the world; using the corruption perceptions index, Singapore ranks between Denmark and Sweden, Hong Kong (China) between Canada and Germany, and Japan between Chile and Spain. Other East Asian economies rank among the most corrupt; Myanmar ranks between Turkmenistan and Haiti, Indonesia between Iraq and Ethiopia, and Cambodia between the Republic of Congo and Burundi.

A second observation is that there is a correlation between corruption indexes and gross domestic product (GDP) per capita. As charts a and b of figure 7.2 illustrate, the level of corruption in many East Asian economies in 2004 appears to be broadly in line with what one might predict based on their GDPs per capita. The data of both the corruption perceptions index (chart a) and the control of corruption index (chart b) suggest that corruption in China, Hong Kong (China), Japan, the Republic of Korea, Mongolia, the Philippines, Thailand, and Vietnam is broadly at the level one might expect based on GDP per capita.

A third observation is that, despite the general correlation between the perception of corruption and GDP per capita, levels of corruption vary widely among economies at similar levels of per capita income. Thus, for example, based on the control of corruption index, Indonesia, with a GDP per capita of US$3,361 (in 2003, in purchasing power parity terms), has a ranking showing it as more corrupt than Vietnam, with a GDP per capita of US$2,490; China, with a GDP per capita of US$5,003, ranks the same in terms of the control of corruption as Mongolia, with a GDP per capita of US$1,850. As figure 7.2 illustrates, both indexes indicate that Malaysia and Singapore exhibit less corruption than one might predict according to their GDPs per capita, whereas Taiwan (China) has rather more corruption than one might so predict. The control of corruption index (figure 7.2, chart b) also indicates that Cambodia, Indonesia, the Democratic People's Republic of Korea, the Lao People's Democratic Republic, and Myanmar are significantly worse in the control of corruption than one might predict based on GDP per capita. Clearly, corruption is not wholly determined by income.

■ FIGURE 7.2 **Richer Economies Show Better Outcomes in Global Corruption Indexes**

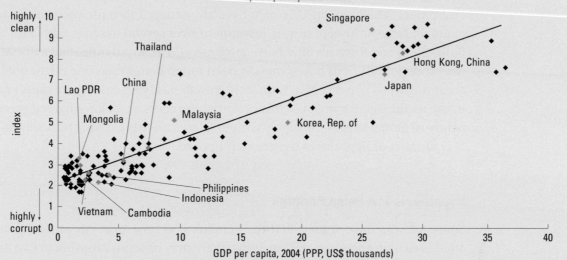

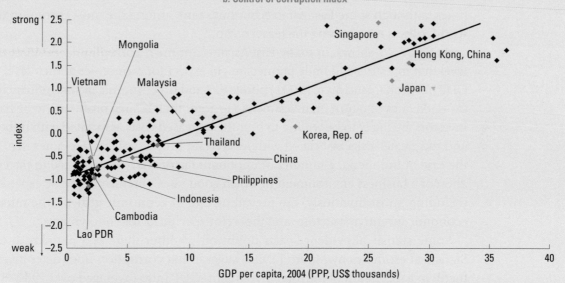

Sources: Transparency International 2005; Kaufmann, Kraay, and Mastruzzi 2005; World Development Indicators Database, World Bank, http://www.worldbank.org/data/datapubs/datapubs.html.
Note: The gold symbols indicate economies in East Asia.

Is There an East Asian Model of Corruption?

As Campos (2001) argues, the corruption in East Asia presents proponents of good governance with a paradox. China, Indonesia, the Republic of Korea, the Philippines, Thailand, and Vietnam have all managed to trade successfully and to attract large inflows of private investment over several decades (although the Philippines and Vietnam have been latecomers). The social outcomes associated with core public goods have generally been much better than one might predict according to GDP per capita. Economic growth has been among the most rapid in the world. Yet, for much of this period, these economies have figured prominently in global lists of the highly corrupt. How can this paradox be resolved?

A number of hypotheses have been proposed.

Hypothesis 1: A False Paradox

Some authors have argued that the paradox is a false one. An aspect of this, alluded to in the previous section, is that there may be less corruption in East Asia than is popularly supposed. In the wake of the East Asian crisis, there was much media discussion of crony capitalism in East Asia. However, as figure 7.1 illustrates, although some East Asian economies rank among the most corrupt in the world, others rank among the least corrupt.

As figure 7.2 shows, in many East Asian economies, corruption is at about the level that investors and trade partners might expect for economies at their level of GDP per capita. MacIntyre (2001) points to standard economic factors influencing expected rates of return on investment. He notes that, if large profits are to be had, investors are likely to be willing to bear the increased costs associated with bribery and the greater risks associated with less certain property rights. He notes that, in the case of Indonesia, a number of important factors have contributed to the creation of a business environment in which good rates of return might be expected, including, most obviously, the prevailing rate of economic growth, the microeconomic incentive structure, and the sector-specific factor endowments.

Some statistical evidence casts doubt on whether there is a paradox at all. Statistical estimates by Mauro (1995) suggest that corruption does deter investment. In a regression of the total investment–GDP ratio (averaged over 1980–85) on a constant and the corruption index, the point estimate of the slope is 0.012. As Wei (1999) remarks, the simple implication of this is that, if the Philippines could reduce its corruption to the Singapore level, other things being equal, it could raise its total investment–GDP ratio by 6.6 percentage points.

Wei (1997) shows that, after controlling for other factors such as GDP per capita, the impact of corruption on foreign direct investment (FDI) is no different in East Asia than it is in other regions. The implication of his cross-country regressions is that, in East Asia, other factors swamp the negative effect that corruption has on FDI. This offers a possible explanation why East Asian economies have grown more rapidly despite significant levels of corruption.

In an article provocatively entitled "Why Does China Attract So Little Foreign Direct Investment?" Wei (2000) argues that, given China's income and population, the amount of foreign investment it attracts falls well below the level that one might predict based on cross-country regressions. This is particularly the case, he argues, if adjustment is made for the significant amount of Chinese investment that is not really foreign, but is Chinese investment round-tripped through Hong Kong (China). Wei attributes the lower than predicted level of FDI in China to corruption, as well as other government-induced barriers to foreign investment.

Against this, Campos, Lien, and Pradhan (2001) argue that Wei's analysis is potentially problematic because FDI is dominated by countries of the Organisation for Economic Co-operation and Development. They propose it is quite possible that the results would be different if these countries were excluded from the sample as hosts of FDI or, alternatively, if the dependent variable used were private investment (both domestic and foreign). They hold that other middle-income and low-income developing countries would be a more appropriate comparator. Furthermore, they note that Wei's observation regarding the importance of FDI from overseas Chinese indicates that informal institutions may be an important omitted variable that affects the nature of corruption and thus the impact of corruption on investment.

Rock and Bonnett (2004) present cross-country regression analysis offering quite different conclusions to those of Wei. They find that corruption slows growth and reduces investment in most developing countries, particularly small developing countries. However, they find that growth may actually have increased with corruption in the large newly industrializing economies of East Asia (a group they construct to include China, Indonesia, Japan, the Republic of Korea, and Thailand and analyze over four different time periods between 1980 and 1996).

Survey evidence presents us with similar contradictions. Evidence from the World Bank and International Finance Corporation investment climate (enterprise) surveys tends to support the idea that corruption is not a major constraint to business in all East Asian economies. As table 7.1 illustrates, less than one-third of the firms surveyed in China, Malaysia, Thailand, and Vietnam considered cor-

■ TABLE 7.1 **Corruption May Not Be a Severe Constraint on Enterprises in All of East Asia**
percent of responses to the question: is corruption a constraint to business?

Country	No	Minor	Severe or major
Cambodia	4.7	39.4	55.9
Indonesia	29.3	29.2	41.5
Philippines	40.6	24.3	35.2
China	24.1	48.5	27.3
Thailand	49.7	32.1	18.3
Malaysia	53.8	31.7	14.5
Vietnam	52.3	17.8	14.2

Source: Investment Climate (Enterprise) Survey Database, World Bank and International Finance Corporation, http://www.enterprisesurveys.org/.
Note: The table reflects unweighted averages.

ruption a severe or major constraint to business. Firms in Cambodia, Indonesia, and the Philippines saw corruption as a more serious constraint.

A rather different trend in perceptions across firms in East Asia may be observed in the World Economic Forum's most recent executive opinion survey. Kaufmann (2006) places the East Asian economies in the survey into two groups: East Asian newly industrializing economies (Hong Kong [China], the Republic of Korea, Singapore, and Taiwan [China]) and developing East Asian economies (Cambodia, China, Indonesia, Malaysia, Mongolia, the Philippines, Thailand, Timor-Leste, and Vietnam). Focusing on survey questions about the top three constraints to business, he compares the responses of firms in these two groups to those of firms in other groups of economies. As illustrated in figure 7.3, chart a, corruption is not perceived as a major constraint in newly industrializing economies. Moreover, firms in this group are the least likely among firms in all regions to report corruption as a major obstacle to business. However, the situation seems to be dramatically different in developing East Asia, where the firms surveyed report corruption as a major obstacle to business. Figure 7.3, chart b shows that the venues of bribery and frequency also sharply contrast between the two groups within the region. While the reported frequency of bribery for permits, utilities, taxation, the awarding of public contracts, and the judiciary is as low in the East Asian newly industrializing economies as in the countries of the Organisation for Economic Co-operation and Development, the reported levels in developing East Asia are more on a par with those in the countries of sub-Saharan Africa and the former Soviet Union.

■ FIGURE 7.3 **Is Corruption a Major Constraint on Business? No Single Answer for East Asia**

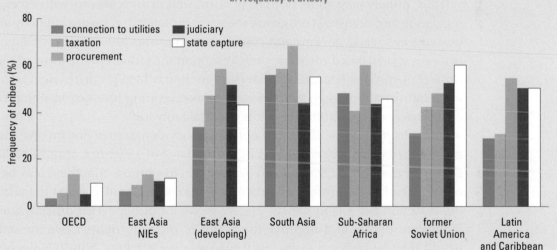

a. Top constraints on business

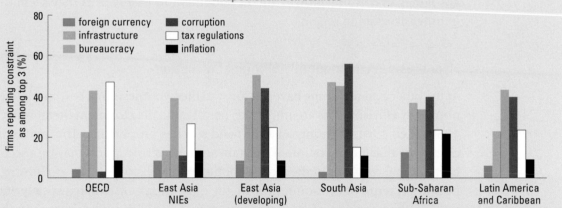

Source: Kaufmann 2006, based on the executive opinion survey 2005 of the World Economic Forum.
Note: The survey covered firms in 117 countries. Chart (a) reflects the case of the survey instruction: select among the above 14 constraints the five most problematic factors for doing business in your country. Chart (b) reflects the case of the survey question: in your industry, how common is it for firms to make undocumented extra payments or bribes connected with permits, utilities, taxation, the awarding of public contracts, or the judiciary? Possible responses included "common," "never occurs," and so on. NIEs = newly industrializing economies. OECD = Organisation for Economic Co-operation and Development.

Even if these somewhat contradictory results may convince us that, in the absence of corruption, GDP growth and FDI flows may have been more spectacular, they still fall short of explaining why high levels of corruption do not absolutely undermine growth and development in East Asia as they seem to do in other developing regions.

Hypothesis 2: Economically Efficient Corruption

At the other extreme, some have put forward the hypothesis that corruption is economically efficient. This argument was prevalent in development literature in the 1960s (Leff 1964; Huntington 1968) and still has proponents. The argument is essentially that the toleration of a certain amount of corruption may be a second-best optimal response in the face of another policy distortion; or, as Huntington puts it, "in terms of economic growth, the only thing worse than a society with a rigid, over-centralized, dishonest bureaucracy is one with a rigid, over-centralized and honest bureaucracy" (p. 386).

Thus, bribery may allow firms to perform well in an economy with excessive regulation and licensing (the grease money argument). It is posited that, by allocating licenses and government contracts to the firms able to pay the highest bribes, a system based on bribery might support the growth of the most efficient firms (Lui 1985). It is suggested that corruption may help get prices right by raising administratively repressed prices to market clearing levels or by enhancing civil service remuneration where it is unsustainably low.

Some have also theorized that optimal policy design may not involve minimizing corruption, since that may imply too large of a sacrifice of other welfare goals. For example, Acemoglu and Verdier (1998) propose that there may be an optimal level of corruption and property rights enforcement that acts to trade off the costs and benefits to society. Higher wages for public sector officials would reduce corruption and improve the extent of property rights since the stakes would then be higher for officials if they get caught taking bribes. However, a strategy of high public sector wages may result in high taxes and attract many talented individuals to the public sector, even though they could have been more productive in the private sector. The authors conclude that it may be optimal to allow some corruption and not enforce property rights fully; less well developed economies may even choose lower levels of property rights enforcement and more corruption.

There are strong counterarguments to most of these efficient corruption propositions. As Myrdal (1968) was the first to point out, corrupt officials may actually cause greater administrative delays so that they may attract more bribes. As Bardhan (1997) puts it, "the distortions are not exogenous to the system and are instead often part of the built-in corrupt practices of a patron-client political system" (p. 1323). Shleifer and Vishny (1993) also make the case that a country's regulatory burden may be endogenously exploited by corruption-prone officials for the purposes of extracting bribes. Tanzi (1999) argues that bribes tend to channel resources not to those who are more efficient in economic activity, but to those who are more skilled at bribery. The *World Development Report 1997* (World Bank 1997) illustrates how a competent and honest civil service is the lifeblood of an effective state and provides empirical evidence that adequate pay and meritocratic recruitment and promotion are correlated with economic growth and the perception of investors of bureaucratic quality even when controlling for other factors.

Such empirical evidence as exists for Asia tends to support these counterarguments. Using data from the *Global Competitiveness Reports* for 1996 and 1997, Kaufmann and Wei (1999) examine the relationship between the payment of bribes and the amount of management time wasted. Contrary to the grease money argument, they find that firms paying more bribes are also likely to spend more, not less, management time negotiating regulations with bureaucrats.

Focusing on a subsample of the Asian economies, Kaufmann and Wei undertake an explicit examination of what they term the Asian exceptionalism hypothesis (whereby, for reasons of Asian culture, corruption facilitates economic growth in Asia). They reject overwhelmingly the hypothesis, concluding that, in fact, the amount of management time wasted increases in parallel with the payment of bribes more rapidly in Asian countries than in the global sample.

Singapore's case is an excellent example of how an effective state and low corruption may be supported through competitive public sector wages, together with the recruitment and promotion of the best and the brightest within the civil service (see box 7.1).

Altogether, the empirical evidence weighs heavily against the grease money argument and against the argument that tolerance of corruption is an effective or fiscally efficient way of motivating civil servants.

Hypothesis 3: An East Asian Model of Corruption?

Between these extremes lies a more balanced hypothesis: corruption has been damaging for East Asia and has discouraged FDI and slowed growth, but "corruption regimes" have generally been more well managed in East Asia than they have in other parts of the world, and the extent of the trade-off has thus been

■ BOX 7.1 **Singapore, Corruption, and the Civil Service**

Singapore, the least corrupt East Asian economy today, was rife with corruption until the 1960s. The low salaries and rapidly rising cost of living during the postwar period, combined with the inadequate supervision of civil servants, created ample incentives and opportunities for corruption.

When the People's Action Party assumed power in 1959, the pay of civil servants was raised significantly, reaching levels competitive with the private sector, as a pillar of a strategy to establish an honest and effective civil service. In Singapore, public sector salaries average 114 percent of those in the private sector, and senior Singaporean civil servants are better paid than their U.S. counterparts.[12] It is often suggested that the salaries of cabinet ministers in Singapore are pegged to those of chief executive officers in the largest multinational firms in the world. The pay of the prime minister of Singapore is several times that of the president of the United States.[13] This is viewed as a safeguard against the polit-

ical corruption seen in other parts of the world. "I'm one of the best paid and probably one of the poorest of the Third World Prime Ministers," Lee Kuan Yew, then prime minister of Singapore, told a cabinet meeting in 1985 (cited in Quah 1988: 93).

Merit-based recruitment and promotion and the maintenance of the prestige of the public service were also pillars in achieving a clean and effective civil service in Singapore. Singapore's civil service is among the best in the world in terms of its coherence and sense of purpose. About 5 percent of the top of the graduating class of the National University of Singapore (and more recently Nanyang Technological University) are admitted each year as prospective civil service recruits and are put through a one-year training program to establish a common understanding of what is expected of them and build trust among them. The meritocratic promotion system ensures that the goals of civil servants and their agencies are aligned.

somewhat dampened. There are both theoretical and empirical arguments to support the idea of an East Asian model of corruption.

Huntington (1968) was an early proponent of the view that the structure of political and bureaucratic institutions and processes is important as a determinant of the level and nature of corruption:

> Corruption thrives on disorganization, the absence of stable relationships among groups and of recognized patterns of authority. The development of political organizations which exercise effective authority and which give rise to organized group interests—the "machine," the "organization," the "party"—transcending those of individual and social groups reduces the opportunity for corruption. Corruption varies inversely with political organization (p. 71).

Shleifer and Vishny (1993) propose an economic model of corruption that posits the existence of different types of political and bureaucratic institutions for the management of corruption. They propose that different regimes may create greater or lesser distortions and costs (see box 7.2).

With regard to East Asia, Shleifer and Vishny consider, as an example, the Philippines before and after President Marcos. They argue that, in the Philippines

■ BOX 7.2 **Corrupt Governments as Joint Monopolists**

In an important paper, Shleifer and Vishny (1993) propose a model of corruption in which the structure of government institutions and the political process is an important determinant of the level of corruption. In particular, they argue, weak governments that do not control their agencies experience high corruption levels, whereas stronger and more centralized governments may experience lower levels of corruption.

Their model builds on an analogy from the literature on industrial organization: the idea of a joint monopolist. A joint monopolist is a firm that has a monopoly over two strongly complementary goods. Such a firm will price differently from multiple independent monopolists, each producing only one of the strongly complementary goods. A joint monopolist will price so as to maximize returns across both markets, whereas independent monopolists will tend to push up the price of their respective products regardless of the demand effects in the complementary markets, and all will suffer.

This simple notion may be extended in a model of corruption to a case in which government officials must be bribed before they will provide licenses or permits. In many situations, a private firm needs several complementary licenses or permits to conduct business. For example, a firm might need an investment license and a planning permit. In the case of a strong, but corrupt government with tight control over its agencies, the value of the bribes for investment licenses will be kept down so as to expand the demand for the complementary planning permits, while the value of the bribes for planning permits will be kept down so as to expand the demand for investment licenses.

Alternatively, under a weak and corrupt government with loose control over its agencies, the investment agency and the planning bureau may set bribes independently. Each agency sets bribes so as to maximize the total bribes, while taking the other agency's output as given; so, the per unit bribe is higher, and the output (the number of investments licensed and plans permitted) is lower. By acting independently, the two agencies actually hurt each other, as well as the private buyers of permits.

This analysis holds that any corruption is distortionary and therefore costly (and more distortionary and costly than taxation because of the need for secrecy). However, since bribes are set at higher levels under the weak government scenario, corruption is more distortionary under weak, decentralized governments than under strong, centralized governments.

under President Marcos, it was always clear who needed to be bribed and for how much. All bribes flowed to the top, and the bribes were then divided among all the relevant government bureaucrats, who did not demand additional bribes from the purchaser of the package of permits. Since the demise of Marcos, the authors argue, the number of independent bribe takers has probably risen, the level of corruption has probably increased, and the efficiency of resource allocation has probably declined.

Shleifer and Vishny also imply that more organized corruption may also reduce uncertainty. For example, they argue that, in the Republic of Korea, although corruption was pervasive (at the time of writing in the early 1990s), the person paying the bribe was assured of getting the government good that was being paid for and would not need to pay additional bribes. By contrast, they believe, in many African countries and in post-communist Russia, not only do numerous bureaucrats need to be bribed to get government permits, but bribing a bureaucrat does not guarantee that some other bureaucrat or even the first one will not demand another bribe.

A similar, almost contemporaneous model is that devised by Olson (1993), who, perhaps significantly, draws his metaphor from Chinese history to argue that "stationary bandits" are preferable to "roving bandits." Through uncoordinated competitive theft (or corruption), roving bandits destroy the incentive for economic agents to invest and produce, leaving little for the population or the bandits. Both might be better off if one bandit sets himself up in a stationary position to monopolize and rationalize his thefts (or corruption). The successful, rational, and stationary bandit, Olson argues, will monopolize theft in his domain and will limit what he steals because he knows that, in the long run, he will be able to extract more if he gives his victims the public goods and incentives they need to invest and produce additional income and wealth. Because of this, Olson posits, there will be less investment and growth in countries governed by roving bandits.

Both quantitative analysis and country case studies tend to support the relevance of these ideas in the East Asian context. The simple scatter charts presented in figure 7.4, prepared using Kaufmann-Kraay indicators for 2004, suggest that East Asian countries generally are perceived as having greater government effectiveness and better regulatory quality than would be predicted by their control of corruption percentile.

The simple scatter charts presented in figure 7.5, have been prepared using the 2003 United Nations Development Program human development index. The corruption perceptions index (chart a), and the control of corruption index (chart b), indicate that East Asian economies generally show better human development outcomes than one might expect based only on the level of the corruption indexes.

The impression these data give is that corruption is widespread but orderly in East Asia and that it goes hand in hand with generally effective, well-regulated, and benign (or, at least, developmental) government. In line with the Shleifer-Vishny model, it seems that East Asian governments have typically managed corruption so as to minimize the adverse impacts on investment and growth, and, in line with the Olson model, it seems East Asian governments have also typically managed corruption so as to minimize the adverse impacts on human development and, hence, growth.

Similarly, the scatter charts in figure 7.6, prepared using data from the World Bank investment climate surveys, suggest that bribes to secure a contract with

(text continues on page 332)

Government Effectiveness Is Greater Than Corruption Indexes Imply, 2004

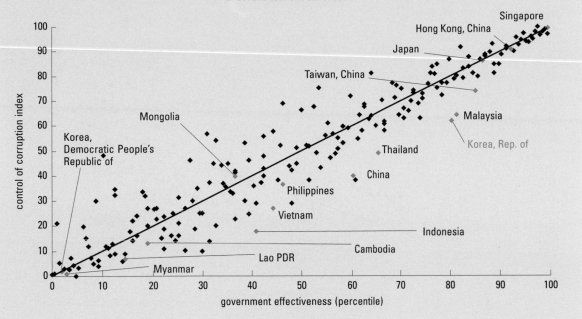

a. Government effectiveness

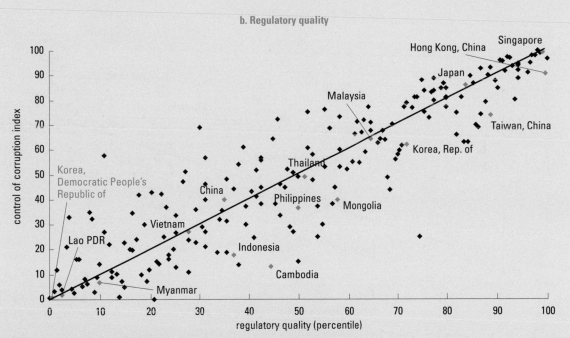

b. Regulatory quality

Source: Calculations of the authors based on data from Kaufmann, Kraay, and Mastruzzi 2005.
Note: The figure shows global percentiles. East Asian economies are highlighted.

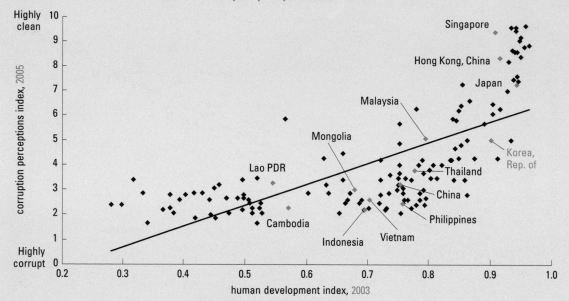

a. Corruption perceptions index and HDI

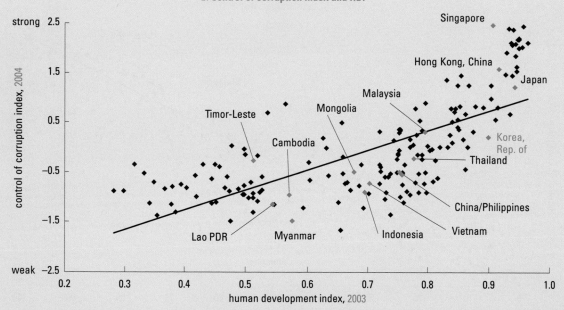

b. Control of corruption index and HDI

Sources: Prepared using data from Transparency International 2005, Kaufmann, Kraay, and Mastruzzi 2005, and UNDP 2003.
Note: HDI = human development index. East Asian economies are highlighted.

■ FIGURE 7.6 **The Bribes Needed to Get Things Done Appear to Be Smaller in East Asia**

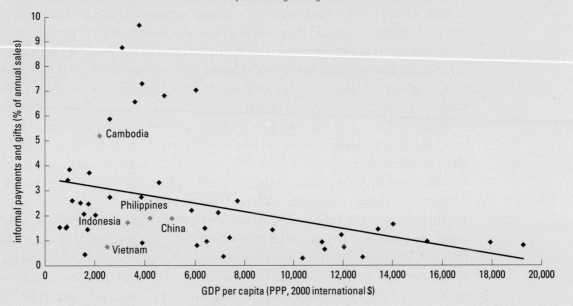

a. Payments to "get things done"

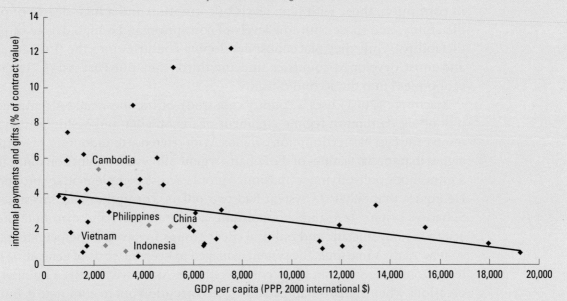

b. Payments to secure a government contract

Sources: Investment Climate (Enterprise) Survey Database, World Bank and International Finance Corporation,
http://www.enterprisesurveys.org/; World Development Indicators Database, World Bank,
http://www.worldbank.org/data/datapubs/datapubs.html.
Note: The figure shows global percentiles and reflects unweighted averages. East Asian economies are highlighted.

government or to "get things done" are lower as a share of contract value or annual sales in most East Asian economies surveyed (China, Indonesia, the Philippines, and Vietnam) than one might predict based on GDP per capita. This finding appears to be consistent with the hypothesis that economies with strong, centralized governments set bribes at lower levels. The exception is Cambodia, which, as box 7.3 illustrates, fits the competitive corruption model more closely than the organized monopoly model.

Campos, Lien, and Pradhan (2001) present cross-country regression analysis to show that, while corruption impacts adversely on investment, it tends to have smaller adverse impacts under regimes in which corruption is predictable (in the sense that the favor, service, or product being sought is more likely to be granted). Using survey data collected for the *World Development Report* of the World Bank (1997), they find that corruption does impact adversely on investment, but that, for any given level of corruption, the predictability of corruption has a positive effect on investment. Other things being equal, countries in which corruption is predictable tend to attract higher relative levels of investment. The authors propose that countries may be classified into three categories: those with high levels of corruption and a low degree of predictability in corruption, those with high levels of corruption and a high degree of predictability, and those with low levels of corruption and a high degree of predictability. While they place most developing countries into the first category and most developed countries into the third, they put East Asia's "miracle economies" into the second category.

MacIntyre (2001) uses a country case study of Indonesia and a centralized monopoly corruption regime argument of the Shleifer and Vishny variety to resolve the East Asian corruption paradox. With reference to Indonesia, MacIntyre argues that special features of the Suharto regime allowed it to function much like a joint monopolist trying to maximize profits across complementary products. He argues that Suharto's system had two pillars: corruption and investment. Suharto's system gave ample opportunity to extract rents and distribute these across the bureaucratic and political client groups involved in perpetuating the system. At the same time, the system managed to keep the costs of generating the rents from squeezing out long-term investment. MacIntyre details a number of occasions when Suharto clamped down on corruption not to eliminate it, but to ensure that it remained under his control. MacIntyre argues that this provided a greater degree of predictability for investors. While investors might have had to pay substantial bribes, they were assured that their investments would be protected from unpredictable and uncoordinated corruption.

■ BOX 7.3 **Competitive Corruption in Cambodia**

At the end of the Khmer Rouge period, no functioning state institutions remained in Cambodia. The legacy of conflict had depleted the country's human talent on which the public sector and entrepreneurship are based and destroyed the social institutions that had glued the society together. After 1979, the Cambodian state and civil society had to be rebuilt. The growth in Cambodia over the past decade has been remarkable in light of the destruction wrought by years of conflict, but it has been heavily dependent upon a narrow base, namely, garment exports and tourism. Corruption may have reduced the rate of growth and the rate at which the economy has been able to diversify.

The problems of Cambodia's weak formal and informal institutions are felt most directly and acutely through corruption. The government has tried to fill the institutional vacuum through administrative measures; these have often proved unsuccessful and have created more opportunities for corruption. Overlapping and expensive regulation has created room for excess discretion and rent seeking, which has added to the cost of doing business.

It takes 86 days to start a business in Cambodia, 36 days more than it takes to start a business in Vietnam and 53 days more than in Thailand.[14] The incentives for the private sector are distorted; staying in the informal sector appears a rational response to the investment climate since informal firms face lower taxes and fewer requests for bribes. The investment climate assessment of the World Bank (2004a) found that doing business in Cambodia involves the most annual inspections, costs the most per capita for the official registration of businesses, and, after China, requires the greatest amount of time among managers for dealing with officials.

Moreover, according to the investment climate assessment survey, unofficial payments do not appear to grease the wheels: bribes do not necessarily expedite services in Cambodia. There is no statistical difference between the speed of administrative procedures for firms reporting higher versus lower ratios of bribes as a share of sales for essential services such as utility connections. Firms of all sizes acknowledge paying bribes; but the larger and more formal the enterprise, the higher the bribes as a share of sales. Private sector firms estimate that unofficial payments cost them an average of 5.2 percent of total sales revenue; for large firms, the figure exceeds 6 percent. Unofficial payments represent a significant component of doing business in Cambodia, to the extent that the share of revenue consumed by unofficial payments is more than double that found in parallel surveys in Bangladesh, China, and Pakistan.

A recent survey found that the institutions considered the most corrupt were the customs service, the courts, the police, and tax collection; among all but the last of these institutions, corruption seems to have worsened between 2000 and 2005.[15] The majority of survey respondents rejected the notion that corruption is acceptable merely because it is so common or that a small salary entitles a civil servant to bribes. To some extent, the perception that corruption has become more severe may be affected by the growing intolerance for corruption.

The same survey found that, on average, each household pays US$24.50 per year for bribes. This represents between 1.4 and 2.2 percent of total household expenditures and 5 percent of total income. The cost of bribes is only a small fraction of the overall burden of corruption. Indirect costs to households range from undelivered services to higher prices for consumption and investment goods and from forgone revenue that would otherwise finance service delivery to the dispossession of poor and poorly connected families from access to common resources because local officials are selling these off as private property.

Sources: World Bank 2004a, 2004b, 2005a.

Indonesia during the Suharto years experienced short-lived, but striking interventions that targeted corruption. Thus, Suharto issued a presidential decree that disempowered the entire customs bureau in 1985 when the corruption became serious enough to jeopardize his whole system of rent extraction. In an unprecedented move, the bureau's bureaucratic functions were outsourced to a foreign company. Similarly, in 1986, when the textile industry was imperiled by the cotton import monopoly, executive action was taken to dismantle the monopoly, and its senior officials were fired.[16] Although none of these interventions were aimed at eliminating corruption, they were seen as necessary to ensure the sustainability of the respective sectors and, hence, of overall rent streams.

Additional evidence exists of the extent of the centralization of corruption in Indonesia under Suharto. In an innovative study, Fisman (2001) created the Suharto dependency index to measure the political connectedness of firms listed with the Jakarta Stock Exchange. He showed that rumors of Suharto's health problems between 1995 and 1997 had a strong negative impact on the share prices of firms that ranked high on the Suharto dependency index, and, furthermore, the impact increased as the rumors grew worse.

Kang (2002) and Chang (2001) present similar arguments in their case studies of corruption in the Republic of Korea. Both find that Korea managed to establish a corruption regime in the postwar period. The regime permitted rapid economic growth despite the extensive corruption it also allowed. Kang says that there was a balance of power among a small and stable set of government and business elites. To fund their operations, political elites took massive donations from the *chaebol* (the dominant firms in Korea). *Chaebol* donations were sometimes used for humanitarian or developmental purposes, but were part of a larger web of money politics. Kang presents evidence that businessmen who did not provide politicians with sufficient "voluntary donations" when they were asked had their loans called by the Bank of Korea, suffered through tax audits, or had their subsidy applications denied. Kang characterizes the arrangement as one of mutual hostages, whereby each side benefits from the arrangement and has strong incentives not to undermine the benefits of the other. The collusion of a powerful business class and a coherent state meant that corruption, though widespread, was constrained.

According to Huntington (1968), most forms of corruption involve an exchange of political action for economic wealth. Where there are many avenues to accumulate wealth, but few positions of political power, he argues, the dominant pattern will be the use of the former to achieve the latter. Huntington held that, in the United States, for example, wealth has commonly been a road to political influence rather than political office a road to wealth. In most modernizing countries, however, the opportunities for the accumulation of wealth through private activity are limited, and politics therefore becomes the road to wealth. Similarly, Kang (2002) concludes that the different development trajectories of the Republic of Korea and the Philippines—though, in both countries, growth and corruption existed side by side for decades—may be explained by the balance of economic and political power. Even during the period of rapid growth in the Republic of Korea, economic power and political power were balanced, and corruption never spiraled out of control. In the Philippines, however, the imbalance in the two factors led to abuses and to corruption that was sufficiently large to choke off growth.

Is East Asian Tolerance of Corruption Declining?

East Asian Values and Corruption

There has been much debate about whether corruption means the same thing in Asia as it does in the West. "What you regard as corruption in your part of the world, we regard as family values," Mohammad Suharto, then president of Indonesia, is reported to have told James Wolfensohn, then president of the World Bank.[17] It is frequently argued, especially with reference to East Asia, that cross-country comparisons of corruption are inappropriate since public ethics are culturally specific.

Some have held that the cultural characteristics of Asia make it more inclined to corruption. For example, Tanzi (1995) has contended that firms in some countries are culturally less inclined to have arm's-length economic relationships, which, in turn, may lead to more ingrained corruption. It is certainly the case that the giving and accepting of gifts are a normal way of doing business in many parts of Asia.

Against this, Mahbubani (2006) writes that a Confucian notion of obligation to society characterizes East Asian elites. Vogel (1991) believes that, while East Asian societies do not focus on binding legal codes as do societies in the West, they have detailed rules about the behavior of the individual with respect to the group. Vogel cites the emphasis on loyalty, the responsiveness of people in organizations to group demands, and the predictability of individual behavior in the group setting as characteristics well suited to the needs of industrialization, particularly in those economies trying to catch up.

Fukuyama (1999) points out that arguments based on Asian values fail to recognize Asia as a diverse location, where values vary significantly from country to country. Thus, Confucianism is interpreted differently in China, Japan, and the

Republic of Korea, and kinship ties vary in importance throughout Asia, playing a minimal role in Japan and a very important one in southern China. Furthermore, as others have highlighted, Eastern religions, including Buddhism, Confucianism, Hinduism, and Islam, each condemn corruption. Fukuyama also says that arguments according to Asian values falsely suggest that values have a direct impact on behavior. He holds that institutions may be at least as significant and that values are mediated through a variety of institutions before becoming manifest.

Neither values nor institutions are static, but may evolve. For example, the long-established tradition of receiving gifts in the Japanese administration has been restricted by the National Public Service Ethics Law of August 1999, which obliges senior officials to report gifts of a value greater than ¥5,000 (roughly US$50 equivalent).

Survey evidence from Thailand shows that people make quite sophisticated distinctions between appropriate and inappropriate gifts. Thus, although Thais set higher limits than those in many other countries on the amount of money officials may take from the private sector before they consider it corruption, they do not tolerate major payoffs involving high-level officials and major investors.[18]

As we discuss in the context of Cambodia, survey evidence shows that households do not agree that corruption is acceptable because it is so common or that low salaries entitle civil servants to bribes. Indeed, the researchers who have conducted the surveys have concluded that, to some extent, the increase in the number of respondents who say corruption has worsened may be affected by their growing intolerance for corruption.[19]

The Demand for New Forms of Governance

Demands for new forms of governance and enhanced anticorruption efforts have been rising across East Asia. Corruption has figured prominently in public discourse and political events, including the convictions of two former presidents of the Republic of Korea, the resignation of President Mohammad Suharto in Indonesia, and the ouster of both President Ferdinand Marcos and President Joseph Estrada in the Philippines. These trends are reflected in the gradual move toward democracy in some countries and a more rapid and general move toward decentralized governance across the region.

There has been a measured spread of political rights and civil liberties around the region. In 1976, only one of the 14 East Asian economies listed in figure 7.7 were considered free (light gold), while four were considered partially free (dark gold), and nine were considered not free (black), according to

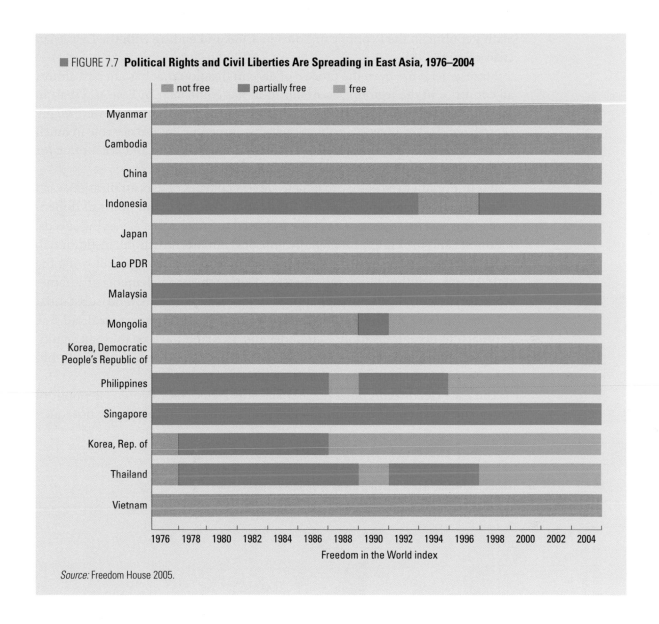

■ FIGURE 7.7 **Political Rights and Civil Liberties Are Spreading in East Asia, 1976–2004**

Source: Freedom House 2005.

the Freedom House freedom in the world index.[20] Since 1998, the equivalent rankings are five free, three partially free, and six not free. Although not all observers would agree with the individual categorizations, it is clear that political democracy and civil liberties have made advances in the region during the period under review (particularly between 1986 and 1997, starting with the fall of Marcos in the Philippines in 1986 and the passage of the Constitution of the

Sixth Republic in the Republic of Korea in 1988 and ending with the East Asian crisis of 1997–98).

More general has been the process of decentralization that has affected almost all countries in the region. Decentralization has come later in East Asia than in many other parts of the world. Before 1990, most East Asian countries were highly centralized. Today, however, subnational governments play a major role in much of the region's development, delivering many critical services and accounting for a significant portion of total public expenditures (see figure 7.8).

It is important to recognize that there are several types of decentralization, each with different formulations on the fiscal, administrative, and political dimensions. The East Asian economies have followed separate paths at varying speeds. Indonesia and the Philippines rapidly introduced major structural, institutional, and fiscal reforms and pushed sweeping decentralization reforms following the sudden end to authoritarian rule, thereby creating the basic elements of a framework for decentralization, subnational democratic elections, and substantial resource sharing. China and Vietnam have taken a more piecemeal, ad hoc approach to decentralization. Cambodia and Thailand have established significant elements of decentralization at the formal policy and legislative levels, but have been slow in implementation.[21]

There are clearly economies in East Asia—the Democratic People's Republic of Korea and Myanmar, for example—that political modernization may not touch

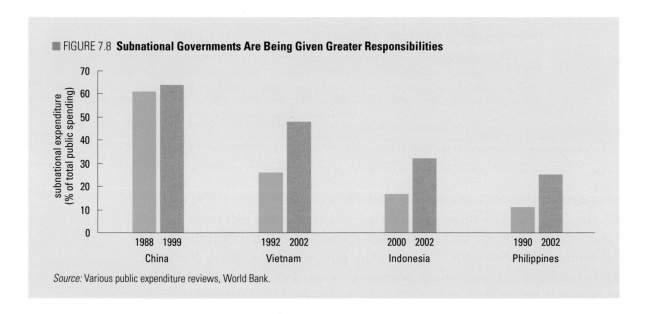

■ FIGURE 7.8 **Subnational Governments Are Being Given Greater Responsibilities**

Source: Various public expenditure reviews, World Bank.

for some time. Taking the region as a whole, however, it seems likely that the demand for political modernization will continue to grow.

With reference to the United States, Friedman (2005) has argued that, historically, economic growth has created conditions conducive to the strengthening of governance. The standard accounts of European history also suggest various connections between the economic and social transformations of the industrial revolution and the process of political modernization. Growing urban populations and better educated and articulate middle classes may make demands for greater political representation, less corruption, and more effective service delivery harder for political leaders to ignore.

As advanced East Asian countries mature, growth rates may be expected gradually to converge with those of advanced countries in the Organisation for Economic Co-operation and Development. Rates of return will eventually become less spectacular and may no longer be adequate to compensate investors for the prevailing levels of corruption. Investors and trade partners may no longer be willing or able to absorb the extra costs and uncertainty associated with corruption. The ability to control corruption may therefore become a binding constraint to growth in a way that it has not hitherto been. Indeed, a mechanism of this kind may well have contributed to the demand for better governance and reduced corruption in Hong Kong (China), Japan, and Singapore over the last half century.

Domestic and global environments have changed drastically across the region; in an era of sweeping economic, political, and social transformations and full-scale integration into the global economy, no East Asian state has a grip on the whole state apparatus and the economy as Suharto did in the 1980s. It is becoming difficult to imagine that East Asian states might maintain corruption regimes of the kind they have had in the past.

Regional and global integration may create demand for reduced corruption from businesses. In the short term, action to tackle the corruption in customs administrations may be necessary to support accession to the World Trade Organization. The requirement to eliminate remaining trade barriers as part of the Free Trade Area of the Association of Southeast Asian Nations or because of World Trade Organization commitments will further reduce policy-induced sources of rents.

In the longer term, economies will become more complex as a result of the integration process and the increased crossborder flows of capital and ideas. The success of East Asian economies will depend less and less on factor endowments, such as cheap labor or natural resources, and more and more on the ability of these economies to address bottlenecks in the availability of human capital, efficient infrastructure, or innovation. The demand for government that helps address these bottlenecks, rather than simply extracting rents, may also grow as a consequence.

FDI may bring with it international accounting and auditing standards that help deter corruption. Integrity and trust may become prerequisites for success in business in a way that they were not hitherto. Corruption may be harder to broker across national and cultural boundaries as FDI becomes ever more significant. Greater intraregional and international exchanges of ideas may expose citizens to other governance models and to debates about governance that are less widely accessible domestically.

Will Political Modernization Reduce Corruption?

If political modernization accelerates across East Asia, how will this impact on corruption? Empirical investigations are ambiguous about the effects of democracy and civil liberties on corruption and about the effects of decentralization on corruption. On balance, the available evidence tends to support the presumption that the spread of political and civil liberties and the development of more decentralized forms of governance will reduce corruption. However, there is also evidence that these effects may take time to play out and that the full benefits may be contingent on a parallel and necessarily more gradual process of institution building.

A Longer-Term View

Most East Asian countries have experienced unprecedented social and economic change in the past few decades. Economic development, the spread of education, and growing, affluent middle classes have been key drivers for better governance. Scott (1972) argues that, with more equal income distribution, a relatively large middle class is able to survive, act to hold elites accountable, and, as a consequence, foster lower levels of corruption. In similar fashion, Glaeser, Scheinkman, and Shleifer (2003) propose that inequality enables the rich to subvert the political, regulatory, and legal institutions of society for their own benefit.

Empirical studies on democracy and corruption draw our attention to complex and often difficult-to-prove links between the two. Rose-Ackerman (1999) has argued that elections increase the accountability of politicians, but also produce new incentives for corruption as the need for political financing rises. Brunetti and Weder (2003) do not find any impact of democracy on corruption in a cross-country analysis. However, Treisman (2000) presents a more subtle picture. He finds that democracy will not reduce corruption significantly in general, but that a long exposure to democracy does appear to decrease corruption: democracies are significantly less corrupt only after 40 years.

Chowdhury (2004) uses cross-country regression analysis to confirm that democracy and press freedom may have a significant impact on corruption. He notes that the two act together. The presence of press freedom brings public corruption cases to public attention, while democracy allows the public to punish corrupt politicians by ousting them from office. Like Treisman, Chowdhury believes there may be a substantial time lag and that, while a shift toward democracy and press freedom may influence the extent of corruption, an immediate improvement is unlikely. Drawing on a cross-country analysis, Montinola and Jackman (2002) conclude that political competition helps reduce corruption, but only beyond a certain threshold of competition. They find that corruption is slightly more prevalent in countries with intermediate levels of political competition than in their less democratic counterparts, but once past the threshold, higher levels of competition are associated with considerably lower levels of corruption.

It is quite possible that, as countries transition to democracy, democratic consolidation will take more time, and institutions will need to be strengthened before corruption levels come down. It is quite possible that, in an environment with weak institutions and poorly established accountability mechanisms, elections will produce new opportunities and incentives for corruption. According to Diamond (1997):

> Democracy may be the most common form of government in the world, but outside of the wealthy industrialized nations it tends to be shallow, illiberal, and poorly institutionalized. If there are no immediate threats of democratic collapse in most of those countries, neither are there clear signs that democracy has become consolidated and stable, truly the only viable political system and method for the foreseeable future. In fact, of the more than 70 new democracies that have come into being since the start of the third wave, only a small number are generally considered to be deeply rooted and secure (p. xv).

Acquiring effective institutions is a slow process. Even the most advanced countries that now rank among the least corrupt in the world were once riddled with corruption in every sphere of public life. Institutions that enable these states to deal with corruption have evolved over time, but it has not been a linear, progressive path. The U.S. experience is a good example (see box 7.4). Legislative corruption in the United States was so serious that President Theodore Roosevelt is known to have lamented that the New York assemblymen who engaged in openly

■ BOX 7.4 **The History of Corruption in the United States**

The incidence of corruption actually increased in the United States for quite some time, in parallel with unprecedented economic growth. Glaeser and Goldin (2006) show this by using public documents—newspapers—to construct an index of reported corruption. Taking advantage of the advent of online searchable editions of long-established U.S. newspapers (including *The New York Times* and a large group of small town newspapers), they searched for the words "corruption" and "fraud" (and their variants, such as "corrupt" and "fraudulent") and counted the number of pages containing these words in newspapers. They adjusted this index to control for the size of the newspapers and the overall amount of attention given to politically relevant stories.

Glaeser and Goldin have found that the extent of corruption increased until the 1870s and then declined between the 1870s and the 1920s, with most of the decline concentrated in the mid-1870s to 1890 and in the 1910s. They argue that the rise in corruption across the 19th century may be explained by the rapidly expanding scale of both government and the economy: the budgets of local governments swelled, thereby increasing the potential benefits of corruption.

Why, then, during the 1870s and the 1920s did corruption in the United States decline despite the continuous

rise in the size of government and the high returns to corruption in the judiciary? Glaeser and Goldin discover the answer in a change in the costs of corruption. Before about 1900, many actions that are considered corrupt and illicit today were legal. Institutional checks and balances were inadequate. Governments rarely prosecuted themselves, and the higher levels of government were sufficiently weak that they could not provide a check on local corruption. The lack of information was also a serious problem; although national newspapers might expose corrupt practices, many smaller city media outlets were tied to the political establishment and did not fulfill their informational role properly.

By the early 20th century, however, the United States was able to establish and implement a fuller apparatus of modern checks on corruption. Rules began replacing discretionary approaches in many areas, including patronage networks. Different levels of government became more effective at patrolling each other. Greater competition and political independence in the news media assured more transparency across the nation, not only in the big cities. Finally, voter expectations about corrupt behavior had changed, and officials caught in corruption became more likely to experience defeat at the polls.

selling votes to lobbying groups "had the same idea about public life and civil service that a vulture has of a dead sheep."[22]

Empirical investigations into the effect of decentralization on corruption show mixed results. Treisman (2000) finds that federal countries exhibit higher rates of corruption. However, Treisman's measure of decentralization is a simple one based on the existence or lack of a federal structure. In contrast, Fisman and Gatti (2002) measure decentralization as the share of government expenditure at the subnational level and use cross-country regression analysis to show that this measure of decentralization is strongly and significantly associated with lower corruption. Fisman and Gatti find that their regression results hold with or without including in the sample the countries that decentralized over the period 1980–95. However, their paper does not set out to investigate whether the impact of decentralization on corruption becomes stronger the longer a country is exposed to decentralization.

Much like democracy, decentralization in weak institutional settings is not a panacea for good governance or for active efforts to curb corruption. Nonetheless, the empirical research is scarce, and the evidence is not definitive. There is thus a heated debate about the links between decentralization and corruption. Table 7.2 summarizes some of the potential benefits and risks of decentralization in the short and long term with respect to corruption. The expected benefits from decentralization are all based on the assumption that local accountability mechanisms are effective and that information is available so local actors may demand better governance. In reality, local institutions are often weak, and mechanisms to ensure satisfactory information flows are frequently dysfunctional.

Shorter-Term Dynamics

Country case studies cast some light on the shorter-term dynamics of the relationships among democratization, decentralization, and corruption. While welcoming

■ TABLE 7.2 **Potential Link between Corruption and Decentralization**

Time span	Benefits of decentralization	Risks of corruption
Short run	Brings governments closer to the people Overcomes information asymmetries Enhances transparency and accountability Allows for local innovation	Local governments may be more susceptible to state capture Local politicians may be more likely to engage in clientelism to win elections Capacity constraints may be a problem for local governments and also for local institutions involved in checks and balances, such as local legislatures, the judiciary, the media, and civil society
Long run	Promotes tax and policy competition Underpins long-term political reform	Creates intergovernmental tension; may increase uncertainty Exacerbates disparities between lagging and advanced regions Fragments economies of scale Intense interregional competition may lead to excessive cuts in tax rates and public goods

Sources: Based on Kaiser 2006; Campos and Hellman 2005.
Note: State capture covers the actions of individuals, groups, or firms in the public or private sectors undertaken to influence the passage of laws, regulations, decrees, and government policies to their advantage through the illicit and nontransparent provision of private benefits to politicians or civil servants. Clientelism refers to politicians who distribute publicly funded goods to selected members of the electorate in return for votes and political support.

Indonesia's transition to democracy as a positive development in the longer run, MacIntyre (2001) writes that corruption may actually become worse during transition. He notes that the transition represents an important step toward more transparent governance and a more independent legal system. However, in the short and medium term, Indonesia's swing from centralized authoritarian rule to more democratic and more decentralized government may be associated with a less attractive investment climate and greater corruption: it has progressed beyond tight centralization, but has not yet developed a truly independent legal system or transparent governance institutions. In terms of the Shleifer-Vishny model, Indonesia is likely to advance from a situation wherein there is a single monopolist who accepts bribes to a more distortionary situation wherein there are multiple independent monopolists who accept bribes.

Decentralization has been driven by political rationale in many countries with a legacy of authoritarian rule; often, it represents an attempt to deal with cross-cutting social and economic tensions and ease local grievances against the central state. It is considered a shorter route toward the establishment of accountability among policy makers, citizens, and service providers in order to improve service delivery. In Indonesia and the Philippines, decentralization was adopted following the sudden collapse of authoritarian regimes (respectively, Suharto in 1998 and Marcos in 1986), which fueled demands for legitimate, local representation. In the region, these two countries have done the most to implement comprehensive decentralization programs.[23]

Indonesia initiated the process of decentralization in the late 1990s, but the climax of the process was the big bang decentralization in 2001. At that time, control of a significant share of public resources and direct authority over nearly 2 million civil servants were transferred to the local level. Recent empirical evidence from Indonesia appears to confirm that corruption may actually have become worse in the first few years following the big bang decentralization. The World Bank's productivity and investment climate survey asked firms about the impact of decentralization on key aspects of the governance and investment climate. As figure 7.9, chart a, illustrates, firms perceived decentralization as negative in four areas: labor regulations, licenses, policy uncertainty, and corruption. Most notably, more than 40 percent of the firms surveyed thought that decentralization had made corruption worse, while only 11 percent thought it had reduced corruption. The survey data also show that corruption is perceived as one of the major obstacles to business in Indonesia and that local corruption is considered even more serious as an obstacle than national corruption (figure 7.9, chart b). According to the survey, as an average share of annual revenues,

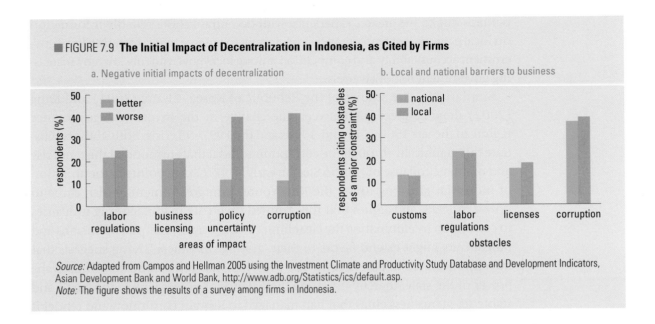

■ FIGURE 7.9 **The Initial Impact of Decentralization in Indonesia, as Cited by Firms**

a. Negative initial impacts of decentralization

b. Local and national barriers to business

Source: Adapted from Campos and Hellman 2005 using the Investment Climate and Productivity Study Database and Development Indicators, Asian Development Bank and World Bank, http://www.adb.org/Statistics/ics/default.asp.
Note: The figure shows the results of a survey among firms in Indonesia.

firms pay 64 percent more in informal payments to local governments than they do to officials at the national level. But informal payments seem not to translate into grease money, because firms also spend 15 percent more of their time dealing with local regulations than they do with national regulations. Although these results are preliminary, it is difficult to argue that decentralization has helped bolster the accountability of the state, at least from the perspective of Indonesian firms.

Clientelism and capture are also a problem at the local level; local legislative candidates are reported to pay national party organizations for ballot slots, and their selection is linked to elite village networks. Voters are often influenced by direct payments and other transfers.

The major decentralization reform in the Philippines took place during 1992–93. Perception-based measures of corruption have consistently improved since then, but it is not clear whether decentralization has been the key driver of this trend. Based on surveys of households and public officials at various levels of government, an extensive study in 2001 by the World Bank and the Center for Institutional Reform and the Informal Sector at the University of Maryland concluded that, while the lower levels of government are perceived to be less corrupt, local governments are no more accountable to local preferences than is the central government.[24] Nonetheless, there are promising developments; in the Philippines, perhaps due to the greater experience with decentralization, reliable information on local government performance is beginning to emerge that is fostering local government accountability and competition among local governments, thereby increasing government responsiveness.

Similarly, in case studies of the Republic of Korea, Chang (2001) and Kang (2002) draw connections between the change in the investment governance regime in the late 1980s and mid-1990s and the 1997–98 crisis. Both authors illustrate this graphically through the corruption scandal that surrounded the rapid rise and dramatic collapse of Hanbo Steel in early 1997. Chang points to the abolition of industrial planning under the Kim Young Sam government, which came to power in 1993, and argues that this exposed even core manufacturing industries to corruption by eliminating the clear limits on the ways influential politicians and bureaucrats might extend favors to their "paying customers." Kang suggests that the crisis occurred in part because the 1987 transition to democracy diffused the power of the state, thereby upsetting the balance of power within the small and stable set of business elites that had managed to restrain corruption and render it (in that context) actually beneficial to growth.

The validity of using corruption indicators to make comparisons over time is subject to some debate. The comparison of corruption rankings is certainly not meaningful. A country or region may stand still in terms of corruption, but slide down the rankings due to advances in other countries or regions. Even comparisons using point estimates need to be made with caution. The surveys used to compile these composite indicators vary from year to year. A change in perception may lag the fundamentals by a number of years. Nevertheless, as figure 7.10 illustrates, the control of corruption index does suggest there has been a decline in the control of corruption in East Asia as a region and in Indonesia and the Republic of Korea as cases in point over the period for which data are available.

Summing up such arguments, MacIntyre (2001) writes that: "the one thing worse than organized corruption is disorganized corruption" (p. 44). This argument is in fact rather similar to that of Huntington (1968) when he said that political modernization, defined as a transition from an autocratic to a more democratic government, is usually accompanied by an increase in corruption because of the underdevelopment of the institutions supporting democracy. Huntington points to the "organizational imperative": the need to assign greater priority to strengthening the political and bureaucratic institutions supporting democracy so that political modernization has a better chance to succeed and corruption will not increase.

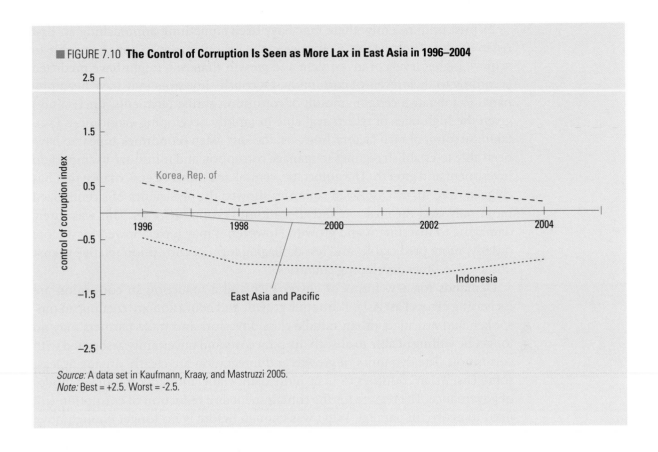

■ FIGURE 7.10 **The Control of Corruption Is Seen as More Lax in East Asia in 1996–2004**

Source: A data set in Kaufmann, Kraay, and Mastruzzi 2005.
Note: Best = +2.5. Worst = -2.5.

Conclusions

Despite the frequent use of terms such as crony capitalism and endemic corruption in connection with East Asia, it is clear that there is no uniform level of corruption in the region. The evidence suggests that there is tremendous variation in the levels of corruption across the region. Although some East Asian economies, such as Cambodia and Myanmar, rank among the most corrupt in the world, others, such as Hong Kong (China) and Singapore, rank among the least corrupt. In many East Asian economies, corruption is at about the level that one might expect based on their GDPs per capita. But there are certainly outliers that are significantly more or less corrupt than one might predict based on GDP. This should serve both as a warning to those who are inclined to ignore the issue and as a source of optimism for would-be reformers.

At least until recently, there may have been something approaching an East Asian model of corruption. Countries in the region appear to have been able to achieve higher levels of investment and growth than one might have predicted according to their levels of corruption. Of course, investors may have been prepared to tolerate a certain amount of corruption (bribe payments, uncertainty) given the high rates of return available in rapidly developing economies. Even taking account of such factors, however, the East Asian economies appear to have been able to establish regimes to manage corruption and minimize its impact on investment and growth. The autocratic, centralized mode of governance that has characterized many East Asian countries allowed the persistence of a centralized monopoly over the creation and allocation of economic rents. This was surely damaging to investment and growth. However, it may have allowed for a more orderly, more predictable, and less damaging form of corruption relative to that observed in other developing countries.

Demands for new forms of governance and a reduction in corruption are increasing across East Asia. Economic growth and education are creating an outspoken and articulate urban middle class. Investors and trade partners may no longer be willing or able to absorb the extra costs and uncertainty associated with corruption. The dynamics of growth and integration are clearly driving at least some East Asian countries to new, more democratic, more decentralized modes of governance. The regime for the containment and reduction of corruption will need to evolve in parallel. What was enough before is no longer enough now. Fighting corruption is moving up the agenda, and East Asian governance is moving from the rule of man (*renzhi*) to the rule of law (*fazhi*).

In the longer term, political modernization will probably bring with it improvements in transparency and accountability and reductions in corruption. At the same time, it would be naive to assume that improvement will be continuous and linear. The regimes established to manage corruption under precrisis models of governance have been swept away in a number of East Asian countries, and new institutions to support the rule of law, transparency, and accountability at the central and local levels will need more time to take hold. The result may well be an increase in corruption in the short and medium term. The imperative for institution building has therefore never been greater.

Notes

1. Wedeman (2002) refers to this as "the East Asian paradox" (p. 34).

2. The terms *renzhi* and *fazhi* differentiate political systems and the relationship between the state and its citizens. *Renzhi* (rule of man) vests rights in the larger community or nation defined according

to the ruler's determination of society's greater good. *Fazhi* is a more ambiguous term. It may be translated as "rule by law" or "rule of law." In this chapter, the term is used to denote rule of law: governmental authority is legitimately exercised only in accordance with written, publicly disclosed laws that have been adopted and are enforced through established procedures. Rule by law may be understood to mean that the state uses laws as a tool of social control without reference to the process of the formulation of law and without any implication about citizen rights or legitimacy. Rule *by* law has existed throughout much of East Asia's history. Emphasis on the rule *of* law as a core element of good governance is more recent.

3. As discussed in detail by Bardhan (1997), not all illegal transactions are corrupt, nor are all instances of corruption or bribery illegal. Bardhan proposes wide-ranging examples of actions that are corrupt, but not necessarily illicit or illegal, from tipping the maitre d' to get a better table at a restaurant to cases of gift-giving to politicians by lobbyists, or the assignment of campaign contributions to political action committees for favors, or the provision of postretirement jobs in private firms to bureaucrats of agencies meant to regulate the firms.

4. For example, in Svensson (2005).

5. As Huntington (1968) notes, in the early 19th century, the United Kingdom accepted the sale of peerages, but not of ambassadorships, whereas the United States accepted the sale of ambassadorships, but not of judgeships.

6. See Transparency International (2004: 13).

7. See Transparency International (2004: 13).

8. Both data sets include standard errors for each observation. Adapting a simple rule of thumb used by Kaufmann, Kraay, and Mastruzzi (2005), only half of the East Asian countries in the Kaufmann-Kraay control of corruption index sample and one-third in the Transparency International corruption perceptions index sample may be placed in their relevant tercile with a 95 percent significance level.

9. See http://www.transparency.org/policy_research/surveys_indices/cpi for the 2005 corruption perceptions index, which is described more fully in Lambsdorff (2005).

10. The control of corruption index and other Kaufmann-Kraay indicators are available at http://info. worldbank.org/governance/kkz2004/ and are described more fully in Kaufmann, Kraay, and Mastruzzi (2005).

11. For the Transparency International corruption perceptions index and the Kaufmann-Kraay governance indicators, changes in trends are subject to measurement error, and these may not be trivial. Kaufmann, Kraay, and Mastruzzi (2005) write: "Over the eight-year period from 1996–2004 spanned by our governance indicators, we find that in about 5 to 7 percent of countries we can be confident (at the 90 percent significance level) that governance has changed substantially. And at a lower 75 percent significance level, roughly 20 percent of all observed changes stand out as significant" (p. 41). They show, however, that many data sources agree about the direction of change in a given country.

12. See World Bank (1997).

13. See Wei (1999).

14. Doing Business Database, World Bank and International Finance Corporation, http://www. doingbusiness.org/.

15. Corruption surveys conducted by the Center for Social Development (Phnom Penh), cited in World Bank (2005a).

16. See MacIntyre (2001).

17. Quoted in Mallaby (2004).

18. See Phongpaichit and Piriyarangsan (1994).

19. Corruption surveys conducted by the Center for Social Development (Phnom Penh), cited in World Bank (2005a).

20. For details on the methodology of the freedom in the world index, see Freedom House (2005).

21. See World Bank (2005b) for a detailed review of decentralization in East Asia.

22. Garrathy and Carnes (2000: 472), cited in Chang (2002).

23. The analysis of decentralization and corruption in Indonesia and the Philippines is based on Campos and Hellman (2005).

24. See Azfar et al. (2000).

References

Acemoglu, Daron, and Thierry Verdier. 1998. "Property Rights, Corruption, and the Allocation of Talent: A General Equilibrium Approach." *Economic Journal* 108 (450): 1381–1403.

Azfar, Omar, Tugrul Gurgur, Satu Kähkönen, Anthony Lanyi, and Patrick Meagher. 2000. "Decentralization and Governance: An Empirical Investigation of Public Service Delivery in the Philippines." Washington, DC: University of Maryland Center for Institutional Reform and the Informal Sector and the World Bank.

Bardhan, Pranab. 1997. "Corruption and Development: A Review of Issues." *Journal of Economic Literature* 35 (3): 1320–46.

Bardhan, Pranab, and Dilip Mookherjee. 2006. "Decentralization, Corruption, and Government Accountability." In *International Handbook on the Economics of Corruption*, ed. Susan Rose-Ackerman, chap. 6. Cheltenham, United Kingdom: Edward Elgar.

Brunetti, Aymo, and Beatrice Weder. 2003. "A Free Press is Bad News for Corruption." *Journal of Public Economics* 87 (7–8): 1801–24.

Campos, José Edgardo, ed. 2001. *Corruption: The Boom and Bust of East Asia.* Manila: Ateneo de Manila University Press.

Campos, José Edgardo, and Joel S. Hellman. 2005. "Governance Gone Local: Does Decentralization Improve Accountability?" In *East Asia Decentralizes: Making Local Government Work*, 237–52. Washington, DC: World Bank.

Campos, José Edgardo, Donald Lien, and Sanjay Pradhan. 2001. "Corruption and Its Implications for Investment." In *Corruption: The Boom and Bust of East Asia*, ed. José Edgardo Campos, 11–24. Manila: Ateneo de Manila University Press.

Chang, Ha-Joon. 2001. "State, Capital, and Investments in Korea." In *Corruption: The Boom and Bust of East Asia*, ed. José Edgardo Campos, 45–68. Manila: Ateneo de Manila University Press.

_____. 2002. "Institutional Development in Developing Countries in a Historical Perspective: Lessons from Developed Countries in Earlier Times." Unpublished working paper. University of Cambridge, Cambridge.

Chowdhury, Shyamal K. 2004. "The Effect of Democracy and Press Freedom on Corruption: An Empirical Test." *Economics Letters* 85 (1): 93–101.

Diamond, Larry. 1997. *Consolidating the Third Wave Democracies.* Baltimore: Johns Hopkins University Press.

Fiorentini, Gianluca, and Sam Peltzman, eds. 1995. *The Economics of Organized Crime.* New York: Cambridge University Press.

Fisman, Raymond. 2001. "Estimating the Value of Political Connections." *American Economic Review* 91 (4): 1095–1102.

Fisman, Raymond, and Roberta Gatti. 2002. "Decentralization and Corruption: Evidence across Countries." *Journal of Public Economics* 83 (3): 325–45.

Freedom House. 2005. *Freedom in the World Comparative Rankings, 1973–2005: The Annual Survey of Political Rights and Civil Liberties.* Washington, DC: Freedom House. http://www.freedomhouse.org/template.cfm?page=15&year=2005.

Friedman, Benjamin M. 2005. *The Moral Consequences of Economic Growth.* New York: Alfred A. Knopf.

Fukuyama, Francis. 1999. "Asian Values and the Current Crisis." *Development Outreach*, Summer. http://www1.worldbank.org/devoutreach/summer99/index.asp.

Garrathy and Carnes. 2000. *The American Nation: A History of the United States.* 10th ed. New York: Addison Wesley Longman.

Gelos, R. Gaston, and Shang-Jin Wei. 2005. "Transparency and International Portfolio Holdings." *Journal of Finance* 60 (6): 2987–3020.

Glaeser, Edward L., and Claudia Goldin. 2006. "Corruption and Reform: Introduction." In *Corruption and Reform: Lessons from America's Economic History*, ed. Edward L. Glaeser and Claudia Goldin, 3–22. Chicago: University of Chicago Press.

Glaeser, Edward L., Jose Scheinkman, and Andrei Shleifer. 2003. "The Injustice of Inequality." *Journal of Monetary Economics* 50 (1): 199–222.

Granovetter, Mark. 2005. "The Social Construction of Corruption." Working Paper, June, Department of Sociology, Stanford University, Stanford, CA.

Hicken, Allen. 2001. "Governance and Growth in Thailand." In *Corruption: The Boom and Bust of East Asia*, ed. José Edgardo Campos, 163–82. Manila: Ateneo de Manila University Press.

Huntington, Samuel P. 1968. *Political Order in Changing Societies*. New Haven, CT: Yale University Press.

Ito, Takatoshi, and Anne O. Krueger, eds. 2000. *The Role of Foreign Direct Investment in East Asian Economic Development*. Chicago: University of Chicago Press.

Kaiser, Kai. 2006. "Decentralization Reforms." In *A Practitioner's Guide to Pension, Health, Labor Market, Public Sector Downsizing, Taxation, Decentralization, and Macroeconomic Modeling*. Vol. 2 of *Analyzing the Distributional Impact of Reforms*, ed. Aline Coudouel and Stefano Paternostro, 313–54. Washington, DC: World Bank.

Kang, David C. 2002. *Crony Capitalism: Corruption and Development in South Korea and the Philippines*. Cambridge: Cambridge University Press.

Kaufmann, Daniel. 2006. "Corporate and Public Sector Corruption Matters for Competitiveness: Empirical Evidence and Implications." Background paper for the United States Agency for International Development "Roundtable on Lessons Learned in Designing Anti-Corruption Interventions in Economic Growth," Washington, DC, June 12.

Kaufmann, Daniel, and Shang-Jin Wei. 1999. "Does 'Grease Money' Speed Up the Wheels of Commerce?" NBER Working Paper 7093, National Bureau of Economic Research, Cambridge, MA.

Kaufmann, Daniel, Aart Kraay, and Massimo Mastruzzi. 2005. "Governance Matters IV: Governance Indicators for 1996–2004." Policy Research Working Paper 3630, World Bank, Washington, DC.

———. 2006. "Measuring Corruption: Myths and Realities." *Development Outreach*, September. Washington, DC: World Bank Institute. http://www1.worldbank.org/devoutreach/september06/article.asp?id=371.

Lambsdorff, Johann Graf. 2005. "The Methodology of the 2005 Corruption Perceptions Index." Report, Transparency International, Berlin; University of Passau, Passau, Germany.

Leff, Nathanial H. 1964. "Economic Development through Bureaucratic Corruption." *American Behavioral Scientist* 82 (2): 337–41.

Lui, Francis T. 1985. "An Equilibrium Queuing Model of Bribery." *Journal of Political Economy* 93 (4): 760–81.

MacIntyre, Angus. 2001. "Investment, Property Rights, and Corruption in Indonesia." In *Corruption: The Boom and Bust of East Asia*, ed. José Edgardo Campos, 25–44. Manila: Ateneo de Manila University Press.

Mahbubani, Kishore. 2006. "From Confucius to Kennedy: Principles of East Asian Governance." In *East Asian Visions: Perspectives on Economic Development*, ed. Indermit S. Gill, Yukon Huang, and Homi Kharas, chap. 11. Washington, DC: World Bank.

Mallaby, Sebastian. 2004. *The World's Banker: A Story of Failed States, Financial Crises, and the Wealth and Poverty of Nations*. New York: Council on Foreign Relations and Penguin Press.

Mauro, Paolo. 1995. "Corruption and Growth." *Quarterly Journal of Economics* 110 (3): 681–712.

Montinola, Gabriella, and Robert Jackman. 2002. "Sources of Corruption: A Cross-Country Study." *British Journal of Political Science* 32 (1): 147–70.

Myrdal, Gunnar. 1968. *Asian Drama: An Enquiry into the Poverty of Nations*. New York: Random House.

Olken, Benjamin A. 2005 "Monitoring Corruption: Evidence from a Field Experiment in Indonesia." NBER Working Paper 11753, National Bureau of Economic Research, Cambridge, MA.

Olson, Mancur. 1993. "Dictatorship, Democracy, and Development." *American Political Science Review* 87 (3): 567–76.

Phongpaichit, Pasuk, and Sungsidh Piriyarangsan. 1994. *Corruption and Democracy in Thailand*. Chiang Mai, Thailand: Silkworm Books.

Quah, Jon S. T. 1988. "Corruption in Asia with Special Reference to Singapore: Patterns and Consequences." *Asian Journal of Public Administration* 10 (1): 80–98.

Rock, Michael T., and Heidi Bonnett. 2004. "The Comparative Politics of Corruption: Accounting for the East Asian Paradox in Empirical Studies of Corruption, Growth, and Investment." *World Development* 32 (6): 999–1017.

Rose-Ackerman, Susan. 1999. *Corruption and Government: Causes, Consequences, and Reform.* New York: Cambridge University Press.

Schiavo-Campo, Salvatore, ed. 1999. *Governance, Corruption, and Public Financial Management.* Manila: Asian Development Bank.

Scott, James C. 1972. *Comparative Political Corruption.* Englewood Cliffs, NJ: Prentice-Hall.

Shleifer, Andrei, and Robert W. Vishny. 1993. "Corruption." *Quarterly Journal of Economics* 108 (3): 599–617.

Svensson, Jakob. 2005. "Eight Questions about Corruption." *Journal of Economic Perspectives* 19 (3): 19–42.

Tanzi, Vito. 1995. "Corruption, Arm's-Length Relationships and Markets." In *The Economics of Organized Crime,* ed. Gianluca Fiorentini and Sam Peltzman, 161–82. New York: Cambridge University Press.

———. 1999. "Governance, Corruption, and Public Finance: An Overview." In *Governance, Corruption, and Public Financial Management,* ed. Salvatore Schiavo-Campo, 1–17. Manila: Asian Development Bank.

Transparency International. 2004. *Global Corruption Report 2004.* London: Pluto Press.

———. 2005. *Corruption Perceptions Index 2005.* Berlin: Transparency International. http://www.transparency.org/policy_research/surveys_indices/cpi.

Treisman, Daniel. 2000. "The Causes of Corruption: A Cross-National Study." *Journal of Public Economics* 76 (3): 399–457.

UNDP (United Nations Development Program). 2003. *Human Development Report 2003: Millennium Development Goals: A Compact Among Nations to End Human Poverty.* New York: Oxford University Press.

Vogel, Ezra F. 1991. *The Four Little Dragons: The Spread of Industrialization in East Asia.* Cambridge, MA: Harvard University Press.

Wedeman, Andrew. 2002. "Development and Corruption: The East Asian Paradox." In *Political Business in East Asia (Politics in Asia),* ed. Edmund Terence Gomez, 34–61. London: Routledge.

Wei, Shang-Jin. 1997. "How Taxing Is Corruption on International Investors?" NBER Working Paper 6030, National Bureau of Economic Research, Cambridge, MA.

———. 1999. "Corruption in Economic Development: Beneficial Grease, Minor Annoyance, or Major Obstacle?" Policy Research Working Paper 2048, World Bank, Washington, DC.

———. 2000. "Why Does China Attract So Little Foreign Direct Investment?" In *The Role of Foreign Direct Investment in East Asian Economic Development,* ed. Takatoshi Ito and Anne O. Krueger, 239–66. Chicago: University of Chicago Press.

World Bank. 1997. *World Development Report 1997: The State in a Changing World.* Washington, DC: World Bank; New York: Oxford University Press.

———. 2004a. *Seizing the Global Opportunity: Investment Climate Assessment and Reform Strategy for Cambodia.* Report Series 27925-KH. Washington, DC: Poverty Reduction and Economic Management Unit, Financial and Private Sector Development Unit, East Asia and Pacific Region, World Bank.

———. 2004b. *Cambodia at the Crossroads: Strengthening Accountability to Reduce Poverty.* Report Series 30636-KH. Washington, DC: East Asia and Pacific Region, World Bank.

———. 2005a. *Cambodia: Halving Poverty by 2015? Poverty Assessment 2006.* Washington, DC: East Asia and Pacific Region, World Bank.

———. 2005b. *East Asia Decentralizes: Making Local Government Work.* Washington, DC: World Bank.

———. 2006. *World Development Indicators 2006.* Washington, DC: World Bank. http://devdata.worldbank.org/wdi2006/contents/cover.htm

INDEX